Sea of Silk

THE MIDDLE AGES SERIES

RUTH MAZO KARRAS, SERIES EDITOR
EDWARD PETERS, FOUNDING EDITOR

A complete list of books in the series is available from the publisher.

Sea of Silk

A Textile Geography of Women's Work in Medieval French Literature

E. Jane Burns

PENN

University of Pennsylvania Press
Philadelphia

Published by
University of Pennsylvania Press
Philadelphia, Pennsylvania 19104-4112

Printed in the United States of America on acid-free paper

10   9   8   7   6   5   4   3   2   1

Library of Congress Cataloging-in-Publication Data
Burns, E. Jane.
    Sea of silk : a textile geography of women's work in medieval French literature /
E. Jane Burns.
        p. cm. — (Middle Ages series)
    Includes bibliographical references and index.
    ISBN 978-0-8122-4154-9 (alk. paper)
    1. French literature—To 1500—History and criticism. 2. Women silk industry
workers in literature. 3. Silk industry in literature. 4. Clothing and dress in
literature. 5. Silk Road—In literature. 6. Women silk industry workers—
Mediterranean Region—History. I. Title.
    PQ155.W6B87 2009
    840.9'3553—dc22   2008050861

To Ned Burns, who graduated from college in May 2008, wearing a cap and gown not of silk but pure polyester. May he continue to read books for the rest of his life.

CONTENTS

INTRODUCTION

Sea of Silk: A Textile Geography

THIS BOOK MAPS a textile geography of silk work done by female protagonists in Old French literary texts. It argues, in brief, that literary portraits of medieval heroines who produce and decorate silk cloth or otherwise manipulate items of silk provide important narrative keyholes onto distant economic and cultural geographies across the medieval Mediterranean. The story of silk is an old and familiar one, a tale of mercantile travel and commercial exchange along the broad land mass that connects ancient China to the west, extending eventually to sites on the eastern Mediterranean and along sea routes to India. But in the Middle Ages, silk traveled over routes that linked Egypt and port cities in North Africa to southern Italy and Muslim Spain, while also joining Constantinople and Levantine sites to northern Italian cities. France itself, especially northern France, does not figure centrally or prominently on this economic map of silk transport. It stands at the edge of the extended process of trans-Mediterranean trade that brought silks to the Champagne fairs, largely through the activities of Italian merchants.

And yet if we shift our focus from economic histories that chart the transport and exchange of silk along both Asian and Mediterranean trade routes to medieval literary depictions of silk, a strikingly different picture comes into view. In literary accounts from the twelfth and thirteenth centuries, emphasis falls on silk production rather than trade and on female protagonists who make, decorate, and handle silk. As this new story of silk production emerges, so too does a metaphorical geography that includes northern France as an important cultural player in the process. Indeed, a number of Old French literary texts contain portraits of heroines whose silk work charts an imaginative textile geography that situates medieval French culture amid an expansive Mediterranean sea of silk that is the subject of this book.

The "sea of silk" I refer to here should, then, be understood in at least two ways. First, it denotes the historical network of medieval trade routes that joined the Christian west, the Muslim world, and Byzantium in a complex system of trans-Mediterranean commercial exchange that David Jacoby has aptly termed "silk economics."[1] Silk functions in this system as more than a simple commodity; it is an economic currency often implicated in a lucrative traffic in gold and slaves while also playing a major role in the movement of luxury goods and relics between Europe and the eastern Mediterranean through pilgrimage and crusade. The second meaning of "sea of silk" as I use it here is literary. It connotes a metaphorical network of fictive female protagonists who are represented as "working" silk in sites along the shores of the Mediterranean. Silk functions in this literary "sea of silk" as a social and cultural currency often represented as enabling the heroines who work it to traverse religious and political barriers while also crossing lines of gender and class.

One of the most salient features of the historical silk trade is that as silk moved across the medieval Mediterranean, it created possibilities for contact with distant lands, foreign peoples, and especially those called "Saracen." In its Old French literary representations, silk also moves constantly, circulating through diverse layers of medieval French culture as it crosses readily between Christians and Muslims, secular and ecclesiastical spheres, and members of distinct social classes. At issue in the literary texts to be examined below is the way that the very silk used to define these diverse sectors of medieval French culture also becomes intimately associated with the female protagonists who are said to "work" it, whether by making, decorating, using, handling, or otherwise manipulating silk cloth or objects made from it. At the same time, it is through women's silk work that the categories of the distant and foreign unknown, so often cast in terms of the feared "Saracen," are brought closer to home. Indeed, in the pages to follow we shall investigate female protagonists across the sea of silk who are positioned as particularly rich sites of cultural crossing between the Christian west, Byzantium, and the Muslim world because they work silk.

This study makes no claim to provide original historical or art historical research. Its contribution lies rather in bringing together the work of economic historians, textile historians, and art historians as a means of reading representations of material culture, specifically representations of silk and silk work, in Old French literary texts. The argument advanced here is that in reading carefully the linguistic details of literary descriptions of silk textiles we can better understand medieval "western" culture as a functional part of the extended Mediterranean society outlined by scholars such as S. D. Goitein and David Abulafia and elaborated more recently in terms of cross-cultural silk production and distribution by David Jacoby.[2] Only faintly mapped out in these accounts of the historical silk trade, however, is the gender of the participants involved. Occasional references to women silk workers in Byzantine, Islamic, or European settings offer welcome and crucial but all-too-brief interruptions in historical accounts that speak more often of ungendered merchants, traders, dyers, weavers, embroiderers, and silk workers.[3] In stark contrast, Sharon Farmer's recent study of silk-making in Parisian factories in the late thirteenth century gives an invaluable, detailed, and gender-specific view of medieval European silk production. She shows that, different from the commercial manufacture of linen and wool, the production of silk in medieval Paris was, in fact, dominated by women workers and entrepreneurs.[4] It should not surprise, then, that Old French literary texts might also stage silk work overtly and exclusively as women's work. But curiously, the location of that work in literary formulations is not typically Paris. Rather, Old French narratives chart a wide geographic expanse of imagined sites across the Mediterranean where women "work" silk physically in commercial or private settings while also deploying it more figuratively and to great effect in highly charged political or legal venues.

Sea of Silk builds upon my earlier research in *Courtly Love Undressed: Reading Through Clothes in Medieval French Culture*, which focused on elite clothes themselves as cultural icons often used to mark courtly protagonists in love as part of a larger Mediterranean culture. Courtly heroines in particular, lavishly wrapped as they are in abundant eastern silks, often function as richly hybrid cultural crossing places: visual maps pointing at one and the same time to the excessive wealth accumulated in western European courts in the early French Middle Ages and to the non-European sites that provided those sumptuous goods.[5] This study shifts the focus from female protagonists who wear silk in the courtly world to those who produce, decorate, or otherwise "work" it in fictive courtly settings across the Mediterranean. The significance of these literary silk workers lies, as we will see, both in the kind of textile work they do and where they are said to do it.

The portraits of Old French heroines featured in this study range widely from representations of women actually weaving or embroidering silk under oppressive and exploitative work conditions to more imaginative scenarios in which women work silk metaphorically as an effective means of gaining social mobility. At times these literary portraits reveal the historical exploitation of women textile workers and the trans-Mediterranean slave trade that accompanied the production and transfer of luxury textiles in the Middle Ages. At other moments, medieval literary depictions of women working silk resonate with the equally lucrative traffic in golden relics that also accompanied the historical transport of luxury silk. In those instances we find a revaluation of women's worth in terms of their deft and often creative manipulation of both silk and gold or silk work infused with valuable gold thread.

Each chapter in this study pairs heroines positioned in France with others, often designated as "foreign" women, who are located in distant sites ranging from Constantinople and Tyre on the eastern Mediterranean to medieval trading sites in North Africa and Muslim Spain along with fictive "islands" that might, in fact, suggest Norman Sicily. Although the literary examples adduced here come from Old French texts, their cultural significance is trans-Mediterranean. By charting the gestures and actions of female protagonists who make, display, and use silk in Old French narratives that range from a little-known *dit* and the single extant example of a *chantefable* to a number of familiar and well-known epic and romance texts, this study reveals a textile map of women's silk work that joins France culturally to sites often demonized as "eastern," "foreign," or "Saracen."

Whereas the ancient trade routes linking China to the Mediterranean have been analyzed most often as a functional block of continuous overland exchange, the network of medieval silk routes traversing the Mediterranean has been addressed through more localized studies.[6] S. D. Goitein charts commerce between Egypt, North Africa, and Muslim Spain in particular, Maurice Lombard and Maya Shatzmiller address Muslim trade, Jacoby's early work, following Robert Lopez, focuses on Constantinople and its Italian connections, Janet Abu-Lughod on Genoa, and Olivia Remie Constable on Muslim Spain.[7] The literary references to women working silk to be examined in the pages that follow tie many of these disparate sites together.

The narrative portraits of these heroines also often extend the meaning of the term "Saracen," commonly used in Old French epic and medieval chronicles to demonize non-Christian others. Indeed, when viewed through the lens of textile production, the highly politicized "Saracen" shifts from designating an unspecified and generic rival enemy (the Saracens) to connoting a category of highly desired luxury textiles ("Saracen work").[8] Used in relation to silk, the term "Saracen" tends to become an inclusive, mobile category that can define Byzantine silk as "porpre sarazinesche," Christian alms purses as "aumosnieres sarrasinoises," and Muslim or Islamicate embroidery as "oeuvre sarrasinoise."[9] In these examples the term "Saracen" loses much of its ascribed anti-Christian designation and becomes instead a mark of the technical skill that can produce highly prized cloth. Indeed, medieval literary depictions of women's silk work replace the facile division of Saracen east versus Christian west with a map that incorporates silk-working sites extending from Muslim Spain and Norman Sicily to North Africa and Constantinople. This textile geography charts a dense and layered cultural expanse rather than a strict ideological divide.

Consideration of silk textiles as they are represented in medieval literary accounts thus confirms recent findings by historians and postcolonial scholars that the term "Saracen" often functions as an open and fluid category in the Middle Ages, readily taking on different inflections rather than being attached to one specific religion, place, or people. Paul Bancourt noted a number of years ago that for Old French epic poets the term "Saracen" referred to more than "pagan and Mohammedan peoples," connoting instead all adversaries of Christendom, including schismatic Byzantine Greeks.[10] Norman chronicles often demonize "heretical" Greeks as displaying the very faults attributed to Saracens in Old French epics: people given to excess, having been corrupted by lavish wealth, luxury goods, and what is viewed as degenerate sexuality or effeminacy.[11] In some twelfth-century accounts, Saracens also tend to take on characteristics of polytheistic, bacchanalian Romans as authors adopt the model of early Christians struggling against idolatrous and wanton Roman pagans to describe the battle between medieval Christians and their contemporary "Saracen" enemies.[12] For many western Europeans in the Middle Ages, then, "Saracens were pagans, and pagans were Saracens," as John Tolan explains.[13] Military enemies of the Franks in the epic cycle of Vivien are most commonly termed "païens" in addition to being "Sarrasins," but they also carry the labels "Turcs, Esclers, Esclavons and Persans" and their geographic range stretches across three continents to include, among other sites, a generic "Orient," India, Persia, Damascus, Nubia, Spain, Sardinia, and Palermo.[14] Jews too become conflated with medieval Saracens in some Old French *chansons de geste* where wealthy, idolatrous "pagans" are said to worship in "synagogues" as well as "mahomeries."[15] And the mobile category of enemy "other" extends readily to additional non-Muslim groups: the English are called "Saracens" in the Battle of Hastings and Vikings and vandals come under the rubric of "gens perfida saracenorum."[16]

Although the word "Saracen" is pre-Islamic, descending from Byzantine Greek where it was used to denote native speakers of Arabic,[17] it comes to represent a large cultural map containing "the diversity of the eastern world," in Jeffrey Jerome Cohen's analysis, or what was perceived and catalogued as "eastern" whether it emerged in fact in Muslim Spain, North Africa, or Constantinople.[18] To be sure, the medieval term "Saracen" was often marshaled with a view to categorize, exclude, and dismiss a highly sophisticated and technologically advanced Arabic culture, as Maria Menocal has shown.[19] But medieval polemical efforts to construct "Saracen" as a monolithic category also record, in Cohen's analysis, the substantial ethnic diversity and geographic scope of the many groups gathered beneath that rubric.[20] Indeed, in the concerted but failed attempt to define a unified Christian west in stark opposition to an equally homogeneous Saracen east, Latin chroniclers from Bede in the eighth century to Guibert de Nogent in the twelfth ironically enumerate within their artificial category of Saracenness people as diverse as the Moors in Spain, Berbers of North Africa, and Persians in the Middle East while also locating Saracens within an even broader geographic expanse ranging from North Africa to the Orient.[21]

The inadequacy of ideological paradigms that attempt to polarize Saracens and Christians becomes even more apparent when we consider the production and exchange of silk textiles across the medieval Mediterranean. David Jacoby's careful documentation of interdependent silk economies reveals the extent to which Byzantium, the Muslim world, and the Christian west were, in fact, tied together through common features of silk making in the Middle Ages, in particular with respect to the "uses, nature and qualities of silk fabrics." He explains that "the manufacturers of high grade Byzantine and Islamic fabrics borrowed motifs, patterns, and pictorial compositions from a common source, namely, Sassanian [Persian] textiles and artifacts." Indeed, because of the economic interaction between the Byzantine Empire and the Muslim world in the field of silk production, it is often "difficult if not impossible to determine the provenance and dating of silks exhibiting such elements."[22] Viewed through the lens of silk production, medieval Christian and Muslim worlds come together more often than they stand apart, joined as they are by trading patterns across the Mediterranean that endure from the tenth through the mid-fourteenth centuries.[23]

It is significant that by the 1260s silk production of small items such as belts and ribbons, often known as narrow ware, was well under way in Parisian workshops and that by the 1290s silk fabrics were also being produced in Paris, as Sharon Farmer has shown.[24] And yet, Old French literary texts of the twelfth and thirteenth centuries do not refer typically to "Parisian silks." Rather, those texts are teeming with references to silks from a conglomerate of eastern Mediterranean locations, often lumped together indiscriminately as "Saracen lands"; silks from Constantinople apparently deemed as "Saracen" as those originating in Damascus, Baghdad, and Alexandria, or those coming from Muslim Spain. Perhaps most interesting for our purposes, even in terms of Parisian silk production, the "Saracen" has come home to reside comfortably in the Frankish heartland specifically through women's silk work. Farmer explains that some of the women workers who manufactured silk in thirteenth-century Paris produced cross-culturally rich items called Saracen alms purses: "aumonières sarrasinoises."[25] The term is highly evocative not only because it suggests a cultural mixture of Christian practice and Saracen decoration, but also because it combines foreign and domestic venues, conflating home and "outremer" through the practice of women's silk work. Thus do historical practices of Parisian silk production function in tandem with twelfth- and thirteenth-century literary portraits of women working silk to provide an important record of yet another venue in which "Saracen" can mean much more than simply "infidel," pagan, suspect, or foreign.

Silk from Unknown Lands

A long tradition of legendary accounts locates silk makers in mysterious and distant lands, at the edge of the earth, even adjoining, in one instance, a strange kingdom governed by women. From the Roman writer Pliny the Elder in the first century C.E. to Marco Polo in the thirteenth century, silk is said to carry great value because it is imported from an unknown and distant place, termed somewhat consistently over time "the Land of the Seres."[26] This faraway place, occupied by people who make silk, hovers in the imagination of many early western writings as a place of odd, if intriguing, practices. Virgil's *Georgics* reports enigmatically that the Seres "comb off" a fine down from the leaves of Ethiopian trees, while Pliny attributes the same process in his *Natural History* to a remote, wild, and savage people known as the Seres who reside vaguely beyond the distant desert lands of the Scythians.[27] Ovid ascribes to these distant people a swarthy complexion (*colorati*), and the Greek geographer Pausanias writing in the second century reiterates prior claims that the Seres are an Ethiopian race while also noting they have been called Scythians crossed with Indians: "Seria is known to be an island lying in a recess of the Red Sea. But I have heard that it is not the Red Sea, but a river called Ser that makes this island, just as in Egypt the Delta is surrounded by the Nile and by no sea. Such another island is Seria said to be. These Seres themselves are of Aethiopian race, as are the inhabitants of the neighbouring islands, Abasa and Sacaea. Some say however that they are not Aethiopians but a mongrel race of Scythians and Indians."[28] Known at first only anecdotally from accounts of trading at the border and in the absence of travel into the actual land of the silk people, the Seres are positioned repeatedly in early Greek and Roman accounts as the extremely distant other, the ultimate dark-skinned foreigners.[29] Ptolemy locates the region of the Seres imprecisely above "Sinae," claiming that both the Seres and the Sinae constitute the easternmost people of the inhabited world, and further detailing the Seres as occupying unknown lands at the edge of the earth. The location of their capital city also remains cryptically unattested.[30]

From the other side of the Chinese border, a counter myth proliferates concerning an equally strange and unknown region, located somewhere south of the capital of neighboring Khotan and south of the Pamir Mountains, seemingly on the route westward from the "Land of the Seres." Recorded in a seventh-century Chinese dynastic history known as the *Beishi*, this odd region is not a land of silk but a kingdom governed by women in which the men, devoted solely to military affairs, are ruled by a principal queen and a surrogate queen. Characterized as practicing human sacrifice to forest divinities, the long-haired inhabitants of the "land of women" wear leather shoes and enjoy hunting. This kingdom, known for local copper, cinnabar, musk, black oxen (yaks), horses, and salt is said to have first made contact with China in 586 when it began to send tribute, or taxes, to the Chinese emperor.[31] The category of the "unknown," associated in early Greco-Roman accounts with distant foreigners who make mysterious silk, shifts in the Chinese account to an equally mysterious province of women.

And indeed, at other moments, Roman accounts attribute the highly skilled process of silk work specifically to women while also characterizing silk and the women who produce the luxurious cloth as a source of moral decay. Seneca the Elder (54 B.C.E. to 39 C.E.) decries the transparency of fine silk as decadent and dangerous since it makes the married women who wear it visually alluring and seemingly available to all comers. He locates the source of such corruption in young women silk workers: "Wretched flocks of maids labour so that the adulteress may be visible through her thin dress, so that her husband has no more acquaintance than any outsider or foreigner with his wife's body."[32] Although silkworm cultivation was not yet known in Rome, Seneca and Pliny after him both describe Roman women's weaving (of presumably imported silk fiber) as a corrupting influence. The problem stems, Pliny explains fancifully, from a land to the east of the "Cannibal Scythians" (the modern-day Caucasus) where people called "the Seres"[33] are famous for a woolen substance obtained from their forests. After steeping the leaves in water and combing off the white down, the Seres then give to "our women" the "double task of unraveling the threads and weaving them together again; so manifold is the labour employed and so distant is the region of the globe drawn upon, to enable the Roman maiden to flaunt transparent raiment in public."[34] Trade with this unknown land of the Seres located on the eastern edge of the world generated for Pliny the image of textile production through which Roman women might clothe other Roman women in flimsy fabric as dangerous to "civilization" as wild animals might be. "The Seres," though "mild in character," Pliny avers, "resemble wild animals, since they shun the remainder of mankind, and wait for trade to come to them"[35]

In another passage, Pliny locates the problematic origin of silk making in a more specific, if mythical, woman. He attributes the unraveling of silk threads and the weaving of them into cloth to Pamphile who lived in Cos. Decrying her invention of silk weaving as "a plan to reduce women's clothing to nakedness,"[36] Pliny also laments the use of this lightweight and transparent fabric by Roman men who, he contends, should be wearing a cuirass instead: "Nor have even men been ashamed to make use of these dresses, because of their lightness in summer; so far have our habits departed from wearing a leather cuirass that even a robe is considered a burden! All the same, we so far leave the Assyrian silk-moth to women."[37] In this view, clingy silk made Roman women, under questionable foreign influence, dangerous agents in transforming wives into adulteresses and maidens into prostitutes, while also threatening to make Roman men effeminate.

Silk in Medieval France

Nothing could be further from the configuration of silk in medieval French literature where it clothes secular and ecclesiastical members of the ruling elite, whether men or women, with equal pomp and prestige. To be sure, moralists from Jerome through Jacques de Vitry and others who follow them call for substantial restrictions on lavish attire.[38] But the literary spectacle of the courtly world tends in general to adopt a Byzantine model of extravagant dress in which silk forms the fiber and fabric of a resplendent and opulent social life.[39] Silk is central to the elaborate dubbing rituals at King Arthur's court where, in the twelfth-century romance *Erec et Enide*, four hundred knights receive lavish silks from the king, who "did not distribute cloaks made of serge, or rabbit fur or coarse wool, but of heavy silk [samite] and ermine, cloaks entirely of fur and silk brocade" (vv. 6606–9; ne dona pas mantiax de sarges,/ ne de conins ne de brunetes,/ mes de samiz et d'erminetes,/ de veir antier et de dïapres).[40] The opulence of silk and furs attests both to the knights' success and to Arthur's own legendary wealth and generosity, which even surpass, we are told, the resources and character of Alexander the Great, the Roman emperor Caesar, and all kings appearing in Old French tales and epics (vv. 6611–19). Silk here signals not effeminacy but masculinity in several registers, connoting feudal prowess and royal liberality along with international power. Alexander in particular is further characterized in this passage as a model manly ruler who had "conquered the entire world and everyone in it" (vv. 6611–12; Alixandres, qui tant conquist/ que desoz lui tot le mont mist). The foreign, in this instance, and eastern opulence specifically, rather than being feared as a lavish contaminant, is revered and emulated as a source of male self-definition and acclaim. Courtly women in particular, as I have argued elsewhere, derive much of their identity and recognition as western icons from lavish eastern silks said to be from Baghdad, Constantinople, Alexandria, and Damascus.[41]

At times, Old French heroines accrue more specific authority and influence by donning silk raiment, evidenced perhaps most strikingly by the astute and legally adept heroine Lienor in Jean Renart's thirteenth-century *Roman de la Rose ou de Guillaume de Dole*.[42] Just prior to the trial scene in which she brilliantly argues her own defense, this courtly protagonist emerges attired in a cloak made "of blue silk and lined with the whitest and finest ermine that ever existed" (vv. 4352–54; d'un samit inde a pene hermine;/ onques si blanche ne si fine/ ne fu nule) along with a tunic made "of green cendal silk fully lined with fur" (vv. 4357–58; d'un cendal vert/ tote forree et cors et manches). She is, however, barely covered by these fine silks: "her hips were low, her waist was slim, and her lovely, firm breasts pressed against the silk" (vv. 4359–62; El ot un poi basses les hansches,/ et grailles flans, et biau le pis./ Un poi fu plus

haust li samis/ desus la mamelete dure).[43] Here, sartorial splendor combines
with elements from the standard catalogue of eroticized courtly beauty to help
stage not lasciviousness but this heroine's extraordinary and ingenious intellectual ability. With Nature, God, and the Holy Spirit on Lienor's side, her
clearly unscrupulous opponent, we are told, does not stand a chance (vv.
4363–66).[44] Indeed, seductive silk here adorns a female exemplar of justice
and moral rectitude who is working against, rather than perpetrating, the
forces of social corruption.

What remains occluded in the brief passages that feature silk-clad protagonists from *Erec et Enide* and *Le Roman de la Rose ou de Guillaume de Dole*
cited above is any cultural ascription of gender, status, ethnicity, or place of
origin to the makers of the silk garments figured in these key scenes. Different
from the Roman accounts that blame women, both foreign and domestic, for
the importation and creation of morally damaging silk attire, the Old French
examples cited above give no indication, however imaginary or exaggerated,
of who might be thought to produce the silk that lavishly and advantageously
adorns the fictive bodies of medieval courtly knights and ladies. However,
other literary passages, some in these same texts, do address the question of
silk making specifically. Indeed, a careful look at key scenes in a range of Old
French texts will reveal silk production, decoration, and display to be firmly
located in the hands of female protagonists. Whereas male characters in Old
French narratives are shown to wear, use, gift, and confer silk cloth and silk
objects, only women are staged as making or embroidering silk.

While the Roman examples discussed above answer the questions of silk's
mysterious origin and production by citing not only foreigners but also foreign women as particularly dangerous influences on their culture, Old French
literary texts map a trans-Mediterranean geography devoid of the polarization
that pits native Romans against foreign populations situated threateningly to
the east. Different too from ideologically driven clerical and political geographies of the Middle Ages that tend to set the medieval Christian west against
a putatively "pagan" or "Saracen" east, the more economically derived, though
still highly imaginary, textile geography of silk to be discussed here constructs
a cultural map of the medieval west in working relation to the larger
Islamicate and Byzantine worlds.[45] The Mediterranean "sea of silk" that ties
medieval France economically to Muslim Spain and Sicily, North Africa, the
Levant, and Constantinople also affords cultural paradigms that cut across
categories of religious, political, and gendered "others." The chapters to follow will show that medieval answers to both "mysteries" concerning the ori-

gin of silk and its producers lie not in the construction of fearsome, unknown, and distant lands nor in dangerously foreign and corrupting women. Rather, the textile geography mapped by women's silk work in Old French narratives effectively revalues the term "Saracen" and the concept of "foreign women" along with it, by staging Saracen silk and Saracen work as desirous and coveted while also positioning female protagonists as highly skilled creators and manipulators of the medieval Mediterranean's most lucrative commodity.

Chapter 1, "Women and Silk: Remapping the Silk Routes from China to France," sets the frame for this study by pairing a popular ancient Chinese legend of the Silk Princess with an anomalous passage in the twelfth-century Arthurian romance *Yvain* that features displaced women as highly skilled weavers of silk. If the well-known silk routes from China to the west tend to map an ungendered terrain of trade and travel, these tales map the terrain of silk production and decoration both in China and the medieval west specifically as women's work.

Chapter 2, "Silk Workers from King Arthur's France to King Roger's Palermo (*Yvain ou Le Chevalier au lion*)," uses a strategy of reading through silk to address head on the longstanding conundrum of three hundred captive and exploited silk workers staged fleetingly in Chrétien's *Yvain*. These putatively foreign women can be seen, in fact, to form the highly significant cultural underside of the courtly luxury enjoyed by the elegant "maiden" whose father and overseer the silk workers "serve" both economically and sexually. Said to be imported from a quasi-mythic "Isle as puceles," these women workers offer a narrative keyhole onto medieval silk production in Palermo where the Norman kings took over silk factories founded by their Muslim predecessors, producing, as do the captive women in *Yvain*, one of the most highly valued commodities in the medieval Mediterranean: cloth of silk and gold.

Chapter 3, "Women Working Silk from Constantinople to Lotharingia (*Le Dit de l'Empereur Constant, Le Roman de la Rose ou de Guillaume de Dole*)," pairs two elite heroines across the Mediterranean: the "pagan" Sebelinne in Constantinople and the Christian Lienor in France, both of whom "work" silk metaphorically in aristocratic settings rather than exploitive factory conditions. Their deft handiwork in manipulating and deploying lavishly decorated and costly silk purses, often known as *aumosnieres sarrasinoises*, enables these aristocratic women to increase their social and political status while also redefining the category of the marriageable daughter.

In Chapter 4, "Following Two 'Ladies of Carthage' from Tyre to North Africa and Spain to France (*Le Roman d'Enéas, Aucassin et Nicolette*)," we trace the story of an astute and capable Tyrian woman, Dido, copiously adorned in Levantine silk, who expires in the North African city of Carthage she founded. The capable queen is incinerated on a silken pyre when the western courtly love story condemns her sartorial extravagance as a sign of corrupt eastern opulence. She falls in love with silk and dies. The Muslim slave girl, Nicolette, by contrast, hails from another Carthage, Cartagena in Muslim Spain, but succeeds in rewriting the narrative of her enslavement by becoming a merchant who trades metaphorically not in silk or cloth of gold, but in costly and ultimately priceless golden relics. This heroine outmaneuvers the traffic in slaves and silk by forging her own traffic in gold.

With Chapter 5, "Women Mapping a Silk Route from Saint-Denis to Jerusalem and Constantinople (*Le Pèlerinage de Charlemagne*)," we turn to the narrative of Charlemagne's fictive pilgrimage and quasi-crusade to the Holy Land and Constantinople, which results in a lavish gift of valuable relics to Saint-Denis. Whereas the text focuses on the putative rivalry between the western Charlemagne and his silk-laden rival King Hugh in Constantinople, we examine the two stationary queens who frame this tale of travel and mercantile exchange. It is, in fact, these barely visible female protagonists who direct our view away from the relic-laden Christian west to focus instead on a silk-filled world across the sea.

Chapter 6, "Silk Between Virgins: Following a Relic from Constantinople to Chartres," closes the book with an account not of golden relics but lead pilgrim badges. These images worn on the clothing of medieval pilgrims represent the legendary Virgin's *chemise* at Chartres Cathedral both as a lavish silk garment associated with the Virgin in Constantinople and as a simple *chemise* produced by domestic linen works in France. In this instance, the "Saracen" is lodged firmly in a silken relic belonging to a woman in the Christian west.

CHAPTER ONE

Women and Silk

Remapping the Silk Routes from China to France

I BEGIN WITH two stories of women "working" silk: two accounts of female protagonists poised at either end of a long chronological spectrum and a wide geographic expanse that stretches from seventh-century China to twelfth-century France. These culturally diverse fictive women are joined across time, place, and social class by complex threads of silk that connect those who wear and display this costly fabric with those who make and decorate it. The first story is a popular Chinese legend concerning the Silk Princess, a woman who is held responsible, along with her two female attendants, for smuggling the invaluable knowledge of sericulture and silk weaving out of China and into the west.[1] The second account, a curious passage in a medieval French romance called *Le Chevalier au lion (Yvain)*, describes three hundred captive women silk workers who transport their knowledge of lucrative silk weaving from the mythic "Isle of Maidens" into the fictive landscape of Arthurian romance.[2]

Both tales chronicle displaced women and cultural border crossings. Both feature female protagonists as knowledgeable carriers of key technological innovations that can potentially generate significant economic wealth. And yet the skilled women silk workers depicted in the Chinese legend are servants and those in the Arthurian romance outright captives. All are foreign women transported against their will. While the Silk Princess travels to a neighboring country as part of a political marriage alliance, the Chinese silk weavers who accompany her are transferred to ensure the continued production of elegant attire for their mistress. The female silk weavers in the French tale are destined similarly to make lavish cloth for elite members of the courtly household where they are held captive. Silk figures in both accounts as a commodity that travels in tandem with the displacement of women who are skilled at producing it.

As a scholar of medieval French literature and culture, I began this project with the story of captive silk workers in Chrétien de Troyes's *Yvain* and came to the Chinese tale of the Silk Princess by reading backward from twelfth-century France to seventh-century China and, simultaneously, by following the historical Silk Road in reverse. My investigation of the abundant references to silk in Old French literature quickly drew me into new intellectual terrain: across the borders of the Arthurian realm and far beyond the frontiers of medieval France, through an extended geography that crosses the Mediterranean to the Levantine coast and continues into Persia, Central Asia, and China, while also traversing the Pyrenees into Spain and North Africa and continuing on to Egypt.[3] It is in this expanded and expansive geography, I discovered, that a gendered story of silk production unfolds, a story of silk cultivation and manufacture, distribution, and consumption that is largely occluded in the familiar account of the Silk Road. For most readers, the network of trade routes known collectively as the Silk Road calls to mind an image of lucrative commerce: a story of commercial travel between imperial China and its neighboring provinces, extending west eventually as far as the Mediterranean. It is also, in many historical accounts and in the popular imagination, a story largely without female participants.

Women and Silk

By contrast, women figure as central players in the two stories of silk workers that provide the framework for this chapter. Tellingly, the skilled women represented as smuggling silk in the Chinese legend of the Silk Princess are not cast as silk traders or merchants. Neither do the young women silk workers transferred into King Arthur's realm in the medieval tale of *Yvain* some five hundred years later actively exchange silk for profit. Rather, all these fictive women are responsible for transporting across cultural borders the highly specialized skill needed to produce silk itself. Indeed, these mythically inflected accounts of women "working" silk add an important component to the more familiar story of the "Silk Road" as a venue of commercial trade. In fact, the Chinese tale of the Silk Princess and the Old French account of women silk workers offer imagined cartographies of silk making that supplement in important ways the historical accounts of commercial trade routes, whether the initial Asian land routes out of China or later sea routes traversing the Mediterranean. In brief, these stories, and others to be analyzed below, chart cultural iconographies that define the elite classes who wear and use silk in relation to the equally salient issue of the gendered production of silk fabric itself.

Many Silk Roads

The story of silk begins, we are told, in the second century B.C.E., when Zhang Qian and Chinese envoys were sent by the Han emperor Wudi to elicit support of the Central Asian Yuezhi against the invading, nomadic Xiongnu.[4] As a result of this foray, diplomatic and economic relations were established and a peace negotiated. The contact then opened a route westward along which a tribute system of exchange developed and flourished under both Han and Tang dynasties (206 B.C.E. to 220 C.E. and 618–907 C.E.).[5] What was traded, initially, was silk fiber (raw silk) and silk goods largely in exchange for horses.[6]

However, silk was not the only commodity exchanged on this route, and goods traded between China and Central Asia did not follow a single path. In fact, the name "Silk Road" was not coined until the late nineteenth century when the Prussian geographer Ferdinand von Richthoven used the term "seidenstrasse" to denote a group of overland routes linking Chang'an (modern-day Xi'an) in China to Samarkand in modern-day Uzbekistan and continuing toward the Caspian Sea and beyond.[7] This network of roads facilitated cultural and commercial communications, in some ways not unlike the network of pilgrimage routes that carried medieval merchants, pilgrims, and travelers across France and Spain toward Santiago de Compostela. As the Asian silk routes developed, caravans departed from Chang'an and followed the Great Wall to the northwest, avoiding the Taklamakan Desert in western China by taking either a southern loop through the ancient city of Khotan (Hotan/Hetian) in the Tarim Basin or a northern loop through Turfan (Turpan).[8] Both routes converged at Kashgar, and from there crossed the

Figure 1. Asian silk routes. © E. Jane Burns.

Pamir Mountains into the Central Asian provinces of Sogdiana in modern-day Uzbekistan and Bactria in modern-day Afghanistan (Figure 1).[9]

The network of trade routes across Central Asia connected a series of desert oases that became market towns, extending westward from Kashgar to Tashkent, Samarkand, Merv (in Iran), and later to Damascus and Mediterranean coastal cities.[10] Few merchants traveled the entire length of these roads, or even the key portion of the route between Chang'an and Samarkand.[11] Most moved back and forth over short distances on limited stretches of a given route.[12] Although in the second century the Greek geographer Ptolemy had mapped a complex network of overland trails extending from the Caspian Sea east to the Pamir Mountains and Romans had been using silk since the first century B.C.E., they did not travel to China itself, but seem to have met on the western shore of the Caspian Sea, in Mesopotamia and the Caucasus, to trade with merchants who had journeyed to the west end of what would later be known as the "Silk Road."[13]

From its earliest use in China and Asia silk functioned not only as a luxury item, as it did subsequently in the west, but also as a currency and a safe investment. Alongside gold, silver, and jewels, silk fiber was used to pay debts and dowries. It served as ransom and as security against loans, as payment for artists or scholars, and as offerings at Buddhist temples.[14] Originally a tax, known as the Tribute of Yu, paid by the Chinese people to the state treasury, silk became so plentiful in government coffers by the fifth century that it was distributed as salary to Chinese civil servants.[15] Spices, of course, were included in the Asian silk trade, although spices were traded in greatest quantities on the sea route to India, and, by the sixth century at least, the term "spices" referred to a range of commodities exchanged in small amounts. In addition to pepper, cloves, and nutmeg, the category of spices could include ambergris, dyes, mordants, scents, pigments, gums, incense, other medicinal items,[16] and, not uncommonly, silk fiber itself. Like spices, raw silk was compact and lightweight, hence easy to transport, and extremely valuable in small quantities. Thus, in addition to exporting silk fabric, China supplied the west with raw silk or silk fiber that traveled along the extended network of overland caravan routes from Central Asia to the Mediterranean, some of it to be worked into cloth in cities such as Antioch and Alexandria.[17]

As silk moved eventually down the eastern Mediterranean coast and into Egypt, it continued to function as currency, serving, according to Goitein, as the "coin of the realm" in international exchange, especially in the textile hub of Alexandria. During the Fatimid period, he explains, all merchants carried some silk as a replacement for cash. Silk fiber was traded in pounds and ounces, according to a standardized price that remained stable from the 1030s to the 1150s.[18] Less valuable was floss silk or waste silk, the outer layers of fiber surrounding the cocoon that cannot be unraveled and reeled, but must be "peeled off" and spun.[19] But silk could also stand in for gold. When Muslim silk-producing states such as Almería sent tribute to the Christian kingdoms in northern Spain, sums specified in gold were often paid, in fact, in silk.[20] The perception and use of silk as currency persists through the high Middle Ages in France, recorded, for example, in the *Dit des Marchéans*, where the extensive catalogue of merchants at the Champagne fairs groups silk together with gold and silver available from "marchéans . . . de soie, et d'or, et d'argent."[21]

In addition to fostering the large-scale transfer of silk and spices, Chinese silk routes enabled the movement of intellectuals, artisans, and technicians, while facilitating at the same time the displacement of prisoners taken in war and conquest, captives exchanged as tribute, and slaves.[22] If Buddhism came to China along the silk routes in the first century, with the first Chinese Buddhist monk traveling west to Khotan two hundred years later in search of missing Buddhist scriptures to be translated into Chinese,[23] so too did slave merchants travel these routes. In fact, the slave trade is one of the few places that women become strikingly visible in the larger story of silk. Documents recording the sale of slaves along the silk routes, for example, include at least one instance in which a slave girl is exchanged specifically for a debt of silk.[24]

It is important to note at this juncture that the historical silk trade depended on two distinct processes that did not always migrate in tandem. Sericulture involved the raising of mulberry trees and silk worms that fed on their leaves, and produced cocoons that were unwound and reeled into silk thread and fiber. That fiber was subsequently woven into silk cloth. Both silk fiber and finished cloth are often referred to by the single term "silk," thus conflating what were actually distinct material products. In fact, however, the ability to weave silk fabric most often preceded the highly prized knowledge of sericulture itself. Initially, the technology of sericulture moved along established silk routes out of China, passing first to the Persians in the third century and then to the Byzantines in the sixth century. But the Persians and Byzantines, like the Romans all enjoyed the pleasure of wearing and using silk cloth long before they were able to produce silk thread.[25] The raising of silk worms and production of silk thread spread widely with the Muslim expansion across North African cities and across the Mediterranean (eighth to eleventh centuries) to al-Andalus, Sicily, and Cyprus, reaching southern Spain in the eighth century and Sicily in the ninth. Sericulture was not, however, adopted in France, where silkworm cultivation proved unsuccessful in the Middle Ages.[26]

Significantly, silk's long-standing reputation as a coveted fabric that falls and moves elegantly in space results from the labor-intensive process of meticulously unwinding a single thread from silkworm cocoons, each one producing an unbroken strand of six hundred to two thousand meters in length. The secrets of this process and other phases of silk production—cultivation of the white mulberry tree (*morus alba*) on which the silkworms feed, raising the worms (*bombyx mori*), and finally unwinding the cocoons—were fiercely guarded by the Chinese, as they would be later by the Persians and subsequently the Byzantines.[27] But in Chinese history and legend, the secrets of silk production were understood to be the province of women. It is women who are credited with the skill, knowledge, and practice of the delicate craft of silk making in all its phases, including the final stage of weaving the exceptionally strong fiber into lengths of luxurious, flowing cloth.[28] In rural China under the Han dynasty (206 B.C.E. to 220 C.E.), sericulture and agriculture were paired in some accounts as balanced and gendered seasonal occupations, the agricultural season of men's work being followed by the winter seclusion in which women's work, especially the weaving of silk, predominated.[29]

Three Chinese Women

The tale of the Chinese Silk Princess confirms this view. Told by a Chinese Buddhist monk, Xuanzang, after he returns from a voyage to India in the seventh century, the story describes a fifth-century King of Khotan who successfully breaks the Chinese monopoly on silk manufacture by requesting a Chinese princess in marriage. The ambassador, sent to accompany the young woman as she voyages to the groom's realm, explains that no silk is made in Khotan. She will thus need to smuggle out of her homeland both the seeds for the cultivation of mulberry trees and silkworm eggs to feed on them if she wishes to have robes of silk for herself. The tale thus characterizes women as vain, greedy, and politically unreliable, subject to the deft political maneuvering of government officials focused on gaining economic advantage over a neighboring country. But if women are figured here as passive and malleable objects of male political intrigue, they also emerge as key links to crucial textile technologies. In the end, the princess cleverly arranges to conceal the two required items in her headdress and succeeds thereby in smuggling past inquisitive border guards the very secrets of Chinese silk production.[30]

A version of the story preserved in oral tradition and found in a compilation of tales from Dunhuang provides a more elaborate and detailed scenario. In this instance, the princess is asked to transport three items: mulberry seeds, silkworm eggs, and technicians skilled in actually producing silk cloth. These things, she is told, will suffice for her dowry, making the delivery of gold, silver, gems, and pearls unnecessary. As in the first version of the tale, the princess conceals the silkworms in her headdress, knowing that it will not be searched at the border because touching the head of a noble is prohibited. In addition, one of her female servants hides the mulberry seeds among herbs in a medicine chest. Seeing these items safely delivered across the border, the Khotanese minister expresses concern that no male technician has accompanied the princess as a specialist in the art of silk making. Her reply is telling. Such technicians have indeed made the journey: before leaving China the princess handpicked three excellent women technicians to be her maidservants, women skilled in planting mulberry trees, breeding and raising silkworms, and also weaving. In China, she explains, these skills are considered to be women's work, and learned by all young girls.[31]

The story of the Silk Princess is used, in this text, to illustrate the transfer of sericulture from China to neighboring Khotan, and its subsequent spread to India and Europe. It offers an interesting alternative to the western account recorded by Procopius that credits two monks with smuggling silk-worm eggs out of a place called Serindia (possibly Sogdania) at the behest of the Emperor Justinian.[32] The tale of the Chinese silk bride also contrasts sharply with earlier Chinese historical accounts that attribute the first official export of silk fabrics from China to the male imperial envoys of the Han dynasty.[33] Legend instead ascribes the stealthy and ingenious transfer of the entire industry of sericulture to women, trained from girlhood to raise silkworms and weave their fibers. Whether the Silk Princess was herself skilled at working textiles is not specified. But the story of women literally carrying the secrets of silk production out of China on their person so captivated the Chinese cultural imagination that it persists in yet another narrative variant surviving from 635, during the Tang Dynasty, even after the knowledge of silk production had reached the Byzantine world and the Middle East. In this version of the story, a Chinese princess named Wencheng is said to have smuggled into Tibet silkworm eggs hidden in her wedding basket when she married the Tibetan king.[34]

The Chinese princess and her servants in the version of the tale elaborated in oral tradition are bound together to the extent that each one emblematizes a facet of the process that yields silk. With the princess carrying the concealed silkworms, one female servant transporting the mulberry seeds, and others adept at weaving, the group of women depicts the transfer of sericulture out of China toward the west. A wood panel discovered by Aurel Stein east of present-day Khotan, on the south branch of the silk routes, offers a portrait of three female figures posed together to tell this story of the transfer of silk production from one culture to another (Figure 2).[35] In this image, a basket full of cocoons records one part of the valuable cargo being transferred. An attendant on the left points to the mistress's headdress, presumably indicating the worm eggs hidden within it. The figure on the far right, positioned behind a loom and possibly in front of a reel, holds a beating comb in her hand.[36] In this visual representation of the Silk Princess's story, a fourth figure accompanies the women: a seated, four-armed male deity who may be the patron or god of weaving.[37] Despite his presence, however, the image preserved on the wooden panel emphasizes, above all, the group of women responsible for the legendary transfer of silk technology to the west, women joined across lines of social class who both produce and display on their bodies a major economic resource of their region and century.

The legend of the Silk Princess provides a useful point of departure for studying the medieval "sea of silk" that is the subject of this book for two rea-

Figure 2. The Silk Princess; wooden votive tablet from Dandan Uiliq. © Trustees of the British Museum. Reproduced with permission.

sons. First, by putting women at the center of the silk story, the tale of the Silk Princess focuses our attention on the labor-intensive manufacture of silk as a highly prized commodity, revealing the extent to which silk production often requires displaced workers, sometimes captives and even slaves. Second, the Chinese legend suggests the importance of considering the seemingly isolated fantasy realm of Arthurian fiction exemplified in the Old French romance *Yvain*—a world as replete with lavish silk as it is with islands of maidens and demons exacting tribute—as situated within an extended textile economy. In the Middle Ages, that economy traverses a sea of silk stretching from Constantinople and the Levant to Egypt and North Africa, Muslim Spain, and Sicily.[38]

Three Hundred Arthurian Captives

Different from the lavishly clad attendants who accompany the Silk Princess in the Chinese legend, the silk workers figured in Chrétien de Troyes's *Yvain* are described not as servants but as prisoners. In the single manuscript illumination that survives, the silk workers are shown to wear simple and unadorned dress (Figure 3).[39] The miniature features a group of women crowded together behind what might appear at first to be a wall or barricade adjoining a castle. While the figures grouped tightly together in the background gesture imploringly to a knight on horseback figured to their left, three women in the foreground, some holding unidentified implements, appear to be "working" the barricade, or on closer inspection they look as though they are weaving a band of cloth stretched out horizontally in front of them. The visual doubling of the apparent barrier with an extended length of cloth gives the sense that

Figure 3. Silk Workers in *Yvain ou Le Chevalier au lion*. Detail. Paris, BnF, ms. fr. 1433, fol. 104. © Bibliothèque nationale de France.

the textile itself and the women's work upon it hold them prisoner. This is precisely the meaning that the Old French text conveys.

In fact, the narrative offers an even starker picture, describing the captive women who transport techniques of silk weaving into King Arthur's realm as impoverished and miserably clad. Like many other young women routinely liberated by questing knights across the Arthurian landscape, these *puceles* are physically confined and economically disadvantaged.[40] They differ significantly from other captive heroines in the Arthurian world, however, because they also weave silk. While dressed in "torn tunics and soiled chemises" (vv. 5193–97), these workers produce the luxurious fabrics that adorn noble players throughout the courtly world, creating the material underpinning of the fantasy realm that knights and ladies inhabit.[41] The spokeswoman for the captives makes the point as follows: "toz jorz dras de soie tistrons,/ ne ja serons mialz vestues" (vv. 5292–93; we weave silk cloth all day but will never be better dressed).

But who are the imported foreign workers and weavers of silk featured in *Yvain* as the underside of courtly luxury? The question goes unanswered in this Arthurian romance, which explains only that the silk workers come from an unspecific and generic "Isle of Maidens" (v. 5251; l'Isle as puceles). Once having arrived at this lord's court, however, the foreign *puceles* become locked together in a fictional dyad with the lord's own unmarried daughter with whom they are subtly paired through a complex dynamic of economic and social dependence, not unlike the tie that binds the Silk Princess to female silk workers in the Chinese tale. As we will see in Chapter 2, the women protagonists in the twelfth-century French tale replicate even more dramatically the class division and cross-class ties that silk work can generate. The stakes are high. The curious scene of three hundred silk workers in *Yvain* assigns to captive foreign workers, all of them women, the technical skill required to produce the textiles that so thoroughly define elite French culture in the twelfth and thirteenth centuries.

Silk in Courtly Culture

Readers of Old French literature are well aware that references to silk cloth and clothing abound. Silks of many kinds festoon courts, towns, churches, and individuals of both genders. Often functioning in lieu of currency, silk garments serve as payment for a troubadour's song, as remuneration for services performed by the lord's retainers, as a mark of courtly *largesse* and hospitality, as a means of fashioning low-born women into courtly ladies, or signaling the status of the wealthy. In ecclesiastical circles, silk adorns priests performing the liturgy and transforms altars into luxurious surfaces. Silk is used for curtains enclosing the altar during mass and for tapestries and wall hangings in churches and monasteries. Silk provides the wrapping for relics before they are placed in reliquaries and the surface on which relics are positioned before the swearing of legal oaths. Silk moves as readily between secular and ecclesiastical spheres as it does between genders, social classes, or across confessional divides, providing an unexpected cultural thread that bridges all of these social categories.

From courtiers to captives, warriors to lovers, both pagan and Christian, literary protagonists in Old French texts wear, use, gift, and trade different grades and types of silk cloth. Romance narratives and epic poems alike feature the all-purpose *paile*, light-weight *cendal*, and heavier *samit* along with even more costly *porpres, osterins*, and *baudequins* that elegantly robe feudal and foreign kings and queens, the courtly members of their extensive retinues, and even their horses.[42] Inhabitants of towns are not without such luxurious trappings; innkeepers, tavern workers, and lower-level knights and squires are described in these tales as wearing silk items of dress that have been handed down to them as gifts or as payment for services rendered. On the field of battle and in military tournaments, silk tunics lie beneath the armor of knights, helmets are said to be affixed by silk laces, and shields are held by grips woven from silk. Members of military councils, whether Christian or pagan, sit together on silk cloth and lavish silk tents house traveling armies or royal retinues. Silk provides funeral shrouds for kings, saints, and military heroes in epic tales. The occasional knight even binds a wound with a *bliaut de soie*.[43] On feast days, coronations, and other special occasions, whole towns are dressed in silk as exterior walls and buildings are hung with large, colorful bands of fabric.

Just who has produced these luscious silk textiles is often occluded in Old French narratives. We hear repeatedly in epic and romance texts that the silks featured there are costly and highly valued, often characterized specifically by the adjective "riche." In addition, these same silks often carry the generic adjective "ouvrés" meaning "worked," either in the sense of being "woven" or, more often, "embellished" with the decorative and ornate embroidery. Why such labor-intensive and coveted fabrics might be expensive needs no explanation. Who has done the highly prized "work" to make them, however, remains, in most cases, obscure. The unattributed adjective "ovré" along with others such as "brusdé" or "bendé" tend to hang in the air with no identifiable subject.[44] Thus do the lavish textiles "made" and "worked" by capable hands recount by omission, or by suggestion only, the untold story of the large numbers of laborers needed to produce them. In addition, repeated allusions in Old French literary texts to silks bearing the names of distant and evocative cities such as *baudequin* (brocade from Baghdad), *paile alexandrine* (silk cloth from Alexandria), and *soie d'aumaire* (silk from Almería) further de-emphasize the process of silk production. Whether these terms are used to indicate a place of manufacture, port of departure, or a style of fabric, they map an international geography of silk trade, travel, and commercial exchange that tends to eclipse those who create and embellish the costly and coveted fabrics. For these silks, no less than for those labeled simply "ouvrés," the gender of the laborers who produced them is nowhere in evidence.

Medieval Silk Routes

A few Old French texts provide tantalizing glimpses of the complex overland and maritime trade routes that brought medieval silk across the

Mediterranean and across the Pyrenees into France. Underscoring patterns of commercial exchange rather than the process of silk making, the accounts tend, in yet another way, to occlude the participation of women in the silk trade. By the early Middle Ages, silks came into France not from China, but from sites extending from the eastern Mediterranean to Muslim Spain. Two main pathways with varied tributaries can be cited as carrying silks to the medieval west and subsequently into France. One trans-Mediterranean network of sea routes joined Constantinople, cities in the Levant, and Alexandria with Italy beginning in the eleventh century. Another set of east-west trade routes linked Egypt to Muslim Spain via Muslim domains in Tunisia and Sicily as early as the tenth century. Although most of that silk moved eastward from al-Andalus, some was transported north into Languedoc and France.[45] Occasional literary references to silk trade and travel along these varied routes tend to seem cryptic, displaced, or comedic.[46]

The twelfth-century mock epic, *Le Pèlerinage de Charlemagne à Jerusalem et à Constantinople*, for example, charts a major silk trading vector between Constantinople and the west within a tale of pilgrimage and political rivalry. We will see in Chapter 5 how the tale foregrounds a complex intersection of commerce and crusading in medieval France by staging a humorous confrontation between Charlemagne as a pilgrim king and his rival in Constantinople lavishly festooned with endless lengths of costly silk. Female protagonists are almost entirely absent from this extended cross-cultural voyage, however, as no women make the trip to Constantinople or trade in Jerusalem where "merchants come to sell their silks, linen, and Syrian silk fabrics" along with eastern spices (v. 210; Il i vendent lur pailes, lur teiles e lur siries). On his return to France, Charlemagne brings relics from the Holy Land rather than silks from Constantinople, allowing the text to draw an exaggerated contrast between eastern silks and western piety, a distinction that actual trade practices do not support.

In fact, Charlemagne's fictive voyage in the *Pèlerinage* evokes long-standing commercial exchanges between France and the eastern Mediterranean. From the time of the Merovingians, Syrian merchants established in Narbonne, Bordeaux, Orléans, and Tours had imported silks used for elite clothing, altar cloths, ecclesiastical vestments, and to wrap relics.[47] Michael McCormick has shown that in the Carolingian era specifically, Byzantine emperors sent substantial quantities of silk cloth from Constantinople as gifts along with gems, pepper, and other precious eastern products to western churches and royal families alike.[48] The transfer of luxury goods from Constantinople and the

Levantine coast during the crusades effectively reinstates these earlier contacts. Frankish crusader colonies in Syria in particular exported large quantities of heavy silks and golden brocades in the twelfth and thirteenth centuries, some carried westward by Italian merchants and others by Christian pilgrims visiting the Holy Land.[49]

The Old French the *Charroi de Nîmes* briefly traces another commercial silk trading route: one that joined medieval France to Muslim Spain. This epic features heroes disguised unconvincingly as silk merchants in a topsy-turvy comic scene in which King Louis's impoverished knights, on a mission to conquer pagan lands in Spain, pretend to be rich traders (vv. 753–57, 1090–91). The knights claim to transport, along with wool textiles and armaments, abundant costly silks:

> Si li demandent: "Quel avoir fetes traire?"
> —Nos, syglatons et dras porpres et pailes
> vv. 1063–64[50]

> (Then they [the Saracens] asked, "What kind of cargo are you carrying?" "Patterned silks, dark colored silks and other silks")

These fraudulent merchants are mocked by the "pagan" inhabitants of the Saracen city of "Nymes" (vv. 914, 1068, 1093–96) who comment ironically that they have "never seen merchants like these," "Ci voi venir de marcheanz grant masse. –Voir, . . . onques mes ne vi tale" (vv. 1060–61; Here comes a great gathering of merchants. In truth, . . . I've never seen any others like these). Claiming not to be from France but from Canterbury, England (v. 1122), Guillaume as head of the supposed cloth merchants cites a wild itinerary of places they have visited to procure what the pagans consider to be their very "substantial goods" (v. 1068, si grant menaie).[51]

In fact, the comic interlude maps terrain traversed by medieval merchants who transported silk northward out of Spain. Muslim Spain produced its own silk fiber and cloth from the time of Charlemagne, and Andalusi fabrics traveled north to both Louis the Pious and Charles the Bald in the ninth century.[52] In 823, Louis the Pious presented a Spanish coverlet to the Abbey of St. Waudrille. His son, Charles the Bald received a variety of textiles as gifts from the silk-producing city of Cordoba in 865.[53] Although Guillaume and his men only travel as far as the Muslim-occupied city of Nîmes, this French epic hero's hasty disguise as a silk merchant gestures toward patterns of commercial exchange between northern France and al-Andalus amply documented in Old French epic and romance texts that refer to prized Almerían and other Spanish silks used by French aristocrats.[54]

The mid-twelfth-century romance *Floire et Blancheflor* sketches a third medieval silk route: one that links Muslim Spain to Egypt. As the Old French text charts this path, however, it alters significantly the narrative patterns of the *Pèlerinage* and the *Charroi* that feature only male merchant-protagonists on silk-related voyages. In this instance, we follow a wealthy Saracen prince from al-Andalus who sets out to recover his Christian French beloved, Blancheflor, from cloth merchants en route to Cairo/Babiloine.[55] The heroine travels, however, only as slave cargo.[56] Blancheflor has been purchased literally by merchants, who transport her along with gold and silks: for twenty silk cloths from Benevento, twenty fur-lined silk cloaks, twenty tunics of blue silk, and a precious golden goblet (vv. 437-41).[57] Disguised as a cloth merchant himself, the Muslim hero-lover, Floire, is appropriately equipped with "ciers pailes et or et argent,/ biax dras et mules en present" (vv. 1137–38; costly silks, gold and silver, beautiful clothes and mules as gifts) along with silver utensils, coins, other costly cloths, and furs (vv. 1141–48).

Floire's journey from Niebla in al-Andalus to the city of Babiloine outside of Cairo reflects important trading exchanges recorded in the lavish documentation of the Cairo Geniza analyzed by S. D. Goitein. Whereas Egypt did not cultivate silk in the Middle Ages, it served as a major manufacturing center for silk fiber imported from Muslim Spain, Muslim Sicily, and Syria, silk thread that it then often exported as finished cloth.[58] Spain figures in documents of the Cairo Geniza as the leading exporter of silks to Egypt, sending cocoons, raw silk, and silk fabrics.[59] The ports of Almería and Malaga are known to have exported lower-quality spun silk to the Muslim Orient, especially to Egypt, silk which was then sometimes transported northward toward Byzantium.[60] En route, some Andalusi silks were delivered to sites on the North African coast. In the 1050s, Tunisia requested garments, including those lined with silk, from al-Andalus, and the twelfth-century geographer Idrisi provides a long list of silks and brocades that were transferred to the Maghreb by merchants from Almería.[61] The lovesick Floire in the medieval tale *Floire et Blancheflor* disguises himself, in the end quite ineffectually, as one such Andalusi silk merchant en route to Egypt. It is equally significant, however, that Blancheflor travels the same route as a displaced captive.

Silk and the Slave Trade

This fictive account of male merchants transporting valuable silk along with female cargo hints at the complex and troubling imbrication of the medieval silk trade with an allied international traffic in slaves. Goitein reports that as early as the tenth century, silk imported to Egypt from Constantinople traveled to Alexandria along with slaves, spices, and foodstuffs from numerous ports on the Syro-Palestinian coast including Acre, Tyre, Tripoli, and Ascalon.[62] Evidence from al-Andalus records northern slaves sent to the Maghreb and the eastern Mediterranean alongside Iberian ambergris, mercury, and silk.[63] Byzantine merchants are also said to have imported slaves from the west in exchange for luxury fabrics.[64]

More specifically, however, the reference to Blancheflor as slave cargo situates this twelfth-century romance amid a protracted history of international silk production, which often relied for its success on the practices of servile labor and slavery in both Byzantine and Muslim worlds. Although the gender and ethnicity of these servile workers most often remains occluded, we do know that in the tenth century Muslim slaves were employed in the imperial workshops in Constantinople as skilled technicians who manufactured silk and were probably also active in various branches of the private silk industry in Constantinople.[65] We know too that women worked in the silk works located in the *gynaeceum* of the Great Palace and are thought to have been wholly servile.[66] Of the five types of silk workers in Byzantium, Lombard lists three that used slaves of unstipulated gender: merchants of raw silk, spinners who reeled and spun the silk, and a group composed of weavers, dyers, and sellers, who bought raw silk from merchants. He notes, in addition, that slaves worked in wealthy Byzantine households tailoring silk garments.[67] In another venue altogether, Jacoby presumes that the luxury silks woven by slaves in tenth-century Fatimid Ifriqiya must have been produced by Byzantine silk weavers captured in Muslim raids.[68] Indeed, the Islamic textile factories known as *tiraz* typically used a mixed labor force of slaves, forced labor recruits, and wage laborers.[69]

In fact, a persistent pattern of forcibly displacing skilled workers was central to the historical process of silk production. As early as the fourth century, a Persian general captured highly skilled Roman Syrians to work in silk factories in the Persian cities of Tustar and Sus.[70] In the twelfth century, the Fatimids in Egypt imported workers from Tustar to weave silk.[71] And as silk making spread throughout the Muslim world, so too were workers displaced from cities in the eastern Mediterranean to Muslim workshops in Spain and Sicily. Later, Muslim textile workers were resettled in China to make lavish robes for the imperial court under the Mongols in the thirteenth century.[72] It is unclear how many of these displaced captives might have been women.

The romance of *Floire et Blancheflor* records only a small part of this vast international story. To be sure, Blancheflor is not a silk worker. And in the Old French account, her purchase by silk merchants in al-Andalus and subsequent sale to the emir in Babiloine (Cairo) is amply shrouded in courtly conventions of rapt, imprisonment, and ultimate liberation, narrative formulations that make the embedded details of the slave and silk trade seem odd and arcane. Blancheflor is, however, not unlike the captive *puceles* in *Yvain*, forcibly displaced to a foreign land as part of a transcultural commerce in silk.

Textile Evidence of Displaced Workers

Some of the most valuable evidence of the widespread relocation of silk workers across the medieval Mediterranean is provided by textiles themselves. Surviving silk fragments often chart the movement of displaced local artisans who carried with them techniques of silk weaving associated with their home sites. Silks named for the original city of manufacture often retain that name even though the cloth is subsequently produced and exported from an entirely different and distant locale.[73] *Attabi*, the heavy silk taffeta first made in and associated with Baghdad, for example, was later produced not only in Damascus, Tyre, and Antioch, but also in distant Almería.[74] The medieval geographer Idrisi reports that imitation silk textiles from Jurjan (a country southeast of the Caspian Sea, today located in Russia) and Isphahan were, in fact, produced in medieval Almería with the result that so-called Jurgani silk ordered in Cairo in the twelfth century could have come either from Jurgan or from al-Andalus.[75] Goitein describes "Tustari" cloth exported from Tunisia to Egypt, presuming that it was manufactured somewhere in the Muslim west rather than in the Iranian city from which it draws its name.[76] In the eastern Mediterranean, a colony of silk workers from Tustar (Iran) was moved in the tenth century to Baghdad where they continued to make *étoffes Tustari*.[77] By the eleventh century, Tustar itself had become famous for its so-called "Rumi" or "Byzantine" silk and gold textiles.[78]

Much as medieval silks often defy their geographically linked names, so too do actual weaving techniques and decorative patterning repeat from one locale to the next, often making it difficult for art historians to distinguish a precise point of origin. Silks woven in Fatimid Egypt can closely resemble those produced in Fatimid Sicily, for example, a situation rendered more complex because silks were traded and transferred in both directions between these two sites as early as the tenth century.[79] Some Almerían textiles, designated as "pallia rotata" in Christian inventories because they include Persian and Sassanian thematic elements of animals enclosed in roundels, are not readily distinguishable from silks produced in either Cairo or Baghdad.[80] The Veil of Hisham, for example, woven in Cordoba for the Umayyad caliph Hisham II, includes woven decoration in colored silk and gold thread that Patricia Baker contends so closely resembles weaving techniques employed at the courts of Cairo and Baghdad that the fabric could, in fact, have been woven in Egypt.[81] As early as the thirteenth century, luxury fabrics known as cloth of gold or Tartar cloths produced in Central Asia, Iran, or Iraq were being preserved in western European churches alongside similar or "imitation" textiles woven not only in Egypt or Syria but also in Spain and Italy.[82] Paula Sanders discusses lavish Fatimid robes embroidered or woven with gold thread in Egypt in the twelfth and thirteenth centuries, along with gold-embroidered and gold-brocaded upholstery, saddle cloths for elephants, and tents[83] reminiscent of gold and silk work in Fatimid Sicily and in the Norman silkworks that continued the textile traditions of earlier Muslim factories in Palermo.[84]

When silk recognized and named as being "from Baghdad" becomes silk made and exported from Almería, and when silks "from Egypt" become silks produced and sold in Sicily, the names of cities, now attached to commodities, patterns, and fabrics as well as to specific geographic locations, help chart an extensive network of displaced textile workers, skilled artisans who are regularly transferred between a number of silk-producing sites across the medieval Mediterranean.[85] To be sure, as medieval Jewish, Arab, and Christian merchants crisscrossed paths from one end of the Mediterranean to the other, trading silk fiber and named silk fabrics as their most valuable commodity,[86] that commercial activity itself produced an effect of shifting cartographies. Silks designated as being from Baghdad, Constantinople, and Damascus came to characterize not only eastern wealth but also western noble identity. And yet, as the medieval European taste for expensive silks and cloth of gold facilitated and fostered the transfer of goods from east to west,[87] the geographical remapping that resulted was further intensified when silk production itself relocated.[88]

Distinctly French Textiles

It is important to note that the westward displacement of medieval silk work-ers differs significantly from the reverse phenomenon in which named French fabrics moved eastward along with other products, often in exchange for im-ported luxury silks. "Draps de Champagne" were especially prized in the Crusader states along with cloth from Languedoc, Avignon, and Paris as well as Flanders and England.[89] By the middle of the thirteenth century, Sayous reports, Marseille had become an *entrepot* between northern France and the east, sending to Syria wool and linen cloth, thread, and garments, mostly coming from the Champagne fairs.[90] Fabrics named in these accounts in-clude: "draps de Champagne, draps de Chalons, toiles de Reims, brunette de Douai, draps rouge d'Ypres, draps de St. Quentin, Cambrai, Louviers" along with wool stamfords from Arras and England, "biffes de Paris, barracans, sai-ettes, capes de Provins, toilettes d'Allemegne et Bale, draps vert et gris d'Avignon, de Tarascon, de Narbonne, de Saint-Pons."[91] The foregoing place names attached to western linen and wool fabrics underscore the foreign na-ture of highly prized imported cloth. In these instances, in contrast to proce-dures followed in the silk trade, sites of production are not displaced. Here fabrics travel but not their manufacturers.

Gendered Silk Work

As place names attached to silk textiles produced across the medieval Mediterranean work in tandem with stylistic imitations of silk fabrics to record widespread displacement of cloth workers as a central feature of histor-ical silk production, they tend also to occlude the gender of those workers. Indeed, the litany of place names distributed widely across the Mediterranean sea of silk, along with the material artifacts they represent, give us a sense of lucrative commercial exchange across diverse and distant geographies, but provide no indication of how the labor needed to produce such luxury goods might have been gendered.

By contrast, a number of Old French narratives tie silk production specif-ically to women's work. Some, like the three hundred silk workers in *Yvain*, are displaced workers. Others are not. But even in examples of elite women working silk, a transcultural and cross-confessional geography dominates their stories. We might consider, for example, the group of women who have handled the heavily embroidered chasuble placed on the altar by the newly wed heroine of Chrétien de Troyes's twelfth-century romance *Erec et Enide*. Having returned to Erec's homeland in Carnant, the young aristocratic couple parade through silk-hung streets, lavishly decorated with costly *tapiz* and *cortines* (vv. 2311–12), to make individual offerings to the local church. In the hope of securing future fertility, Enide places on the altar, along with an extraordinary "paisle vert," a stunningly decorated chasuble:

> Puis a ofert desor l'autel
> un paisle vert, nus ne vit tel,
> Et une grant chasuble ovree;
> Tote a fin or estoit brosdee.
> vv. 2353–56

(No one had seen anything like the green silk cloth she placed on the altar as an offering along with an impressive chasuble completely embroidered in fine gold thread.)

References to "pailes" are commonplace in twelfth-century French romance texts where they refer either to lengths of silk fabric or items of silk clothing. In *Erec et Enide* itself, the term "paile" ranges in meaning from the silk used to make Erec's leggings (v. 99; chauces de paile) to the more generally luxurious attire of knights attending Erec and Enide's wedding, described as men "vestuz de paisle, et de cendax,/ mantiax et chauces et blïax" (vv. 1915–16; wearing garments of silk and lighter weight silk used for mantles, hose, and tunics). The term "paile" also denotes the elegant silk coverlet—said specifically to be from silk-producing Thessaly—on which the courtly Enide is seated:

> An une chanbre fu assise
> desor une coute de paile
> qui venue estoit de Tessaile.
> vv. 2402–4

(She was seated in a room on a silk coverlet that had come from Thessaly.)

The green "paile" that Enide donates to the church carries no such indication of putative origin. But the gold-embroidered chasuble accompanying it does.

Queen Guenevere had the chasuble made, we are told, from a preexist-
ing garment, which she had obtained somewhat mysteriously from the emperor Gassa. The resulting ecclesiastical vestment was as stunning as it was
costly: valued at more than one hundred marks of silver (vv. 2367–76).[92] The
garment's formidable worth results, in part, from the "work" of embellishing
the original silk, work credited specifically in this instance not to professional
silk workers, but to Morgan the Fay. The fairy had "done" the demanding
gold embroidery on a "riche vestemant" that she intended for an unnamed
lover:

Et ce fut veritez provee
que l'uevre an fist Morgue la fee

la fee fet ne l'avoit mie
a oes chasuble por chanter,
mes son ami la volt doner
por feire riche vestemant.[93]
vv. 2357–58; 2362–65

(It was a proven fact that Morgan the Fay had done the work on it. . . .
The fairy had not made it as a chasuble for singing mass but wanted to
give it to her lover as a rich garment.)

However, this lavish garment presented eventually as a chasuble to the
church bears an even more densely layered history, as Sharon Kinoshita has
shown.[94] The silk vestment ornately decorated by the skilled hands of a fairy
located in the quasi-mythical site of the Perilous Valley is also, we are told just
three lines later, fashioned from gold-infused silk made in Muslim Spain:
D'or fu de soie d'Aumarie" (v. 2361; "It was made of cloth of silk and gold
from Almería"). Within the narrative space of this brief description, the mythically inflected process of silk making, figured here as the work of fairies,
comes together with the international commercial world of silk production.
And the resulting garment placed by Enide on the altar at Carnant is a rich
cultural hybrid: a Christian chasuble made of Islamicate silk embellished by a
semipagan fairy.
    Equally important, the cultural crossings between Muslim, pagan, and
Christian spheres recorded in the gold-embroidered chasuble are staged
specifically in this medieval romance around women working silk. The silk

garment made from fabric produced initially by the invisible hands of unnamed workers in al-Andalus has been crafted, decorated, remade, and finally
displayed publicly by a long chain of fictive Arthurian women, having been
"worked" by Morgan, redone by the queen, and handed on to the young bride
Enide for presentation at the church.[95] The varied gestures of these female
protagonists, as they "work" silk in a number of ways—whether manipulating, embroidering, transferring, or conferring it—complicate the commercial
production of "soie d'Aumaire" with a gendered lineage of unexpected den-
sity and dimensions. If a priest eventually ends up wearing this ornate display
of costly silk originally designed for Morgan the Fay's male lover, it comes to
him not only from the world of secular attire and imported fabric but also
from a complex line of female descent. Beginning at a historical site of
Islamicate silk production in al-Andalus, this silk has moved through an
imaginary land of fairies and into the courtly terrain of King Arthur's realm
all because of female protagonists who "work" it in varied ways.

Thus does a single silk garment circulate metaphorically in this brief passage from *Erec et Enide* through diverse layers of medieval French culture,
shifting between social classes and among gendered protagonists, while also
passing from secular to religious spheres. The movement of that single item
of silk highlights the importance of following the narrative trail of silk
"worked" by women as we read Old French literary texts. In many instances,
those narrative threads will carry us far beyond familiar Arthurian or courtly
landscapes, directing our attention to a cross-cultural realm of silk production
and decoration. Indeed, the discussion of female protagonists who work silk
in the Old French narratives to be examined below will open important narrative keyholes onto a number of distant, silk-producing worlds, complicat-
ing, in so doing, the ideological division often used facilely in Old French
epics and chronicles to map a reified Muslim east in stark opposition to a
falsely homogenous Christian west.

Closer examination of the curious scene depicting captive women workers in the Arthurian romance *Yvain* will take us to a second site of historical
silk production where the threads of Muslim and Christian textiles join.

CHAPTER TWO

Women Silk Workers from King Arthur's France to King Roger's Palermo

(*Yvain ou Le Chevalier au lion*)

THE FICTIVE WOMEN silk workers in Chrétien de Troyes's romance *Yvain* move fleetingly in and out of this tale of Arthurian quest and conquest, creating a seemingly anachronistic story within the story, a truncated and intriguing account of foreign women workers, skilled and exploited, who are usually invisible in Old French romance. The tale as a whole follows recognizable conventions of the romance genre, staging the chivalric hero's development amid subplots of love and marriage in which elite women figure both centrally and as displaced participants.[1] Not uncommonly in this genre, the feudal setting that courtly ladies inhabit is infused with mythic or magical elements. Intrusions from the commercial worlds of work or trade are, however, extremely rare.[2]

How, then, are we to read this odd account of commercially exploited textile workers placed inexplicably in a castle located somewhere in King Arthur's realm? The passage occurs near the end of the romance and forms part of an important testing sequence for the chivalric hero Yvain. His goal at the dangerous fortress called the Chastel de Pesme Aventure (Castle of Most Ill Adventure) is to defeat the two demon-devils who hold the silk workers prisoner or suffer devastating shame and humiliation. And yet, the workhouse scene makes us wonder to what extent we should imagine the three hundred silk workers at the unnamed noble's court in Chrétien's *Yvain* as actually weaving silk cloth on the premises. That is, to what extent should we understand the captive women as silk workers physically transferred to Arthurian lands from an enigmatic "elsewhere," as the text claims, or consider their story instead as a displaced narrative, a tale itself imported into the Arthurian world from another cultural landscape? The captives' eventual liberator, Yvain, contends his sole purpose in visiting the castle is to discover who the imprisoned women are (vv. 5247–49) by understanding where they are from:

> Dameiseles qui j'ai veües
> An cest chastel, *don* sont venues
> vv. 5221–22

> (*Where* did the young women I saw in this castle come from? [my emphasis].)[3]

And yet ironically, the answer to questions about the identity and origin of these Arthurian silk workers might lie less in considerations of physical location than in an examination of the kind of clothwork the imprisoned women undertake.[4]

To be sure, the enclosed silk workers diverge starkly from the more standard portraits of other protagonists in this romance. The noble lord of the castle where the women toil appears at first to be a familiar stock character, a beleaguered ruler claiming he cannot overcome the resident evil demons who require tribute payments that bring thirty new maidens to his castle annually.[5] Predictably, he prevails upon the valiant knight errant, Yvain, invoking the long-established custom of the Pesme Aventure. By fighting the demons and freeing the maidens, the capable quester will restore the young womens' honor while establishing his own chivalric reputation. The lord's daughter also plays a staple role readily familiar to readers of Arthurian romance: the unmarried *pucele* poised to fall in love. Providing one of the very few references to female literacy in this genre, the young noble woman reads aloud to her parents from a romance written by an undisclosed author (vv. 5358–64). Although the contents of the tale she reads remain unspecified, the narrator invokes a recognizable Ovidian topos when he describes this maiden's own extreme beauty:

> Li deus d'Amors, s'il la veïst,
> Ne ja amer ne la feïst

autrui se lui meïsmes non.
Por li servir devenist hon,
S'issist de sa deité fors
Et ferist lui meïsme el cors
Del dart don la plaie sainne.
vv. 5371–77

(If the God of love had seen her, he would have made her fall in love with no one but himself. He would have served her as a liegeman and, leaving aside his divinity, he would have shot into his own body the arrow whose wound never heals.)

This is a story of captive love: the male suitor hopelessly trapped by a young woman's alleged perfection.

And yet, the elegant *pucele* who incites these musings in Chrétien's romance sits on lavish silk produced by captives of a very different sort: impoverished maidens forcibly transferred to the castle/workshop. Physically confined to a space marked out by the barrier of stakes enclosing their courtyard, these prisoners live and work in "une grant sale haute et nueve;/ s'avoit devant un prael clos/ de pex aguz reonz et gros;/ et par entre les pex leanz" (vv. 5184–87; a large hall, high and recently built, with a courtyard in front enclosed by thick, round, sharp stakes). They differ significantly from any number of maidens said to inhabit the mythically vague "chastiaus as puceles" scattered throughout the landscape of Arthurian romance.[6] No silk gowns, tournaments, quests, or courtly suitors structure their lives. These women speak of exploitation and physical abuse, shame, poverty, and hunger, not in their island home, but once they are locked up in a putatively courtly castle. Theirs is a story we do not recognize readily, but a story, nonetheless, that seeps uncomfortably through the cover of its Arthurian wrapping in this romance.

Puceles of a Feather and the Arthurian Marriage Plot

Oddly, these women silk workers seem to have been displaced from one island locale to another. Having left the mythical "Isle of Maidens" (v. 5251), a site characterized most distinctively by gender rather than location, they now inhabit another equally gendered site: a kind of socially constructed island of women held in physical isolation from other protagonists in the Arthurian world. And yet, the silk workers are not as distanced from the court life that surrounds them as it might appear. Although the lord's daughter acknowledges no overt connection between herself and the captives, the Old French romance underscores in other ways an unexpected conjunction between the socially distinct *puceles*. Yvain himself notes that had circumstances been different, the beleaguered captives would have been "beautiful and noble" (vv. 5228–29; si m'est vis que beles et gentes/ fussent molt . . .), the precise terms used later in the scene to characterize the lord's daughter herself as a "pucele bele et gente" (vv. 5720, 5369).[7]

Even more telling, the Old French text specifies that the fate and fortune of the marriageable elite maiden hinges precisely, like that of the three hundred captives, on the defeat of the loathsome demons. The lord of the castle explains to the questing knight in no uncertain terms that the lord's daughter will not be free to marry until the demons exacting the yearly tribute are "dead or vanquished" (vv. 5498–99). But why? She is not part of the group of women comprising the annual tribute payment, women who are sent from a foreign land to work in the silk factory (vv. 5275–78). And yet, we are told that the *puceles* of both social ranks, elite and impoverished, will be liberated together, when the monstrous demons, born of a woman and the devil (v. 5267), are defeated. What joins these women together? The captive workers characterized as poor and poorly dressed have thin bodies and pale faces that indicate an emaciated state of exploited prisoners (vv. 5198–99). We learn nothing further concerning their physical attributes, skin color, ethnicity, or religion. What they share most obviously with the wealthy lord's daughter is their status as unmarried *puceles*.

Indeed, a number of narrative clues seem to suggest that we read this scene of displaced and abused single women against the seemingly courtly tradition of handing off marriageable daughters to traveling knights who will take them away to "another land" and dress them in silk. One has only to think of Enide in Chrétien de Troyes's *Erec et Enide* as an example of the latter phenomenon, a *pucele* carried off by Erec to King Arthur's court where Queen Guenevere reclothes her in appropriately ornate courtly finery. In *Yvain*, by contrast, the marriageable daughter is not whisked away into an advantageous silk-clad marriage. Rather, she is made to retain the status of *pucele* that allows the narrator to paint a conjoined portrait of the noble woman and the impoverished silk workers enclosed in her father's castle despite stark differences in social class.

The surprising conjunction of these *puceles* across lines of class and status becomes perhaps most apparent when we consider them in relation to the production and consumption of silk. Indeed, by reading through silk in Chrétien's *Yvain*, we can begin to understand the story of the "other *puceles*" not as peripheral or misplaced in its Arthurian setting, but as crucial to the dominant narrative that features elegant ladies, knights, and nobles draped in costly silks at court.

The issue is complicated by the dense layering of Arthurian romance, which stages elements of French twelfth-century chivalry and aristocratic marriage within mythic geographies of King Arthur's Britain.[8] The genre itself refuses to provide a single answer to the question: "where are we?"—thus rendering especially problematic Yvain's initial query about where exactly the captive maidens might be from. Indeed, when the prologue to Chrétien's *Yvain* indicates that this tale will recount the deeds of another time: "mes or parlons de cez qui furent" (v. 29; But now let us speak of those who lived before), it also situates that highly indefinite past within a quasi-historical and quasi-fictive geography. Invoking in the first few pages of the romance the legendary feats of Arthur, King of the Britains, and his knights, formerly memorialized by Breton storytellers, the romance will later take us from the king's court in Carduel, Wales (vv. 1–7, 37) to a number of evocatively magical sites such as the forest of Broceliande.

Narrative Keyholes

Such is the case with the "Chastel de Pesme-Aventure" (v. 5103) where the three hundred captive silk workers toil. A recognizably courtly castle located in an Arthurian landscape, it is both from "another time" and from the twelfth century, reflecting simultaneously a fanciful, legendary terrain and the sociocultural contours of feudal France. Here, both mythic custom and historical practice are folded together in an unexplained and often curious mix. But we might better understand the geography of the "Chastel de Pesme-Aventure," taken together with its counterpart in the "Isle as puceles," if we think of them as creating a kind of narrative keyhole onto other cultural geographies. That is, focusing our attention on these two fictive sites might provide a fragmentary glimpse of silk works and silk workers outside medieval France that have been "threaded" into the generic conventions of this Arthurian narrative, leaving a number of frayed ends and visible seams. Indeed, looking through the narrative keyhole created by these oddly paired locations in Chrétien de Troyes's classic romance *Yvain* will situate the Arthurian marriage plot within an expansive international geography mapped by the historical transfer and production of silk across the medieval Mediterranean.

Traffic in Silk

Roberta L. Krueger showed convincingly a number of years ago that the tales of love and marriage told in *Yvain* and its companion piece the *Chevalier de la charette* are imbricated in a complex cultural scenario of the exchange of women. Revealing the double bind of courtly heroines' relationships to the knights who ostensibly protect them, Krueger argued that Chrétien's courtly romance *Yvain* in particular transformed the unchivalrous practice of *rapt* into an artfully negotiated marriage alliance.[9] In this chapter, we will see further how the social transactions of courtly love and marriage staged in *Yvain* are closely allied with another kind of traffic in women: the importation of foreign women workers involved in the production and exchange of costly and ornate silk fabrics.

David Herlihy has read this passage in relation to *gynaecea* staffed by servile labor that existed on estates, *demesnes*, and manors beginning in the Carolingian period. Citing evidence of women's workshops that were separate from living spaces and probably used for weaving and dyeing, he describes Carolingian workshops of twenty-four and forty women, but nothing on the scale of the seemingly fanciful three hundred workers depicted in *Yvain*.[10] Observing that women often predominate in the serf lists of manor houses, Herlihy speculates that the staff of these houses likely included cloth workers.[11] But did they work silk? The survey of estates Herlihy uses from St. Germain des Prés near Paris lists fourteen slave girls (*ancillae*) who make cloth (*camisilos*) of linen along with nineteen *lidae*, women of a status lower than free but higher than servile, who make cloth for monks. The latter fabric would likely also be linen, or possibly wool. References to Carolingian workshops in which both weaving and dyeing took place would likely apply to the production of wool alone.[12] Nowhere in these examples is silk indicated.[13]

The scene featuring textile workers in Chrétien's *Yvain*, however, speaks only of silk, while emphasizing at the same time the foreignness of the women workers who produce it.[14] Krijnie Ciggaar has argued that we should look toward Byzantium for a solution to the anomalous silk workers in *Yvain*, and in particular to the Norman King Roger II's raids on Thebes and Corinth in 1147, when workers were taken captive and transported to the silk factory in Palermo. Roger's invasion of Thebes and plunder of its silk workers were known in both east and west, according to Ciggaar, having been recorded by Odo of Deuil in his *Croisade de Louis 7, roi de France*, among other western sources.[15]

But the Norman silk works in Palermo cannot be understood as "Byzantine" alone. Those workshops provide a remarkable western example of the direct transfer to Christian control of silk works established by earlier Muslim rulers of Sicily who had also introduced the silkworm, mulberry trees, and gold and silver production to the island.[16] Records from the Cairo Geniza reveal the dominance of Palermo, often termed simply "Siqilliyya," as a center of Mediterranean industry, trade, shipping, and finance thoughout the eleventh century.[17] In this period, silk fabrics termed "Sicilian" were exported from Palermo, Mazara, and Syracuse, and raw silk itself bore the label "Sicilian."[18] If the forced resettlement of Greek workers to Palermo injected Byzantine elements into the textiles manufactured at the Norman royal atelier, those fabrics were also embellished through a tradition of Muslim embroidery that dates, according to the geographer Ibn Hawqal, to the tenth century.[19]

Extant examples of medieval silks provide ample evidence of joint Muslim and Christian contributions to silk production in Palermo. It has long been recognized that Roger II's famous red silk cape, later used as a coronation mantle for rulers of the Holy Roman Empire, attests to the complex positioning of Palermo as a nexus of Mediterranean silk production and trade. The plain kermes-dyed samite comprising the cloak, which appears to be of Byzantine origin, was subsequently heavily decorated and embroidered with an Arabic inscription in 1133–34 by Muslim embroiderers working in the royal textile workshop in Palermo.[20] Additional surviving Palermitan silks prove even more significant in recording Muslim silk work under the Normans in Sicily, as we will see.

Cloth of Silk and Gold

First, however, we might look carefully at the kinds of cloth produced by the three hundred fictive captives in *Yvain*. Those women workers, who are confined and closely guarded, possess the knowledge and skill to make one of the most highly valued and high-volume commercial commodities in the medieval Mediterranean.[21] Indeed, the imprisoned silk workers in Chrétien's romance are said to produce three distinct versions of the extremely costly textile known as "cloth of silk and gold." We learn first that they "work" gold and silk thread:

> Vit puceles jusqu'a trois cenz
> qui diverses oevres fesioient:
> de fil d'or et de soie ovroient
> chascune au mialz qu'ele savoit.
> vv. 5188–91

(He saw three hundred maidens doing various kinds of cloth work: they worked gold and silk thread, each to the best of her ability.)

In Old French texts of this period the verb *ovrer* means "to work cloth" generally, but is also often used to connote embroidery, and specifically embroidery in gold and silk thread on previously woven silk fabric. In one of the thirteenth-century *chansons de toile* or Old French "sewing songs," for example, the protagonist Bele Yolanz is said to spread open a piece of silk on her lap and sew with one gold thread and another of silk: "sor ses genouz pailes desploie/ Cost un fil d'or, l'autre de soie."[22] In addition to doing embroidery, the women workers in *Yvain* weave silk cloth, as a spokeswoman for the group indicates: "toz jorz dras de soie tistrons" (v. 5292; We are always weaving silk fabrics). As they make silk cloth and adorn it with embroidery, these captive women workers produce the kind of *dras de soie à or ouvrés* (gold-embroidered silk) used specifically to connote the wealth and splendor of the Norman Kings in the *Roman de Guillaume de Palerne*. That late twelfth-century text characterizes the Norman palace in Palermo in terms of its exquisite textile adornments as follows:

> Tot entor fu encortinés
> *De dras de soie a or ouvrés*
> A oevres d'or et a paintures,
> A maintes diverses figures
> D'oisiax, de bestes et de gens
> Les chambres furent par dedens
> Paintes et bien enluminees
> Ainc nus ne vit mix atornees.

(It was completely decorated with *silks worked in gold*, with gold work and images of different figures: birds, beasts, and humans. The interiors were thus well embellished and enlivened/brightened. No one had ever seen any better ornamentation; my italics).[23]

The passage reflects a tradition in place at least since the time of Walter Map's *De Nugis curialium* which attests to the reputation of the Norman kings of Sicily as excessively enamored of silk and gold textiles. Map records King Louis VII chiding the Sicilian kings, along with the Byzantine emperor, for their opulent raiment of "gold and silk cloth."[24] Figure 4 provides an example of cloth of silk and gold produced in Palermo at the end of the twelfth or beginning of the thirteenth century now held at the Musée national du Moyen Age, Thermes de Cluny in Paris.[25]

Equally important, the staging of the three hundred captives in *Yvain* as weaving *dras de soie* and working silk with gold thread also marks these women as producers of a medieval textile of trans-Mediterranean scope, a costly fabric that will eventually be called simply *dras d'or*. More highly prized than the basic *paile d'Orient*, the light weight *cendal*, or heavier *samit* and *siglaton*, gold brocades originally from Baghdad and other sites in the Middle East carried many different names in the medieval west, but by the thirteenth century were often referred to generically, along with *dras d'Arest* and later the *dras de Tartarie*, simply as "cloth of gold" (*dras d'or; dras dorez; tissu d'or*) or "cloth of silk and gold."[26]

The names come into Old French texts of the thirteenth century often without clear differentiation, serving an evocative function of indicating cultural prestige and high cost. In the *Roman de la Rose ou de Guillaume de Dole*, the emperor Conrad's knights who sleep in silk tents (v. 193; paveillons de draz de soie) with maidens clad in *cendal* (v. 203; puceles en cendez) are accompanied by countesses wearing "silk and imperial cloth of gold," "Et ces contesses en samiz/ et en draz d'or emperials." (vv. 200–201). In Guillaume de Lorris's *Roman de la Rose* the allegorical character Deduit wears a "samit portret a oisiaus/ qui ere touz a or batu" (Strubel, vv. 819–20; a heavy silk patterned with bird motifs in beaten gold) and his partner Liesse a "drap qui ere touz dorez" (v. 860; fabric shot through with gold thread). In the more urban settings of the Old French fabliaux too we find mention of "tissu d'or" and "draz dorez."[27]

In fact, Francisque Michel's compendium of literary references to precious medieval textiles indicates that even the basic *dras de soie*, like that woven by

Figure 4. Tapestry. Twelfth to thirteenth century. Gold thread and silk. Made in Palermo, Sicily. Photo: Jean-Gilles Berizzi. Musée national du Moyen Age—Thermes de Cluny, Paris, France. © Réunion des Musées Nationaux/Art Resource, NY.

the silk workers in *Yvain*, or the *paile d'Orient* along with fabrics called *cendal* and *samit*, could become brocades in the Levantine style by having gold thread woven into them, thus producing *samit* or *cendal* "broché" (shot through with gold threads), *samit* or *paile* "à or batu" (with beaten gold decoration), or simply *samit* "doré" (golden).[28] Lombard explains that from the eighth to the eleventh centuries, when Muslim trade dominated the Mediterranean and gold from Sudan was plentiful, most luxury textiles were infused with "brochage de fil d'or."[29] Although by the thirteenth century cloth of gold was produced in the western cities of Genoa, Venice, and Lucca as well as earlier Islamic sites,"[30] Palermo participated in the trans-Mediterranean production and trading of silk from at least the eleventh century.[31]

When Marco Polo Goes "East"

The term "cloth of silk and gold" finds an even wider geographic distribution in Marco Polo's *Description of the World*, where it recurs like a leitmotif, connoting a number of sumptuous silk brocades seen by this Italian merchant as he traveled from the Mediterranean to Beijing, noting the production of "cloths of silk and gold" in modern-day Georgia, Iraq, and Iran among other places. Cloths of "gold and silk" (here called by the Arabic-derived terms *nakh* and *nasij*,[32] also appear in Polo's travels once he reaches northern China, where he claims that the inhabitants "live by trade and crafts, for there are made cloths of silk and gold, which one calls *nascici* [*nasij*], very fine, and another kind of cloth which is called *nac* [*nakh*], and cloth of silk of many different kinds. For just as we have the woolen cloths in our countries of many kinds, just so they have cloths of gold and silk of many kinds."[33] Also known as Tartar cloths, these sumptuous silks came to symbolize the opulence and success of the Mongol Empire under the great khans beginning in the thirteenth century.[34] Gold brocade was their fabric of choice for tents, pavilions, wagon coverings, horse, camel, and elephant caparisons; garments attiring those in attendance at imperial functions; elegant robes given as gifts; and lengths of cloth delivered to clerics, envoys, and foreign rulers.[35] But there is more.

Orfrois

In addition to weaving silk cloth, sometimes decorated with gold thread or gold "work," the captive workers in *Yvain* produce another textile that further ties their labor to silk production in Palermo while also linking it to Islamicate silk production across the Mediterranean. In a passage we considered earlier the quester Yvain explains that the enclosed, captive women weave "orfrois":

> Dameiseles que j'ai veües
> an cest chastel, don sont venues
> qui dras de soie et orfrois tissent.
> vv. 5221–23

(The young women I saw weaving silk cloth and golden bands [*orfrois*] in this castle, where did they come from?)

The term "orfrois," thought to derive from "aurifrigium," is used broadly in Old French epic and romance texts to refer to two different products, both of which include the key ingredient of gold thread.[36] When courtly protagonists are said to wear a garment "d'orfrois," or more simply "un orfrois," the term refers to clothing made from cloth of silk and gold.[37] However, the Old French term "orfrois" refers more often to the silk and gold banded decoration that characterizes costly cloth and items of courtly dress in Old French romance texts. This kind of "orfrois" can be either woven or embroidered, although the technique often remains unspecified. Guenevere gives a belt of "orfrois" to Enide, for example, as part of a full wardrobe of lavish garments befitting the heroine's new status as countess in *Erec et Enide*, "Puis vest son blïaut, si s'estraint,/ d'un orfrois molt riche se ceint" (vv. 1627–28; Then she put on her tunic and tightened it around her with a very rich, decorative gold embroidered/woven belt).

We are also told that King Erec's elaborate coronation robe, fashioned not of commonplace materials such as "serge" or "brunette" but of heavy silk, ermine, and brocade, is further enhanced with bands of "orfrois":

> Molt fu li rois puissanz et larges
> ne dona pas mantiax de sarges,
> ne de conins ne de brunetes,

mes de samiz et d'erminetes,
de veir antier et de dïapres,
listez d'orfrois roides er aspres.
vv. 6605–10

(The king was wealthy and generous. He did not distribute cloaks of
serge, or rabbit fur or rough wool but of heavy silk and ermine, of
whole fur and brocade banded with heavy gold embroidery.)[38]

The hero's shield in *Guillaume de Dole* is fitted with silk and *orfrois* (v. 1959),
equipped more precisely with "guige d'orfrois": "et met l'escu au col, tot
noef,/ par la bele guige d'orfrois," (vv. 2628–29; and he hung his new shield
around his neck from a fine gold embroidered/woven strap). The knight's
tomb in Marie de France's "Yonec" is covered with silk bearing patterned
roundels and banded with costly *orfrois*, "Coverte d'un palie roé,/ D'un chier
orfreis par mi bendé" (vv. 501–2; covered with a *pallia rotata* [silk with patterned roundels] and banded in the middle with expensive embroidered/
woven gold bands).[39]

    While a distinctive part of the courtly wardrobe and repertoire, the term
"orfrois" is commonly defined within a medieval Christian context as "gold
embroidered work or cloth of gold fastened to or embroidered on chasubles
or copes."[40] The "orfrois" found on a number of surviving liturgical vestments
have been defined succinctly as "a band either woven or embroidered in gold
thread"[41] and classified among the many decorations added to liturgical vestments such as ribbons, fringes, pearls, gems, and gold and silk embroidery on
the silk cloth itself.[42] Textile historians distinguish early medieval *orfrois*, from
the tenth to twelfth centuries, from later "orfrois florentins": mid-fifteenth-
to sixteenth-century elaborately woven patterned fabrics with a substantial
component of gold thread but not necessarily patterned banding.[43] Extant examples of Sicilian silks, specifically the "tapisseries de soie et d'or de Palerme"
(considered to have been made in the Norman royal workshop), take both
forms indicated above: appearing either as narrow woven bands of silk and
gold or as decorative patterned bands woven into silk fabrics. Some bear Kufic
inscriptions, as do related silks produced in Muslim Spain. A stunning example is provided by the tapestry-woven *orfrois* bands attached to the rim of
King William II's hose.[44] The green *orfrois* bands are embellished with golden
letters in Tulut Arabic script that correspond to the script used on an alb made
for William II between 1166 and 1189. Like many extant examples of medieval

Figure 5. Detail. *Orfois* border of hose made for King William II of Sicily. Reproduced with permission of the Kunsthistorisches Museum, Wien oder KHM, Vienna.

orfrois, they stand testament to the way Islamicate silks passed effortlessly into Christian usage. (Figure 5).

Textile historians are careful to underscore the difficulty of distinguishing "soies d'or" produced in Palermo from those manufactured in Muslim Spain.[45] Florence May explains that cloth of silk and gold was produced in Almería from the tenth century at least and subsequently in Sevilla, Malaga, and Valencia.[46] By the end of the tenth century, Sicily enjoyed a thriving commerce with these cities and participated in the development of a shared textile heritage among countries of the Islamic west, which included Spain, Sicily, and North Africa.[47] Thus does the attribution of medieval silk to specific sites of production remain highly problematic. A fragment of decorative detail from the alb of the Abbey Biure, for example, a band of silk and gold, historically assigned alternately to both Spain and Sicily, has only recently been deemed Andalusian, although it remains related by numerous traits to Palermitan "tapisseries de soie et d'or."[48] Conversely, the motif of confronted peacocks on a late twelfth-century Andalusian-patterned silk appears, according to Florence May, "possibly more Palermitan than Andalusian."[49]

Most important for our purposes, however, if "orphreys" are typically defined within a Christian context as "gold-embroidered work or cloth," they were often transferred to ecclesiastical vestments from Muslim garments or Muslim fabrics. Piponnier explains that reuse of highly worked silks or fragments of them was not uncommon in the Middle Ages. Indeed, it is in this way that "strange or foreign letters" become an integral part of liturgical vestments, carrying the name "ouvrage sarrazinois." The term used initially to indicate foreign script eventually simply describes the elaborate silk and gold weaving and embroidery used to record those "Saracen" messages.[50] The chasuble of Fermo attributed to Thomas à Becket, for example, was fashioned from worn pieces of gold-embroidered silk produced in Almería, the principal textile center for Almoravid Spain.[51] An Arabic inscription invoking Allah's blessing on the original fabric was subsequently transformed into an "orphrey" centered vertically on the back of the garment in full view of the Christian congregation during mass.[52] Thus was the prestigious and valuable silk textile transferred from Muslim to Christian use, its previously meaningful banded inscription having become ornamental, but no less powerful.[53]

References to "orfrois" on secular garments in the Old French texts do not typically include an indication of writing. And yet the use of banded inscriptions on Islamic (and some Byzantine) silks could explain otherwise curious passages such as the description in Marie de France's "Laustic" of the piece of heavy silk (*samit*) embroidered with gold and with writing "En une piece de samit/ a or brusdé e *tut escrit*/ Ad l'oiselet envolupé" (vv. 135–36; She wrapped the bird in a piece of heavy silk, embroidered in gold and with *writing*; my emphasis).[54] We know too that cloths of silk and gold, many bearing Kufic inscriptions, were frequently used for lining Christian tombs and wrapping relics.[55] The thirteenth-century inventory of silks held in the treasury of Sens cathedral records shrouds made from "tissu sarrasinois" and "soierie sarrasinoises" as well as reliquary pouches either fashioned from "tissue d'or et de soie" and "tissu sarrasinois" or embroidered with "soie et or."[56] And indeed this is the fate of the slaughtered bird in Marie de France's "Laustic." The lover who receives the silk-wrapped corpse places it in a reliquary to be honored and venerated.[57]

Palermitan Silks

Some especially striking examples of gold-embroidered work, cloth of gold, and *orfrois* attest to Muslim participation in the Norman silkworks in Palermo. Of the ten extant pieces comprising the coronation robes of the Norman kings in Sicily, three are thought to have been made in Palermo in the twelfth century: Roger II's famous mantle, the alb made for William II (1166–89), and the hose banded with *orfrois* discussed above.[58] The mantle's well-known inscription embroidered in Kufic letters refers, tellingly, not to the king but to the royal workshop that produced the garment. The alb, adapted in Palermo in 1181 for William II, by contrast, has an ornamental border at the hem that does bear the name of the ruler, King William, in Latin and in Arabic script, stating further that the garment was made in Palermo.[59] Even more striking evidence of Muslim craftsmanship is provided by Arabic inscriptions recorded on linen bands that were concealed beneath the garment's decorative sleeve embroidery. Dated to 1156, when the original garment was repaired for the second coronation of William I, these messages in Tulut script name three embroiderers, Marzuq, Ali of Malta, and Mushin, who are said to have worked under the direction of a Christian called Damyan and a master craftsman named Thomas.[60] The tradition continues through the late twelfth century when Ibn Jubayr, an Andalusian writer who visited the Norman factory in Palermo in 1184, describes Muslim embroiderers in the royal workshops, stating that the elite slave Yahya ibn Fityan was embroidering in gold at the royal factory where gold textiles were produced.[61] In stark contrast to the women silk workers figured in *Yvain*, all the embroiderers in the foregoing examples are male, a point to which we will return.

For the moment, we should note, in addition to the examples of cloth of silk and gold produced at the royal workshop in Palermo cited above, three equally intriguing tapestry-woven gold and silk textiles used as linings at the front and behind the neck of Roger II's famous mantle. These silks suggest a close association between the workshop in Palermo and Fatimid silk production in Egypt. The reused gold fabrics were affixed to Roger II's mantle, Ruth Grönwoldt surmises, as "relics" refashioned from a pallium made earlier in Palermo. Their purpose was to produce a glimmer of golden color as the wearer of the garment gestured with his arms. Moreover, the fine tapestry weave and ample gold threads constitute evidence, Grönwoldt contends, of their close relation to *tiraz* production in Fatimid Sicily and Egypt.[62]

Tiraz

Indeed, medieval banded gold decoration generally, whether appearing on elite secular or religious vestments, often bears close visual resemblance to that specific item of Islamicate silk production known by the Arabic term "tiraz" (Figure 6). Produced intitially in Sassanian Persia and then in textile factories of Muslim caliphs across the Mediterranean, spreading to Syria, Egypt, North Africa, Spain, and Sicily,[63] *tiraz* bands, either woven or embroidered with gold thread, appeared on the border of fabrics or as decorative detailing on garments: at the neck, sleeves, upper arm, and wrist. Many included decorative script that recorded pious formulas or blessings, or indicated the place of manufacture and the name of a vizier or other local official. Only occasionally did the name of the artist appear.[64] Patricia Baker cites administrator and philosopher Ibn Khaldun (d. 1406) to explain the courtly function of the bands woven into garments produced in the Islamic "tiraz," or court workshops: "It is part of royal and governmental pomp and dynastic custom to have the names of rulers or their peculiar marks . . . put on . . . the silk. The writing is brought out by weaving a gold thread or some other colored thread of a color different from the fabric itself into it. Royal fabrics are embellished with such a *tiraz*, in order to increase the prestige . . . of those whom the ruler distinguishes by bestowing on them his own garment."[65] R. B. Serjeant cites an account of the state silk factory in Alexandria, known from Roman times and into the Islamic era, that emphasizes the key role of embroidery in fashioning *tiraz* borders: "One of the royal appurtenances is the royal embroidery (*naksh*) of the sultan's name on clothing (*kuwsa*) which is woven and inscribed (*markum*), and the embroidered borders (*tiraz*) made of silk (*harir*) or gold, with a color different from the cloth (on which it was embroidered) or the tiraz borders, in order that the royal garments and embroideries (*tiraz*) may be distinguished from others, to draw attention to the power of its royal owner or that of the person whom he so honors by the investiture."[66]

Although the typical pre-eleventh-century *tiraz* is made of linen or cotton with a line of woven or embroidered calligraphy, particularly those produced in Egypt (Figure 6), the techniques of embroidering and weaving gold and colored inscriptions were soon applied to silk fabric as well, characteristically in the western Mediterranean.[67] The celebrated Veil of Saint Anne, now housed in the Cathedral of Apt in the Vaulcuse in France, provides an early example of Islamic *tiraz* with gold thread woven into silk banding on a linen garment thought to have been acquired as booty in the First Crusade.[68] Inscriptions in Arabic sewn in red silk on the central roundels include a profession of Islamic faith and a blessing for the Fatimid Caliph of Egypt, while two side bands indicate they were produced in the royal factory in Damietta in 1096–97.[69] Islamic-style banded decoration appears in another important western European venue: on twelfth-century sculpted representations of Christian garments, especially at the hem and sleeves, as Janet Snyder has shown.[70] Her studies of the sculptured clothing represented on French cathedral façades from the 1130s to the 1160s reveal a number of garments adorning western Christian figures that have *tiraz*-like bands bearing intricate geometric patterns rather than actual script.

In many ways, then, the brief reference in Chrétien's *Yvain* to captive silk

Figure 6. Detail of linen cloth with an embroidered band, 1013–21. Linen and silk. Egyptian. Photo: Franck Raux. Cl. 21955. Musée national du Moyen Age—Thermes de Cluny, Paris, France. © Réunion des Musées Nationaux/Art Resource, NY.

workers making *orfrois* and "cloth of silk and gold" positions those fictive women within a thriving commercial network of silk production and decoration that extends between once-Muslim lands in the western Mediterranean and their corollary textile producers on Levantine shores. But there is more.

Although the Arabic word "tiraz" in its original usage probably meant embroidery in general and came in time to refer to robes produced in royal textile factories that bore banded inscriptions displaying the name of the ruling caliph, the term also applies eventually to the weaving workshop itself.[71] The establishment of *tiraz* workshops begins with the Umayyads who took over Byzantine *gynaecea* in Syria and Alexandria among other cites and continued the Sassanian practice of weaving garments that included royal insignia. Both Umayyad and Abassid dynasties valued *tiraz* highly, but the custom flourished especially under the Fatimids in Egypt, North Africa, and Sicily.[72] The Fatimids established two kinds of workshops, according to Patricia Baker: those that produced clothing, tents, furnishings, and other textiles solely for the court and those that manufactured cloth items for public sale.[73] Both were controlled by government officials, partly because of the need to supervise the highly valuable bullion that was spun into metal thread.[74] The gold thread used for both weaving and embroidery, Lombard explains, could be of two types: actual metal thread or a film of gold wrapped around an inner thread of wool or silk.[75] Some *tiraz* workshops were located inside the caliph's palace (as is the courtyard workshop attached to a castle in *Yvain*). All were overseen, Baker explains, by a powerful master responsible for the weavers and other staff, for payment of their wages, equipment, and the inspection of finished work.[76] To be sure, the silk works figured in Chrétien's *Yvain* is not itself an Islamic *tiraz*. And yet, all three procedures in evidence at the silk factory in *Yvain*—whether weaving "dras de soie et orfrois" or embroidering with "fil d'or et de soie"—were used in Islamic *tiraz* factories across the medieval Mediterranean: from al-Andalus and Sicily to Egypt and Syria.[77]

In addition, a shadowy but powerful overseer appears behind the lord of the castle in the silk worker's scene in *Yvain*, marking yet another uneasy confrontation of commercial and courtly worlds in this romance. A spokeswoman for the imprisoned workers, who explained initially that they could be liberated only when the two demons collecting tribute had been killed (vv. 5280–87), alludes to a vicious human employer, distinct from the mythic demons, as "the man we work for" (v. 5313; cil por cui nos nos traveillons), a human who exploits the workers financially. It is never made clear in the seemingly anomalous courtly silk works who really holds the women workers prisoner, or precisely how the lord of the castle, the two monstrous *fils de netun* who exact the tribute, and the exploitive foreman overseeing the women's work might be related.

Scholars have generally understood the lord of this castle as a somewhat skewed version of a courtly nobleman, a feudal aristocrat whose seemingly beneficent veneer conceals the exploitation practiced by a privileged social class.[78] In this reading, the noble lord and hostile foreman are assumed to be one and the same. At times, the lord speaks in a courtly mode, as when he claims to be troubled by the unseemly "custom" that forces him against his will to make visiting knights combat hideous, black demons (vv. 5458–63, 5500–5507).[79] And yet, these same demons are described at one point as the lord's own *sergenz* (v. 5465), as if they were men in his employ. One wonders, then, whether the cruel overseer is also in some sense, like the demon *sergenz*, actually working for the lord in the key position as manager of the silk works.[80]

In any event, the women workers accuse "the man we work for" of more than financial exploitation. The spokeswoman for the group tells a tale of abuse and mortification that implicates the ambiguously conjoined figures of the lord of the castle and its foreman in the practice of sexual exploitation as well. She explains that the women are unable to rest during the night or day for fear that their cruel employer will "injure their members," Des nuiz grant partie veillons/ et toz les jorz por gaaignier/ qu'il nos menace a mahaignier/des manbres, quant nos reposons;/ et por ce reposer n'osons," (vv. 5314–18; We stay awake a good part of the night and all day long to prevent him from threatening to maim our members while we are at rest. For this reason we dare not rest). Here we learn that "the man we work for" exploits the workers financially and harasses them physically, threatening specifically to "maim their limbs," in a thinly veiled reference to the violation of rape.[81]

One thinks here of Lienor's claim in *Le Roman de la Rose ou de Guillaume de Dole* that she was raped while working "in the sewing room." Even though Lienor's account is fictitious, forming part of the masterful legal case she presents against the devious seneschal in court, as we will see in Chapter 3, her allegation of "lost honor and virginity" (vv. 4788–89; et m'onor et mon pucelage) while working in the sewing room resonates with the characterization of female silk workers in *Yvain* as sexually exploitable. Lienor states:

> Il fu uns jors, qui passez est,
> que cil la, vostres seneschaus
> (lors le mostre as emperiaus),
> vint un un lieu, par aventure,
> ou ge fesoie ma cousture.
> Si me fist mout let et outrage,
> qu'il me toli mon pucelage.
> vv. 4778–84

(It happened one day, some time ago, that that man, your seneschal [as she pointed him out to the emperor], came by chance to the place where I was sewing. He badly mistreated and dishonored me by taking my virginity.)

The fact that the silk workers in *Yvain* continue to be called *puceles* throughout the narrative does not negate the possibility that they have suffered sexual assault in secret, a secret effectively maintained by the prolongation of their "virginal" epithet. Indeed, the spokeswoman for the group tells Yvain that she cannot recount the full extent of the extremely shameful treatment the workers have endured. It remains hidden:

> De honte et de mal nos avons tant
> Que le quint ne vos an sai dire.
> vv. 5320–21

(We have suffered so much shame and harm that I cannot tell you even a fifth of it.)

We might, then also consider the plight of these workers in relation to lower-class women in the Islamic tiraz system who carried out the work of weaving, embroidery, and spinning on a commercial scale, comprising the largest female labor force at those sites. Maya Shatzmiller has explained that the *tiraz* system operated in medieval cities with a mixed labor force of slaves, forced labor recruits, and wage laborers including women who embroidered and wove silk and brocades along with threads of flax, cotton, and wool. These female workers were also typically considered morally suspect and often labeled "harlots."[82]

The association of women's silk work and sexual exploitation is documented even more specifically in Palermo. Karla Mallette describes Norman rule of Sicily in the eleventh and twelfth centuries as a tense balance between tolerance and repression of the island's Muslim population whose culture was both respected and patronized by the Christian colonizers. Mallette invokes the late twelfth-century account of Ibn Jubayr who "consistently describes Christian tolerance of Muslim Sicilians in general" while he also "dwells on the suffering of Muslim Sicilians, and the difficulties of their lives under Norman occupation."[83] This Muslim eyewitness traveler, who mentions a male servant of King William the Good (William II) employed in the silk works embroidering with gold,[84] also tells of Muslim slavegirls and Frankish Christian women who worked at the factory in Palermo during William the Good's reign (1166–89) and secretly converted to Islam under the influence of Muslim slave girls working there: "As for the slave girls and concubines in his palace, they are all Muslim. One of the most wonderful things that his aforesaid slave—Yahya ibn Fityan the Embroiderer, who embroiders in gold in the king's *tiraz*—told us about him was that the Frankish Christian women who enter his palace become Muslims, being converted to Islam by the aforesaid slave girls. But they do all this in secret from their king."[85]

Immediately preceding this passage Ibn Jubayr says of William the Good, "The king has imposing palaces and elegant gardens, especially in the capital of his kingdom, the aforementioned al-Madīna [Palermo]. . . . He makes great use of eunuchs and slave girls."[86] The earlier reign of Willliam I is characterized by both a "harem" and the silk works famed in particular for lavish gold cloth. A letter written to Peter, Treasurer of the Church in Palermo (ca. 1190), upon the death of Roger's successor, William I, and appended to the so-called Hugo Falcandus's *History of Tyrants of Sicily* (1189), laments the future demise of a number of Sicilian cities subjected to "foreign" influence while extolling the virtues of Palermo, describing among other things its architectural distinctiveness. The author of the letter claims further that the middle portion of the New Palace, called Joharia: "is particularly beautiful, sparkling with the glory of many kinds of adornment, and the king used to spend his time there intimately when he wanted to enjoy peace and quiet. Over the rest of the site there are various mansions placed all around for the married ladies, the [slave] girls of the harem,[87] and the eunuchs who are assigned to serve the king and queen. . . . Nor is it appropriate to pass over in silence the high-quality workshops which belong to the palace, where the threads of silkworms are spun most finely in separate threads of different colors before being knitted together to make multiple strands."[88]

After describing how six-stranded thread requires more skill and expense than single-, double-, and triple-stranded thread, and how threads of red and green please the eye, the author notes the extreme costliness of "damask cloth marked by circles of different kinds [that] requires greater application from the [workers] and richness of raw material, and is consequently finished at greater cost. You may see many other adornments of different colours and types there, among them *gold threaded into the silk*, and a variety of different shaped representations made by sparkling gems."[89]

The tradition of female silk workers, documented under the twelfth-century rule of William I and II, continues into the thirteenth century under the Emperor Frederick II Hohenstaufen, who maintained a staff of female slaves at several palaces in southern Italy and Sicily, although not specifically Palermo. Herlihy cites administrative directives from 1239 and 1240 that distinguish between "ancille camere nostre," slave girls of our chambers, and *domicelle* and *garcie* (meaning young girls) who should be kept busy with spinning or some other work. Although Herlihy finds no proof to substantiate the view held by many modern historians that the emperor's workshop was a "harem," he concedes that the young women therein seem "sexually available."[90] It is not difficult to imagine that from the enslaved women's perspective such "sexual availability" could have been imposed or forced. In any event, these examples offer the same conjunction of captivity and sexual exploitation that characterizes the women silk workers so startlingly featured in Chrétien's *Yvain*.

When we take into account all the details of the brief scene of three hundred silk workers in Chrétien's *Yvain*, a dense and complex image emerges. We find a story of displaced women, silk work, servile labor, and sexual predation that makes less sense in an Arthurian landscape than in the international geography mapped by a conjoined trafficking in silk and slaves that dominates the medieval Mediterranean.

Women Workers

If the workhouse scene in *Yvain* can be understood to represent some oddly fantasized hybrid place that draws elements from the conjoined Muslim-Christian silk works in Palermo, the Old French romance foregrounds the sexualized aspect of that silk production. It does so by casting all the captives in the courtly workhouse as women. The Arthurian romance departs significantly in this regard from the historical account of Roger II's relocation to Sicily of skilled Greek and Jewish silk workers from Thebes, as we have seen.[91] That group is thought to have included male and female technicians. Indeed, by the twelfth century, Thebes had become a manufacturing center famous for silk production where many tasks, it seems, were performed by men.[92] Other, perhaps more legendary, narratives from the Peloponese, however, continue to reinforce a cultural association of silk weaving and women. Nicetas Chionates reports that in 1147 the Norman commander who plundered Thebes kidnapped women skilled at weaving and installed them in Palermo because "it was the women of Thebes who were renowned for the 'daintiness of their weaving.'"[93] If the Greek chronicler here draws on a literary topos, as David Jacoby suggests, the allusion forms part of a tradition dating to the ninth century, as Jacoby also notes, in which women silk workers in the Peloponese are characterized yet again as forcefully displaced. The *Vita Basilii* records gifts given by the wealthy widow Danelina, a Slav from Patras, to the emperor Basil I that included, along with precious textiles called "sidonia" or sendal, one hundred female weavers.[94]

The three hundred silk workers in Chrétien's *Yvain* offer only a partial and highly fictionalized glimpse of the complex migrations of captive and exploited female textile workers across the medieval Mediterranean. The force and importance of this odd passage, seemingly so ill-fitted into the Arthurian romance that surrounds it, is that it does provide that gesture. Opening a kind of narrative keyhole in the fabric of Arthurian romance, the scene of the three hundred silk workers gives us perhaps a fleeting view of a foreign landscape that, historically, would have included Frankish and Muslim women along with Greeks and Jews working silk at a site like the Norman factory in Palermo. No precise clues are provided in the Old French text concerning the ethnicity or religious affiliation of the enclosed workers. We know only that they come from "elsewhere" and generate great profits. Indeed, the silk workers' spokeswoman explains pointedly "we do enough work to make a duke wealthy" (v. 5310; De ce seroit riches uns dus!). A duke, or more precisely in this instance, a lord.

The Arthurian Marriage Plot

As the workhouse scene in *Yvain* pointedly reveals the crucial intersection between two seemingly dissonant narratives—the stories of the *courtly* pucele reclining comfortably on an elegant silk *paile* and the other *puceles* whose exploited labor produces such luxuries—it also highlights an important wrinkle in the Arthurian marriage plot. Indeed, we witness in this scene a curious intersection of the feudal lord committed to marrying off his daughter and a seemingly more commercial employer intent on keeping *puceles* imprisoned for profit. In this instance, the marriage option fails to yield a profitable alliance while the silk workers produce sizable economic gain. The scenario deviates starkly from the more standard Arthurian plotline found, for example, in *Erec et Enide*, in which the questing knight bestows substantial wealth on the marriageable *pucele* and her family. In *Yvain*, by contrast, the quester, already married, takes no bride. Rather, when the victorious Yvain refuses for the third time to "take" the lord's daughter in marriage, along with all the noble's land (vv. 5709–10), the knight-liberator takes instead the skilled workers, who are handed over to him by the lord of the castle much as a daughter would be, "Tantost mes sire Yvains s'an torne/ qui el chastel plus ne sejorne,/ et s'en a avoec soi menees/ les cheitives desprisonees;/ et li sires li a bailliees" (vv. 5765–69; Soon, lord Yvain takes his leave from the castle, leading away with him the liberated captives that the lord had handed over to him). As the plotlines of courtly and working *puceles* tend increasingly to converge in this tale, exploited women workers are shown to displace the noble daughter as a potential source of revenue for the feudal lord.

And yet we might pause here to reconsider the courtly heroine Enide, another unmarried *pucele*, in Chrétien's romance *Erec et Enide*. The daughter not of a lord but of an impoverished vavasor, Enide appears initially, not unlike the captive silk workers in *Yvain*, as "poorly dressed" (vv. 405–9). This forlorn young woman is characterized further by the narrator, again like the bedraggled captive silk workers, as potentially "bele" (v. 398). More to the point, however, when the silent and pitiful Enide first encounters the newly arrived Erec, she emerges from a "workshop" (v. 442; Issue fu de l'ovreor) where she is said to have been "working" (in this instance, alongside her mother): "Li

vavasors sa fame apele/ et sa fille qui molt fu bele,/ qui an un ovreor ovroient"
(vv. 397–99; The vavasor called to his wife and very beautiful daughter who
were working in a workshop). Although the narrator makes a point of pro-
claiming ignorance about the kind of work done in this workshop "mes ne sai
quele oevre i feisoient" (v. 400; But I do not know what sort of work they do
there), one wonders whether this too could be a place of silk production, a
kind of workhouse for unmarried *puceles*, or perhaps yet another narrative
keyhole to distant sites of silk manufacture. Certainly, the presence of Enide's
mother and the loving disposition of Enide's parents provide story elements
that diverge significantly from the scenario of three hundred isolated maiden
silk workers held captive in *Yvain*. We have no indication that Enide has been
transplanted from "elsewhere," nor do we hear of profits derived from her
work. But this heroine's rags-to-riches story might provide yet another
glimpse of the larger cultural narrative linking elite women in the Arthurian
world who wear silk to those who weave it. At the very least, we are left to
wonder what Enide's work in this *ovreor* has to do with the surrounding world
of courtly romance and Arthurian opulence that she later enters effortlessly
through marriage.

Courtly Silk Work

The highly lucrative and large-scale production of the silk workers in *Yvain*
stands in stark contrast to examples in other Old French narratives of elite
women who "work" silk on an intimate scale not for profit but for pleasure.
Lienor's mother, for example, bears the title "ovriere," in Jean Renart's *Le
Roman de la Rose ou de Guillaume de Dole* because she "knows all about the
mestier" of embellishing decorative fabrics for the monastery, "quel ovriere il
a en ma dame./ C'est une mervellouse fame/ et set assez de cest mestier"(vv.
1131–33; The lady is such an accomplished cloth worker, a wondrous woman
who knows all about this craft). She and Lienor have often "worked" chasubles and beautifully decorated *aubes* as a form of pleasurable almsgiving, as
Guillaume explains to Conrad's messenger: "chasubles, bele aubes parees/ ont
amdeus maintes foiz ouvrees./ Frere, c'est aumosne et *deduis*" (vv. 1134–36;
Both of them had often worked/embroidered chasubles and beautifully decorated albs, brother. It is their charity and their *pleasure*; my emphasis). Of further significance, as Lienor and her mother sew, they sing the *chanson de toile*
that features a mother/daughter who are said specifically to produce "orfrois."

In the song entitled "Fille et la mere se sieent a l'orfrois," the women embroider golden crosses with a "fil d'or": "a un fil d'or i font orïeuls croiz" (vv. 1159–60).

But physical abuse is also part of this story. I have shown elsewhere how the demure decorative clothwork undertaken by female protagonists in the Old French *chanson de toile* is often accompanied by physical confinement and corporeal punishment. A number of the singer/sewers in the *chanson de toile* are forcibly enclosed by their father or husband and in some instances even beaten until they are black and blue. At the same time, many of the sewing songs recount the formulation of unconventional marriage alliances chosen not by restrictive parents or overlords, but designed independently by women who sing and work cloth.[95] These heroines use clothwork as a subtle means of expressing their thwarted desire and to challenge the system of arranged marriages by engineering a match of their own choosing.

By contrast, the forced labor of physically and sexually exploited silk workers in *Yvain* seems, in some sense, a perverted form of these familiar paradigms. Indeed, the captive victims of monetary exploitation and forced sex in *Yvain* are women working in the stark absence of pleasure and with no chance to use clothwork to improve their situation. They recall more closely the highly accomplished weaver Philomena in Chrétien's tale by the same name. An unassuming *pucele* (v. 205), Philomena was handed off by her father to the exploitive and sexually rapacious tyrant Tereus, as her sister had been handed to him in marriage earlier. While held captive in isolation, she marshals her considerable skills in "working" cloth (v. 1135; *ovrer*) to "write" the story of her abduction and gory mutilation into a tapestry bed curtain: "Tot ot escrit en la cortine" (v. 1131; She wrote everything into the bed curtain).[96] Providing yet another cryptic reference to writing in cloth work that might be explained in terms of the writing found in Islamicate *tiraz*, this tale shows how Philomena's skilled hands save her from perpetual imprisonment and forced sex with Tereus.[97] The captive silk workers in *Yvain* do not seem to have this option.

Neither do these skilled women resemble other elite female protagonists like Soredamors in Chrétien de Troyes's *Cligès* who works gold and silk thread on an intimate and noncommercial scale. Preparing an unusually lavish silk *chemise* as a love token for the hero Alixandre, this romance ladylove sews strands of her golden hair into the *chemise* already sewn with gold thread at the neck and sleeves:

Tant c'une chemise en a treite;
De soie fu, blanche et bien feite,

Molt delïee et molt soutil.
Es costures n'avoit un fil
Ne fust d'or ou d'argent au mains.
Au queudre avoit mises les mains
Soredamors, de leus en leus;
S'avoit antrecosu par leus
Lez l'or de son chief un chevol,
Et as dues manches et au col.
vv. 1145–54

(She pulled out a finely made white silk shift that was very soft and delicate. Among the embroidered threads there was not one that was not either gold or at least silver. On certain occasions, Soredamors's own hands had done the stitching and in certain places, on both sleeves and at the neck, she had sewn along with the golden thread a strand of her own hair.)[98]

In this instance, the kind of banded decoration that resonates with the *orfrois* produced by silk workers in *Yvain* (and the embroidery of *tiraz* bands in Islamicate textiles) has fused materially with the identity of the courtly lady as a valued treasure. As the heroine's "golden hair" is described precisely in the language of textile production and decoration, as "fil d'or," the commercial value of cloth of gold becomes metaphorized into female protagonists often rendered as golden treasure troves: "Fils d'or ne gette tel lur/ Cum si chevel cuntre le jur!" (vv. 569–70; Golden thread does not reflect as much light as does her hair in the daytime).

To be sure, the silkworker scene in *Yvain* remains distinctive in scale from the small groups of women enclosed in towers or households in the *chanson de toile*, the tiny forest hut where Philomena, the *vilaine*, and her daughter work together on a single, joint tapestry story, or the courtly setting of Soredamor's embroidery in *Cligès*. Indeed, the immense workshop said to house three hundred silk workers in *Yvain* suggests a level of commercial production returning substantial revenues that the women workers generate but do not control. Of further significance, the captive silk workers in *Yvain* are cast specifically as "foreign" women.

Foreign Women?

And yet, although they hail from an intriguingly unknown island inhabited largely, it seems, by women, the imported silk workers do not appear especially foreign. Purportedly "beles and gentes" in *Yvain*'s description of them, these women workers appear potentially, if not actually, marriageable, "beautiful" and even "noble," as we have seen. But the text makes us wonder what the women workers would gain if they fulfilled that role, becoming ladies in the courtly world and taking up the position of the "other" *pucele*. The lord's beautiful daughter, though rich, seems trapped in yet another way: by the conventions of aristocratic marriage that restrict her. Visually framed and physically confined within the square of silk fabric (*paile*) on which she sits, this female protagonist seems to hang before our eyes, oddly suspended like an icon of courtly marriageability woven into a romance tapestry.

Indeed, in an interesting twist on the paradigm of courtly love service to the chosen lady invoked earlier in the passage,[99] this *pucele* awaiting an interested suitor is caught up in service of another kind. The courtly code of hospitality requires that she "serve" Yvain, "Meïsmes la fille au seignor/ le sert et porte grant enor/ com an doit feire a son boen oste" (vv. 5405–7; Even the lord's daughter served him, treating him with great respect, as one should do to a guest). And she does so in part by sewing. In addition to washing and dressing the visiting knight as expected, this *pucele*, "so courtly, noble, and well-born" (vv. 5426–27; tant cortoise,/ et si franche, et si deboneire), takes needle and thread in hand to sew up his sleeves. As the verb *cosdre/coutre* (to sew) is made to rime here with *coster* (to cost), the traveling knight errant raises, however metaphorically, the issue of the price of this *pucele*'s labor:

> Et fil et aguille a ses manches
> Si li vest, et ses braz li cost.
> Or doint Dex que trop ne li cost
> ceste losenge et cist servise!
> vv. 5416–19

(And taking needle and thread to sew his sleeves, she dresses him. God grant that this attentive service not cost him too much.)

Her labor is free.

We know that the three hundred captive silk workers, for their part, suffer a nearly mythic fate: to weave ceaselessly (v. 5292), like an odd parody of the patient Penelope, while an endless string of "chevaliers juenes et prodomes" (v. 5324) fail to defeat the ever-ominous demon captors. Abandoned by their own young king, who at age eighteen chose to send thirty silk workers annually as tribute instead of fighting the formidable *fils de netun* himself, the women silk workers are paid only a pittance of what their abundant cloth work is worth. And yet, that might be in the end the most telling detail of their story. They are, above all, endlessly productive throughout the narrative, making "diverses oevres" (v. 5189) of the most highly valuable medieval textile: cloth of silk and gold that is said to generate high profits for a shadowy employer we never see. What we observe in sum, indeed what *Yvain* sees when he first encounters the imprisoned women workers (v. 5200), are two distinct tableaux of women's labor. One records the intensely seductive beauty of the silk they produce, while the other conveys the unsightliness of the workers' plight.

Yvain casts the dichotomy in terms of pleasure and displeasure, noting first that the "silk cloth and gold bands" made by these women are "pleasing" to the eye (vv. 5223–24; qui dras de soie et orfrois tissent,/ et oevres font qui *m'abelissent*; They weave silk cloth and *orfrois* and produce works that *are agreeable to me*; my emphasis). He then explains the image as "displeasing" to the viewer: "Mes ce me *desabelist* mout" (v. 5225; But this *displeased me* greatly; my emphasis), because in body and face these women are thin, pale, and sad (vv. 5226–27; qu'eles sont de cors et de vout/ meigres, et pales, et dolantes). They would have been "beles et gentes" (v. 5228) Yvain contends if only they had "itex choses qui lor pleüssent" (v. 5230) that is, if only they had "things that pleased them" or, more literally, things that *they* found pleasing: "qui *lor* pleüssent" (v. 5229).

Whose Pleasure?

As we read this telling phrase, the captive workers, known to us previously as exploited, abused, shamed, and dishonored become, for a passing moment at least, the subject of the sentence: women who might possibly experience pleasure. What they might "want" can only be imagined by reversing the terms of their current condition in which, as their spokeswoman describes it, "ja mes n'avrons rien qui nos *pleise*" (v. 5288; we will never have anything that pleases us). That is, they will never be liberated (v. 5290) or be able to leave this place, to weave luxurious silk without themselves being ill-clad, poor, naked, hungry, and thirsty:

> Que ja mes de ceanz n'istrons;
> toz jorz dras de soie tistrons
> ne ja n'en serons mialz vestues;
> toz jorz serons povres et nues
> et toz jorz fain et soif avrons.
> vv. 5291–95

(We will never leave this place. We will always weave silk cloth and never be any better dressed. We will always be poor and naked, hungry and thirsty.)

Most important, they will never be able to earn by the work of their own hands more than a trifle of what their silk work is worth, here stated as four meager *deniers* to the pound, "que ja de l'uevre de noz mains/ n'avra chascune por son vivre/ que quatre deniers de la livre" (vv. 5300–5302). They will never be able to provide for themselves: "Ja tant chevir ne nos savrons" (v. 5296).[100]

And yet, contrary to these dire predictions, the *puceles* are liberated and they do leave the exploitive silk works. It is a "fairy-tale" ending, to be sure. But continuing in that same vein could we not imagine that, in addition to these putatively impossible reversals, the remaining terms of their confinement might also be overturned: that they might in fact eventually be able to weave luxurious silk to clothe themselves richly, and to profit from the fruits of their own labors?

That would be a different story, indeed; certainly not the standard love story featuring endlessly festering Ovidian wounds that the narrator says he might have pursued if such a tale *had pleased* his audience, "de ces plaies molt vos deïsse/ tant qu'a une fin an venisse/ si l'estoire bien vos *pleüst* (vv. 5383–85; I would have told you much about these wounds before ending the tale, if such a story had pleased you). Nor would it be a story of successfully arranged marriage, like the one between Laudine and Yvain, so *pleasing* to the go-between Lunete at the close of this romance that she "has everything she could want" (v. 6800; ne li faut chose qui *li pleise*). Indeed, the stinging remarks of the silk workers' spokeswoman suggest that "the things that might please them" (v. 5230; itex choses qui lor pleüssent) would not be the elegant clothes, silk brocades, and *cointises* typically lavished upon courtly *puceles* by a father intent on marrying them off or by a rich husband eager to parade them in public. Rather, these foreign silk workers yearn to deploy their considerable skills to different ends: to make their own costly fabrics and earn profits by the work of their hands (v. 5300; de l'uevre de noz mains). To do so would mean to become *subjects* of their weaving and embroidery. That is, not to abandon clothwork as necessarily exploitive—for indeed, it is shown here to be highly remunerative—but to take control of silk work and use it for their own benefit and profit. We witness such a scenario in the thirteenth-century romance *Galeran de Bretagne* where the heroine Fresne knows how to "faire oeuvres de manieres" including "laz et tissuz, et aulmosnieres" (v. 1162; to make diverse objects [like] laces, belts, and alms purses) such that "N'ot telle ouvriere jusqu'en Pouille/ Com elle est de tistre de d'aiguille" (vv. 1159–60; there was no finer worker in weaving or needlework as far as Puglia). She escapes from a convent, travels to Rouen, and turns a widow's house into a shop producing luxury cloth of silk and gold from which she earns a sizable profit: "Et draz ouvrés de soye et d'or/ Qui bien valoient ung tresor" (vv. 1163–64; cloth worked with silk and gold that was worth a treasure).[101]

For the newly freed silk workers in Chrétien's tale to begin profiting from their highly valued silk work would mean to emerge from the position of the unnamed agents hidden behind all those dangling adjectival references to "worked cloth" (*dras ouvré*) in Old French literary texts and to take up a position of working women: *ouvrières* who are not subject to economic exploitation or physical attack in the "sewing room." Tellingly, those exploitive and dangerous conditions seem only to be associated in this romance with the foreign silk workers once they enter the Arthurian landscape, not beforehand. Indeed, the freed captives return to the elusively mythic "Isle of Maidens" without hesitation or apprehension. They express only joy:

"Alez, fet il, Dex vos conduie
En voz païs sainnes et liees."
Maintenant se sont avoiees;
Si s'an vont grant joie menant.
vv. 5800–5803

("Farewell," he [Yvain] said, "may God lead you to your country healthy and happy." Then they departed in great joy.)

More specifically, when they depart from the lord's castle, the "cheitives desprisonees" (v. 5768) are said to feel "rich" although still clad in rags:

Povres, et mal apareilliees,
Mes or sont riches, ce lor sanble.
vv. 5770–71

(Although poor and poorly dressed, it seems to them that they are rich.)

Despite the prior actions of their weak and inexperienced king, who stumbled ignorantly into the perilous customs of the Arthurian world and traded his freedom for the *puceles*' imprisonment, these workers remain highly skilled and capable of producing a most valuable commodity.[102] It is in this single detail that the three hundred *puceles* differ most significantly in the end from the Arthurian lord's daughter whose textile skills are not at all marketable. That courtly *pucele* can only sew up the decorative sleeves of the knightly suitor to whom she renders a service free of charge. These women, by contrast, can work silk and gold.

Indeed, more is liberated at the close of this brief scene than female captives. When the *puceles* in Chrétien's *Yvain* are freed by the questing knight, so too is their silk working skill liberated along with them. If the provocative passage featuring three hundred silk workers in this romance offers a narrative keyhole onto distant silk working sites scattered across the medieval Mediterranean, it also invites us to imagine an alternate scenario staged on the elusive and indistinct "Isle as puceles." While this text lets us see the kind of exploitation that might have characterized workshops like those in Palermo, it allows us to conceptualize at the same time an antidote fashioned in a mythic elsewhere. Potent with historical and legendary resonances of women and silk making across the Mediterranean, this story is also about women's skill and knowledge being first appropriated but then restored.

Perhaps, then, we might revise our earlier query concerning where these foreign women came from and consider the more salient question: where does their skilled work go? How can we as readers of Old French texts attempt to keep women's ability to work silk in view as we read further, looking for the complex threads of the textile geography that results from their gestures and movements? That is the task of the chapters that follow: to take a close look at instances of women working silk in a variety of subtle ways across a range of Old French texts. We will find them in the most unlikely places.

CHAPTER THREE

Women Working Silk from Constantinople to Lotharingia (*Le Dit de l'Empereur Constant, Le Roman de la Rose ou de Guillaume de Dole*)

Two FICTIVE WOMEN occupying lands separated by the medieval Mediterranean form the focal points of this chapter: the little-known heroine Sebelinne, daughter of the emperor of Constantinople in the anonymous *Dit de l'Empereur Constant*, and the more familiar Lienor, sister to Guillaume de Dole in Jean Renart's *Roman de la Rose ou de Guillaume de Dole*. Distinctly different from the impoverished and captive women who weave and embroider without significant material gain in Chrétien de Troyes's *Yvain*, these privileged women "work" silk to their considerable advantage. Both Sebelinne and Lienor use cloth work astutely to refashion their sociopolitical identities and gain, as a result, increased social mobility and status. In fact, both heroines, although separated by the geographical expanse between their home cities of Constantinople and Dole, forge unexpected narrative identities by "working" a small trans-Mediterranean material object. Commonly known in the French Middle Ages as an *aumosniere*, the medieval alms purse that ties these disparate heroines together is also often termed *sarrasinoise*.

Whether damask or velvet, decorated with silk or gold embroidery, Old French *aumosnieres* described in romance texts and trade accounts of the thirteenth century are fashioned typically from costly silk and hung from a belt that is itself often made of rich silk fabric. Thus do we find the oft-repeated

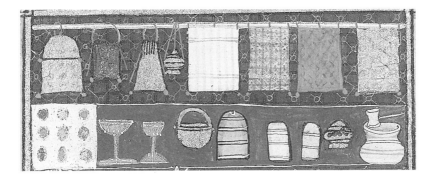

Figure 7. Detail of French Apocalypse, Northern France, thirteenth century. Household goods in decreasing order of value: *aumonières*, precious textiles, and furs; precious gems and glassware; metal, wood, and ceramic containers. Paris. BnF, ms. fr. 13096, fol. 62. (© Bibliothèque nationale de France).

couplet "aumosniere et ceinture" or alternately "aumosniere et tiessu" used to describe items of dress worn by courtly protagonists of both genders. Although these small purses can serve the practical function of holding anything from herbs, unguents, and medicines to holy bread or even sewing supplies,[1] Old French literary texts often feature silk purses as lavishly embroidered receptacles for carrying small change and keys, valued rings, brooches, and jewels. The depiction of household goods from a French Apocalypse in Figure 7 above features a series of differently shaped *aumosnieres* hanging alongside valued silks and costly gemstones. At times, these highly decorative items of elite clothing are bestowed as luxury gifts or love tokens. In the extreme, the silk *aumosniere* becomes a signifying mark of the male courtly lover as in Guillaume de Lorris's *Roman de la Rose*, where the God of Love stipulates as requisite attire for the aspiring Amant: gloves, a belt, and an "aumoniere de soie" (vv. 2153–54).[2]

The term *aumosniere* itself takes us in another direction entirely, however, suggesting a religious function for the silk purse as a pouch that might hold alms for the poor or money to be donated at Christian pilgrimage shrines. A number of historical *aumosnieres* inventoried in the substantial relic collections of Sens and Chelles[3] attest to the ability of these small material objects to perform both secular and religious functions. Many of the lavish silk purses catalogued at Sens and Chelles once served as reliquary pouches. And yet, despite their Christian contents, these *aumosnieres* were termed not infrequently "aumosnieres sarrasinoises." In this instance, the term likely connotes textile technique rather than an Islamicate site of production. Indeed, as we have seen, some of the *aumosnieres* made in thirteenth-century Parisian workshops and described in guild regulations also bear the name "aumosnieres sarrasinoises."[4] Here, the attribution "Saracen" is thought to refer to the lush adornment of the purses in question, whether connoting gold thread woven into the silk fabric or gold embroidery applied to it. In both cases, the cross-cultural and cross-confessional resonances contained within the oxymoronic "aumosnieres sarrasinoises" map a broad trans-Mediterranean scope for these decorative items of elite dress. That scope is confirmed for historical *aumosnieres*, which figure among the many small silk items such as ribbons, belts, veils, and headscarves that were widely used in all three major regions of David Jacoby's study of silk economics, that is: Byzantium, the Christian west, and the Muslim world.[5]

Recent research by Sharon Farmer shows that thirteenth-century Paris had a lively silk industry dominated in fact by women, both as workers and as entrepreneurs, as we have seen. Etienne Boileau's *Livre des métiers* lists women spinners (*fileresses*) who prepared silk fiber for weaving (lv), women silk weavers (*tisserandes de soie*) who produced headscarfs and linings (lviv), women who worked silk as *chapelieres* and *mercieres* (lxxvii), and female *tissutiers* and *rubaniers* who wove silk ribbons, perhaps adding embroidered detail (lviii).[6] In the narrative of the *Empereur Constant*, Sebelinne works her influence through a cloth object that is said obliquely to have already been "worked" or heavily "decorated" (v. 355; une aumousniere de rice oevre), perhaps by other women.[7]

It is significant, however, that Sebelinne is not situated in a Parisian workshop like the women mentioned in the *Livre des métiers*. Nor is she located in a household or castle in medieval France, as are the protagonists in the Old French *chanson de toile*. Rather, this heroine's father has enclosed her in the company of a nurse and under the guardianship of local nobles in a castle situated cryptically at the edge of his realm (v. 89; el cief de sa tierre) while he travels to Bisence. Sebelinne is positioned, then, somewhere in the distant and geographically vague Byzantine Empire, understood anachronistically in this tale as a "pagan" land.[8] Descended from the kings of Greece on her father's side and from Roman emperors on her mother's, Sebelinne, who displays the hallmark beauty and nobility of the western courtly lady, also stands geographically in the quintessentially eastern city of Constantinople: a pagan princess who chooses to marry a future Christian emperor. She engineers that union herself through her personalized and individual "work" on an iconic object of courtliness, the *aumosniere*.

Whereas not all the decorative *aumosnieres* featured in Old French literary texts carry the label "sarrasinoises," they tend, nonetheless, to be characterized specifically by rich adornment. The belt and purse, for example, that figure among the items of clothing laid out for the courtly hero Yvain in Chrétien de Troyes's *Le Chevalier au lion*, are described as "et ceinturete, et aumosniere/ qui fu d'une riche sainiere" (vv. 1893–94; a small belt and purse of rich luxury cloth)[9] and the belt and purse adorning Pygmalion's ivory beloved in Jean de Meun's *Roman de la Rose* typically appear as exceedingly lavish, highly valuable, and costly: "Mais c'est d'un si tres riche ceint/ c'onques pucele tel ne ceint/ E pent au ceint une aumosniere,/ Qui mout est precieuse e chiere" (vv. 20987–89; No maiden had ever worn such an exceedingly lavish belt. And hanging from the belt there was a highly valuable and costly purse).[10] At times, the opulence of this signature article of aristocratic clothing is marked specifically by its association with "orfrois," as in Jean Renart's *L'Escoufle*, when the *pucele* Ysabiaus depicts the gift she will present to the lady of Montpellier, "Je li ferai une çainture/ et une mout riche aumosniere/ d'orfroi; et s'iert d'une maniere/ Et aumosniere et la ceinture (vv. 6560–63; I will make her a belt and lavish purse of gold-worked cloth and both will be made in the same style, the purse and the belt).[11]

So too are the individual *aumosnieres* "worked" by the hands of Sebelinne and Lienor designated as highly decorative: Sebelinne deftly handles an "aumosniere de rice oeuvre" while Lienor manipulates an *aumosniere* said to bear highly distinctive motifs embroidered in gold.

Thus do the *Dit de l'Empereur Constant* and *Guillaume de Dole* draw our attention to two key features of Old French *aumosnieres*: their cultural association with women's work on the one hand and the opulent decoration that was sometimes termed "Saracen work" (*opere saraceno*) on the other.[12] In so doing, they reveal the extent to which the eastern and putatively pagan Sebelinne and the western Christian Lienor might be joined across the medieval Mediterranean through their deft manipulation of the richly adorned small purses that they "work" in different ways. If the ocean separating these heroines geographically was known in the Middle Ages to be teeming with the profits of a highly lucrative silk trade, the silk "work" of these women is shown to return profits of a different sort. Indeed, it is through their individual interactions with a rich and costly *aumosniere* that Sebelinne and Lienor exert substantial legal and political influence. In both narratives, the handiwork of elite women creates a kind of social language allowing them to accrue authority and status as they work to redefine, through the use of luxury textiles, the category of the "marriageable" woman.

Sebelinne

The *aumosniere* in the thirteenth-century *Dit de l'Empereur Constant* is perhaps most significant as a material object from which the heroine Sebelinne pulls, almost magically, a brief plot of monumental proportions. The tale recounts no less than the legendary transformation of Byzantium into Constantinople, ostensibly by a lowly youth, Constant, who is himself changed unpredictably in the course of the tale from a low-born son into an emperor.[13] When the boy called Constant is perceived by Sebelinne's father, Florien, emperor of Byzantium, as a threat to royal succession in the eastern capitol, he is kidnapped and severely mutilated. Saved by a chamberlain who wraps the infant in silk, swaddling him in a "vermeil couvertoir de soie" (v. 201; red silk coverlet), Constant is delivered to an abbey, baptized, and raised as a Christian (v. 233). Not unlike the heroine Fresne in Marie de France's *lai* by the same name, this protagonist is later recognized because of the lavish silk cloth which, in this instance, documents his capture and his stay in the royal household while also presaging his future status as emperor (vv. 273–80).[14] As this Christian convert modeled on feudal nobility replaces the former emperor of a people here cast as "pagan" (vv. 192–93), he is credited with giving the famed eastern city a new name derived from his own hybrid identity: "Constant le noble" (vv. 627–28). The city called "Constantinnoble" suggests both the costly (*coustant*) opulence typically associated in the medieval west with Byzantine splendor and the requisite nobility (*le noble*) of a Christian courtly hero who might predictably perform such a daunting task.[15]

And yet, the conversion of the dazzlingly rich eastern city and the surprising creation of its new ruler are actually affected by a woman, the Byzantine emperor's unassuming daughter Sebelinne, who is associated with rich cloth in a very different way. In fact, this heroine successfully lays claim to a trans-Mediterranean political identity by manipulating a small, ornate purse. Sebelinne's father Florien, hoping to dispose once and for all of the troublesome rival Constant, sends him away with a secret message ordering Constant's own death. It is Sebelinne who intercepts the message, cancels the order, and saves the messenger's life. Thus does she obtain her every wish, we are told (vv. 382–83, 427, 599), for Sebelinne has fallen suddenly and inexplicably in love with this "noble damoisiaus" (v. 251).

On the advice of a woman servant (vv. 384–94), Sebelinne performs a breathtaking act of ventriloquism, replacing her father's written message with one of her own devising. Sebelinne writes in her father's place and literally in his name, inserting into the "aumousniere" a message that begins, "Jou, empereres de Bisence, de Griesse et de Sesille rois" (vv. 406–7; I, Emperor of Byzantium and Greece and King of Sicily). Usurping the functions of Florien as both emperor and father, Sebelinne boldly instructs the emperor's provost at one and the same time not only to spare the young Constant's life but also to arrange for him to marry her.

Different from the prose version of the *Empereur Constant*, in which Sebelinne notices and then seizes the messenger's letter directly,[16] the *dit* draws our attention pointedly to the lavish silk purse in which the letter is enclosed. What catches Sebelinne's eye in this account is the messenger's belt and the "richly worked" *aumosniere* attached to it:

Tant qu'elle vit a sa çainture
Une aumousniere de rice *oevre*;
La pucielle le prist, se l'*uevre*.
vv. 354–56 (my emphasis)

(As soon as she saw a richly worked purse attached to his belt, the maiden took it and opened it.)

Although this "aumousniere de rice oeuvre" is not said specifically to be made of silk, its characterization as "richly worked" situates it squarely among any number of lavish silk purses typically described in literary texts of the period as an "aumoniere de soie" "aumosniere" of "samit vermeil," or "aumonniere/ qui de soie estoit boinne et ciere."[17] In the *Dit de l'Empereur Constant*, Sebelinne's gesture of opening that *aumosniere* opens her future, as the homophony between "oeuvre" and "l'uevre" in the passage quoted above suggests. Hers is a future cast within the folds of richly worked cloth.

If the story of the *Empereur Constant* begins by asking "who can be emperor?" in terms of religion and class status—a Christian or a pagan, a "fils de vilain" or a noble—it later asks that question in terms of gender and place: Could the emperor, in some sense, if only temporarily or in effect, be a woman? To what extent could the signature on a message behind the

name of the "Emperor of Byzantium, the King of Greece and Sicily" be
penned not by a man's hand but by a woman's? The question resonates historically with an infamous Byzantine empress from an earlier period, the
Empress Irene who, after serving as co-regent with her son, Constantine
VI, took the unprecedented step of displacing him entirely and adopting
for herself the title of *basileus* traditionally reserved only for the male
emperor.[18]

The subtle narrative nod to Irene, who ruled Byzantium at the time of
Charlemagne, should not surprise. It forms part of the larger anachronistic
and fanciful mix of historical eras and legendary figures that create the backdrop of the *Dit de l'Empereur Constant*. As a conversion story of mythic proportions, this tale draws indirectly on overlapping elements in medieval epic
cycles that feature Charlemagne and Constantine, respectively, positing both
men as sovereign Christians, protectors of the Church, and enemies of paganism in the East.[19] One epic in the Charlemagne cycle from the end of the
twelfth century, *La Chanson de la Reine Sibile* (entitled *Macaire* in this version), describes Charlemagne's wife, Sebile, as daughter of the emperor of
Constantinople,[20] much as the heroine Sebeline in the *Dit de l'Empereur
Constant* also bears that name officially, "Et Sebille en droit non nommée" (v.
78). We are told in addition that the hero Constant in this tale will eventually
father Constantine.[21] As the historical conversion narrative of Constantinople
becomes highly fictionalized and distended across a broad chronological expanse in the *Dit de l'Empereur Constant*, so too is the tale's geography extended in ways that reflect political ideologies and cultural developments in
the medieval Mediterranean. In particular, Sebelinne's signal claim to replacing her father as "Emperor of Byzantium and Greece and King of Sicily,"
draws our attention to the "royaume de Secile," a region only formed historically with the advent of the Norman kings of Sicily. If at the time of
Constantine no kingdom of Sicily existed, by the Middle Ages, as we have
seen, Norman Sicily played an important role along with key cities in
Byzantium and Greece in the production of the kind of luxury fabrics used to
fashion the narrative identities of both Sebelinne and Constant in this tale.
When Sebelinne is said pointedly to have put her authoritative and ventrilo-
quized decree "dedens l'aumosniere" (v. 429), the reference to luxury silks locates this heroine cross-culturally between the mythically potent site of silk
production in Byzantium and the more local silk factories in Norman Sicily.
Indeed, the highly charged political questions posed by this tale regarding
who can be emperor, a Christian or pagan, noble or commoner, man or

woman, are used to foreground a more culturally charged question: in what sense could a courtly female protagonist orchestrate the plot of this story, determining the course of its events and the pattern of her future life? And by what means?

In many of its details, the *Dit de l'Empereur Constant* stages courtly protagonists in an eastern venue, drawing heavily on courtly vocabulary to characterize not only Sebelinne (vv. 336, 470–72) and Constant (vv. 245, 251, 344–46, 478), but also the heroine's mother (vv. 101–2) and even, on one occasion, the pagan emperor Florien (v. 263).[22] Indeed, a scenario of seemingly impossible love at first sight structures the turning point in the tale when the delicate courtly heroine transforms herself almost effortlessly into something else entirely: "empereres de Bisence, de Griesse et de Sesille rois." Not only do Sebelinne's authoritative written instructions to the provost indicate her "commandement" (v. 456) that he carry out, under penalty of death, the incontrovertible expression of "her will" (v. 427; tout son vouloir), she employs in her message the recognized legal formula of "manç et commanç."[23] Using these words, the heroine, posing as the emperor, directs the provost to substitute her very body for that of the messenger, recognizing and paying deference to it:

A vous, mes fiables prouvos,
Manç et commanç que aussitos
Que ces letters avés oÿes,
Que del messagier, qui baillies
[A] vous les avra de par moi,
Faciés autant dou corps de soi
Que de moi meïsmes feriés.
vv. 409–15

(I order and command you, my faithful provost, that as soon as you have heard this letter delivered to you by a messenger on my behalf, you take it as seriously coming from his body/person as you would from me/mine.)

All this is contained within a single, decorative "aumosniere de rice oeuvre": a small, material item that allows this heroine to assume metaphorically, but also with legal force, both the voice and body of her father the emperor.

Thus do the transfigured contents of the "richly worked" purse enable

Sebelinne to step boldly out of the gendered categories of governance and marriage. At tale's end, the emperor gives his wholehearted consent to the marriage as soon as the provost explains that it was sanctioned in fact by a letter from the emperor himself, that the wedding was arranged specifically and only because of *his* command, "Car a vo prouvost le mandastes/ Par vos lettres et commandastes/ Que on li fesist espouser" (vv. 567–69; Because you instructed and ordered your provost in your letter that she should marry him). And yet "his" command was of course actually "hers." We as reader/listeners know that the message was penned by Sebelinne. In agreeing absolutely with the provost's contention that the emperor's orders must be followed (vv. 572–73), Florien, Emperor of Constantinople and Greece and King of Sicily, subtly cedes his authority in the matter of marriage to his daughter, the young woman turned emperor through the contents of an *aumosniere*. Rather than object that *his* words have been stolen or *his* wishes misrepresented, Florien insists instead that Sebelinne's orders must be followed. Through the emperor's declaration, the contents of the *aumosniere* stand as an official and authoritative document, created through this heroine's handiwork with a small silk purse.

In one sense we might understand Sebelinne as "working" the *aumosniere* much as heroines in the Old French *chanson de toile* work fabric, rewriting the male-voiced songs of love and romance in a different key, often recasting the traditional male lament into a story of shared desire and consensual marriage. The female protagonists of the *chanson de toile* effect this transformation while performing cloth work: sewing, spinning, and embroidering.[24] In the *Dit de l'Empereur Constant*, Sebelinne rewrites her own marriage plot by recasting the role and function of what was historically, in western Europe, often a product of such women's work: a decorative *aumosniere*.

Aumosnieres *and* Bourses

The aristocratic *aumosniere* that appears in romance narratives as a costly dress accessory worn atop other articles of lavish clothing can be distinguished from the leather money pouches or small satchels called *bourses* that hung from the belts of peasants and tradesmen. Leather *bourses* designed to carry coins such as *deniers* or *mailles* are portrayed in the fabliaux as being used by merchants at fairs, customers in the marketplace, clients at the tavern, or shopkeepers and tradesmen in town settings.[25] Two surviving archaeological examples of medieval French purses, reproduced in *Le Quotidien au temps des fabliaux* by Danièle Alexandre-Bidon and Marie-Thérèse Lorcin, aptly illustrate the distinction.[26] The first is a leather *bourse* from the thirteenth century discovered in Brussels, a simple money pouch closed with a drawstring. The second is a silk *aumosniere* from Chelles, dated to the twelfth century. The leather pouch resembles the everyday coin purse hanging from a peasant woman's belt in the Luttrell Psalter or the "bourses et ceintures" displayed for sale in a fourteenth-century manuscript drawing of the mercer's stall, both reproduced in *Le Quotidien au temps des fabliaux.*[27] By contrast, the *aumosniere* of red silk from Chelles (Seine et Marne) dated between 1170–80 is heavily embroidered and bedecked with tassels, pompons, and decorative buttons.[28] An item of luxury attire, this silk purse resembles more closely the highly ornamented and apparently expensive *aumosnieres* displayed alongside furs and precious textiles, gemstones, and glassware in a thirteenth-century miniature of "household goods" from a northern French Apocalypse (Figure 7). And yet the *aumosniere* from Chelles is thought to have served, at one time at least, as an envelope for Christian relics.[29] Further attesting to the ability of *aumosnieres* generally to fulfill both secular and religious functions, Brian Spencer catalogues English *aumosnieres* that actually served as reliquaries, indicating also that miniature versions of these purses in lead, whether hung as necklaces or affixed to clothing as were many medieval pilgrim badges, sometimes also functioned as reliquary pendants.[30]

At times, the Old French terms *bourse* and *aumosniere* are not entirely distinct. We see the aristocratic *aumosniere* in context, for example, in the fourteenth-century *Roman de Baudoin de Sebourc* when the Rouge Lion has his sister dressed for marriage: the lavish outfit of rich silk fabrics and cloth of gold is completed appropriately by an elegant purse, here called a "bourse ovree" (v. 770).[31] More commonly, however, the term *bourse* appears in comical and ribald fabliau, accompanying visual images of male sexual potency and lustful gaming. The erotic connotations of the Old French *bourse* emerge clearly, for example, in the fourteenth-century manuscript image of a merchant's stall, reproduced by Alexandre-Bidon, where *bourses* and belts displayed for sale are juxtaposed with an image of a fornicating couple.[32] A fourteenth-century courtly variation on the motif features a lady offering her heart to her lover while a husband offers his wife a more tangible *bourse*, the latter suggesting both monetary and sexual abundance.[33]

Reliques *and* Coilles

Medieval audiences would have been familiar with the conflation of the erot-
ically charged *bourse* and the religiously and ritually oriented *aumosniere*, for
they appear in one of the most widely circulated thirteenth-century narratives, the *Roman de la Rose*. In that text, purses serve a wide array of functions.
When the God of Love proscribes the requisite attire for an aspiring courtly
lover in Guillaume de Lorris's portion of the romance, the *aumosniere*
emerges, as we have seen, as a necessary and integral part of the male courtly
lover's self display. Along with the gloves and belt that complete his rich attire, this costly *aumosniere* contributes to the "bel robe et bel garnemant" (v.
2141) that will ensure, we are told, Amant's elegance or "cointerie" (v. 2134):

> De ganz, d'aumoniere de soie
> Et de ceinture te contoie.
> vv. 2153–54

(Dress yourself up in gloves, a silk purse and a belt.)

Fashioned from silk, this *aumosniere* marks the nobleman wearing it in this
instance specifically as a lover.

The association becomes complicated, however, in the infamous passage
from Jean de Meun's section of the *Roman de la Rose* in which Raison, responding to Amant's objection to the use of "vulgar" language by a "cortoise
pucele . . . sage et bele" (vv. 6927–28), evokes the linguistic dyad positing a
potential confusion of male genitalia and relics, specifically, *coilles* and
reliques. Raison says, in effect, that if the names of these two objects had been
switched, the lover would have considered the word "reliques" to be lowly and
disgusting while understanding "coilles" as a lovely word, so esteemed in fact
that he would have venerated *coilles* as if they were relics and kissed them in
churches where they would be set in gold and silver (vv. 7107–20).[34] At the
end of Jean de Meun's portion of the romance, the courtly-lover-turned-
pilgrim approaches the Rose in precisely this way, but with a significant
substitution of metaphorical genitalia. In the closing scene, Jean de Meun's
pilgrim/lover venerates not *coilles* at all but, in some readings at least, female
labia-turned-relics. In an extended description of this pilgrim's sexualized
"equipment" (vv. 21587–21676; *hernois*), his "bourdon"(v. 21592) first touches
the relics (v. 21589) that stand in for female genital lips and then enters the

"reliquary" (v. 21597; *saintuaire*) itself. In this instance it is the pilgrim's *escharpe*, a purse slung typically around the neck and shoulders, that functions in the metaphorical and violent defloration of the Rose. The male lover's purse is here said to hang behind the advancing, thrusting *bourdon* (vv. 21609–10).[35]

Are we to imagine, then, that in addition to the metaphorical pilgrim garb of "bourdon et escharpe" the "properly dressed" Amant, having finally arrived at the desired Rose, is still wearing the costly silk *aumosniere* that the God of Love declared to be necessary for amorous success? If so, the bawdy *bourse* (*escharpe*) and the decorative *aumosniere* would come together in this final scene, allowing images of base lust and refined love to collide irreverently with the practice of purportedly honoring relics in religious devotion. As the lover explains, "Car mout oi grant fain d'aorer/ Le biau saintuaire honorable/ De cuer devost et piteable" (vv. 21596–98; I had a great hunger to venerate, with a devout and pious heart, the beautiful and honored reliquary). The female beloved, here reduced to sanctified labia, would then be both revered and violated by two culturally charged material objects: the pilgrim's *escharpe* and courtly lover's *aumosniere*.

In an important sense, Sebelinne's very different use of another kind of *bourse*, the lavishly decorated "aumosniere de rice oeuvre," offers a powerful alternative to this story of violation parading as reverence.[36] Although Sebelinne too inserts part of her body into an object made potentially to hold valued relics, hers is not a pseudo-religious gesture, and the body part in question here is not a metaphorical male member represented by the pilgrim's *bourdon*. Rather, this heroine "enters" the *aumosniere* with her hand in order to deposit a sealed, handwritten message claiming the Byzantine emperor's rank and trans-Mediterranean authority as her own. What is honored irreverently in the *Empereur Constant* is not the genitalia of either gender, but the heroine's invaluable and transgressive hands that enact a crucial transgendered performance. Interestingly, this heroine's bold substitution of her letter for her father's is not condemned as a forgery but hailed as a legally binding document that the emperor endorses (vv. 572–73). Sebelinne, much like Reason in Jean de Meun's *Roman de la Rose*, emerges here as both "sage" and "bele." And if her speech bears no terms "inappropriate" for a courtly lady, her writing, enclosed and delivered in silk, certainly does. These words transmitted in their luxurious textile enclosure are her currency, a considerable asset in a world where unwed daughters might otherwise have little purchase.

If the relic/testicles mentioned in the bawdy passage of the *Rose* are set in silver and in gold (vv. 7120), Sebelinne's words lie within a pouch of equally precious fabric. Her cultural currency is safeguarded in an envelope of cloth whose shape and substance would normally spell, for a medieval French audience, courtly wealth and opulence, while also signaling the amorous prerogatives of the *Rose*'s male courtly lover or the erotic antics of male lovers in Old French fabliau. Through Sebelinne's concerted handiwork, however, the potential violation of women in courtly copulation is transformed into a potential for female-initiated marriage.

But there is more. The "aumosniere de rice oeuvre" so ably "exploited" or "worked" by the astute heroine Sebelinne, becomes a narrative crossing place for a number of cultural threads that wind their way through this brief tale. When Sebelinne introduces her hand into the *aumosniere* hanging from Constant's belt, we witness not only a potentially sexualized woman's hand willfully entering a man's purse, but a pagan hand depositing a message of love and marriage into the purse of a Christian, and the hand of the emperor's daughter signaling a desire to combine her lineage with that of a commoner (*fils de villain*). In brief, the *aumosniere* "worked" by Sebelinne into a site where gender identities can shift and cross, also offers a crossing place for bloodlines and political alliances, the unexpected mixing of social class and rank, the effortless joining of religious affiliations, and the effective blurring of economic distinctions between east and west that the prose version of this tale more overtly holds apart.

Indeed, the conversion narrative that merely forms the backdrop for courtly, amorous, and marital events in the *Dit de l'Empereur Constant* takes center stage in the prose version of the tale, which deploys a highly religious vocabulary to underscore the triumph of Christianity over a demonized pagan emperor.[37] Here Florien becomes Muselins (l. 472), a ruler who invokes Mahomet and Tervagant (ll. 26–27) while disparaging and mocking Christianity (ll. 152–53).[38] In the *Dit*, Florien seems surprisingly uncommitted to maintaining paganism in his realm. Happening unexpectedly upon the wedding celebration to which he has not been invited, Florien embraces the Christian Constant as his son and heir without apparent hesitation, as we have seen.[39] Whereas the prose text directly stages the baptism and conversion of Sebelinne, both events are only implied in the *Dit*, which emphasizes instead Sebelinne's ability to facilitate cultural crossings between the two faiths.

Crucial to conveying these substantial differences in each text's ideological positioning of Christians and Muslims is the "aumosniere de rice oeuvre." So central to the *dit* and entirely omitted from the prose text, the lavishly decorated purse maps a trans-Mediterranean scope for this tale through its cultural association with "aumosnieres sarrasinoises." The functional and unadorned "boiste" (v. 296) said to hold the emperor's letter in the prose text implies no such cross-cultural scope. In addition, the prose text makes no mention of the Kingdom of Sicily among the titles given to the Byzantine emperor.[40] Muselin is labeled simply as Emperor of Greece and Byzantium. Thus is the foreignness and isolation of the distant emperor emphasized, positioning him geographically as a dreaded easterner who lacks contact with the western Mediterranean.

In the *dit*, by contrast, the *aumosniere* of richly worked cloth tells a complex story of protagonists who succeed in crossing lines of class, gender, and religious affiliation. In so doing the brief tale of the *Empereur Constant* attests to the ability of luxury fabric and the woman who deploys it to rewrite a number of familiar medieval plotlines. Using an item of luxury dress designated not as Christian, Muslim, or Byzantine, and not named for an eastern city or a western site of production, but frequently called in other contexts by the hybrid and geographically inclusive term "sarrasinois," Sebelinne subtly hedges the narratives of arranged marriage and paternal authority that would typically prescribe the future of the European-style "courtly heroine" on which she is patterned. By opening and closing a heavily "worked" *aumosniere* this heroine is able to critique literary scenarios of courtly copulation and the love reputed to accompany it. Her "silk work" , reveals how female protagonists can use trans-Mediterranean luxury textiles to disrupt highly gendered cultural and legal paradigms that govern medieval marriage and political succession.

Lienor

Far from Constantinople in the city of Dole, the heroine Lienor in Jean Renart's *Roman de la Rose ou de Guillaume de Dole* also forges an unexpected narrative subjectivity by manipulating richly worked cloth that has been made into an *aumosniere*. Not unlike Sebelinne, Lienor conforms in many respects to the profile of the courtly lady well known from Old French romance. And yet the question of Lienor's identity is fundamentally challenged in this tale by an unfounded accusation that she is not a virgin and, thus, not an eligible bride for the Emperor Conrad.

The accusation, as readers know well, issues from the Emperor's "cruel and wicked" seneschal (v. 3524), the hapless cur in this romance, who claims falsely to have deflowered Conrad's future bride, offering as proof of his conquest a description of the rose on her thigh that gives the romance its name. The seneschal made the "outrageous claim":

> Qu'il a eü son pucelage;
> Et por ce que croire l'an puise
> De la rose desor la cuisse
> li a dit mout veraie ensaigne
> vv. 3586–89

(That he had robbed her of her virginity and to make it believable he gave as proof the rose on her thigh.)[41]

A rich array of scholarly readings have focused on the tangled terms of this heroine's identity as "la pucele a la rose," analyzing the complex attempts by different players in this tale to establish the status of Lienor's courtly body as either virginal or defiled. Is this heroine an innocent *pucele*, sister of Guillaume de Dole and possible future wife of the Emperor Conrad, who just happens, according to a tale told by her mother, to have the mark of a rose on her thigh? Or is she a *pucele* no longer because the seneschal knows her marked body intimately, and thus a woman only parading as a virginal flower, the fictive image of courtly purity now cast as a sexually active and therefore guilty vaginal flower?[42] Or is Lienor the conniving daughter of a shrewd mother who invents the story of the rose on Lienor's thigh to use the seneschal in her own plot of financial gain?[43]

Scholars have also noted the importance of Lienor's name and its association with gold in particular reflected in the golden color of her hair and her value as a "treasured" beauty beyond compare.[44] But little attention has been paid to the specific gold embroidered motifs that decorate the *aumosniere* skillfully deployed by this heroine to refute the charge that she is "la pucele a la rose." Indeed, this highly decorated, "richly worked" *aumosniere* and the belt attached to it raise, from a different angle, the fundamental question posed by this romance: Who is Lienor?

To answer this question, I propose that we shift our attention away from the image of the rose on this heroine's thigh and consider instead the ways she forges for herself an unexpected subjectivity that stems specifically from her handling of a small item of elite dress. If Sebelinne uses an *aumosniere* in the

Dit de L'Empereur Constant to appropriate imperial authority and engineer a marriage with far-reaching political and social consequences, Lienor deploys her own distinctive *aumosniere* to craft a social and legal identity for herself quite apart from the "unmarriageable" status imputed to her by the senechal's false charge. I would argue in fact that, based on the material evidence that Lienor presents at her trial and the very specific kinds of silk this heroine manipulates with her hands, we might best understand her not as the sexually marked "pucele à la rose" but a legally astute "pucele à l'aumosniere."

Indeed, it is through this small silk purse that intimate questions of virginity and female sexuality are recontextualized within an expanded, cross-cultural geography that bridges categories of Frenchness and foreignness. Lienor's silk work in particular calls into question the effectiveness of these categories. Earlier in the romance, the same seneschal who defines Lienor as "la pucele a la rose" also raises the pointed question about this heroine's place of origin:

—Dont est ele dame de France,
ou fille le roi ou sa suer?
vv. 3514–15

(Is she, then, a noble lady from France, or the king's daughter or his sister?)

The guileful seneschal's purported concern is with the wealth, status, and land that might accrue to his lord, Conrad, should the marriage take place: "Prendrez vos i terre, ou avoir,/ ou amis?" (vv. 3517–18; Will you gain land or wealth or friends?). And yet, the question about Lienor's place of origin and her status as a "dame de France" also foregrounds the problem of foreign queens.

Conrad never says specifically whether Lienor is a "dame de France" or not. We know that she and her brother come from a small town outside the city of Dole in what is now the Franche-comté but which stood at the time this tale was composed within the Holy Roman Empire.[45] We learn only that Lienor is not wealthy, not anything like the sister of the kings of England (v. 3575) or France, but sister to the struggling knight Guillaume, a man nagged by creditors at home and forced to buy provisions for the tournament from Liège on credit (vv. 1935, 1955). However, the knights who join Guillaume at the tournament at St. Trond come from the French regions of Perche, Poitou, Maine, and the county of Champagne, among others (vv. 2087–88). The geographical precision of place references in *Guillaume de Dole* has enabled John Baldwin to locate the bulk of the action in the romance's early scenes in Lotharingia, the middle territory between France and the Empire, especially the diocese and principality of Liège, an area lying at the linguistic frontier between Germanic and French-speaking populations.[46]

Yet many of the text's references to clothes, food, armor, ecclesiastical practices, and royal politics remain, according to Baldwin, distinctively French.[47] Certainly the splendor of Conrad's generosity in providing his many knights with "joiax, dras de soie et destriers" (v. 94) and the ladies' luxurious clothing cut from costly silks—*samite* and *cendal* along with coveted cloth of gold (vv. 200–203)[48]—all ring of King Arthur's lavish courtly abundance as it is figured in an array of twelfth- and thirteenth-century Old French romances. More specifically, the elegant and costly silks that fashion the knights and ladies of Conrad's court into "genz acesmer," including golden silks bearing the name of Baghdad, point to "outremer," eastern sites "across the sea", much as they do in any number of Old French romances of this period: "Lors veïssiez genz acesmer:/ de samiz, de dras d'outremer,/ de baudequins d'or a oiseaus/ orent et cotes et manteaus (vv. 233–36; There you would see people adorned in heavy silk and cloth from across the sea. They had tunics and cloaks made of gold-infused Baghdad-style silks with bird motifs). Although we receive no direct answer at this point regarding Lienor's status as a "French" lady, these imported and sometimes golden silks are an important harbinger of later narrative developments that will establish a hybrid, trans-Mediterranean identity for the tale's golden-haired heroine.

At the trial, Lienor denounces the seneschal directly as an outrageous liar and traitor (vv. 5062–65) claiming herself to be an unsullied innocent beauty: "ce sui ge bele Lïenors"(v. 5097; I am the fair Lienor), while also deploying the consummate skills of an accomplished lawyer to set the stage for the seneschal's downfall (vv. 4768–73). Most important, however, she makes her case and exonerates herself through the deft manipulation of intimate items of her own clothing: the sartorial duo of her belt and its attached alms purse, objects that she had shrewdly arranged to have planted on the senechal's person as if they were love tokens from the Chastelaine de Dijon. In preparation for the trial, Lienor had given precise instructions to her messenger:

Vos m'en irez au seneschal,
si porterez cest affichal,
cest tiessu et ceste aumosniere [49]

Si li direz que le envoie
La chastelaine de Dijon:

Si li mande la chastelaine
que, s'il ja mes veut q'el le voie,
que cest tiessu que li envoie
ceigne a sa char soz sa chemise.
vv. 4290–92, 4297–98, 4315–18 ·

(Go to the seneschal for me and take him this brooch, belt, and alms
purse . . . Tell him they were sent by the chatelaine of Dijon. . . . Thus
does the *chastelaine* ask that, if he ever wants her to receive him, he
must wear the belt that she has sent him under his shirt.)

When the seneschal claims at the trial that he has robbed Lienor of her virginity (vv. 3585–86), Lienor asserts that he stole that and much more: her *aumosniere, ceinture* and her jewelry:

Qu'il me toli mon pucelage
Et aprés cele grant ledure,
Si m'a tolue ma ceinture
et m'aumosniere et mon fermal.
vv. 4783–87

(He robbed me of my virginity. And after committing that hateful
crime, he robbed me of my belt, my purse, and my brooch.)

In fact, the seneschal took none of these items, and in claiming his own in-
nocence of this charge—asserting he has not "taken" her virginity or her belt
or alms purse "by force" —he disproves his own earlier claim to have "taken"
her virginity, presumably with her consent, at all.

Material Evidence

The difference between the two accusations of lost virginity made successively by the seneschal and Lienor lies tellingly in the decorative items he is
made to wear: the conjoined *aumosniere* and *ceinture*. Whereas the seneschal

can provide no tangible proof of his allegation of deflowerment based only on his putative knowledge that a "rose" decorates the virgin's thigh, Lienor has the material evidence of luxury textiles on her side. Although she fabricates the story of the stolen belt and purse, the items themselves can be produced in court. If Lienor's case succeeds in part because she deftly outmaneuvers the seneschal on his own ground of verbal deceit,[50] her success also hinges crucially on the visible proof that textiles provide.[51] The narrator observes crucially that, as "everyone could see," the seneschal was wearing her belt:

> Or li taint et palist li vis
> Por sa parole qui empire.
>
> que chascuns vit qu'il l'avoit mise
> et çainte estroit a sa char nue
> vv. 4844–45, 4864–65

(Then the seneschal's face paled and lost color because of her speech, which had turned things against him . . . And everyone saw that he was wearing the belt tightly fastened around his bare body.)

In this instance it is the combined *aumosniere* and belt, here called most often by the single term "ceinture," that enable this heroine to demand justice:

> G'en serai voir tote honoree,
> se Deu plest, ainz que ge m'en aille,
> se vostre cort ne me fet faille.
> Car, quant il nia ma *ceinture*,
> s'en li eüst lors fet *droiture*
> quant il en fu trovez sesiz,
> il fust lués penduz et honiz
> com cil qui toz estoit jugiez.
> vv. 5068–75, italics mine

(God willing, before I leave, my honor will be completely restored, unless your court fails me. If *justice* had been done, when he was caught wearing my *belt*, even though he had denied having it, he would have been hanged and shamed, as a proven criminal.)

Justice from a belt. That is Lienor's plea as *droiture* is made to rime here tellingly with *ceinture*. Conrad's barons, as Lienor explains, profess to being unconvinced by the staggeringly condemnatory evidence. The seneschal's friends accuse Lienor of having used magic to plant the belt with attached *aumosniere* on his body (vv. 4911, 4962). Although the barons remain "concerned" by the disturbing implications of that belt and purse (vv. 4880–81), they denounce it as inconclusive evidence because, they claim, such belts are common, "Font li un: 'De tel feture/ en porroit l'en assez trover'" (vv. 4882–83; Some of them said, "One can find any number of belts made like that").[52]

The Significance of Feture

And yet this is precisely the point made repeatedly by the infinitely capable Lienor, who asserts in no uncertain terms that the *feture* of this belt does matter:

> Bons rois, por Dieu, ne vos griet mie;
> vos dites ci qu'il le me nie,
> qu'il onqes n'ot mon pucelage,
> et dit qu'onqes a mon domage
> n'ot mon joial ne ma ceinture:
> savez vos de quele *feture*
> cele ceinture estoit ouvree?
> vv. 4819–25, my emphasis

> (Good king, I do not wish to grieve you. You say that he denies it, that he never took my virginity and that he never harmed me by taking my jewelry or my belt. Do you know by what handiwork that belt was embroidered?)[53]

It is the "handiwork" of the belt, its elaborate embroidery, that not only makes it distinctive but also marks it unequivocally as "hers." In advancing this claim, Lienor implies the importance of the belt's creator, quite possibly Lienor herself, who is figured earlier in a *chanson de toile* embedded in this narrative as embroidering church vestments with her highly accomplished mother. Indeed, Lienor's mother is characterized as a woman who "set assez de cest mestier" (v. 1133): "Fanons, garnemenz de moustier,/ chasubles, bele aubes parees,/ ont amdeus maintes foiz ouvrees" (vv. 1134–35; Both of them embroider clerical vestments for the Church, maniples, chasubles, and beautifully decorated aubes). These "richly worked" garments, presented as alms to the church (c'est aumosne, v. 1137), resonate with the richly worked *ausmoniere* and *tiessu* (alms purse and belt) that Lienor later gives to the messenger as putative tokens of the Chasteleine de Dijon's love (vv. 4291–93). She states specifically that both this belt and purse are embroidered in a single distinctive way: "cest tiessu et ceste aumosniere./ Tot est brodé d'une maniere" (vv. 4292–93). But what does this mean?

Answering her own rhetorical question to Conrad, "savez vos de quele feture/ cele ceinture estoit *ouvree*?" (vv. 4824–25; Do you know by what handiwork that belt was *embroidered*? my emphasis), Lienor describes delicate gold embroidery reminiscent of the gold work done by the three hundred captive silk workers in *Yvain* who work "fil d'or et de soie" (v. 5190) or the "grant chasuble ovree" (v. 2355) in fine gold handed from Morgan to Guenevere to Enide in the passage from *Erec et Enide* discussed in Chapter 1. In the case of Lienor's *ceinture* and *aumosniere*, however, additional distinctive details are mentioned. These items were not only embroidered in gold, she explains, but also bore two specific motifs, those of fish/shellfish and birds:

El estoit de fin or broudee
a poisonnez et a oisiaus.
vv. 4826–27

This is not the first time we have heard these details. Earlier in the narrative, when Lienor instructed her messenger to carry the fateful *tiessu* and *aumosniere*, "brode d'une maniere," to the unsuspecting seneschal, she explained that the combined purse and belt included images of birds and fish designed expressly "for him":

si li direz que li envoie
la chastelaine de Dijon:
por li i sont cil oisillon
ou tiessu, et cil poisonnet. (italics mine)
vv. 4297–4300

(And tell him that the Chastelaine de Dijon sends [these items] and that the birds and fish on the belt/purse are *for him*.)

For him, indeed. One thinks here of the meal prepared "just for" Tereus, the equally unsuspecting and conniving assailant in the Old French *Philomena*, who finds himself caught in an elaborate revenge plot engineered by the heroine Procne and her wronged sister, Philomena, to exact justice for Tereus's brutal rape and mutilation of the young virgin Philomena. The sisters jointly prepare a meal designed solely and expressly "for him," in the sense of meting out due punishment for crimes Tereus has committed and hidden. In that text, we see women achieving justice from a meal made by their own hands, a kind of female handiwork that follows directly from Philomena's earlier handiwork in weaving and working a tapestry used to communicate her plight to Procne.[54]

In *Guillaume de Dole* we find a heroine's dedication to exact justice from other items worked by a woman's hands: a belt and *aumosniere* used here also to right a sexual violation. These decorative items of dress provide a stark contrast to the oral accounts circulated earlier in the tale both by Lienor's mother and the seneschal, accounts that characterized her as a woman marked by the image of a rose on her thigh. Indeed, Lienor emerges in the trial scene as a woman who has herself marked the material items that now stand in for her purportedly defiled body with other, very specific images: motifs of fish and birds. If these images "worked" in costly gold were crafted purposefully "for the seneschal" earlier in the tale, as Lienor claims, their function at the trial scene is to provide an indisputable authentication of *her* identity, not his.

Interestingly, that identity is not rendered in recognizably French heraldic coats of arms or signs of family lineage, but through patterned motifs that appear on Islamicate textiles across the medieval Mediterranean. We have seen how silks woven with patterned birds in gold thread figure among the *dras d'outremer* that adorn Conrad's guests when the story opens:

Lors veïssiez genz acesmer:
de samiz, de dras d'outremer,
de baudequins d'or a oiseaus
orent et cotes et manteaus.
vv. 233–36

(There one could see people dressed up in heavy silk and fabrics from across the sea. They had tunics and cloaks made of gold-infused, Baghdad-style silks with bird motifs.)[55]

At tale's end, when the barons escort Lienor to her wedding, we hear again of a remarkable abundance of costly and eastern-style silks that robe those in attendance, some woven with motifs of birds as well as fish:

> Tant baudequin, tant ciglaton,
> Tant bon dïaspre, tant samit
> Onques nuls emsamble ne vit.
> Tant robes de plusors façons,
> l'une a oiseax, l'autre a poisons.
> vv. 5364–68

(No one had ever seen so much Baghdad-style brocaded silk, so much light silk cloth with patterned roundels, so much brocaded silk, and so much heavy silk cloth in one place; so many gowns of different kinds, some patterned with birds, others with fish.)

In one sense, the allusion should not surprise. Indeed, silks patterned with golden bird motifs appear with regularity in medieval French courtly romances as part of the standard repertoire of costly silk. The allegorical figure Deduit in Guillaume de Lorris's *Roman de la Rose*, for example, wears a "samit portret a oiseaus/ qui ere touz a or batu/ Fu ses cors richement vestuz (vv. 819–21; He was richly dressed in a heavy silk garment, shot through with golden bird motifs). Even the God of Love, whose gown is not silk but made entirely of flowers following the model of patterned silks, is decorated with bird motifs that accompany images of escutcheons and fierce animals: "a lozenges et a escusiaus,/ A oissiaus et a lionciaus,/ A bestes et a lieparz,/ Fu la robe de toutes parz/ Portraite, et ovree de flors (vv. 879–83; The gown was decorated all over with images, worked in flowers, of diamond shapes and escutcheons, birds and lions, other animals and leopards).

In these examples, we hear nothing of cloth coming from or imitating textiles in "outremer" or "Baghdad." Rather, silk has become an identifying mark of European courtliness itself. Other Old French texts, however, record the trans-Mediterranean character of similarly patterned silk more overtly. In the *Chanson d'Antioche*, for example, the character Corbarans d'Oliferne, the Emir of Mossoul and military chief of the sultan of Persia, who leads one hundred thousand "Turcs de la gent païennes" (vv. 393–94) into battle against the Franks for control of Jerusalem and Syria, also wears costly silks decorated

with images of birds and fish. Interestingly, they are said to come not from
Constantinople or silk-producing cities in the Levant, but from the ambigu-
ous "Carthage":

> Vestus fu d'un cier paile qui fu fais en Cartage,
> A bestes et a flors, nes li oisel volage
> Par furent entissu et li posson marage.
> vv. 8387–89[56]

([He] was dressed in a costly silk made in Cartagena/Carthage. Images
of animals and flowers, even flying birds and shellfish were woven into
it.)

This, then, is the wardrobe of the fearsome "pagan" enemy: luxurious silk
from a place called "Cartage," which could refer, as we will see in Chapter 4,
either to the north-African city of Carthage or Cartagena in Muslim Spain.
No longer associated only with Baghdad or Damascus, as in the descriptions
of silks worn by Conrad's courtiers (vv. 5364–68), the geographic range of silks
patterned with birds and fish extends in this instance across the
Mediterranean reaching perhaps as far as Muslim Spain, which produced
Baghdadi silks in large numbers.[57] The spatial spread of this luxury fabric is
further reinforced by the epithet of the emir who wears it. This military chief
of the sultan of Persia is said to be "the richest pagan from here to Almería"
(v. 405; N'ot plus riche paien desci qu'en Almarie). His identity as both
wealthy and powerful is cast specifically as trans-Mediterranean, extending
from Mossoul to Almería, the latter a key Muslim silk-producing venue as
early as the eighth century.[58]

What does it mean that the courtly French Lienor from Dole, transplanted to the Emperor Conrad's courts in Mainz and Cologne, uses items of
dress to identify herself that also mark, in Old French fictions about enemy
pagans, a prominent military leader whose influence extends from the
Muslim Middle East to Muslim Spain? And how significant is it that whereas
the sultan's emir, Corbarans, simply wears silks patterned with birds and fish,
Lienor claims to know how to make them and to recognize their distinctive
feture?

Bird motifs appear with great frequency in medieval Islamicate textiles,
often accompanied by Kufic script. Patricia Baker offers a number of exam-

ples, among which are a ninth-century Egyptian silk bearing patterned bird
motifs alongside a Kufic inscription, or the famous silk patterned in peacocks
found at St. Sernin in Toulouse but generally dated to twelfth-century Iberia,
also with an inscription in Kufic letters.[59] Sophie Desrosiers provides additional examples of silks with bird motifs from eleventh-century Spain,
eleventh- to twelfth-century Sicily (Palermo), and twelfth-century Fatimid
Egypt.[60]

But what of Lienor's reference to fish? Unlike birds, fish do not appear as
a common motif in Islamicate textiles. However, the fishbone (or herringbone) patterned weave does. Textile scholars of the elusive and problematic
"drap d'arest," also called "draps d'ache," have suggested most recently that
these silks, which derive their name from fish-skeleton shapes that form
chevron patterns, might well have been produced in Muslim Spain if not also
in Languedoc. Known to have been traded at the fairs in Champagne, these
silks are thought to have been produced by Muslim weavers of unspecified
gender.[61] Anne Wardwell cites two examples of extant thirteenth-century
Tartary cloth, silks probably produced in central Asia but often preserved in
western churches alongside textiles woven in Spain and Italy or Egypt and
Syria, described by Boniface VIII in 1295 as bearing a herringbone design: "ad
modum spine piscus," and "ad spinum piscis."[62]

If Lienor's *aumosniere* and *ceinture* are not termed Saracen per se, they position her, nonetheless, between distant shores of the medieval silk-producing
Mediterranean. Like the historical *aumonières* in David Jacoby's account of
Mediterranean "silk economics," Lienor's fictive *aumosniere*, decorated in this
case with a distinctive *feture* of birds and fish, locates the golden-haired heroine somewhere between the former Byzantine Empire (Persia), the Islamic
east, Muslim Spain, and the Christian west in one fell swoop. If Lienor is in
one sense a "dame de France" she is a French woman defined by handiwork
that has a distinctively trans-Mediterranean pedigree. The special *feture* of
Lienor's hand-embroidered *aumosniere* and *ceinture* situates this heroine, then,
as both French and foreign.

Other Ceintures

Other *ceintures* figure in this text, as do other *aumosnieres*. But in contrast to
the defensive assertions by Conrad's barons that the evidence displayed on the

seneschal's body is "commonplace" and of ordinary "feture" (vv. 4882–85, 4964–65), no other *ceinture* or *aumosniere* seen in this tale bears the distinctive motifs that Lienor ascribes to her incriminating evidence. Those motifs seem indeed, as she claims, to have been crafted expressly for the seneschal. Early in the romance, Conrad's messenger Nicole received as a gift from Lienor's mother a seemingly unadorned purse, an item named only generically as "une aumosniere" (v. 1228). The *aumosnieres* carried by the *puceles* cavorting among Conrad's fancily dressed knights during the summertime festivities in *Guillaume de Dole*, small purses containing spools of thread used to sew closed the retinue's sleeves, carry no distinctive markings (vv. 274–76). Although the word *aumosniere* in this instance is made to rime with *filieres*, thus further reinforcing the association of the aristocratic purse with needlework by women, the *aumosnieres* themselves bear no indication of being "worked" with any specific designs or patterns:

Les puceles, ce m'est avis,
Lor atornent fil de filieres
Qu'eles ont en lor aumosnieres.
vv. 274–76

(The young women, I believe, prepared spools of thread that they carried in their alms purses.)

Even the belt worn by Lienor herself is similarly unmarked and undistinguished, although the gold brooch attached to her chemise is said to be "ouvré par grande maiestrise/ riche d'or et bel de feture" (vv. 4375–76; worked with great mastery, rich in gold and beautifully crafted). The heroine's belt appears remarkable only for its costly gold buckle (vv. 4383–84). Guillaume gives a similarly valuable belt, decorated with silver but without embroidered motifs, to a young lady singer at the innkeeper's tavern, "sa ceinture d'argent ferree" (v. 1842). The "corroie" and "fermail" he sends to Lienor in the following scene carry no unique markings (v. 1931), nor does the "ceinture" Conrad exchanges for a "corroiete blanche" in the opening scene; its jewels and gold alone make it invaluable (vv. 252–56). When Lienor later outfits her knights in elegant furs and silks and white gloves (vv. 4342–45), the belts she provides are distinctively embroidered in gold, predictably with coats of arms but not patterned animal motifs:

Blans ganz et une ceinturete
broudee d'or, a escuciaus
a doné a chascun de ciaus
en l'onor des robes noveles
vv. 4345–48

(She gave each of them white gloves and a narrow belt, embroidered
with a coat of arms in gold, to go with their new outfits.)

One other belt bears mentioning since it stands in for the heroine Lienor
in a sense. During a private conversation between Guillaume and Conrad, the
devious and plotting seneschal overhears the emperor reply favorably to
Guillaume's mention of his sister and then sees that he "exchanged
Guillaume's belt for one of his own" (vv. 3173–74; et si chanja la ceinture/ a
une qui soe ot esté) before bursting into song, a love song about the treasured
ladylove he seeks (vv. 3184–87). The seneschal concludes from the eavesdrop-
ping incident that Conrad's apparent interest in Guillaume's "chevalerie"
masks a greater interest in "his sister":

Fet il: "De ce sui get toz fis
que n'est pas por chevalerie/
qu'il li porte tel druerie:
ce n'est que por sa seror non.
vv. 3200–3203

(He said, now I am certain: it is not chivalric prowess that wins him
such favor, but merely his sister.)

This exchange of belts of unspecified design and decoration suggests to the
seneschal an expression of Conrad's love for Lienor while also symbolizing his
feudal bond with Guillaume. Yet, different from the love tokens marshaled by
Lienor to represent gifts from the Chastelaine de Dijon to the seneschal,
Conrad's gift belt bears no singular "feture."

Lienor's Wedding Gown

It is significant that the trans-Mediterranean motifs on Lienor's *aumosniere* and *ceinture* differ significantly from the complex embroidery covering this heroine's wedding gown. The gown, placed on Lienor by the highborn wives of knights who adorn and dress her once she has "won" her legal case against the seneschal (vv. 5315–19), is utterly unique and remarkable, we are told, so much so that, like other garments we have seen, it is said to have been made by fairies. In addition, the cloth has been meticulously adorned over seven or eight years by the accomplished needlework of a queen of Apulia:

> D'un drap que une fee ouvra
> fu vestue l'empereriz;
> il n'iert ne tiessuz ne tresliz,
> ainçois l'ot tot fet o agulle
> jadis une roine en Puille,
> vv. 5324–28

> (The empress was dressed in fabric embroidered/worked by a fairy. It had not been woven, whether in tight or loose fashion, but rather completely embroidered [covered completely in needlework] long ago, by a queen of Apulia.)

Indeed, we are told, "no one alive could have made such a fabric" (vv. 5350–51; or n'est en vie/hom qui si biau drap seüst faire); that is, no one could depict in thread the elaborate narrative portrayed on this garment: the story of Helen of Troy, her capture by Paris, and the Trojan war it provoked when the Greeks came to retrieve her (vv. 5332–50).[63] This extended account of rapt and ravishment, well known to medieval audiences from Benoit de St. Maure's *Roman de Troie*, is here rendered in visual images, completely embroidered in gold thread: "i sont d'or fetes les ymages" (v. 5339). Distinct from the Islamicate patterned motifs of birds and fish that decorate the *aumosniere* and *ceinture* so skillfully employed by Lienor in the trial scene, this embroidery tells a story.

Thus does an odd dissonance result from the festive enfolding of the heroine Lienor in this grandiose and elaborately embroidered garment, for Helen's story could not be more different from hers.[64] Although Lienor's name might resonate in important ways with Helen's,[65] this heroine with the golden hair and known for her beauty is not captured and carried off as a war prize. Rather, as we have just witnessed in the trial scene, she escapes entrapment by the seneschal, in part through her verbal skill, but more specifically by deploying what she claims to be highly distinctive textile motifs of her own. The well-known Greco-Roman tale of Helen's rapt makes no reference to the kinds of skill at "working" cloth displayed by Lienor, whether in the direct sense of embroidering thread on fabric or more metaphorically in manipulating cloth accessories. Indeed, the distinctive *feture* of Lienor's *aumosniere* and *ceinture* asserts a kind of justice, if only temporary, forged by women for women, a kind of justice glaringly absent from the legendary account of Helen of Troy's rapt.

If the wedding gown asserts a classical heritage for Lienor, wrapping this courtly heroine in the trappings of a borrowed and dissonant mythic past, the *ceinture* and *aumosniere* she works suggest another cultural vector altogether: drawing not on classical narrative but on the cultural language of Islamicate silk production across the Mediterranean: from the Levant to Muslim Spain. It is as if this important dissonance between the story of Helen's rapt and Lienor's escape from the seneschal's charge of ravishment has been recorded visibly and tangibly in distinctive modes of cloth work. It seems in a sense that Lienor's deft performance in the trial scene, now covered over and occluded by the lavish wedding gown, offered a glimpse of an alternative narrative to the story of Helen's rapt and sexual violation. At the trial, Lienor deployed the distinctive non-narrative *feture* of two items of elite dress to gain justice for a wronged woman in a court of law. By manipulating the silk *aumosniere* and *ceinture*, Lienor drew on a non-western textile tradition to revalue a female body marked from the outset of this text as virginal and ravishable. All that is now hidden beneath the imposing wedding cloak, which reinstates the more standard narrative of rapt and ravishment, of women traded. But we have witnessed in the course of this complex tale something else, something quite extraordinary, a western courtly heroine who has successfully thrown off the charge of being the embodied and sexually available "pucele a la rose" by enacting instead her identity as a *pucele* who knows the *feture* of golden Islamicate silks.

For both Sebelinne and Lienor, working "richly decorated" luxury objects offers a narrative path for forging alternate gendered subjectivities: different from the daughter married off by her father in *Erec et Enide*; different too from the woman fought over, captured, and seized again as the prize in the heroic battle for Helen of Troy. Standing at two outposts across a sea of silk, both heroines, one putatively Greek and the other nominally French, come together through their work on lavishly decorated alms purses, known widely in the trans-Mediterranean language of silk as neither Greek nor French, but as a crossing place between the Christian west and Islamicate cultures: as "*aumosnieres* sarrasinoises."

CHAPTER FOUR

Following Two "Ladies of Carthage" from Tyre to North Africa and Spain to France (*Le Roman d'Enéas, Aucassin et Nicolette*)

FOR READERS OF medieval French literature, the epithet "la dame de Carthage" evokes two distinct heroines, not generally discussed together since they hail from different countries, indeed different continents, yet their respective cities face one another across the western Mediterranean. Dido, the tragically abandoned pagan woman in Virgil's *Aeneid* and the mid-twelfth-century *Roman d'Enéas* that derives from the classical text, flees her Phoenician home in Tyre after the brutal murder of her husband to become a revered and capable empire builder in what this text calls the Lybian city of Carthage (v. 295). Nicolette, the Saracen princess, abducted, enslaved, and eventually converted to Christianity in the thirteenth-century *chantefable Aucassin et Nicolette*, suffers captivity and sale to a French count and further abduction by Saracen merchants before being returned to her lost homeland in Cartagena, Spain. Both the North African city of Carthage and Iberian Cartagena are rendered in the Old French texts that feature them as "Cartage," a name that signals their parallel colonial histories.[1] The historical Cartagena, called Qart Hadast, "the new city," was founded in 230 B.C.E. as a second Carthage by colonizers who had migrated from the "other" Carthage, itself already established as a North African colony by Phoenicians from Tyre in 814 B.C.E.[2]

Reading the stories of Dido and Nicolette together will reveal yet another way in which Old French literary texts map the vast trading empire of the medieval Mediterranean, in this instance the geographic triangle formed by the two Carthages—one African, the other Andalusian—and the earlier Phoenician settlement in Tyre.

To be sure, Dido and Nicolette represent two very different narrative trajectories. The capable Carthagian queen who eventually suffocates under the opulence of seductive and dangerous silk stands in stark contrast to the slave girl from Cartagena who manipulates gold and the cult of relics to escape subjugation and servitude. Both of these "dames de Cartage," however, effectively rewrite established narratives of the problematic "foreign" woman. They do so not by producing cloth of gold, as do the captives in Chrétien's *Yvain*, but by manipulating metaphorical forms of cloth and gold, respectively.

Dido: Dame de Cartage, Dame Tyrienne

Dido, as she appears in the Old French *Roman d'Enéas*, actually bears two titles, which seem at first to mark the endpoints of her movement from Tyre on the eastern Mediterranean to Carthage in the west. But in fact when "Dydo la Tirïaine" (v. 576) moves to the North African coast and establishes a magnificently luxurious city that she then governs expertly as "la dame de Cartaje" (v. 741), she brings the commercial essence of Tyre with her, transporting the riches and elegance of her highly civilized homeland to what is called a "savage terre" (v. 241). The "substantial treasure" she imports includes significantly, along with gold and silver, opulent "silks and fabrics":

> Par mer s'en est Dydo fouïe,
> moult ot grant gent en compaignie;
> porté en a moult grant tresor,
> pailes et dras, argent et or.
> vv. 274–77

(Dido fled by sea with a large retinue. She took with her substantial wealth in silk and fabric, silver and gold.)

If Tyre was a rich commercial center, Carthage under Dido's queenship is teeming with the abundant merchandise that indicates a thriving trade in luxury goods:

> Moult par sont riche li bourjois,
> de leur avoir ne set nulz prois;
> bien est la ville replainie,
> assez y a marcheandise.
> vv. 360–63

(The town's inhabitants are very wealthy. No one knows the value of their goods. The town is well stocked with ample merchandise.)

The city's "unimaginable riches" are cast specifically, in terms of furs and varied silks: quilts and coverlets, colored silk fabrics, costly curtains and rugs, silk cendal and samite, imperial silks, and authentic expensive, dark-colored silks:

> Illuec vent l'en le vair, le gris
> que l'en aporte en cez paÿs,
> coutes de paile, couvertoirs,
> les dras de soie de colours,
> les chiers dossez et les tapis,
> et les cendaulz et les samis,
> et les pailes emperëaus,
> les chieres porpres naturaus:
> ne scet richece homme penser
> qu'il ne puisse illuec trouver.
> vv. 364–73

(There, one sells imported furs, silk coverlets and bed covers, colored silks, costly curtains and wall coverings, lightweight and heavy silks, imperial silks, authentic precious purple silks. It would be impossible to imagine a kind of wealth not found there.)

Dido's city, as a place of astounding wealth and opulence (vv. 386–87), is further emblematized by the cultivation of sea creatures that produce the rarefied dye used to color the famed Byzantine "porpres."

En celle mer, jouste Cartaige,
illuec prent l'en sor le rivage
d'une maniere poissonnés
ne gaires granz, mais petités;
l'en les taille sor les coetes,
si en cheent rouges goutetes;
de ce taint l'en la porpre chiere
poy sont poisson de lor maniere.
Li vermeil sont de cel poisson,
ens en Cartaige les taint l'on.
vv. 374–83

(In the ocean near Carthage one catches, at the water's edge, a
particular kind of shellfish: not large but smallish ones. When one cuts
into their small tails, small red drops flow out of them. With this
substance they dye the costly dark silks. This type of shellfish is rare.
The dark red silks are made from it. They are dyed in Carthage.)

Indeed, all three of the features asserted in this text as distinctive of
Carthage—wealth, silk, and purple dye—were associated typically in the
French Middle Ages with the mythically rich city of Constantinople.

Tyrian Purple

Has the "dame Tiriane" (v. 1568) of the twelfth-century *Roman d'Enéas* thus
fashioned a kind of Constantinople on the African coast? Is her lavish
Carthage, as a new colonial outpost of Tyre, cast here as a western version of
the famed eastern capital? Yes and no. For Tyre itself held the reputation of producing an extremely costly dye called "Tyrian purple," one of the most highly
valued commodities in the ancient Mediterranean, also produced eventually in
the Carthagian colony.[3] John H. Munro explains that the famous "Tyrian purple," which referred to deep violet and scarlet-hued purple dyes, was sometimes confused with the scarlet color cochineal, also called "punicus," because
the ancient Phoenicians originated scarlet dyeing. Whereas "Tyrian purple,"
along with the prized and highly controlled Byzantine purple, or royal purple,
was produced from shellfish (murex and purpura mollusks), scarlet dyes from
the cochineal insect, sometimes referred to as "vermillion" in color, were less

closely controlled.[4] Thus when Dido appears in the famous hunting scene of the *Roman d'Enéas* clad in a "porpre vermeille," the garment signals more than wealth. To be sure, this queen's "porpre vermeille" is heavily laden with gold, as is her "cher mantel," opulently decorated in gold thread and golden pearls:

> La roÿne se fu vestue
> d'une chiere porpre vermeille
> d'or bendee a grant merveille
> trestout le cors des que as hances,
> et ensement toutes les manches.
> .I. chier mantel ot afublé
> menuement a or gouté.
> vv. 1549–55

(The queen was dressed in an expensive red silk lavishly banded in gold across the entire bodice to the hips and including the sleeves. She was wearing a costly mantle delicately beaded with gold.)[5]

While this lavish attire forms part of the exceedingly elegant hunting gear that makes Dido resemble Diana, goddess of the hunt (vv. 1568–71), the "porpre" also points to Dido's origins in Tyre. The narrative makes this clear in the scene when Dido first encounters Enéas's men bearing news of their escape from Troy. At that moment, the heroine wears not only a tight-fitting "porpre alexandrine" against her skin but also a costly mantle of white ermine covered with fabric described specifically as beautiful "dark silk from Tyre":

> Devant le temple ert la roÿne:
> D'une porpore alexandrine,
> tout senglement a sa char nue,
> estroitement estoit vestue.
> Afublee fu la roÿne
> d'un chier mantel d'un blanc ermine
> couvert d'un bon tyret porprin.
> vv. 526–32

(The queen stood before the temple, dressed only in Alexandrine silk against her naked skin. The queen wore an expensive mantle of white ermine covered with a dark silk from Tyre.)

Faced with Dido's stunning clothes and magnificently decorated imperial palace, Enéas fails to make this connection, interpreting the capable queen's silks and gold not as a transposition of eastern opulence to North African shores, but, predictably, in line with medieval portraits of French romance heroines generally, as an indication of this lady's recognizably western courtliness:

> Eneas entra au palays:
> onc en si bel ne entra mais
>
> perçut que celle ert moult cortoise
> ·qui ert dame de tel richoise.
> vv. 690–91, 696–97

(Eneas entered the palace. Never had he been in such a beautiful one . . . He saw that the lady who possessed all this luxury was very courtly.)

Equally awestruck by Dido's wealth, the Trojans accompanying Enéas concur, characterizing this Tyrian/Carthagian queen as the exceedingly capable leader of a "noble, courtly, and refined" entourage:

> Si Troïen moult se merveillerent:
> entr'euz dïent et conseillerent:
> "Moult est la dame preus et saige
> qui se deduit a tel barnaige!
> Veez quel salle et quel maisnie,
> gentilz, courtoise, afaitie.
> Bien doit celle terre tenir
> qui tel gent a a son servir."
> vv. 698–705

(The Trojans were amazed and said among themselves, "The lady who enjoys such an entourage is of extraordinary worth and wisdom. Look what a hall and what people: so noble, courtly and refined. A woman who has such people as servants must govern her land well.")

Capable, indeed. But this is also the precise narrative moment at which Dido's fortune and success begin to turn. Marilynn Desmond has shown convincingly how the Enéas poet transforms Virgil's story of Dido in the fourth book of the *Aeneid* into a twelfth-century vision that reflects the feudal traffic in women and literary patterns of courtly lovesickness.[6] Dido's sexual agency challenges the economy of desire that structures both feudal romance and the assumptions of gender in Norman culture, Desmond argues, making the appropriation of Dido into a romance narrative especially difficult. Instead, she comes to represent here, and in the depiction of the Dido episode inscribed on Enide's saddlebow in Chrétien's *Erec et Enide*, an illustration of the dangers of socially unregulated female desire.[7]

Indeed, as the anonymous narrator of the *Enéas* subtly rimes the Old French "richoise" with "cortoise" (vv. 696–97), Dido as the ingenious, respected, and astute silk-clad ruler enters the realm of courtliness: a western world where love can kill. Enéas, the heroic warrior escaped from Troy and destined to continue further west to found Rome, is her fateful guide on the journey into the courtly world and the poisoned love that issues from his kiss (via Cupid, v. 888), his clothes, and the bed sheets they share (vv. 2120–21, 2134, 2153).

Dido and Cloth

In one sense, Dido's brief life in Carthage is framed by two telling encounters with variant forms of cloth. The first, which actually involves a primal kind of cloth, an animal skin, occurs when the Tyrian queen, laden with her treasure of gold, silver, and "pailes et dras" as we have seen (vv. 276–77), arrives in Carthage and cleverly asks the ruling prince of Lybia to sell her as much land as could be covered by the hide of a bull:

> En cel paÿs est arrivee;
> au prince vint de la contree
> par grant engin li ala querre
> qu'il li vendist tant de sa terre
> com pourprendroit .I. cuir de tor;
> donna l'en et argent et or,
> et li princes li octroia,
> qui de l'engin ne se garda.
> vv. 278–85

(She arrived in this country and went to find the prince of the land. Very cleverly, she asked that he sell her some land: only as much as an ox hide could cover. She gave him silver and gold and the prince accepted, not realizing the trick.)

The unsuspecting prince imagines, of course, that the land in question will be no larger than the size of a single animal skin. But the ingenious Dido cuts and shapes that skin into thin strips that she then uses to outline the extensive boundaries of an entire city:

Dydo trencha par coroietes
le cuir, qui moult erent graillettes,
a celi a tant terre prise
qu'une cité y a assise.
vv. 286–89

(Dido cut the hide in very narrow strips and took enough land from him to found a city.)

A version of the tale appears in Geoffrey of Monmouth's *Historia Regum Britanniae* and the issue, there too, is one of crafty foreigners laying claim to ancestral land. In Geoffrey's account, the sly interloper Hengist asks King Vortigern for as much land as he can surround with a single leather thong cut from a bull's hide.[8] In the *Roman d'Enéas*, however, the figure of the sly foreigner becomes a woman, an eastern woman, threatening because of her political astuteness and the silken wealth that connotes it.

Although the utilitarian ox hide that Dido deploys differs significantly from the luxury fabrics deftly manipulated by Sebelinne and Lienor, all three heroines use their handiwork effectively to recast an inauspicious future. In this instance, the heroine rewrites the story of dishonor and exile that other protagonists had assumed to be hers. Here, the tale of a widow wronged by a conniving and ambitious brother who murders her husband for political gain becomes, as a direct result of this heroine's skilled hand, a story featuring her foundation and successful governance of a thriving and prosperous city. As this "dame de Carthage" succeeds at the task by exercising her knowledge and skill, the queen's "richece" is made to rime with "prouecse," the skill that enables her to captivate and control the considerable resources of the "superb" and "impregnable" city of Carthage:

Puis conquist tant par sa richece,
par son savoir, par sa prouesce,
qu'elle avoit tout le paÿs,
et les barons a souz soy mis.
La cite ot a non Cartaige,
en Libe sist sor le rivaige,
moult par fu belle et bien assise,
ja par siege ne sera prise.
vv. 290–97

(Then she conquered so much through her wealth, knowledge, and skill
that she had the entire country and its barons under her control. The
city was called Carthage, situated on the shore in Lybia. It was beautiful
and well positioned so as never to be taken in siege.)[9]

This tale of the Dame de Carthage triumphant, represented graphically
by a cloth-like animal skin that maps a thriving and wealthy city, flits before
our eyes in a few passing lines. The enduring image of Dido for most readers
is that which follows: the lovesick and abandoned woman who expires on a
pile of clothes. Once Enéas enters the scene, the Trojan warrior cast in the role
of western courtly lover, Dido herself is pulled further west metaphorically as
she is drawn into a French courtly narrative of foolish love. Overcome by the
anguish, despair, and helplessness that are standard Ovidian conceits in
Andreas Capellanus's *Art of Courtly Love* and lyrics of the Provençal troubadours, the "dame de Carthage" can no longer govern (vv. 1494–1501) and
leaves her Carthagian/Tyrian legacy behind. Although Queen Dido continues
to be clad in the formidable "porpre vermeille" of her Tyrian homeland, the
threads of another narrative have wrapped fatally around her. In this instance,
the courtly love story gives silk a new meaning.

Dido's Silk Pyre

Dido's tragic demise in the *Roman d'Enéas* focuses on the gifts offered by
Cupid on Enéas's behalf and at the behest of Venus to make the unsuspecting
Carthagian queen fall in love. Dido is fascinated, almost spellbound by the
presents, we are told:

Dydo commence a merveillier
Les garnemenz et lor bonté
vv. 873–74

(Dido became awestruck by the precious objects/items of dress and
their worth.)

Unaware of the love "poison" these "garnemenz" carry (v. 893), she swallows,
along with the fatal kisses from Cupid's lips (vv. 875–91), the mortal effects of
Enéas's three sartorial gifts: a necklace adorned with enamelwork (v. 748, une
nosche faite a esmaus) that is worth a fortune (v. 756), a golden crown, and, most
important for our purposes, a costly silk fabric, brought from Thessaly, woven
and beautifully embroidered with gold thread, that is, a cloth of silk and gold:

Une corronne de fin or
rueve aporter et .I. chier paille
qui aportez fu de Tessaille,
a or cousu et bien broudé
vv. 757–60

(He had brought in a crown of fine gold and an expensive silk cloth
imported from Thessaly, sewn and embroidered with gold.)

One thinks here of the cloth work done by the captive silk workers in
Chrétien's *Yvain*, who both weave and embroider with gold thread. What is
the significance in this instance of specifying imported cloth of silk and gold
as a gift from the Trojan Enéas to signal his love for the "dame de Cartage"?
Tellingly, the *paille* from Thessaly does not figure among the gifts proffered
by the suitor Aeneas in Virgil's text. In the *Aeneid*, Dido receives gifts representing royal governance: a scepter, and the necklace and the crown of
Illionee, Priam's eldest daughter.[10] The Old French text shifts the emphasis to
focus on the decorative sumptuousness of the costly enameled necklace and
gold crown. In addition it substitutes for the scepter an elegant piece of foreign silk called "paille." To be sure, references to "pailes" are commonplace in
later twelfth-century French romance where they often provide the setting for
courtly love stories, as we saw in Chapter 2. For Dido, however, that same
paille proves deadly.

A suggestion of covetousness accompanies the Old French portrayal of Dido's fall and suicide: a hint that this ingenious and capable ruler of a major metropolis falls prey to "loving" gold and silk instead of her city. Indeed, it is under the seductive influence of the wondrous gifts of silk and gold, termed collectively "garnemenz" throughout this text, that Dido's magnificently civilized city at Carthage is reduced to a site of "debauchery" because, as she herself says: "Sez garnemenz ay moult amez" (v. 2124; I so loved his items of dress). In the Old French text it is luscious, amorous silk, which has taken the place of the scepter of governance, as much as the gold crown or jewelry, that draws Dido into a fateful love affair and marks the end of her ability to rule:

> Par Lybe nonce ceste Fame
> la fellonie de la dame,
> dist que de Troye estoit venu
> .I. hom, Dydo l'a retenu
> ensamble o li enz en Cartaige;
> Or la maintient cil en putaige.
> En luxure ambedui mainent
> Le temps d'yver, d'el ne se painent,
> La dame en laisse son affaire,
> Nulle autre rien ne prise gaire,
> Et cil en a guerpi sa voie,
> Et l'un et l'autre se foloie.
> Moult est la dame defanmee
> Par toute Libe la contree.
> vv. 1650–63

(The lady's reputation for treason spreads through Lybia. They say that a man came from Troy and that Dido kept him with her in Carthage. He caused her to live a debauched life. They spent the winter together in lust, with no other cares. The lady neglected her duties. She was interested in nothing else. And he abandoned his mission. They lost their minds. The lady was defamed throughout all of Lybia.)

Thus does the extraordinarily elegant Carthagian queen, clad in lavish Tyrian purple silks, sink into debauchery as her city founders without guidance or direction. In Dido's own words, at the moment of her self-imposed death, all is lost: her kingdom and her power, her reputation and all her glory:

Ci lais m'onnor et mon barnaje,
ci deguerpi sanz hoir Cartaige,
ci pert mon non, toute ma gloire
vv. 2136–38

(Here, I lose my honor and power. Here, I leave behind Carthage without an heir. Here, I lose my name and all my glory.)

More specifically, it is on the site of the very *garnemenz* that drew her into love initially that Dido breathes her last, "les garnemenz au Troÿen" (vv. 2026–27, 2120–21) which include the fateful necklace, crown, and silk "paille" Enéas gave her along with his sword (v. 2018) and the bed on which she was dishonored (v. 2019). These "garnemenz," she explains, were the beginning of her death and destruction:

Mar vi onques ces garnemens.
Il me furent commencemens
de mort et de destructïon:
mar vi cil qui m'en fist le don;
comme folle ay trop amé,
a grant contraire m'est torné.
vv. 2128–33

(To my peril I first saw these items of dress. They were the beginning of my death and destruction. To my peril I looked upon the one who made me a present of them. Like a mad woman, I loved him too much. It has turned fatally against me.)

The Old French "garnemenz" carries a range of meanings, which are exploited and also at times richly conflated in this layered portrayal of Dido's demise. The term can signify equipment, armor, clothing, or ornament and decoration.[11] The *Roman d'Enéas* adds another dimension to this constellation by associating the clothing and ornamentation of "garnemenz" with a generic term for clothing—*dras*—itself a homonym of bed sheets. As the "dras du lit" of Dido's ostensibly adulterous passion fuse thematically with the "gar-nemenz" offered as love tokens and the clothing worn by the armed Trojan lover, Dido expires on a site of multilayered "dras" that accompany the other key textile in this scene: the silk *paille* from Thessaly:

> Sor ces dras veul fenir ma vie
> Et sor ce lit ou fui honnie.
> vv. 2134–45

(On these sheets and items of dress I want to end my life, and on this bed where I was dishonored.)

It is significant, however, that the funeral pyre of clothing and bedsheets is not prepared by Dido herself, but arranged by her sister according to the instruction of a sorceress who has suggested how to expunge the wrongs of Enéas's visit (vv. 2010–37). Decidedly different from the astute handiwork Dido performed when shaping the bull's hide to outline her newly founded city, the "dame de Carthage" can no longer use her hands to fashion anything. Once ravaged by love, she can only pull out her hair or gesture desperately with her ermine sleeve to call Enéas back from the sea:

> Elle tort poinz et ront sa crine,
> A la manche du blanc ermine
> Le racenne .C. foys et cent,
> Mais ce ne li monte nïent
> vv. 2044–47

(She wrings her hands and pulls her hair. With her white ermine sleeve, she makes hundreds of signs to him. But these gestures are in vain.)

Dying on a bed of "les garnemenz au Troyen" (vv. 2120–21), Dido makes the point explicit: her hands are worthless for anything but dealing death:

> Sez garnemenz ay moult amez,
> tant com Dieu plot les ay gardez,
> ne puis avant ma main estendre;
> desor ces dras veul ma vie rendre.
> vv. 2124–27

(I cherished these items of clothing, and kept them, as long as it pleased God. I cannot extend my hand. I want to surrender my life on these clothes and bedclothes.)

The final gesture of the betrayed and abandoned heroine comes from her lips, not her hands, as she kisses the "garnemenz" to signal reconciliation, we are told, and further pardons Enéas by kissing the bed and all the "dras" piled upon it:

> Par fin acordement de pays,
> Ces garnemens yci en bais;
> Jel vous pardoins, sire Eneas"
> Le lit baise et touz les dras;
> vv. 2150–53

(As a sign of reconciliation, I kiss these clothes. I pardon you, lord Enéas. She covers the bed and all the clothes/bedclothes with kisses.)

In embracing his clothes, his bed, and the silk coverlet he gave her, Dido embraces a material rendering of love gone tragically wrong. Her amorous alliance with Enéas is here reduced to a sartorial rendering of her own demise: a pile of fabric that connotes the end of her handiwork along with her kisses.

Maps of Cloth

The image provides a stark contrast to the silk *chemise* embraced and kissed fervently, if also somewhat comically, by the love-struck Alixandre in Chrétien de Troyes's *Cligès*. That silk garment, carefully embroidered by the heroine Soredamors with golden thread and strands of her own golden hair, communicates female desire in love and effectively joins the socially distanced lovers together.[12] In Dido's case, sartorial love tokens do not stand for an absent lover who will return, but for absence itself—the hero's and heroine's alike. By the end of this scene, the "dame Tirïane" has been reduced to ashes, the site identified previously with her keen political acumen having shrunk progressively over the course of the narrative from the circumference of Carthage, to the funereal pile of clothes, to a handful of cinders contained in a small urn:

Quant li cors fu devenu cendre,
sa serror fait la poudre prendre;
en une assez petite cane
metent la dame tyrïanne.
vv. 2214–17

(When her body had become ashes, her sister collected the powder.
They put the lady from Tyre in a small urn.)

The ever-expansive fabric/skin that once mapped Dido's expert ability to
found and govern a thriving commercial center now dissipates into a powder
of ruination, formed by the wispy remains of the Trojan lover's "dras." The
cinders define a Dido defamed and debauched (vv. 1650-51, 1674-75) in a "savage terre" previously civilized by her but now gone wild with "luxure" and
"love" under the corrupting influence of a Trojan lover. Enéas bears the pedigree of adulterous Trojans like the famed Paris, we are told (vv. 3370–79). But
readers of medieval romance will also recognize in him the persuasive gift-
bearing courtly lovers of twelfth-century French romance.

What happened to the "porpre vermeille" and "porpre de Tyre" of Dido's
venerated heritage? Where are the silks that marked her as regal, authoritative,
and capable, even ingenious and quick-witted, a woman amply endowed not
only with "richece" but even more so with *savoir* and *prouece*? The "paille de
Tessaille" that should have served as the trysting place for these displaced
lovers, like silk coverlets that adorn the beds of amorous couples in so many
Old French romances and *chanson de toiles*, here mercilessly engulfs and swallows up the Tyrian queen. This "dame de Carthage" is ruined in silk.

But why? If it is ultimately love, and specifically a version of courtly love,
that brings Dido down in the *Roman d'Enéas*, to what extent does her fatal
end result as much from what is cast here as the dangerous seduction of luxury goods as from an amorous attraction to Enéas?

Dangerous Foreign Luxury

To be sure, practitioners of courtly love in the French Middle Ages often drew
fire from preachers and moralists who condemned their proclivity for expensive and ostentatious clothing as an indication of "luxure."[13] From gold
adorning knights' spurs to the long gowns trailing behind ladies, courtly cul-

ture generally and the illicit and adulterous love it promoted were often cast as corrupting, too materially based, and dangerously worldly. While moralizing tirades often targeted women specifically, they also indicated at times a fear of the foreign. One can hear in comments by Lady Reason and the staunchly antifeminist Jealous Husband in Jean de Meun's *Roman de la Rose*, for example, subtle echoes of Tertullian's blanket condemnation of luxury goods such as gold, silver, jewelry, and costly clothes as provoking excessive desire simply because they are "imported from a foreign country."[14] The allegorical Ami in Jean's text states specifically that contact with "the foreign" through pilgrimage and travel generates avarice, envy, and fraud, a kind of corruption absent in former times:

> Paisiblement sanz vilonnie
> S'entreportoient compaignie,
> N'il ne donnassent pas franchise
> Pour l'or d'Arrabie ne de Frise,
> Car qui tout l'or en porroit prendre,
> Ne la porroit il pas bien vendre.
> N'estoit lors nul pelerinage,
> N'issoit nus hors de son rivage
> Pour tracier estrange contrée.
>
> Trestuit trouvoient de en leur terre
> Quanque leur sembloit bon a querre.
> vv. 9499–9507, 9523–24[15]

(They lived peacefully as a group without villainous acts. They would not have given their freedom for all the gold in Araby or Phrygia because even if one could obtain all this gold, it would not be possible to profit from it. At that time, there was no pilgrimage, no one left his own shores to search for foreign lands . . . They found everything deemed worth searching for in their own land.)

From the vantage point of twelfth-century France, Tyre was just such a source of imported luxury goods, responsible in particular, along with the cities of Damascus, Antioch, and Tripoli, for the production and shipment of large quantities of dangerously seductive silk to the west. Under Fatimid control until 1124, Tyre continued to produce lavish silks after passing to Frankish rule. Heavy silks, brocaded or woven with gold and silver and decorated with Islamicate motifs of birds and animals, were especially prized in the west for making clerical vestments and adorning chuches.[16] Western church inventories often cite the receipt of *vela tyrea*, indicating Tyre as a major point of export for silks from French colonies in Syria during the twelfth and thirteenth centuries, whether they were produced there or not.[17]

The emphasis on Dido's *porpre* in the mid-twelfth century *Roman d'Enéas* calls to our attention, then, the potential dilution of western identities that could result from the medieval colonization of crusader states in the Latin east. Michel Balard explains that the Christian colonial society of "outremer," established in large part by peaceful immigrations after the first crusade and the descendents of those immigrants, posed a particular threat to continued European crusading efforts. Franks born in the Holy Land and known as "poulains" were critiqued by western chroniclers at the end of the twelfth century for having adapted too readily to the excesses of eastern splendor.[18] They had become, in a word, too much like the amorphous eastern rivals, often called "Saracens," that crusading Franks were attempting to subdue. As Steven Runciman explains, crusaders landing in the Frankish east generally had to embrace an oddly hybrid place, "When he landed at Acre or Tyre or St Symeon, the traveler found himself at once in a strange atmosphere. Beneath the feudal superstructure, Outremer was an eastern land."[19] In the case of Tyre specifically, Fulcher of Chartres attempts to minimize that disparity, claiming assimilation to be so effortless that the Franks had actually become "Tyrians": "For we who are Occidentals have now become Orientals. He who was a Roman or a Frank has in this land been made into a Galilean or a Palestinean. He who was of Rheims or Chartres has now become a citizen of Tyre or Antioch. We have already forgotten the places of our birth; already these are not known to many of us, or not mentioned anymore."[20]

Exhorting new arrivals to embrace the putative success of colonial Occidentals, Fulcher actually asserts that "God had transformed the Occident into the Orient."[21] For our purposes, his mention of the cities of Rheims and Chartres is significant in this context since it indexes transformations in western identity in terms of site-specific cloth production. Rheims and Chartres were known in the Middle Ages as producers of linen—examples of Rhemois linen in particular being prized in the east and sent to Crusader states.[22] The medieval cities of Tyre and Antioch, by contrast, were premier centers of silk production in the Levant, where Muslim techniques of silk weaving, that had themselves previously incorporated Byzantine styles, continued to dominate

Syrian silk industries under Christian control.[23] Fulcher's use of these particular geographic locations to claim that Franks had shed their western identities and become "orientals" draws indirectly on familiar distinctions in cloth production to underscore his point. Linen was known in France as an indigenous fabric, made of locally produced flax, whereas putatively "foreign" silks were often marked linguistically, as we have seen, as having been imported from "outremer."

As Dido's lavish garb of silk and gold, her Tyrian purple, is set ablaze and incinerated when she moves westward and enters the courtly love story with a suitor hailed as the founder of Roman and later Frankish civilization in the west, the *Roman d'Enéas* takes a stand against Dido, the powerful Tyrian woman ruler whose luxurious silks display the economic success of their country of origin. These costly silks are perceived by many medieval clerical writers as engulfing and swallowing up Franks who have traveled haplessly eastward and fallen prey to the temptations and seductions of life among what many texts called "Saracens." If the colonial Franks described by Fulcher represent God's absorbtion of the Occident into the Orient, Dido's movement westward to become the Dame de Carthage charts a different transformation: an invasion of eastern splendor into North Africa as it moved ever closer to France.

As Dido expires in the Old French *Roman d'Enéas*, so too is the westward movement of silken luxury that tempts her iconically truncated and its potential cultural threat expunged. When the Tyrian silks that once marked Dido's success become her downfall, we witness a woman once skilled at manipulating an ox hide in order to build, control, and govern a splendid eastern-style city succumb to the deadly effects of excess luxury and opulence. Not only is this heroine's dangerous sexuality thus removed from the tale but also, along with it, the seductive power of the silk-making world so often associated in the cultural imagination of texts from the *Enéas* to the *Roman de la Rose* with the foreign situated in a vast and vague "outremer."

Nicolette: Dame de Carthage, Dame de Biaucaire

The "other" "dame de Carthage," Nicolette in the thirteenth-century chantefable *Aucassin et Nicolette*, is not, like Dido, a pagan heroine from Antiquity, but a Saracen princess from medieval Spain. Both are foreign women forcibly displaced from their individual homelands, but under starkly different circumstances. Whereas Queen Dido fled her Tyrian home to found the lush commercial city of Carthage in North Africa, Nicolette is abducted from the Muslim city of Cartagena in Spain (rendered as "Cartage" in Old French) and transported to France as precious slave cargo. Although both narratives tell stories of star-crossed lovers, the *Roman d'Enéas* plays out the tragic consequences of medieval courtly conventions while *Aucassin et Nicolette* often mocks courtliness in a comedically light tone. And yet, the humorous love story in *Aucassin et Nicolette* carries with it a serious narrative cargo that lets us see more fully the darker world of Mediterranean commerce only suggested in the scene of captive silk workers from Chrétien de Troyes's *Yvain*. Love in this anomalous Old French tale is shown specifically to result from geographic displacements wrought by the medieval slave trade, commerce that often occurred historically in tandem with the trading of silk.

We have seen the conjunction of slaves and silk clearly in the twelfth-century romance *Floire et Blancheflor* when the courtly French heroine, Blancheflor, is sold in Niebla to Saracen merchants for silks and gold: ".xxx. mars d'or et .xx. d'argent/ et .xx. pailes de Bonivent,/ et .xx. mantiax vairs osterins,/ et .xx. bliaus indes porprins,/ et une ciere coupe d'or" (vv. 437–41; thirty marcs of gold and twenty of silver, twenty silks from Benevento, twenty fur-lined silk cloaks, twenty tunics of blue silk, and a costly golden goblet), and traded again to the emir of Babiloine in Egypt (vv. 1311–14, 1542).[24] By contrast, however, the love story infused with Mediterranean commerce in *Aucassin et Nicolette* is not entirely displaced to luxury-rich Saracen lands in Spain or Egypt. This tale's reference to buying and selling women involves France itself. As such it offers important insights into the brief suggestion of slave trading contained in the scene of captive silk workers in *Yvain*.

In *Aucassin et Nicolette* we witness not only culturally demonized "Moors" and corrupt "emirs" who practice the slave trade but also a French count who traffics in women. The Viscount of Biaucaire has purchased Nicolette from Saracen merchants and transported her to France as a "captive" from "Cartage": "ce est une caitive qui fu amenee d'estrange terre, si l'acata li visquens de ceste vile a Sarasins, si l'amena en ceste vile" (II, 29–31; She is a captive/slave brought from a foreign land. The viscount of this city bought her from Saracens and transported her to this city).[25] By the end of the tale, this seeming slave from Cartage is wrapped in sumptuous silk attire provided by her former adoptive French mother in preparation for an unlikely marriage: "le viscontesse le recounut et seut bien que c'estoit Nicolete et qu'ele l'avoit norrie . . . se se vesti de rices dras de soie" (XL, 31–32, 35–36; The vi-countess recognized her, knew she was Nicolette, and that she had raised her . . . and she dressed her in rich silks). As the French courtly lover Aucassin comes together with the Saracen slave-turned-princess, Nicolette is placed iconically, as Dido might have been, on a silk coverlet, "s'assist en le canbre sor une cueute pointe de drap de soie" (XL, 36–37; She sat in the chamber on a coverlet of silk cloth). However, silk in this instance, signals the fruits of love rather than its fatalities:

> Quant or le voit Aucassins,
> Andex ses bras li tendi,
> Doucement le recoulli,
> Les eus li baise et le vis.
> La nuit le laissent ensi,
> Tresqu'au demain par matin
> Que l'espousa Aucassins.
> XLI, 12–18

(When Aucassin saw her, he held out both arms and enfolded her gently, kissing her eyes and face. That night, they left it at that until the next morning when Aucassin married her.)

In stark contrast to Dido's demise amid silk that seduces and kills, Nicolette's story uses silk to mark the unlikely transformation of the putative slave woman from Cartage into the "dame de Biaucaire" (XLI, 19). Silk in this narrative connotes, it would seem, not the foreignness of ancient Mediterranean civilizations or the seductive dangers of Frankish crusading colonies in the Levant, but rather a hybrid existence, used here most overtly to mark Nicolette's transformation from a Saracen slave into a proper and marriageable courtly lady.

And yet the degree to which Nicolette has become a courtly woman in the course of this *chantefable* remains subject to debate. To be sure, the heroine's transformation from imported slave to courtly beloved and bride is attributed predominantly to the baptism and conversion to Christianity imposed upon her by the Viscount of Biaucaire. In addition, the text's copious and detailed depictions of Nicolette as the courtly lady par excellence,[26] the eventual revelation of her noble heritage and the courtly romance conventions that structure the love liaison all work together in this tale to create the portrait of what has been called a "white" Saracen princess.[27] More nuanced readings have shown, however, the further complexity of Nicolette's hybrid identity as a Spanish Arab princess who chooses at one point to disguise her blond self as dark in order to secure her assimilation into French society.[28]

In fact the category of the Saracen princess is, by definition, a hybrid category that generates heroines whose conflicted and complex rhetorical positioning defies the very dichotomization of east against west that the narratives containing them, whether epic or romance, tend to promulgate.[29] Indeed, as Maria Rosa Menocal argued a number of years ago, this seemingly lightweight love story, which relentlessly parodies any number of Old French literary genres, also offers a trenchant analysis of the largest historico-cultural issues of its time: the Arabic "other" and its degree of assimilation into French cultural identity. In Menocal's reading, *Aucassin et Nicolette* reveals the extent to which the putative "Arabic other" is no more alien, foreign or distant than the highly courtly, white-skinned Nicolette.[30] And yet, less attention has been paid to the story of slavery encased within the courtly veneer of *Aucassin et Nicolette*. The layered rhetorical strategies that mark this heroine as western and courtly tend to make the initial account of her enslavement seem foreign and incidental, as if slavery were a pagan practice easily erased by Christian conversion. And yet, the *chantefable* reveals something quite different.

To understand more fully the allusions this tale makes to the medieval slave trade, we might pay closer attention to its references to silk cloth, silk clothing, and the heroine who wears them. We might ask to what extent this curious *chantefable*'s allusions to slave trading and its association with silk trading prove central to the highly anomalous love story and to our understanding of its complex, culturally hybrid heroine.?

It is well known that Nicolette, shortly after arriving in France, sheds the role of "captive woman" to play, metaphorically at least, the part of questing knight in a courtly love scenario with roles reversed. Often acting as the capable "hero" in contrast to the hapless Aucassin's tearful damsel in distress, Nicolette appears skilled, astute, and effective. In many instances, it is her initiative that moves the narrative forward: first by escaping the tower prison where the viscount has enclosed her, by undertaking the search for Aucassin, by building the hut in the forest, healing the hero's wounded shoulder, effectively escaping captivity in Carthage through *engin*, and finally playing the *jongleur* as Aucassin listens. While he sits and waits–in his bedchamber-prison and elsewhere, she travels extensively, moving twice from Spain to France. In

many ways, Nicolette enacts the role of a capable Gauvain to Aucassin's beleaguered courtly damsel in need of rescue or liberation.

In the majority of these scenes the heroine's attire is not detailed. Before
setting out from the tower to rescue the helpless Aucassin, however, Nicolette
dons a "bliaut de drap de soie" (XII, 12), silk clothing appropriate for the
courtly lady generally and reminiscent in particular of the very silk made by
the imprisoned workers in Chrétien's *Yvain*. By implication, then, if not direct description, this heroine's series of chivalric-like adventures seem to be
performed in a silk tunic (XII, 12; bliaut de drap de soie), which announces,
in a sense, the "rices dras de soie" (XL, 35–36) that mark her as the courtly
ladylove at the tale's close. And yet, during the intervening moments, as this
complex and anomalous story unfolds, Nicolette also seems defined by something else entirely.

The Captive

From the outset, Nicolette's story is that of a young child, abducted and sold
to a French viscount who kept her, as Aucassin's father tells it initially, to be
"nurtured, trained, and brought up" by the viscount, "si l'amena en ceste vile,
si l'a levee" (II, 30-31 and IV, 4, 12; He brought her to this city and raised her)
and as the viscount himself reiterates, "si l'ai levee . . . si l'ai nourie" (VI,
14–15; I raised and nourished her). What does this mean? The viscount's version of events situates the slave's "training" within the context of a putatively
beneficent conversion and baptism used to transform the captive woman into
his "goddaughter": "si l'amena en ceste vile, si l'a levee et bautisie et faite sa
fillole" (II, 30–31; He brought her to this city, raised her and baptized her and
made her his goddaughter). Nicolette's account, by contrast, emphasizes the
repeated abductions and imprisonments that have structured her travels as a
captive woman.

Elaborating her version of the story at the end of the *chantefable* when she
takes up the role of *jongleur*, dressed not in the silks of a courtly lady but in a
man's "cote et mantel et cemisse et braies" (tunic and cloak and under-tunic
and under breeches) Nicolette-as-*jongleur* explains to the lovesick Aucassin
and to other members of the audience at his father's castle in Biaucaire that
her initial capture and sale to the French count was followed by a second abduction and imprisonment by her own father. Speaking of herself in the third

person, with her face artificially darkened to enhance the disguise, Nicolette explains:

> . . . Nicholete la prous . . .

> A Torelore u dongon
> Les prissent paiien un jor
> D'Aucassin rien ne savons,
> Mais Nicolete la prous
> Est a Cartage el donjon
> Car ses pere l'ainme mout
> Qui sire est de cel roion.
> XXXIX, 18, 21–27

(The skilled and capable Nicolete [*la prous*] . . . Pagans seized her one day along with Aucassin from the prison tower in Torelore. Although we know nothing of him, the skilled and capable Nicolette is now held in the castle keep in Carthage, by her loving father, who is lord of that realm.)

A second capture by a second putatively caring father figure. Having first been purchased from unnamed Saracen merchants and transported from an "estrange tere" (VI, 15) by the viscount of Biaucaire, as we have been told earlier, the blonde, comely, highly courtly "Saracen" Nicolette was then taken captive a second time, she now explains, when a flotilla of Saracens attacked the castle at Torelore, seizing its valuable contents, money and slaves, which included the courtly couple: "Et uns estores de Sarrasins vinrent par mer, s'asalirent au castel, si il prissent par force; il prissent l'avoir, s'en menerent caitis et kaitives; il prissent Nicolete et Aucassin" (XXXIV, 4–7; A fleet of Saracens arrived by sea and besieged the castle; they took goods/treasure/valuables; carried away male and female captives, they took Nicolete and Aucassin).

One of these Saracen ships belonged coincidentally to the King of Carthage, Nicolette's long-lost father, who was himself plundering captives: "La nes u Nicolete estoit estoit le roi de Cartage, et cil estoit ses peres" (XXXVI, 2–3; The ship Nicolette was on belonged to the king of Carthage, who was her father). Having been placed by chance into his slave-carrying ship, the heroine was again transferred as cargo, this time toward her homeland, tellingly unable to explain to those on board ship "who she was": "ele ne lor sot a dire qui ele estoit" (XXXVI, 6–7; She was unable to tell them who she was).[31] Indeed, it is only after coming face to face with the "cité de Cartage" as if looking in a mirror, that this "dame de Cartage" recognizes herself, literally, in the contours of her natal city: "Il nagierent tant qu'il ariverent desox le cité de Cartage, et quant Nicolete vit les murs del castel et le païs, *ele se reconnut*" (XXXVI, 8–10; They sailed until they came upon the city of Carthage, and when Nicolette saw the walls of the castle and countryside, she recognized herself).

But what does she recognize? In one and the same breath Nicolette claims her identity as a noblewoman from Carthage and a captive: she is the daughter of the King of Carthage and she was also taken away as a young child, many years earlier: "je sui fille au roi de Cartage et fui preée petis/ enfes, bien a quinse ans" (XXXVIII, 5–6; I am the daughter of the king of Carthage and was taken away as a young child, a good fifteen years ago).

It is not surprising that readers of *Aucassin et Nicolette* have not paid more attention to the heroine's tale of repeated enslavement. The potential rhetorical force of the term "caitive," indicating forced capture, is effectively attenuated at several turns in the narrative. The tale's anonymous author sometimes transposes the word's meaning into the courtly register, using it to connote the misery of lovesickness. In addition to the descriptions of Nicolette as a "caitive" bought and transported from an "estrange terre" (II, 29) and the subsequent capture of the courtly couple as "caitis et kaitives," meaning slaves forcibly seized by "pagan" sea men (XXXIV, 6), we hear Nicolette lament imprisonment of a different kind when she is enclosed in a "cambre" by the viscount of Biaucaire who hopes to end her amorous liaison with Aucassin. Her sigh, "Ah mi! lasse moi, caitive!/ por coi sui en prison misse?" (V, 15–16; "Woe is me! Unfortunate captive; why have I been put in prison?") is later magnified in the dolorous complaints and sobs that issue from Aucassin's "chamber," as the failed knight laments his beloved's absence while neglecting his knightly duty to defend his father's besieged lands (VIII, 1–6). His father calls him "caitis"—miserable and wretched—the term used metaphorically in this instance to mean "a captive to love": "Ha! fix, fait il, con par es caitis et maleurox" (VIII, 12; Alas! My son, he said, you are a miserable captive).

The reference provides a stark contrast to Nicolette's physical enslavement as a miserable captive, cast out from her home city (III, 9; "jetee fu de Cartage") and bought by a Christian French count at pains to insist at several junctures that he spent good money on her.[32] He claims, as we have seen, to have baptized and raised this young girl, making her his *fillole*, with a plan to give her one day to a young man who will toil honorably for her: "si la donasce un de ces jors un baceler qui del pain li gaegnast par honor (VI, 17–18). Are we to understand, then, that this slaveholder has turned thoroughly familial, a slave buyer casting himself as a well-meaning and protective father figure? Is Nicolette's capture and incarceration then free of the sexualized overtones that accompany the captivity of silk workers in *Yvain*, also "overseen," if in a different way, by a courtly lord?

To be sure, Nicolette's body is eroticized throughout this tale, generally within the recognizable and predictable parameters of courtly encounter: as the lovely heroine whose "gens cors" and "biautés" (III, 15–16) steal the heart of the lovesick Aucassin, or as the "doce amie, flors de lis" (XI, 32) whose comely leg, Aucassin imagines, could heal an ailing pilgrim (XI, 26–28).[33] But this female body is not made for refined loving alone, as Aucassin himself explains in a little-noted passage a few lines earlier. Here the erotic connotations of the heroine's body are replaced by a suggestion of vulnerability to violation, as Nicolette announces her plans to separate herself from Aucassin, saying "I will cross the ocean on your account and travel to another land" (Por vous passerai le mer,/ s'irai en autre regné" (XIII, 13–14).[34] Aucassin responds in no uncertain terms that such travel will put the heroine at risk of being *taken* by the first man who sees her, "Li premiers qui vos verroit ne qui vous porroit, il vos *prenderoit* lués" (XIV, 4–5), taken in a sense perhaps latent in the text's earlier reference to Nicolette being "taken" from Carthage (II, 29–31). Here the implications of women being taken captive are made explicit: "et vos meteroit a son lit, si vos asoignenteroit" (XIV, 5–6; and he will put you in his bed and thus make you his mistress).

In a courtly context, one would think of the "coutume de Logres" in which women traveling alone through the forest, unaccompanied by a knight protector, are characterized as being subject to attack, vulnerable to having men (knights included) "do as they please" with them.[35] But Nicolette specifies that she intends to cross the sea and venture into another country altogether, a trajectory that invokes Mediterranean commerce more than courtly adventure, commerce that historically included trading in slaves along with silk, slaves who often became house servants and were also used as concubines.[36] Indeed, we might ask how closely the Old French "asoignenter" (to take as a mistress) used in the quotation above resonates with the verb "soignier," used by the Viscount of Biaucaire, meaning "to take care of, to watch over, to occupy oneself with, to be preoccupied by."[37] This is the word he uses to indicate his preoccupation with the slave girl Nicolette, brought as a captive from an "estrange terre" and sold to the count by Saracens from "Cartage" (XXXVIII, 5–6). The reference, although less overt than mention of the overlord's sexual threats against the captive silk workers in *Yvain*, remains nonetheless highly suggestive.

Cartagena

The portrait of Cartagena as an "estrange terre" framing the love story of *Aucassin et Nicolette* corresponds to the view of "Cartage" articulated in Old French epics such as the twelfth-century *Couronnement de Louis*. There, the city is cast as a generic Saracen fief located in lands held nebulously by the Moors of Spain."[38] John Tolan has explained, however, that Carthaginians in Africa were also often conflated with Moors from the time of Alfonso X in chronicles that expressed the royal ideology of reconquest. One chronicle in particular, the *Estoria de España*, attempted to justify Alfonso's supremacy as a Gothic king by claiming the Romans and Visigoths as the only legitimate dynasties that had ruled Spain.[39] Especially reviled in this account were Spanish colonizers who had come from Africa and were labeled in this instance as both "Carthaginians" and "Moors." This chronicler's version of the Arab invasion of Spain, Tolan explains, decried African invaders with "black faces" as semi-diabolical creatures marred by trickery and cleverness, much the same characterization as was visited upon dark-skinned Muslims generally.[40] This view reflects a more general tendency, as P. K. Hitti has explained, in evidence by the mid-thirteenth century when the reconquest was nearly complete, to recast the historical struggle of Romans against Phoenicians in the Punic Wars into a medieval ideological battle of Christians against the forces of Islam.[41] Thus do the Carthaginians—both African and Iberian—come to represent, in the medieval imagination of certain Old French literary works, one amalgamated block of "Saracens." In *Aucassin et Nicolette*, those Saracens are further marked as merchants involved in the Mediterranean slave trade.

The casting of Nicolette herself as a Saracen woman with blonde hair and white skin "jetee de Cartage" for unexplained reasons and sold by "Saracen" merchants to a Christian French count represents yet another literary amalgamation, suggesting a possible conflation of two distinct phases of the Andalusi slave trade. Constable explains that by the mid-thirteenth

century, al-Andalus, which had previously distributed "white slaves" to other
parts of the Islamic world—Christian and pagan slaves largely from eastern
Europe and Christian Spain—began to engage in a new trade: the sale of
Muslim slaves to Christian buyers. As early as the tenth century, male and female slaves from Frankish and Galician regions, not unlike the light-skinned
and blonde Nicolette, had figured among the most famous exports from al-
Andalus to other Muslim lands.[42] By the thirteenth century, however,
Muslims slaves were being exported from al-Andalus to Christian cities in
southern Europe,[43] as is the captive Nicolette. Constable notes that the shift
to trafficking in Muslims in the thirteenth century was often linked directly
to Christian victories in Islamic lands where slaves were taken as war booty.
She explains, for example, that once Christian armies reached Cordoba in
1236, the city's Muslim traffic in northern Christian slaves effectively came to
an end, but large numbers of Muslim slaves began to appear for sale in
Christian cities.[44] Simultaneously, as Christians regained control of the
Mediterranean in the thirteenth century, the Andalusi export of silk, which
for so long had been the preeminent export of Muslim Spain, decreased
markedly.[45] Is it possible that *Aucassin et Nicolette* gestures in some measure
toward this shift, featuring as it does the dizzying portrait of a heroine who
constantly swings between identities: a European slave with blonde hair,
light skin and grey eyes (XXI, 9–10) and white legs and feet (XII, 28) or a
darker "cousine of the Aumaffle" and daughter of the "roi de Cartage"
(XXXVII, 7–8) who wishes to marry her to a rich "pagan" king in Spain
(XXXVIII, 13)? Nicolette is presented as being all these things, a kind of
generic "Andalusi" slave "other." But there is more.

Nicolette's Linen Handiwork

The gradual transformation of the slave girl from Carthage into the "dame de
Biaucaire," is often rendered in this text through Nicolette's varied skills at
healing, many of them involving not "foreign" silk but indigenous linen.
When Nicolette cures the pilgrim's madness in Aucassin's imagined scenario,
it is by raising her "pelican" and the "cemisse de blanc lin" beneath to reveal
her putatively therapeutic "ganbete" (XI, 25–26). When she later heals
Aucassin's wounded shoulder with a mixture of herbs and flowers, those healing agents are tied in place by a "pan de sa cemisse" (XXVI, 14). And at the
end of the tale, as we have seen, when Nicolette, cross-dressed as a *jongleur*,

sings the curative story of "Aucassin and Nicolette," which is said to heal those who are "de grant mal amaladis" (I, 12–13), she wears a man's "cemisse" and "braies" along with outer garments of "cote" and "mantel" (XXXVIII, 17). These recurrent references to the heroine's "chemise," a simple garment most often emblematic of domestic linen production, resonate more broadly with another form of linen, the bedsheets that feature so prominently in Nicolette's initial act of escape from the "canbre vautie" where the viscount holds her prisoner (V, 1–2, 15–21). In this first expression of independence and strength, the "caitive" from Carthage fashions a cord from "dras de lit et touailes" and sets herself free: "Si prist dras de lit et touailes, si noua l'un a l'autre, si fist une corde, si longe conme ele pot, si le noua au piler de le fenestre; si s'avala contreval le gardin" (XII, 13–15; She took bed sheets and linens, tied them together and made as long a rope as she could, tied it to a pillar at the window and descended into the garden).

Indeed, from the moment she wraps those bed linens together, we can see that Nicolette's otherwise delicate and "lily white hands" continually work to fashion the couple's eventual reunion on a silk coverlet. Whether applying linen bandages, weaving together leaves of the hut she constructs, or bowing the *viele* that transforms her story into musical notes, Nicolette, who portrays herself to Aucassin at tale's end as one "who came from far away to find you" (XL 44–45; qui de longes terres vos est venue querre) has also, throughout her travels, accomplished a series of remarkable signature feats with her hands.

Gold

Most notable in terms of the Mediterranean slave trade that subtends this narrative, however, is the way this heroine works not linen or even silk, but gold. Although the transformation is metaphorical, it carries important material consequences for the heroine Nicolette who effectively redefines her embodied value as a slave, transposing her initial worth as commercial cargo into a golden object beyond commercial circulation. The fact that the "very rich" Viscount of Biaucaire in his "very rich palace" uses his considerable "avoir" (VI, 16; IV, 20) to buy Nicolette initially, provides some indication of her "worth" as a captive. Aucassin's first assessment of the slave girl's courtliness retains this allusion to her incomparable worth as he negotiates a "couvens" with his father (VIII, 31; X, 43, 47, 51), promising to exchange his military service for an opportunity to speak to the "caitive" (VI, 15) and receive a single kiss worth more than 100,000 marks of pure gold. The narrator explains:

> Aucassins ot du baisier
> qu'il ara au repairier:
> por cent mile mars d'or mier
> ne le fesist on si lié.

> (IX, 1–4; Aucassin heard of the kiss he would have on his return and he could not have been happier if someone had given him 100,000 marks of gold.)

With appropriate hyperbole, the lovesick suitor values the kiss from the woman he calls "Nicolette me douce amie" (VIII, 35) more highly than gold that might be gained from a substantial commercial venture. Tellingly, Nicolette later negotiates a bargain of her own, setting out into the dangerous forest, *borse* in hand (XVIII, 32), to transact business with a group of bewildered shepherds. Offering them payment to deliver a cryptic message to her beloved Aucassin, Nicolette describes herself as an inordinately valuable beast possessing a single limb worth more than five hundred marks: "Se Dix vos aït, bel enfant, fait ele, dites li qu'il a une beste en ceste forest et qu'i le viegne cacier, et s'il l'i puet prendre, il n'en donroit mie un menbre por cent mars d'or, non por cinc cens, ne por nul avoir" (XVIII, 17–20; So help you God, my children, she said, tell him [Aucassin] that there is a beast in this forest that he should hunt. If he could capture it, he would not part with a single one of its limbs for one hundred marks of gold, not even for five hundred, or for any amount of money).[46]

Nicolette La Bête

The passage has often been read as a send up of excessively elaborate courtly language that makes little sense to rural workers.[47] And yet the precise terms used by Nicolette have important ramifications for the commercial register of this narrative. Speaking metaphorically of herself as the highly desirable "beste" to be taken (*prendre*) now in a very different sense from when she was "taken" captive (that is, bought as a slave) by the Viscount of Biaucaire, Nicolette characterizes herself in terms quite beyond extravagant sums of gold. She is now literally a priceless object. No longer the courtly lady whose kiss Aucassin values in terms of gold, Nicolette has transposed herself into a being who will not be traded or exchanged "for any amount of money" (XVIII, 20; por nul avoir). The awestruck shepherds miss this crucial point, exclaiming that Nicolette must be a fairy reciting "fantosmes!" (XVIII, 24) since there is no beast in the forest, whether stag, lion, or wild boar "dont un des menbres vaille plus de dex deniers u de trios au plus, et vos parlés de si grant avoir" (XVIII, 26–27; that has a single limb worth more than two deniers or three at the most, and you speak of such great wealth). But Nicolette has not, in fact, equated this magical "member" with "si grant avoir" any more than her comments reflect the marketplace prices of "deniers" that the shepherds quote. Her message is not that the beast is so costly, but quite the opposite: that no amount of gold would be sufficient to purchase this extraordinary limb or the woman who possesses it, "il n'en donroit mie un menbre por cent mars d'or, non por cinc cens, ne por nul avoir" (XVIII, 19–20; He would not give up a single limb for a hundred marks of gold or five hundred or for any amount of money). Focusing on the potential value of a single golden limb, "un menbre," Nicolette has refashioned the courtly lady's coveted and fetishized "gent cors" described earlier (XXIII, 2, 9, 13) into a "menbre d'or" that expresses her incomparable worth precisely because it cannot be assigned a monetary value.

We have here a literary example of an Andalusi Muslim slave escaped from her Christian captor who begins trading in her own right, first literally, by paying the shepherds to deliver her message, and then narratively, by telling her tale of a single leg worth more than gold. If Sebelinne in the *Dit de l'Empereur Constant* casts herself as the "emperor of Constantinople" in a message penned by her hand, Nicolette composes an oral message asserting her value and status as even more incalculable. Rather than being bought, perhaps for gold, she has assigned herself the highest value possible—safely beyond the precious metal currency needed, along with silk, to make the slave trade run.

Michael McCormick has shown that patterns of Muslim slave trade based on the exchange of European slaves for African and Asian coins and silk, among other commodities, began in the Carolingian period and persisted long afterward.[48] The marked influx of Arab gold into western Europe in the decades around Charlemagne's coronation coincides, he claims, with the large quantities of silk textiles that crossed the Mediterranean, especially into Italy, as Europeans sold to Muslim merchants large numbers of "captivi," meaning slaves, as mobile merchandise rather than slaves linked to land. As the Arab slave trade developed in the ninth century, it fueled the expansion of commerce between Europe and the Muslim world, a commerce dominated by the silk trade.[49] These patterns persist, McCormick asserts, with the Mediterranean slave trade negotiating large sums of gold, as a necessary supplement to costly silks, spices, and gems, which were insufficient to purchase highly valued human beings.[50] To be sure, prized silk was routinely carried like cash by many Mediterranean merchants in the tenth and eleventh centuries, as recorded in the Cairo Geniza.[51] But silk alone, McCormick surmises, was insufficient to purchase slaves. Constable explains further that under the Almoravids and then the Almohads, when the Andalusi silk industry flourished, substantial quantities of gold were channeled through the western Maghreb into Muslim Spain. At the same time, slaves coming into al-Andalus from eastern Europe and Christian Spain were then reexported to other parts of the Islamic world.[52]

The Old French romance of *Floire et Blancheflor* stages just such a confluence of silk and gold trading across the Mediterranean when the French heroine Blancheflor is sold in Muslim Spain to foreign merchants for ample quantities of eastern luxury goods, as we have seen. But Nicolette's assertion of her extraordinary "worth" in terms of a single "menbre" also takes us back to the exceedingly vulnerable "menbres" of the silk workers in Chrétien's *Yvain*, captive women who fear bodily harm and abuse at the hand of their unnamed employer. They fear specifically that he will "maim their members": "Des nuiz grant partie veillons/ et toz les jorz por gaaignier/ qu'il nos menace a mahaignier/des manbres, quant nos reposons;/ et por ce reposer n'osons" (vv. 5314–18; We stay awake a good part of the night and all day long to prevent him from threatening to maim our members while we are at rest. For this reason we dare not rest). Nicolette's "members" have seemingly escaped such a fate. But the story she tells contains a number of key elements that resonate with the narrative recounted by the three hundred silk workers. Nicolette tells the tale of a woman enslaved and transported to France who escapes initial imprisonment by her "lord" and manages to revalue her bodily worth outside of the slave trade. Yet, unlike the silk workers in *Yvain*, whose primary economic resource is their ability to weave the most highly valued cloth of silk and gold, Nicolette's ultimate resource lies in gold itself, that is, in configuring her bodily worth quite apart from the system that bound silk and gold together as commodities of exchange in the slave trade.

Nicolette the Relic

When Nicolette, the captive of Carthage, claims to have a single limb worth more than one hundred or five hundred marks of gold, or indeed, as she says, worth more than any amount of gold, she speaks not in commercial terms, invoking money that might be paid for purchasing slave women, nor in a courtly register where gold often signifies golden hair or golden kisses. If Aucassin is cast throughout this tale as a "rice home" (XXII, 16), Nicolette, characterized as the "beste" with the golden limb, embodies the extraordinary value of riches transposed into another sphere altogether, riches transformed into relics. On one level, Nicolette's seemingly odd and comical description of herself as a golden "beste" has alchemized the most costly metal, gold, into a spiritually potent icon, while retaining all the while the association of material value with female physicality. Earlier in the narrative, we heard Aucassin describe Nicolette's incomparably beautiful leg as capable of healing, of curing the madness of a pilgrim: "Tant que ta ganbete vit:/ garis fu li pelerins/ et tos sains, ainc ne fu si" (XI, 26–28; As soon as he saw your leg, the pilgrim was cured and healthier than ever before). Now the heroine herself claims to have a golden limb of priceless value, a limb that evokes the many dismembered fingers and hands of saints, often encased in gold, that were believed to heal pilgrims and travelers across medieval France. In the mid-twelfth-century *Couronnement de Louis*, for example, St. Peter's arm, encased in gold and silver, is brought out from the church for the hero Guillaume to kiss, thereby gaining protection from harm "by any man."[53] The first relic offered to Charlemagne in the *Pèlerinage de Charlemagne à Jerusalem et à Constantinople*, and later enclosed in a lavish gold reliquary, is St. Simeon's arm (v. 163).

If relics like these consistently attracted monetary donations to parish churches across medieval France, Nicolette's metaphorical *menbre d'or* invests its heroine with similarly potent value. Profits from this kind of gold will not accrue to merchants or slavers. But neither is this a simple case of gold transferred to spiritual or religious use. Most important in Nicolette's refashioning of herself as the "beast with the golden leg" is that having created the curious and powerful "beste" rhetorically, Nicolette will literally deliver its curative powers more valuable than gold. As the shepherds explain to Aucassin, "car li beste a tel mecine que se vos le poés prendre, vos serés garis de vo mehaig" (XXII, 36–37; because the beast has such curative powers that if you could catch it, you would be healed of your wound).[54] To be sure, Aucassin will gain in the transaction, being cured of the love sickness that assails and imperils him. Once healed of love's stranglehold, Aucassin will be released from his beleaguered state as a "miserable captive" (VIII, 12; caitis et maleurox). But Nicolette alone can provide the priceless golden cure. Significantly different from the immobilized and gold-encrusted "members" of so many medieval saints' relics, however, Nicolette is distinguished throughout this tale, as we have seen, by arms and legs, hands and toes that move, whether working linen or other material objects.[55]

Once a valued commodity of exchange bought and sold by others, Nicolette now positions herself as a curious kind of subject, a relic that can cure lovesickness not by being venerated or touched physically, but through a sequence of purposeful actions here rendered by a long string of active verbs. When Aucassin arrives at the forest hut carefully prepared by Nicolette's "bele mains," it is she, the astute and capable heroine, figured earlier as that incomparably valuable golden limb, who succeeds in capturing him: "Quant Nicolette oï Aucassin, ele vint a lui, car ele n'estoit mie lonc; ele entra en la loge, si li jeta ses bras au col, si le baisa et acola" (XXVI, 1–3; When Nicolette heard Aucassin, she came to him, since she was not far off, she entered the bower, threw her arms around him and kissed and hugged him). Similarly in the final reunion scene, we see Nicolette beautifully groomed and dressed in "rices dras de soie," posed iconically on a "cuete pointe de drap de soie," much like the noble *pucele* sitting on the *dras de soie* in Chrétien's *Yvain*. And yet, this heroine remains still only until Aucassin enters the room. Nicolette then springs into action, a silk-clad woman in motion:

> Quant ele voit son ami,
> or fu lie, ainc ne fu si
> contre lui en piés sali.
> XLI, 9–11

(When she saw her beloved, she was full of joy as never before. She jumped up to greet him.)

As a foreign woman who heals lovesickness, Nicolette seems in many ways an embodied variation of the Provençal troubadours' desired but distant "amor de lonh." If so, she would be that "amor de lonh" come home. Recasting the familiar far-off beloved of early troubadour lyric, Nicolette as a lady captured and tamed, could, it seems, resolve on French soil the troubadour's rhetorical dilemma of unrequited love. Does this thirteenth-century heroine then provide, in some sense, an answer to Jaufré Rudel's wish to be a pilgrim in the "far-off land" so that "far-off love" might in fact become close at hand?

> Be tenc lo seignor per verai
> Per qu'ieu veirai l'amor de loing;
> Mas per un ben que m'en eschai
> N'ai dos mals, quar tant m'es de loing.
> Ah! car me fos lai peleris,
> Si que mos fustz e mos tapis
> Fos pels sieus bels huoills remiratz!
> vv. 29–35[56]

(I shall consider him in truth my Lord, the man who lets me see this far-off love. But for each good thing that befalls me, I get two evils, for this love is so far away. Ah! I wish I were a pilgrim there so that my staff and my cloak might be reflected in her beautiful eyes.)

Jaufré wants, he contends, to occupy the very position that Aucassin seeks to shed: living as a prisoner in love's embrace, a captive termed specifically "chaitius" in this song, and located "over there" (*lai*) in the kingdom of Saracens:

> Qe lai el renc del Sarrazis,
> Fos eu per lieis *chaitius* clamatz!
> vv. 13–14 (my emphasis)

(For over there in the kingdom of the Saracens, I wish I were a prisoner for her.)

So too does Bernart de Ventadorn portray the problematic ladylove as a foreign woman, residing in an unattainable place, a woman who realizes, Bernart claims, how much she is worth and therefore holds herself aloof: "Ja.l jorn qu'ela.s mire/ ni pens de sa valor,/ no serai jauzire/ de leis ni de s'amor?" (# 25, vv. 45–48; As soon as she looks at herself and realizes how much she's worth, it won't be me who enjoys her or her love).[57] She will leave him, like the pilgrim in Jaufré's song, with nothing but the longing of a madman: "que can vei la bela/ que.m soli' acolhir,/ ara no m'apela . . . Als non sai que dire/ mas: mout fatz gran folor" (vv. 15–17, 37–38; When I see my beautiful lady who used to receive me, she does not call me now . . . I cannot say anything but this: I am crazy).

In these poems of unrequited desire, the male lover's longing persists unabated because the geographical distance between "lai" where the ladylove resides and "sai" where the lover waits cannot be bridged, as in the following passage from Bernart de Ventadorn:

> Mo cor ai pres d'Amor
> Que l'esperitz lai cor,
> Mas lo cors es sai, alhor,
> Lonh de leis, en Fransa.
> # 44, vv. 33–36

(My heart stays close to Love, my spirit runs to it there, but my body is here, in another place, far from her, in France.)

The metaphor is spun out differently in Chrétien's *Cligès*, where the lovers are said in fact to be together, even when they are apart, as Cligès explains to Fenice:

> Ausi com escorce sanz fust,
> Fu mes cors sanz cuer an Bretainge.
> Puis que je parti d'Alemainge,
> Ne soi que mes cuers se devint,
> Mes que ça aprés vos s'an vint,
> ça fu mes cuers, et la mes cors.
> N'estoie pas de Grece fors,
> Car mes cuers i estoit venuz,
> Por cui je sui ça revenuz.
> vv. 5120–28[58]

(In Britain, my body without its heart was like bark without a tree. After I left Germany, I don't know what became of my heart except that it returned to you. My heart was here and my body there. I was not away from Greece because my heart returned there, which is why I have returned here [to you].)

In this instance, as with the troubadour poets, the familiar conceit "vostre est mes cuers, vostre est mon cors" (*Cligès*, v. 5190; my heart and body are yours) is rendered specifically in geographic terms as the lover's heart and body are temporarily split between two discreet countries.

Poet/lovers like Jaufré and Bernart also sometimes cast physical proximity with the beloved metaphorically in terms of heavenly payment, specifically as manna:

> Car anc genser Crestiana
> No fo, ni Dieus non la vol,
> Juzenza ni Sarrazina;
> Et es ben paisutz de manna,
> Qui ren de s'amor gazaaigna. vv. 17–21[59]

(There never was a gentler woman, Christian, Jew, or Saracen—God does not want it: He is fed on manna who wins a little of her love.)

Nicolette the Merchant

By contrast, Nicolette, the once-distant "foreign" woman now living alongside the lover whom she alone can cure, equates her curative powers not with spiritually based manna but with commercially resonant gold. If she is the *amor de lonh* come home, she is cast less as a lady than a merchant, but the merchant of a commodity not for sale from a woman not for purchase. No payment, heavenly or otherwise, is indicated here. And this female merchant's trade is not in silk or slaves. Rather, Nicolette has redefined herself as a silk-clad woman merchant trading in goods of incomparable value: a female body that cannot be bought literally or metaphorized into a purchasable commodity. Definitely a woman who, in Bernart de Ventadorn's terms, "knows how much she is worth" (#25, vv. 45–48), this heroine, in stark contrast to Blancheflor, is so costly she has no price.

In all of Nicolette's traveling, then, what kind of a map have her movements drawn? In contrast to Dido's displacement westward from Levantine Tyre to North African Carthage, Nicolette travels in circles: from Spain to France to the upside-down world of Torelore, then to Spain again and back to France. It is significant that the second trajectory repeats the first while also rewriting it. First traded and transported as cargo on her initial journey from

Cartage to Biaucaire, Nicolette makes the second voyage between these same sites as an independent and wily quester adept at *engin*. Her successful machinations seem initially to portray her abandoned natal town of Carthage as a Saracen prison to be escaped and the French town of Biaucaire as a Christian site of desirable conversion and resettlement. Indeed, Nicolette returns to France for the second time not only as a baptized, Christianized woman soon to marry a French count's son, but also as a cross-dressed *jongleur* who has skillfully first liberated and then "captured" and cured the tale's long-suffering hero. In the end, she has in fact "taken" him. And yet, if Nicolette's story eschews the westward journey toward incineration that Dido suffered, her circular path between al-Andalus and southern France reveals that Christians as well as Muslims are traders in slaves, captors of women, and thus occupiers of equally problematic venues.

Most important, that seemingly "French" and Christianized courtly lady seated on an elegant "dras de soie" when the lovers meet at tale's end carries the legacy of her earlier *dras de lit*, reminding us of all the ways her hands have worked in the interim: how they have enabled the captive *fille au roi de Cartage*, who was "taken" into slavery, to escape imprisonment and later to transform herself almost magically into a "beast" with priceless golden limbs belonging to no one. A mythical beast? A fairy? A woman from elsewhere, perhaps foreign and imported like the captive silk workers in Chrétien's *Yvain*? Nicolette's metaphorical "beste" has no known religious affiliation or nationality, no specified ethnicity. Its key characteristic is that it cannot be bought. If the captive silk workers in Chrétien's *Yvain* work with their hands to produce one of the most highly valued commodities traded across the medieval Mediterranean—cloth of silk and gold—Nicolette spins a verbal tale of gold itself, and even more specifically a form of gold so valuable that it purports to be beyond commodification: it is literally priceless.[60]

CHAPTER FIVE

Women Mapping a Silk Route from Saint-Denis to Jerusalem and Constantinople (*Le Pèlerinage de Charlemagne*)

THE ANOMALOUS OLD French epic bearing the double title *Le Pèlerinage de Charlemagne à Jerusalem et à Constantinople* is, in a sense, all about travel in the conspicuous absence of women.[1] The mid-twelfth-century narrative charts the displacement of the Frankish monarch from west to east as he undertakes both a pilgrimage to Jerusalem to secure valuable relics and a further voyage to Constantinople to engage his putative rival King Hugh. When Charlemagne and his band of fighting-men-turned-pilgrim-crusaders set off for Jerusalem, they make a point of leaving behind the emperor's wife.[2] Because no women undertake the quasi-crusading journey in this tale, it is easy to forget that the *Pèlerinage* is framed iconographically by two female protagonists. They are not unmarried *puceles*, as in the narratives we have studied previously, but married women: the unnamed wives of two powerful kings who are staged in this narrative as ideological enemies, one representing the Christian west and the other the demonized rival east. Although King Hugh of Constantinople is not overtly called a pagan or Saracen in this epic, the *Pèlerinage* constructs him relentlessly as the feared opponent of the crusading Christian Charlemagne, thus reiterating the commonly held medieval view of the eastern church as disreputable and less than Christian, while viewing Constantinople itself, as did Odo of Deuil, as "arrogant in her wealth, treacherous in her practices, corrupt in her faith."[3] As the plot of the *Pèlerinage* focuses our attention on the political and cultural standoff between the emperor Charlemagne and King Hugh, the female protagonists allied to these rulers appear insignificant.

And yet, as Alexandre Leupin argued a number of years ago, it is the pointed and disruptive speech of Charlemagne's "unruly" wife that actually sets the entire tale in motion, spurring the rivalry between Charlemagne and Hugh that drives the plot.[4] But what of the second woman, King Hugh's wife? And how might our reading of this account of pilgrimage, crusade, and the resultant transfer of relics to the west change if we examined the two un-named wives together? What if we considered the relation between the Frankish queen and the Byzantine empress in terms of silk?[5]

The *Pèlerinage* is often read as a reflection of the disastrous Second Crusade undertaken by Louis VII and Eleanor of Aquitaine, who retraced in large part the itinerary through Byzantine territory en route to Jerusalem that had been followed by their predecessors on the First Crusade.[6] To be sure, the complex layering of Capetian and Carolingian worlds in this highly fanciful text adds a rich texture to all its protagonists, as we will see below. The allu-sion to the Second Crusade explains the oddly dual itinerary that takes Charlemagne to both Constantinople and Jerusalem in this account, although the order of the two stops is reversed in the epic. But there is another expla-nation for including Constantinople in Charlemagne's putative pilgrimage to the Holy Land. The "east" constructed here as Charlemagne's ideological, mil-itary, and quasi-religious rival was also, in both Carolingian and Capetian eras, an economic rival of Franks in the "west." One of the most coveted com-modities involved was silk; not silk seen as the corrupting and extravagant luxury item that many medieval moralists decried, but silk as a vibrant com-mercial commodity and a key diplomatic currency: a mark of both mercan-tile success and political power. As we have seen, Charles's overall journey in the *Pèlerinage* follows one of the major east-west vectors of the Mediterranean silk trade between Constantinople and France established in the Carolingian era and expanded substantially during the crusades to include Latin colonies in the Levant. It is the complex world of silk economics that the barely glimpsed female protagonists in the *Pèlerinage* bring to our attention. Although the women featured in this text do not travel, they are joined, nonetheless, by a textile map that ties east to west through the lavish display, sale, and production of costly silk.

Charlemagne's wife introduces this expansive geography in the initial exchange that sets the parameters for the king's journey. Responding to the emperor's seemingly rhetorical question: "Dame, veïstes unkes hume dedesuz ceil/ Tant ben seïst espee, ne la corune el chef?" (vv. 9–10; Lady, have you ever seen another man who wears the sword and crown as well as I do?), the lady provides a literal answer, telling the emperor that his authority may be less infallible than he imagines: "Emperere, dist ele, trop vus poez priser./ Uncore en sai jo un ki plus se fait leger/ Quant il porte corune entre ses chevalers" (vv. 13–15; "Emperor," she said, "you think too highly of yourself. I know of one man who wears his crown more elegantly when among his knights").[7] Tellingly, Charlemagne replies not by asking "who" this rival king might be, but rather "where" he resides: "E, dame, u est cil reis?" (v. 19; "And, where is this king, my lady?"). The Frankish queen too couches her answer in terms of place: "Del rei Hugun le Fort ai mult oï parole./ Emperere est de Grece e de Costantinoble,/ Et si tent tute Perse tresque en Capadoce" (vv. 46–48; "I have heard much about King Hugh the Strong, Emperor of Greece and Constantinople who holds all of Persia as far as Capadocia"). Even Hugh's prowess is indicated, in this female protagonist's account, in geographic terms: "N'at tant bel chevaler de ci en Antioche" (v. 49; "There is no finer knight from here to Antioch"). Charlemagne and his barons take the queen's words as a mark of insubordination, a kind of unruliness not becoming the emperor's wife. And in the end, part of her purportedly outrageous claim is proven, literally, wrong. When King Hugh and Charlemagne march side by side in Constantinople, the eastern emperor's gold crown is visibly "lower" than Charlemagne's, tangibly marking the eastern king's inferiority: "Karlemaine portat la grant corone a or,/ Li reis Hugue la sue, plus basement un poi:/ Karlemaine fud graindre de plein ped e .iii. pouz" (vv. 809–11; Charlemagne wore the large golden crown and King Hugh wore his, somewhat lower. Charlemagne was taller by a full foot and three fingers).

Looking Eastward

And yet, of all the people assembled at Charlemagne's court at the outset of the *Pèlerinage*, the Frankish queen alone looks beyond the court's perimeter. Her remarks, though characterized by the narrator and Charles's courtiers as "foolish, foolhardy, inaccurate, and silly," are instrumental in directing Charlemagne's attention—and our own—to other places, specifically eastern places.[8] The queen's words open this text to sites beyond western Europe, not only to destinations of pilgrimage and crusade but also to points of international commercial exchange. Even though the queen's initial words seem to pit Charlemagne against Hugh in an oppositional contest of crowns, her remarks imply at the same time that Charlemagne's geographical frame of reference might be too limited to "see" all that lies within what this text calls "foreign lands" (v. 861; estrange regnez).[9]

To be sure, the narrator of the *Pèlerinage* emphasizes the queen's dire fate, detailing the futility of her attempts to repent her outburst, her falling pitiably at Charlemagne's feet to request forgiveness and further offering to fling herself from a high tower to prove her loyalty (vv. 34–38). As the troops depart, the outspoken queen cast aside by her husband appears pathetic: "La reïne remeint, doloruse e plauraunt" (v. 92; The queen stays behind, sad and sobbing). And yet, even though the queen remains absent from the momentous journey and barely visible in the text, her comments suggest a sense of geography beyond Saint-Denis and the French court, a geography stretching from Constantinople and Antioch to Greece, Persia, and Cappadocia, and indeed, as we will see, a terrain mapped ultimately in terms of silk.

The *Pèlerinage* can be seen to chart an even more expansive economic geography when we consider the text's allusion to the historical Charlemagne's forays into Muslim Spain. It is the patriarch in Jerusalem who instructs the fictive emperor later in the epic to pursue Saracens "en Espaigne" after returning home. And yet, both routes outlined for the pilgrim/crusader Charlemagne in this narrative—whether across the Mediterranean or across the Pyrenees— reflect two crucial vectors of the medieval silk trade, as we saw in Chapter 1. It is those routes of commercial contact with lands often considered "pagan" or "Saracen" in the High Middle Ages that the reputedly "foolish, foolhardy, and silly" voice of Charlemagne's disruptive wife brings to our attention in the *Pèlerinage*. Her remarks focus our sights first on Constantinople.

When Charlemagne's wife admonishes him metaphorically to "look eastward" by comparing himself to King Hugh, her words suggest that he take a longer view of medieval kingship and other related cultural formations, thus beginning to consider the west not in isolation but in relation to points east. Her comments also reveal to the Frankish emperor that wealth can be calculated in various ways. In addition to formulating east-west relations in terms of golden crowns displayed on royal male heads, Charlemagne might want to consider other resources as well.

Indeed, when we look eastward in the *Pèlerinage*, we see most emphati-

cally that King Hugh's wealth derives not only from the gold and riches used
to fashion royal crowns, gold that both kings display in abundance throughout in this text, but also from highly prized silk. Different from
Charlemagne, King Hugh of Constantinople, Greece, and Persia is identified
specifically and recognized visually as the man seated under "a silk tent" (v.
281; A cel paile tendut verrez lu rei seant). Although the narrator notes in
passing that Charles's men carry silk tents among numerous other provisions
as they depart, the silk of Hugh's canopy serves a more symbolic function.[10]
The silk suspended above the seated King Hugh's royal head provides a visual flag connoting a particular kind of wealth that is repeated in the silks of
Hugh's throne (v. 294), the silks hanging from his palace walls (v. 332), the
silks adorning his daughter's bedchamber (v. 706),[11] and the silks of knights
and ladies featured in the opening view of the wealthy city of
Constantinople: "Vint mile chevalers i troverent seant,/ E sunt vestut de
pailes e de heremins blans" (vv. 267–68; Twenty thousand knights were
seated there, dressed in silks and white ermine). We even hear of *orfrois*
alongside silk *pailes*: "E treis mile puceles a orfreis relusaant/ Vestues sunt de
pailes, ount les cors avenanz" (vv. 272–73; And three thousand maidens, their
attractive bodies dressed in silks and shimmering gold-embroidered
bands/ribbons). Charlemagne, by contrast, as depicted in this epic, represents the worlds of Jerusalem, Saint-Denis, and Paris, a culture rich in relics,
gold, and silver, but not in silk per se. We as reader/listeners can recognize
this crucial difference even though Charlemagne, who focuses only on the
contest of crowns, does not. The text conveys the message visually in no uncertain terms as we witness King Hugh, the ostentatiously wealthy king of
Constantinople and the noble inhabitants of his realm, all lavishly wrapped
in sumptuous silk.

Joinville's account of the Seventh Crusade sums up the paradigm already
in evidence in the twelfth-century epic, repeating the model that figures
pagan wealth in terms of silk. When Joinville explains how the Count of
Brienne, Lord of Jaffa, appropriated golden and silk fabrics from "Saracen"
caravans, he uses the term less to indicate religious affiliation than ample mercantile wealth: "sarrazins qui menoient grant foison de dras d'or, et de soie"
(Saracens carrying great quantities of cloth of silk and gold).[12] Much earlier
epic descriptions of Saracens in Spain evince a comparable stereotype of hea-
then wealth registered in silk that is often played off against Christian piety.
In the *Prise d'Orange*, for example, the Saracen queen Orable is bedecked with
paile, *soie*, and *samit* from the outset of the narrative:

La sist Orable, la dame d'Aufriquant;
Et ot vestu un paile escarinant,
Estoit lacié par le cors qu'ele ot gent
De riche soie cousue par les pans.[13]
vv. 660–67, 683–84

(Here sits Orable, the lady of Ifriqyia, wearing expensive silk. Her comely body laced up with costly silk sewn along the sides.)

However, when the French hero Guillaume captures the wonderfully rich city of Orange (vv. 416–17, 460–66, 1104, 1319) and marries its newly converted queen, Orable's identity shifts from the elegantly dressed pagan "gentil dame" (v. 692) to the properly Christian "cortoise moillier" (v. 1581). She sheds not only her pagan name but also her clothes:

Orable firent de ses dras desnuër
Il la batisent en l'enor Damedé

A nostre loi la font Guibor nomer.
vv. 1867–69, 72

(They had Orable remove her clothes and baptized her in God's name . . . According to our law they named her Guiborc.)

The newly Christianized city of Orange, a site rivaling Constantinople in its abundant riches, remains decked out in "dras de soie" (v. 1884) on the model of its former Muslim queen.

The *Pseudo-Turpin Chronicle* (1160–75), on which the *Pèlerinage* may be based in part, also casts the ideological battle between Christian and Saracens specifically in terms of differential dress, but from the Saracen perspective. When the Saracen commander Agoulant, "roi d'Aufrique," who had twice conquered Spain according to this account, cedes to the victorious Charlemagne, he refuses baptism because Charlemagne's men are so "poorly dressed" (*povrement vestu*), a state inappropriate, he contends, for messengers of God.[14] The figure of Charlemagne himself articulates the opposing view in an anecdote recounted in Notker's highly legendary biography of the Frankish emperor, where Charles reprimands his retainers for wearing anything but wool or linen. Those who dared to dress in silk, gold, or silver would only contribute, Charles asserts, to pagan idolatry: "Why are you dolled up in gold, silver, and scarlet?" they are asked. "Why hand over your worldly goods to an enemy who will use them to adorn idols?"[15] Yet another passage from Notker's text recounts Charlemagne's denunciation of the eastern finery imported by Venetians from "lands beyond the sea" as he ridicules ostentatious pheasant skins and peacock feathers sewn on silk along with ribbons dyed in Tyrian purple and lemon-colored hues. Belittling such ornate attire as costly, useless, and impractical, Charles, cast here as the "most devout Christian emperor," calls those who wear such extravagant clothing "fools."[16] The model for the simplicity of Christian dress is of course Christ himself, as the Old French *Couronnement de Louis* makes clear. That "Christ forsook riches" was most evident in his humble attire: "Christ wore a wretched mantle" (vv. 745, 763). In this view, it is Saracens and those who deign to wear their lavish exports who indulge in the sartorial excess of silk.

I have argued elsewhere that the ideological divide between a Saracen east and Christian west, posited in so many Old French epic, chronicle, and clerical accounts, is actually systematically undermined by the figure of the courtly lady herself, dressed as she is by definition in "Saracen" silks and gemstones that in many instances make her a map for points of convergence between western Europe and the eastern Mediterranean.[17] In directing our gaze toward Constantinople and its overly abundant silks, the female protagonist whose frank words launch the *Pèlerinage de Charlemagne* further unsettles the pat dichotomy between Christianity and Islam that the epic narrator of this text and others try insistently to convey. Sarah Kay has shown how epics of the later period in the Old French corpus tend to undermine the schematized polarization of Saracen against Christian that typically dominates the earlier *chansons de geste*.[18] But the *Pèlerinage* curiously resists this literary paradigm by being an early epic that also critiques strict confessional dichotomies. It does so specifically through subtle references to international trading practices, at the heart of which lies the commerce in silk.

Indeed, the Frankish queen's insistence on looking toward the silk-laden Constantinople in the *Pèlerinage* spurs us to consider specifically the extent to which this text's purported opposition between east and west might shift if the full implications of silk are considered. We have noted previously that the commercial movement of silk along medieval trade routes throughout the Middle East and across the Mediterranean ties east and west together in defiance of ideological or confessional divides. To see how the *Pèlerinage* stages this crucial movement, we will need to consider not only the text's portrayal of Constantinople but also its depiction of Jerusalem.

Relics

Charlemagne's initial boast in the *Pèlerinage* and his calculus for victory situate King Hugh's rival domain in Constantinople against three Christian sites claimed by the western emperor: Paris and Saint-Denis, official loci of royal power for Capetian kings of the twelfth century, and of equal importance, Jerusalem. Since positioning Jerusalem on the "western" side of this ideological divide makes little sense geographically, the *Pèlerinage* tries insistently to locate the holy city at a clear visual remove from the luxuriously silk-clad Constantinople. The Jerusalem depicted here is marked visually not by silk but by Christian gold. Charles has come to Jerusalem, a "citez antive" (v. 108) of "grant bealté" (v. 123), as he explains to the patriarch, as a humble pilgrim seeking relics to take back to France:

> Vinc en Jerusalem, pur l'amistet de Deu:
> La croiz e le sepulcre sui venuz aürer
>
> De voz saintes reliques, si vus plaist, me donez,
> Que porterai en France qu'en voil enluminer!
> vv. 154–55, 160–61
>
> (I have come to Jerusalem, for the love of God, to venerate the cross and the holy sepulchre. . . . If you please, give me some of your holy relics to take back to France. I want to make it sparkle with them.)

In addition to St. Simeon's arm, St. Lazare's head, and St. Stephen's blood, the patriarch offers even more valued relics: Jesus' *sudarium*, one of the nails from the cross, the crown worn by the crucified Christ, the chalice and silver paten that he blessed, the knife Jesus used at meals, and St. Peter's beard and some of his hair (vv. 163–81). This wealth of religious "treasures," as the patriarch calls them, is further enhanced by still other relics of "grant vertuz": Mary's milk, and her "sainte chemise" (vv. 186, 187, 189),[19] all eventually encased in gold.

The extreme symbolic value of these relics, composed of body parts formerly belonging to Christ, the saints, or the Virgin, or of items like nails of the cross or the Virgin's *chemise*, which had direct contact with venerated bodies, is recognized by housing them inside casings of gold. Immediately upon receiving the relics in Jerusalem, Charlemagne had them enclosed in a spectacular "fertre" fashioned from pure Arabian gold: "Li reis fait faire un fertre—unkes meldre ne fud—/ Del plus fin or d'Arabe i out mil mars fundud" (vv. 198–99; The king had a reliquary made—the best ever—by melting a thousand marks of the finest Arabian gold).

These are the relics that enable Charles's men to triumph in unarmed combat against the reputedly incomparable Hugh of Constantinople at tale's end, thus seeming, from the eastern king's perspective, to avoid "magically" (vv. 756) the decapitation he repeatedly threatens (vv. 633, 647, 698, 742). An extended series of comically exaggerated boasts fills about one quarter of this epic (pp. 59–69), inducing Charlemagne to put the patriarch's highly prized relics to fanciful use: "Et ad fait les reliques aporter devant lüi:/ A ureisuns se getent, unt lur culpes batud,/ E prient Deu del cel e la sue vertud,/ Del rei Hugun le fort que les garisset üi,/ Que encuntre lur est si forment irascud" (vv. 667–71; He had the relics brought before him. They began praying, confessed their sins, and prayed God in Heaven and his power to protect them that day against King Hugh the Strong, who had been greatly angered by them). In response, an angel of God appears, scolding Charlemagne for his men's foolhardy "gabs" (v. 676) but promising, nonetheless, to protect them from the eastern king (v. 677). Indeed, as Charles's men successively make good on each of their ridiculous claims,[20] it is "not by force, but by God's grace" (v. 751) working through the powerful relics in Charles's possession that the Franks triumph (v. 774).[21]

Hugh, as we know, has put his gold to very different use, in keeping with his extravagant display of silk, the most ostentatious example being the golden plow on which he sits (beneath the silken tent) when Charlemagne first meets him:

> Chevalchet li emperere, ne se vait atargeant:
> Truvat lu rei Hugun a sa carue arant.
> Les conjugles en sunt a or fin relusant
> Les essués e les röes e li cultres arant.
> vv. 282–85

(Without delay, the emperor rode off and found King Hugh plowing with his plow. The yoke was made of fine shimmering gold along with the axles, the wheels, and the cutting blade.)

As if in direct defiance of Tertullian's admonition to avoid the elaborate excess of making practical utensils of gold and silver, Hugh sits on a plow containing an unfathomable amount of gold: "Tant i at de fin or que jo n'en sai mesure" (v. 321; There is so much gold in it that I could never determine the amount). In his treatise "On the Apparel of Women," designed specifically to discourage women from wearing overly attractive, ostentatious garb and immodest adornments, Tertullian prohibits the use of gold for plowing in particular: "Certainly you will never plow a field with a golden plow nor will any ship be held together by silver bolts."[22] Thus does silk figure in Tertullian's view, alongside gold and silver as one of "the principal materials" of worldly excess.[23] In this context, the *Pèlerinage*'s portrait of King Hugh sitting beneath a silk canopy astride a golden plow connotes morally corrupt "worldliness" par excellence.

The Christian economy depicted in this text operates on different terms. Although the patriarch in Jerusalem soundly rejects Charles's offer of payment for the invaluable relics (vv. 220–21),[24] he does request compensation of a different sort, rendered not in gold but in the death of Saracens who threaten to destroy Christianity: "E dist li pastriarches: "Savez dunt jo vus priz?/ De Sarazins destrure, ki nus ount en despit! (vv. 226–27; And the patriarch asked, "Do you know what I ask of you? To destroy the Saracens who hold us in contempt").[25] The exchange is clear: the patriarch offers his considerable treasures (v. 222; "Tuz li mens granz tresors vus seit abandunez") to Charles, now a passive and unarmed pilgrim in the Holy Land, who promises upon his return to France to take as many fighting men as he can muster and destroy the advancing Saracens in Spain: "Jo manderrai mes humes, quant qu'en purrai aver,/ E irrai en Espaine: ne purat remaner!" (vv. 229–30; I will summon my men, as many as I can gather, and go to Spain without delay).[26] The *Pèlerinage* thus superimposes holy wars on two continents, reflecting the position that had been articulated by Pope Urban II in preaching the First Crusade and throughout his pontificate, a stance that equated "the war in the east with the reconquest of Spain," as Jonathan Riley-Smith explains.[27]

Even more specifically, the remarks of the two Christian leaders in the *Pèlerinage*, an emperor and a patriarch, outline an economy of holy relics exchanged for military victory and religious triumph that spans the Mediterranean. The patriarch's ideologically polarized vision of Christians against Muslims in al-Andalus subtly replays the initial clash of golden crowns that pitted Charlemagne's Christian west against Hugh's demonized east in the opening lines of the *Pèlerinage*. Casting Charlemagne as the savior of

Christendom in both venues, the *Pèlerinage* represents the Frankish monarch in a circuit in which wealth and military might are traded for protective and potent golden relics. In this economy of Christian conquest, silk plays no role.

Trading Silk in Jerusalem

And yet, another economy is in evidence during Charles's prolonged stay in Jerusalem, an economy that also benefits from the Christian emperor's enormous wealth and commitment as a religious leader, while intersecting tellingly at the same time with the international commerce in silk. During his four-month stay in Jerusalem, we are told, the "rich" emperor (v. 206) Charlemagne founds a church dedicated to the Virgin, a holy site characterized specifically by the trade in silks and spices that takes place there:

> Comencent un muster k'est de sainte Marie:
> Li hume de la terre le claimant la Latinie,
> Car li language i venent de trestute la vile,
> Il I vendent lur pailes, lur teiles, lur siries,
> Coste, canele e peivre, altres bones espices.
> vv. 207–11

> ([The emperor and the twelve peers] begin building a church dedicated to Mary. Local inhabitants call it the Latin church because people of different cultures come there from all over the city to sell their silks, linens, and Syrian silks, alecost (ginger), cinnamon, pepper, and other fine spices.)[28]

Merchants come from the varied sectors of this international city apparently to buy and sell, in addition to costly imported spices and prized linens, the very *pailes* used to characterize, in later scenes of the *Pèlerinage*, King Hugh's eastern opulence: that is, the *pailes* that lavishly clothe twenty thousand knights and three thousand *puceles* in King Hugh's palace, the luxurious *pailes* used to adorn his castle walls, and the *paile* that forms a distinctive silk tent, emblematic of the imposing eastern emperor who sits beneath it (vv. 267–68, 272–73, 301, 332). We hear nothing about the Church of the Latanie that Charlemagne has established in Jerusalem except its spectacular role as a mercantile center for the international Mediterranean cloth trade.

Historian Jean Richard reads the brief market scene in the *Pèlerinage* as a remarkably accurate reflection of the Latin city of Jerusalem as it would have been seen by pilgrims in the second quarter of the twelfth century: a city divided physically between Latin and Syrian shopkeepers, with the Syrian cloth merchants having recently relocated to a site adjacent to the Latin church the *Pèlerinage* describes.[29] The inclusion of "siries" in the brief list of fabrics sold at this Jerusalem market in the *Pèlerinage* further suggests commerce with silk-producing sites along the Levantine coast and with Syria more specifically. Whereas the Old French "siries" could be a form of *series*, or *seres* both from Latin *sericum* simply meaning "silk," as Glynn Burgess and others suggest, Tobler-Lommatsch also gives at least one example in which "drap de syre" might in fact indicate the silk's provenance as Syre or Syria.[30]

Medieval Syria is known to have produced both Byzantine- and Persian-style silks, destined largely for Christian pilgrims to transport home to western Europe. During the twelfth and thirteenth centuries, the French colonies in Syria exported large quantities of heavy silks and golden brocades to western Europe.[31] Trade fostered by Italian merchants from the 1180s onward favored the Syro-Palestinian coast, leading to a golden age of commerce with the Frankish states of Acre, Tyre, and Tripoli in the first half of the thirteenth century.[32] Purchases made by Christian pilgrims in Syria included *siglatons* and *baudequins* imported from Baghdad, and brocades from Mossoul.[33] *Samite* was made at Acre and Beirut, while Tyre was famous for *cendal*.[34] Exports from Syria also included products brought from Alexandria and oriental "spices" such as perfume and dyes that traveled with the high-volume, famed silks.[35]

As we chart the westward movement of these Islamicate textiles, some of which are later used as Christian altar pieces or made into elegant and delicate carrying cases for Christian relics, the oppositional weight of the terms east and west begins to lessen.[36] And the attempt in the *Pèlerinage* to pit an eastern realm of extravagant silk against a western empire committed to transforming gold into relics falters. What this text charts instead, at least in part, is a pattern of silk trading and transfer that tends to bridge the opposing cultural identities represented in this epic by Constantinople on the one hand and Jerusalem and Saint-Denis on the other. The rival rulers Charles and Hugh come together iconically in this tale through depictions of silk: the *pailes* festooning the Byzantine emperor's palace and the silks sold in Charles's Latin church in Jerusalem. Silk economics here trumps political and cultural rivalries through trade across the Mediterranean.[37]

A number of years ago, Joseph Bédier characterized the *Pèlerinage* as a comic rendition of a serious story: an ideologically potent tale of the translation of Christian relics from east to west recast in a form designed to amuse pilgrims, merchants, and others gathered at market fairs such as the *foire du Lendit*.[38] As part of his larger thesis that the Old French *chansons de geste*, born in the eleventh century from the everyday business of local churches, recorded crusading forays into Spain and the Holy Land, Bédier read the *Pèlerinage* in tandem with the *Descriptio*, the *Pseudo-Turpin Chronicle*, and other versions of the legend as a product of local ecclesiastical efforts to promote pilgrimage.[39] Bédier's analysis of Old French epic revealed the extent to which pious observance could intersect productively with mercantile concerns along medieval French pilgrimage routes.[40] Indeed, the thirteenth-century *Dit du Lendit rimé*, which he cites, shows a bustling market economy at Saint-Denis and a number of other Northern French market towns, including three key locations of the Champagne fairs: Troyes, Provins, and Lagny.[41] The celebrated Champagne fairs are also known to have participated in a vast network of international trade, featuring a mix of local goods and those imported, largely by Italian merchants, from sites across the Mediterranean. Most prominent among the imported products was fabric, in particular highly prized silk.[42]

King Hugh's Unnamed Wife

And what of the other wife in this tale, the seemingly compliant and utterly silent queen who appears only briefly beside King Hugh of Constantinople at the close of the *Pèlerinage*? She appears as the nearly invisible wife and mother, a consort mentioned only as holding her daughter's hand:

> La femme al rei Hugun, ke sa corune enporte,
> Par la main tent sa fille, que ad la crigne bloie.
> vv. 822–23

(King Hugh's wife, wearing her crown, leads her fair-haired daughter by the hand.)

To be sure, King Hugh's unnamed wife could provide a vague allusion to Michael Comnenus's German first wife, Berthe-Eirene, as Eugene Vance has shown.[43] Historian Michael Angold reports that this foreign bride's "stolid, pious, and obstinate" nature seemed to jar with the lavish and lively opulence of the Byzantine court, where in fact it was a matter of jest that she "had no time for rouge, eye-liner, and other cosmetics."[44]

But the *Pèlerinage*'s heavy-handed insistence on the abundance of silk festooning King Hugh and his court in Constantinople also directs us elsewhere, to Constantinople in an earlier era, in fact, as early as the time of Charlemagne. Angold asserts that by the mid-twelfth century Constantinople had almost certainly been outstripped by Thebes as the main producer of silks in the Byzantine empire.[45] Indeed, according to the chronicler Nicetas Choniates, as we saw in Chapter 2, it is because the women of Thebes were so renowned for "their weaving" that they were driven into exile in Sicily by the invading Normans in 1146–47.[46] By the time of Manuel Comnenus, Byzantine silk production was no longer centered in the capital.[47]

And yet, if we look toward Byzantium at the time Charlemagne is emperor (800–14) rather than during Louis VII's reign, we find something quite different from the submissive Byzantine queen figured at the end of the *Pèlerinage*, and nothing equivalent to King Hugh. In fact, we see no king or emperor at all, but a headstrong and politically astute woman who has taken for herself the title of *basileus*: the Empress Irene. Not a wifely queen, but a commanding empress and the first woman to preside over the Byzantine Empire in her own right, Irene reigned from 797 to 802. She was known in particular, along with Theodora, for her role in restoring the cult of Christian icons that lasted through the final six hundred years of the Byzantine empire.[48] But this formidable eastern ruler also attempted to engineer one of the most ambitious foreign marriages: to join the Frankish and Byzantine Empires by arranging in 781 to marry her son, Constantine VI to one of Charlemagne's daughters, Rotrud. When negotiations faltered, Irene herself proposed to marry the widower Charlemagne.[49] Most important for our purposes, however, the empress Irene played a key role in promoting and expanding the very source of Byzantine splendor that was later both coveted and condemned in medieval France: the silk industry.[50]

Byzantine Silk Workers?

Known as a lavish builder and a pious ruler dedicated to good works, Irene the Athenian restored a number of churches and secured the return of a significant collection of relics to Constantinople.[51] But key among her building projects was a new palace called the Eleutherios located in the center of the city near the commercial port, part of a large complex that included workshops and bakeries and, after the fire of 792, silk-weaving shops. Judith Herrin speculates that the building of new workshops attached to the Eleutherios might in fact indicate an attempt on Irene's part to keep control of the place where highly valued and closely monitored imperial silks were produced.[52] Large numbers of valuable purple silks decorated with secular images were woven in Constantinople in the eighth and ninth centuries, some sent as diplomatic gifts to the Franks, including the famous charioteer silk used for Charlemagne's own burial shroud.[53] Many other Byzantine silks exported to France were used for secular and ecclesiastical garments, to cover liturgical vessels and icons, and to wrap relics. Irene appears to have continued the custom well-established during Constantine V's long reign of sending silks west as diplomatic gifts.[54] The Byzantine embassy to Frankia in 824 presented ten different types of silks as gifts to Charlemagne's son and heir, Louis the Pious.[55]

Irene had come to Constantinople as a foreign woman decorated in silken clothes, an Athenian brought from Hellas as a wife for Constantine V's son, Leo IV.[56] It appears that she soon quarreled with the hard-line iconoclast Leo, who accused her of venerating icons secretly and denounced her in public, contributing to her reputation as a headstrong and wily wife,[57] When Leo IV died, Irene ruled as regent for her son until he tried to rule without her and she had him blinded. From 797 to 802 Irene not only ruled alone, minting new gold *solidi* that represented her as empress, but also adopting for the first time the male title of "basileus" on legal documents, citing her authority as "the great emperor, faithful in Christ."[58] Even more interesting in terms of the *Pèlerinage*'s emphasis on royal crowns, this female emperor acceded to the throne literally because of Leo's odd habit of wearing a specific crown. Leo IV died suddenly and unexpectedly at age thirty from uncertain causes, although he was known to have had an excessive fascination with jewels and a particular attachment to a jeweled crown belonging to Hagia Sophia. His constant wearing of that crown was thought to have induced the growth of carbuncles on his head, which led in turn to a fatal fever. Irene became emperor, then, because of the way her husband obsessively wore his crown.[59] If Charlemagne emerges victorious in the *Pèlerinage* from an obsessive rivalry of crowns with a fictive Byzantine emperor named Hugh, legendary accounts of Charlemagne's contemporary

Leo portray the eastern ruler as having literally lost his empire and his life to an upstart woman because of an equally inexplicable obsession with royal headgear.

Historical Fictionalizing

As a twelfth-century narrative featuring Charlemagne, the *Pèlerinage de Charlemagne* moves deftly, if unpredictably, between Carolingian and Capetian worlds, often producing a story layered with different chronological strata that combine and clash in evocative, if illogical, configurations. The historical Charlemagne, for example, although he carries the reputation in twelfth-century France as a model crusader, never traveled to the Holy Land or to Constantinople, making his only pilgrimage to Rome.[60] By contrast, Louis VII did voyage to Jerusalem, Constantinople, and other Levantine cities during the second crusade in the company of Eleanor of Aquitaine.[61] Indeed, the portrait of the disputatious royal couple figured in the opening lines of the *Pèlerinage* carries a number of overtones resonant of Louis VII and his strong-willed and independent wife.[62] Theodor Heinermann argued long ago that the *Pèlerinage* offers a compensatory narrative of the Second Crusade, staging Charlemagne as a successful version of the failed Louis VII in his standoff against the Byzantine emperor Manuel Comnenus.[63]

However, Eleanor might figure in the background of the *Pèlerinage* in yet another way: in terms of her extravagant taste for the carnal and sartorial pleasures and excesses that western clerical writers often attributed to Constantinople.

Eleanor as a "Foreign" Queen?

Eleanor, known in medieval legend and chronicle as a bawdy and impenitent queen with extravagant tastes who was unhappily married to the demure and devout Louis, represents in many ways the scandal of an uncontrollable foreign woman. Imported as she was to Paris from the lively court culture of southern France, Eleanor spoke Occitan, a language foreign to the French king and courtiers but shared by Eleanor's close childhood friend and young uncle then living "outremer": Raymond, King of Antioch.[64] Occitan was also, of course, the language of the men and women troubadour poets, not the least of whom was Guillaume IX of Poitiers, Eleanor's infamous grandfather who had himself traveled to the Holy Land on the First Crusade.

In a number of popular legends and chronicles, especially among English chroniclers from the late twelfth and early thirteenth centuries, Eleanor figures as a wildly adulterous queen whose contagious sexual promiscuity was responsible for the failure of the Second Crusade.[65] John of Salisbury gives prominence to a narrative of Eleanor's supposed adulterous incest with Raymond of Antioch. Walter Map and Gerald of Wales also speak of her supposed adultery with Henry II's father, Count Geoffrey of Anjou.[66] To be sure, Eleanor's cultural affiliation with Raymond of Antioch raised questions about her political sympathies, since Raymond had long-standing ties with the Greeks and the Byzantine emperors, an alliance that might even have influenced the young queen to argue that the crusading party follow the land route to Constantinople rather than travel eastward by sea.[67] In any event, once having arrived in Antioch, Eleanor is said to have reveled in the excessive splendor and court festivities of eastern life.[68] Allegations of her reputed love affair with eastern extravagance persist long past the composition of the *Pèlerinage* and are rendered perhaps most graphically in the mid-thirteenth-century *Ménestrel de Reims*. That account claims that Eleanor, seduced by Saladin's remarkable courtliness, declared her love for him, promising to convert to Islam and elope.[69] From this perspective the historico-legendary Eleanor emerges as a difficult and unruly wife of the French monarch, a woman with known ties to lands lying "outremer," and a particular eye for eastern splendor. Within this extended narrative of Eleanor as a problematic woman, the queen's sartorial excess played a significant role. One twelfth-century Greek chronicler reports that Eleanor dressed as extravagantly as Penthisilea, the women in her retinue playing the part of Amazons.[70] The chronicler Odo of Deuil details the excessive accoutrements accompanying Queen Eleanor on her crusading voyage, and those required by other women on the journey. Whereas Louis departed for the crusade somberly clad in penitent's garb, Eleanor required the equivalent of Saracen opulence: "too many locked chests containing cloaks, gowns, women's veils, ointments, basins, table ware and large quantities of linens and beautifying accessories: wash basins, soaps, mirrors, combs, brushes, containers of powder and creams, jewels, bracelets, necklaces, brooches, tiaras . . ."[71] Although silk is not specified here, the extravagance of self-display is. From the French perspective, Eleanor's political sympathies with the Byzantines were doubled by her interest in lavish dress, her unruliness as an untamed wife indexed by her choosing to dress in the opulent style that had been deemed the province of a corrupt eastern enemy.

I do not mean to suggest that the *Pèlerinage* contains purposefully coded references to specific historical figures, whether in the ninth century or the twelfth. It should be clear from the text's presentation of Charlemagne that historical accuracy is not the goal of this highly imaginative and often comic narrative.[72] And yet, once we begin to read "for silk" in this epic and other Old French tales that might appear on the surface to bear little connection to the medieval traffic in cloth across the Mediterranean, resonances of cultural and historical figures can be seen to move in and out of the narrative, not as keys to decoding an accurate story of past events, but as pieces of a narrative layered richly and often quirkily with bits of history rewritten as fiction. In the anomalous mix, Queen Eleanor of France and the Byzantine Empress Irene face off across the Mediterranean and across the three hundred years that separate them historically in an unexpected narrative couplet: two women joined metaphorically by the opulence of luxury goods considered to be the cultural hallmark of the seductive and dangerous Constantinople as opposed to the more austerely devout Saint-Denis.

The *Pèlerinage* closes with Charlemagne's triumphant return to France, having traveled across "estrange regnez" (v. 861) to Paris, the fair city, and into the church at Saint-Denis:

> Mult fu lied e joius Carlemaine li ber,
> Ki tel rei ad cunquis sanz bataille campel.
> Que vus en ai jo mès lunc plait a acunter?
> Il passent les païs, les estrange regnez,
> Venuz sunt a Paris, a la bone citet
> E vunt a Saint Denis, al muster sunt entrez.
> vv. 858–63

(The noble Charlemagne was overjoyed because he had vanquished such a king without physical battle. Should I tell you my long story? They traveled through various countries, through foreign realms; they came to Paris, the fair city, and then went to Saint-Denis and entered the church.)

Charlemagne kneels in prayer and then stands to offer his prized relics on the altar: Christ's crown and a nail from the cross, along with others (vv.

864–67).[73] But this extended tale of the transfer of Christian relics from east
to west does not end there. The narrative closes, as it began, with the Frankish
queen, now silenced as she falls once again at the emperor's feet, her earlier
verbal transgression pardoned by a forgiving Christian emperor:

> Iloec fud la reïne, al pied li est caiet:
> Sun mautalent li ad li reis tut perdunet,
> Pur l'amur del sepulcre que il ad aüret.
> vv. 868–70

(The queen was there; she fell to his feet. The king pardoned her
completely for her misdeed, out of love of the sepulcher he had
venerated.)

The sin of a woman's speech with which this narrative began is thus pardoned, but thereby also effectively erased. Gone too are all traces of the eastern lands that Charlemagne's wife earlier signaled as a way to understanding
the Frankish realm within a larger, international scope. The lavish silks that
characterized King Hugh's realm are nowhere to be seen. Despite the eastern
king's generous offer to give the departing Charlemagne "trestuz mes granz
tresor" (v. 839), the Christian emperor in this epic categorically refuses to
allow his men to bring any eastern wealth westward. As Charles explains to
the King of Constantinople, "Ja n'en prendrunt del vostre un dener muneëd"
(v. 842; They will never take a single coin from you). Apparently no silk was
to be exchanged either. Thus is the expanded textile geography, heretofore in-
termittently woven into the fabric of this epic text, effectively occluded at
tale's end by the transfer of relics rather than silk to Saint-Denis. And yet the
textile map evoked from the outset by the Frankish queen's unladylike and
unwifely language has not been entirely unraveled. We have traveled across
that textile map and understood from its articulation over the course of the
narrative that the *Pèlerinage* is as much about the use and sale of silk as the
transfer of relics. We have seen too that the seemingly absent female protagonists in this epic, however stationary, play an important role in focusing our
attention on the ability of medieval silk to challenge and restructure the falsely
polarizing cultural divisions that the contest of crowns underwrites.

CHAPTER SIX

Silk Between Virgins

Following a Relic from Constantinople to Chartres

THE FEMALE FIGURES who frame this chapter are not drawn exclusively from literary texts. Appearing in Old French Marian legends and miracle stories, the medieval Virgin of Chartres and the Virgin of Constantinople come together around a material object reputed to be made of costly silk: the intriguing western relic of the Virgin's *chemise*. Rather than a case of crusader-pilgrims traveling to distant sites across the Mediterranean, like those represented by Charlemagne's band of warrior followers in the *Pèlerinage de Charlemagne à Jérusalem et à Constantinople* discussed in Chapter 5, in this instance we have a record of local pilgrimage: travelers visiting Chartres cathedral to venerate the Virgin whose image was widely distributed on pilgrim badges they wore and carried. The extant badges, taken together with images of the Virgin sculpted on the cathedral's exterior, tell a story that links pilgrimage to the international commerce in textiles yet again, but with a very different emphasis. In this instance, iconic female figures lie at the center, not the periphery, of the process. And if at first it seems that textiles are used in these literary and material representations of the Virgin to distinguish Chartres as a western site known for its production of simple linen cloth from a distant Constantinople famed for its lavish and costly eastern silk, analysis of the complex relic of the Virgin's *chemise* reveals this geographic and confessional divide to be, in fact, insubstantial. The story of the Virgin's *chemise* at Chartres cathedral is, in the end, a story both local and international. Indeed, the practice of venerating the Chartrain relic in medieval France sends us across the metaphorical sea of silk to confront a Virgin in Constantinople who wears silk with golden decoration ("pourpre a or batue") not unlike the "porpre vermeille d'or bendee" (dark red silk with gold banding) that the Tyrian Dido wears in the *Roman d'Enéas* discussed in Chapter 4. In the case of the Virgin of Constantinople, however, the opulent silk is not feared as a mark of corrupting secular extravagance to be expunged. Lavish silk is here transformed into an icon of western piety and veneration as it becomes the relic of the Virgin's *chemise*.

Chartrain Pilgrimage

Pilgrims who visited Chartres cathedral in the Middle Ages were most often drawn to the site by a single, famed article of clothing they would never see. Miracle stories that narrate the legendary feats of the cathedral's principal relic describe the item of dress in question as an undergarment belonging to the Virgin: a *sainte chemise*. Jean Le Marchant's thirteenth-century account, *Les Miracles de Notre Dame de Chartres*, characterizes the relic in this way, translating the "sancta camisia" of an anonymous Latin source. Although Jean also alludes in passing to a second textile banner called the Virgin's veil,[1] it was the holy *chemise* that became the most highly prized of all the relics attributed to the Virgin in medieval France. The garment was especially worthy of veneration, we are told, because the Virgin was reputed to have worn it at the conception and birth of Christ, key moments when the *chemise* had lain "against her naked skin."[2] This characterization of the Chartrain relic sparked an understanding in the popular imagination of the Virgin's *chemise* as a sanctified version of the common undergarment typically worn "next to the skin" of men and women in medieval France: a long, loose-fitting shift usually made of linen.[3] A historical example of the medieval linen undergarment is provided by the thirteenth-century *chemise* attributed to Saint Louis, now held in the treasury of Notre-Dame Cathedral in Paris.[4] No comparable material artifact, however, survives for the Virgin's *chemise* at Chartres. Some time after the relic was donated to the cathedral, reputedly by Charles the Bald in 876, the holy garment was enclosed in a reliquary that concealed it from view.[5]

Nonetheless, visual representations of the *sainte chemise* proliferated in the high Middle Ages. They appeared on small lead pilgrim badges worn on the hats of visitors who departed from the shrine.[6] Six extant badges dating from the thirteenth through the fifteenth centuries picture the *sainte chemise* from

Chartres with sleeves extended, as if it were suspended or on display, often accompanied by a smaller image of the reliquary itself. Local artisans responsible for portraying the relic on these badges fashioned, in the main, a *chemise* resembling garments that appeared on cathedral façades as clothing for lay people and clerics, garments that also figured in manuscript illuminations and vernacular literature as unassuming everyday items of dress (Figures 8–10).[7]

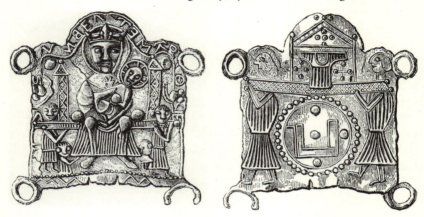

Figure 8. Reproduced from Arthur Forgeais, *Collection de plombs historiés trouvés dans la Seine* (Paris: Chez Aubry, 1863), 2:28–29.

Figure 9. Reproduced from Arthur Forgeais, *Collection de plombs historiés trouvés dans la Seine* (Paris: Chez Aubry, 1865), 4:115–18.

Figure 10. Brian Spencer, *Pilgrim Souvenies and Secular Badges: Medieval Finds from Excavations in London*: 7. (London: Stationery Office, 1998), 224. © Museum of London; reproduced with permission.

Most important, images of the famed *chemise* figured on lead pilgrim badges along with replicas of the garment fashioned in cloth eventually functioned as surrogate versions of the relic itself. Serving originally as purely testimonial objects, the metal *chemisettes*, as they were called later, eventually became endowed with protective and curative properties of their own, as did actual garments designed as replicas of the *sainte chemise*.[8] The *Vieille chronique* of 1389 describes kings, princes, and soldiers flocking to Chartres where they had made for themselves *chemises* that they then touched to the "sainte châsse" and wore under their cuirasses for protection in combat.[9] We know that the Count of Poitiers, dubbed in 1241, paid for "XII ulnis telae ad faciendas camisias de Carnoto,"[10] and an inventory of Charles V in 1380 mentions an actual "chemise de Chartres."[11] The duchess of Orléans was said to possess four "chemises de Chartres" in 1409, and the Duke de Berry was ascribed two in 1416.[12] Beginning in 1531, French queens are reputed to have received an image or likeness of the Virgin's *chemise*, often in white silk with gold embroidery, to honor and facilitate pregnancy and childbirth.[13] Whether lead badge or cloth copy, used to guarantee military protection or promote fertility, images of the holy *chemise* dressed the bodies of French believers from the twelfth through the sixteenth century and beyond.[14]

And yet, when the reliquary at Chartres was opened in 1712, no *chemise* was found. Although the ornately decorated *châsse*, encased in gold and covered with precious gems, was itself studded with small metal tokens in the shape of a medieval *chemise*, suggesting what the contents of the coffer were presumed to be, no *chemise* and in fact no sizable article of clothing lay within it.[15] What emerged instead, as the secreted and legendary referent for miraculous descriptions of the Virgin's humble *chemise*, were two bands of luxury cloth: the first, measuring about five meters and appearing to be of silk, was wrapped in another cloth of silk and linen, decorated with embroidery; the second was said to be a banded fabric in gold and colors patterned with birds, quadripeds, vegetal and geometric motifs.[16] Oddly, it is these two lengths of luxury cloth that the *procès verbal* of 1712 refers to as a "Sacra Camisia."[17] But why? The language derives most probably from medieval Latin accounts of the relic's miraculous performances provided by authors from William of Malmesbury to John of Garland, including Jean Le Marchant's anonymous source, which described the relic as a "sancta camisia."

In line with the *procès verbal* of 1712, a spate of eighteenth- and nineteenth-century attestations consistently attribute the Chartrain relic's provenance to eastern lands and foreign silk. An evaluation sometime after 1793, when the reliquary was opened again and its precious metals melted down, describes the cloth inside as a thousand-year-old silk fabric resembling women's veils "in the Orient."[18] By 1820, the highly venerated undergarment had become known as the Virgin's "veil," detailed in the *procès verbal* of that year as two lengths of silk fabric, now severely reduced in size to "two veils."[19] In 1849, the contents of the reliquary are recorded as "la tunique" (although still composed of two pieces of white silk) and the "voile oriental" wrapped around it.[20] The latter, made of a lighter-weight fabric with Byzantine ornamentation, was attributed at this juncture to the Empress Irene.[21] In 1886 Fernand de Mély published an undated engraving of what he termed the "voile de la vierge (d'après Villemain)": a banded cloth or, in his terms, an Egyptian-like "droguet rayé" ("striped cloth," Figure 11).[22] According to an analysis in 1927, the embroidered cloth is Syrian work from the eighth or ninth century.[23] Most recently, Annemarie Weyl Carr has identified the *tiraz*-like fabric now called the Virgin's veil as Byzantine, dating it to the tenth or eleventh century.[24]

These depictions of the relic at Chartres in terms of foreign silks, oriental embroideries, and Egyptian-like fabric are not merely a product of post-medieval exoticism. They reflect an important detail of the medieval legendary accounts themselves in which, in many instances, the holy *chemise*, so often portrayed in keeping with its Latin name as a simple, western, linen garment, is said in fact to have been imported from the east. Specifically, Charles the Bald is credited with transporting the Virgin's *chemise* to Chartres from Constantinople, a place known widely in the Middle Ages for its wealth, its relics, and its production of lavish and costly silk fabrics.[25] In addition, a thirteenth-century fresco, now destroyed, from the Maison de Dieu in Chartres, shows two figures carrying a long, banded fabric that resembles closely the holy relic depicted in the engraving by Villemain (Figure 12).[26]

From the very beginning, then, the Virgin's *chemise* at Chartres stages an important conundrum: it offers at one and the same time a record of what appears to be a simple, domestic, western linen garment and a competing and equally elaborate narrative of that garment's pedigree as highly decorated, costly fabric imported from the eastern Mediterranean. What can these divergent characterizations of textiles, made sacred because of their reputed proximity to the Virgin's flesh, tell us about the medieval Virgin at Chartres Cathedral? And more specifically, what light might these representations of textiles shed on our understanding of the Virgin who was venerated by medieval pilgrims journeying to Chartres?

The Virgin at Chartres

Art historians have amply documented a wide array of visual representations of the Virgin in stained glass and stone carving at Chartres cathedral that follow the tradition of the *sedes sapientiae*. The theme has an old iconography, drawing on the related topics of Mary as the Virgin Mother, Mary as Theotokos, and Mary as the Throne of Solomon, as Ilene Forsyth has explained.[27] At Chartres, the *sedes sapientiae* appears in varied form from the enthroned Virgin on the twelfth-century right tympanum of the cathedral's west façade[28] to stained-glass images of the thirteenth-century Virgin and child in the apse clerestory window and elsewhere.[29] All of these images provide possible echoes of a wooden statue of Nostre-Dame-sous-Terre, allied in legend to a cultic pre-Christian statue of the *Virgo paritura*, and now preserved only in early modern engravings.[30] From the twelfth century on, this statue, a carved Romanesque Madonna in Majesty,

Figure 11. Reproduced from Fernand de Mély, *Le Trésor de Chartres: 1310–1793* (Paris, 1886), pl. XI, "Le voile de la Vierge (d'après Villemain)."

Figure 12. Reproduced from Marcel Bulteau, *Monographie de la cathédrale de Chartres*, vol. 1 (Chartres: R. Selleret, 1887), 106.

is thought to have been carried in procession along with the reliquary containing the holy *chemise*, both objects together drawing large crowds of medieval pilgrims to Chartres.[31] When the historian Alexandre Pintard enumerated the statue's garments in 1681, listing a tunic, a mantle of classical style in the form of a dalmatic, and a veil covering her head,[32] he mentioned no *chemise*.

Interestingly, this same text and another dated a decade earlier depict the Virgin and Child as black-skinned, presumably in the tradition of "Black Virgins" found throughout southern France. They derive, it is thought by some, from contact with sculptural traditions in the eastern Mediterranean and are exemplified in France by the extant statue at Rocamador among many others.[33] Forsyth notes that a darkened skin color could have resulted from borrowing, at least in part, from an eastern tradition of Byzantine icons of the Virgin painted on wood, including most famously the Virgin of Blachernai at Constantinople. Popular tradition in the Romanesque period, she explains, associated Mary with the dark beauty of the Queen of Sheba, as described in the *Song of Songs* and reflected in commentary on that text by Alain de Lille and the chancellor of the School of Chartres.[34] A number of medieval legends attribute the actual provenance of certain statues of black Virgins to Palestine and the Holy Land,[35] even though the types of wood used in their composition can be identified as indigenous to specific regions in France.[36] Did medieval pilgrims at Chartres cathedral then worship an eastern, black Virgin and, if so, what would that say about their veneration of her holy *chemise*, ostensibly brought from Constantinople?

Stained glass and stone carving at Chartres provide few clues to help answer these questions. Several stained glass images do exist of a later statue venerated by Chartrain pilgrims: a silver-sheathed cult statue of the Virgin and child also in the *sedes sapientiae* pose, a statue installed on the main altar in the choir along with the holy relic when the Gothic church was built.[37] Yet nowhere in these scenes of veneration is the famed relic portrayed. The *sancta camisia*, which played such a crucial role in attracting pilgrims to the shrine at Chartres, that cloth, whether linen or silk, whether western or eastern, which came specifically to represent this western European Virgin, proves to be as elusive as the purportedly black statue itself.

Pilgrim Badges and Textiles

That double absence makes the pilgrim badges from Chartres all the more significant. The locally produced lead badges provide, in the end, the most extensive available representations of the Chartrain relic. They also help draw a portrait of the Virgin at Chartres unlike those available in stained glass or sculpted stone.

Inexpensive and mass-produced pilgrim badges appeared in France as early as the twelfth century and reached a peak of popularity in the fourteenth and fifteenth centuries, with the earliest extant examples dating from the thirteenth century, as Denis Bruna explains.[38] Created initially as an indication of religious commitment, attesting to the completion of a pious journey, medieval *enseignes de pèlerinage* also functioned as a form of popular and public art, becoming highly visible items of dress in their own right.[39] We owe the survival of French pilgrim badges—along with a number of secular *enseignes* and trade medallions, ecclesiastical badges, and coins—to Arthur Forgeais, an antiquarian who preserved them when the Seine was dredged in 1861 and again in 1863–64. Forgeais reproduced engraved images of religious and secular badges with brief textual notations in five volumes before dispersing his collection to museums and private individuals in France.[40] Pilgrim badges from Chartres differed significantly from those distributed at other Marian shrines throughout France in that they depicted the cathedral's principal relic, thus providing an imagined visualization of the hidden *chemise*.[41]

In this chapter we will read the Virgin at Chartres through the iconic chemise that represents her at this site by drawing on eighteenth- and nineteenth-century Church narratives of the absent relic, medieval Marian legends that record the holy garment's miraculous deeds, and most especially the surviving "chemisettes" that pair the well-known image of the Virgin as *sedes sapientiae* with telling depictions of her *chemise* in its relation to local textile production and the international cloth trade.

In assessing the varied representations of the Virgin's *chemise* at Chartres, I want to keep in mind the importance of place that medieval textiles and clothing can so effectively convey. My concern is not with dress as an indication of social place or status—although medieval clothing does often function to display wealth, luxury, or social status—but with geographical location: with what clothes can tell us about movement between culturally specific sites and about the generation of cross-cultural identities that can be fashioned in fabric. The Virgin's *chemise* at Chartres raises important questions about the cultural specificity and identity of the Virgin at that pilgrimage site. In investigating the relation between linen and silk that is staged by the Virgin's chemise at Chartres, we will see that behind the story of that potent icon of western femininity and maternity, or perhaps more accurately within it, lies another story: a story of textile production and international trade, a story that twines together threads of locally produced linen and imported foreign silk. That story maps an important site of cultural crossing between the Chartrain Virgin and the Virgin of Constantinople.

The Relic: French Linen or Saracen Silk?

The medieval legends that indicate Constantinople as the source of the Virgin's *chemise* are thought to derive from an eastern account of a wildly heroic Virgin protecting the city of Constantinople with her cloak. Annemarie Weyl Carr has shown that the legend of what she calls the Virgin's "veil" at Chartres builds on stories of the *maphorion* worn by the warrior goddess Virgin in the Byzantine empire who, by the sixth and seventh centuries, had become the "embodiment of the imperial virtue of eternal victory." Her veil-like cloak is said to have defended Constantinople in a series of battles from the seventh to the ninth centuries. From the tenth to the twelfth centuries, Mary becomes the "invincible general," protector of Constantinople in times of war.[42] Engaged, active, and interventionist, this Virgin is no *sedes sapientiae* and her garment is not linen.

Versions of this account travel to the west and are perhaps best documented in Old French in *Les Miracles de Nostre Dame* by the thirteenth-century poet Gautier de Coinci (1210–25). His narrative, "Comment Nostre Dame desfendi la cité de Constantinnoble," describes Constantinople under fierce attack by an unspecified Saracen king hoping to usurp the city's great wealth and treasure (vv. 6–9 and 44–48).[43] The story focuses on a beautiful, glorious, and wondrous woman who protects the besieged city by descending from the clouds in a dark-colored garment decorated lavishly in gold and fashioned of silk:

> Une dame si mervilleuse
> Si tres bele, si glorïeuse,
> Et d'une pourpre a or batue

Si acesmee et si vestue.
vv. 127–30

(A wondrous woman, so beautiful and glorious, so comely and dressed
up in a dark silk fabric with beaten gold detailing)

She uses a single corner of her silk cloak to cover the city. Miraculously, the
enemy blows bounce off:

D'un des corons de son mantel
Cele dame grant et plaigniere
Desfent la vile en tel maniere.

Cele roÿne glorïeuse,
Cele grans dame mervilleuse
En son mantel reçoit les colz
Et rebondist la pierre entr'olz.
Dou myracle, de la merveille
Li roys paiens mout se merveille.
vv. 140–42, 147–52

(With one corner of her mantle, this great and beneficent lady defends
the city. . . . This glorious queen, this great and wondrous lady, receives
the blows with her cloak and sends the stones back to them. The pagan
king marvels greatly at this miracle and wonder.)

Central to the miracle performed by the Virgin in Gautier de Coinci's account
is not an everyday linen *chemise* but a garment made from much more costly
fabric—a fabric often associated with Constantinople and Levantine shores:
silk.[44]

That the association of silk with the Virgin at Constantinople might
readily carry over to the Virgin at Chartres would not be surprising. We
know from the *Catalogue des reliques et joyaux de Notre-Dame de Chartres* that
"draps d'or et de soie" were among the most common gifts made to the
cathedral throughout the twelfth and thirteenth centuries, becoming so numerous, in fact, that the church began to sell them as shrouds to wealthy
parishioners. Lucien Merlet gives three examples from the *registres cartular-
ies* of 1298, one of "pannum sericum decoratum," and cites an inventory

from 1353 that lists—among ecclesiastical vestments including chasubles, tunics, and dalmatics—seventeen fabrics of gold or silk, some with images, along with "une grande toaille," a white altar cloth, decorated with silk, and with linen at each end.[45] The cathedral was teeming, it seems, with imported silks—whether as vestments, diplomatic gifts, spoils from crusade, or donations from travelers. If the precise point of origin of these silks remains unspecified in Merlet's account—and they could well have come by this time from places as close as Italy, Spain, or even France itself—they held the cachet of foreign imports.[46]

In terms of surviving textiles, Dominique Cardon has analyzed an array of extant oblong silks with banded patterns of figures and geometric shapes, now dispersed in France, Italy, Switzerland, and Brussels, that resemble most closely the engraving of the Virgin's *chemise* made by Villemain.[47] These surviving silks bear strong visual resemblance as well to a 1927 photo of the "oriental embroidery" wrapper for the white silk at Chartres provided by Delaporte.[48] Cardon assesses the silks she analyzes as having been woven in Spain in the twelfth and thirteenth centuries.[49] Thinking again of medieval designations of the Virgin's *chemise* as a gift from Charles the Bald, we should note that Charles himself is thought to have received a variety of textiles as gifts from Spain, specifically from the silk-producing Andalusian city of Cordoba in 865.[50] And Charles the Bald holds the legendary reputation in a number of thirteenth-century French literary and pseudo-historical texts as the founder of the very fairs that facilitated commercial exchange between Muslim Spain and northern France: the fairs of Champagne.[51]

Marian Legends: The *Sainte Chemise* in Action

Strikingly, however, the Chartrain legends themselves feature no silk, emphasizing instead the homespun quality of a common garment that could miraculously protect individual men in battle or be transformed into a stunningly effective military battle flag. Perhaps the best-known legend documenting the miraculous powers attributed to the Virgin's *chemise* at Chartres recounts a military triumph against invading Norsemen in 911, secured by the inspired use of the Virgin's *chemise* in combat.[52] As we might expect, there are a number of competing versions of the story. Recorded first in Latin by chroniclers Dudo of St. Quentin and William of Jumièges, the accounts are taken up subsequently by William of Malmesbury, Vincent of

Beauvais, Etienne de Bourbon, and John of Garland. Old French versions appear in Wace's *Roman de Rou* and in later tales by Jean le Marchant, William Adgar, and others.[53] In some versions of the tale, the inhabitants of Chartres gain a military victory against the invading pagans (alternately called Saracens) by displaying the Virgin's *chemise* on the ramparts. In others, the bishop of Chartres carries the holy *chemise* aloft into battle as a standard attached to a lance. Jean Le Marchant's thirteenth-century poem records both actions in sequence. First:

> Li Chartrin la chemise pristrent,
> Sus les murs au quarneaus la mistrent
> En leu d'enseigne et de benniere.
> 28.63–65

(The Chartrains took the *chemise* and placed it on the crenellated walls in place of a flag or banner.)

Then, they left Chartres and entered the fray against the pagans:

> Ovec leur evesque Gousseaumes,
> Qui portoit la seinte chemise,
> Por deffense et por garantise.
> 28.84–86

(With their bishop Gousseaumes, who was carrying the holy *chemise* for defense and protection.)

Nowhere is the fabric of the miraculous *chemise* specified. But perhaps more important, the Virgin herself is absent from the fray in this account. Starkly different from Gautier de Coinci's tale of the elegant and invincible Virgin boldly defending the city of Constantinople with her steely silk mantle, this legend and its counterparts transfer those powers to the holy garment itself. The Virgin's physical presence is effectively replaced by the miracle-wielding *chemise*-turned-flag that represents her.[54]

Another legend in Jean Le Marchant's *Miracles de Notre Dame de Chartres* suggests even more clearly that the relic was understood to be a medieval linen undergarment, although here again the fabric of the *chemise* remains unstated. In this story, a besieged knight from Aquitaine visits Chartres as a pilgrim, carrying with him a coffer full of his own *chemises*.[55] Having touched each one to the reliquary containing the "seinte chemise," he returns to battle (21.48–49), where the fiercest blows from lance and sword bounce off the man's undergarment, as if it were two hauberks:

> Que la robe li ont perciee
> Mes la chemise delïee
> Ne fu (pas) perciee n'entamee
>
> Ne li fist mal ne fer ne fust
> La montance de deus festus.
> S'il eüt deus haubers vestus.
> 21.87–89 and 98–100[56]

(They pierced his outer garment, but the delicate *chemise* was not pierced or cut. . . . He was not harmed at all by shaft or blade. It was as if he were wearing two hauberks.)

This pilgrim-knight's thin *chemise* has been made impenetrable by contact with the Virgin's *chemise*, which had itself successfully repelled the blows of Norsemen advancing on the cathedral early in the tenth century.

In the Chartrain miracle stories, not only does the eastern Virgin's lavish silk mantle become a lowly and simple *chemise*, the Virgin's absence from these tales allows the textile itself to grow in prominence. In the accounts given by Le Marchant, both the city of Chartres and the knight from Aquitaine are saved from annihilation by a simple piece of cloth.

Pilgrim Badges I

This, too, is the emphasis conveyed by the pilgrim badges from Chartres, which are equally distinctive in giving marked visual prominence to the holy *chemise*. As we noted earlier, surviving French pilgrim badges from other sites do not typically represent local relics. They show only the Virgin crowned and haloed, enthroned in the pose of the Romanesque *sedes sapientiae*, holding the Christ Child on her knees and the *fleur de lys* in one hand.[57] Few medieval French pilgrim badges carry representations of clothing at all. Obvious exceptions are the "sainte tunique" reputedly worn by Christ on the day of the

Passion, figured on badges from Argenteuil, and the Virgin's tunic at Aachen, which appears on pilgrimage badges from that site beginning in 1334.[58] Typically, the space on the reverse side of the badge is used to indicate the name of the city in which the Virgin's shrine was located.[59] Badges from Chartres, however, pair the traditional image of the seated Virgin holding the Christ Child with sizable depictions of the holy *chemise* on the reverse (see Figures 8 through 10).

At Chartres, the representation of the garment-relic is facilitated by the badges' unconventional shape. Rather than follow the model of Rocamador, in which both pilgrim badge and Church seal bear the "navette" form, a conjunction that has led scholars to deduce that pilgrim badges may have been based originally on cathedral seals,[60] Chartrain badges feature a distinctive and ample architectural outline. Their more capacious shape allows enough space on the reverse of each badge to portray not only the *chemise* but also, often above it, the reliquary that contains the *chemise*. Equally prominent is a third image we will discuss below: a fictional representation of local coinage: the *denier chartrain*.

If we attempt to read the six extant badges from Chartres in terms of the way they depict the *sainte chemise* and the Virgin represented by that holy relic, at least two visual types can be discerned. In Figures 8 through 10 we find the Virgin seated, crowned, and haloed, looking straight ahead, reflecting a variation on the *sedes sapientiae*, in this instance with the Christ Child held off to the side.[61] At Chartres itself, one stained glass image presents the seated Virgin and Child in a similarly altered pose: the north rose window where she and the child are both shown frontally but, different from the Belle Verrière and others mentioned earlier, not centrally aligned.[62] Rather than being seated on the throne, however, the Virgin figured on the Chartrain badges sits on a platform carried by two walking figures, suggesting perhaps that this image represents not the Virgin herself but the now-lost statue of Notre Dame-sous-Terre as it was paraded before believers to raise donations for the cathedral. Indeed, the reverse of the badge in Figure 8 shows the relic itself and the reliquary containing it (figured as a rectangular coffer with pitched roof at the top of the badge) both carried aloft by two walking figures.

The *chemise* on this badge, along with those depicted in Figures 9 and 10, is less a garment to be worn than a textile to be venerated. Clearly different from the elaborate and highly pleated drapery that characterizes the

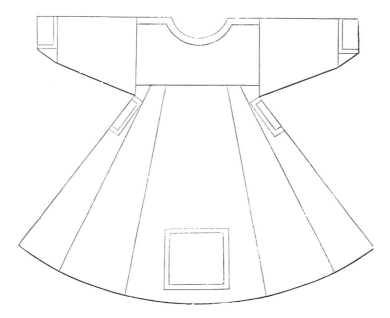

Figure 13. Reproduced from Arthur Forgeais, *Collection de plombs historiés trouvés dans la Seine* (Paris: Chez Aubry, 1865), 4:103.

Madonnas in Majesty studied by Forsyth, in which the clothing conforms to the shape of the figure beneath,[63] the *chemises* represented on the pilgrim badges from Chartres are rendered in two dimensions only. Their shape and form, however, are distinctly western. Figure 8 makes especially clear that the garment representing the relic is sewn from two separate pieces of fabric, the sleeves joined to the bodice by a horizontal seam. The *chemises* figured on these three badges suggest a western European garment: a full, gathered, loose-fitting item of dress, much like the garment schematized by Forgeais (Figure 13).[64] The second type of *chemise*, which follows a different cultural model, will be discussed below.

But first we should consider the full ramifications of the depiction of a cloth garment on badges attesting to local piety and pilgrimage in terms of clothwork at Chartres.

The Virgin and Domestic Clothwork

The Virgin's legendary role in local cloth production at Chartres, especially in the weaving of linen, is attested in a number of Marian legends. One tale in Le Marchant's collection features the work of a diligent "bien preude fame" (27.15) who, after vowing to make a "toaille" and offer it at the Virgin's altar, produces a beautiful and refined piece of clothwork ("La toile . . . belle et delïee," 27.21 and 25).[65] In preparation for her pilgrimage to Chartres, the Virgin's devotee wraps the "toaille" in another piece of linen ("drap linge," 27.26–27) and places both in a wooden chest used to store garments and other things (27.31). When the devil sets fire to the chest, the "toaille," protected by the Virgin for whom it was made, survives intact, although the "linge" and cloth ties wrapped around the offering are all consumed in flames (27.60–64 and 89–95). Thus, when the woman finally sets out on her pilgrimage to Chartres (27.106), she carries more than a sample of her own weaving. The "toaille" she fashioned for the Virgin has now been "seintefïee" (27.61) and qualifies to become a relic in its own right. Having arrived at Chartres, the pilgrim recounts the story of the cloth's miraculous survival to the visiting Bishop of Angers, who kisses it devoutly and insists that this "touaille" be enclosed in a "chasse" and honored as a relic ("Et cum reliques ennouree," 27.140).[66]

André Chédeville has shown that from the end of the thirteenth century, Chartres was well known for its linen production, some of it woven in the town, but a large portion produced by rural weavers. Although the expansion of the textile industry at Chartres and the neighboring region from Etampes to Orléans beginning in the second half of the twelfth century centered on the production of wool, linen production also increased significantly and was often undertaken by women in the countryside.[67] The story of the woman pilgrim who offered a "toaille" of her own making to the Virgin is especially significant because it links the local, small-scale manufacture of linen cloth by women to a Virgin who is herself depicted in the sculptural programs at Chartres cathedral as presiding over women doing clothwork.

The façade of the thirteenth-century Virgin's portal on the north porch of Chartres cathedral contains, in the inner archivolts of the left bay, representations of the active and contemplative life, both of which the Virgin was thought to embody. The sculptural figures representing the active life are all women involved in different phases of working linen, according to Katzenellenbogen: washing and carding, stripping and combing flax, spinning and winding, although Dominique Cardon joins earlier scholars in assessing two of the women as working wool.[68] At one time, below these figures there was also a large statue further representing the active life in the form of a woman sewing, perhaps Martha or Leah.[69]

Other legends portray the Virgin herself as a clothmaker. One text tells of Bonitus, a bishop in Auvergne, asked by the Virgin to say mass at a special service.[70] When he hesitates, an angel places before him a "saint vestement" (v. 110), a garment that Notre Dame had withdrawn from her own "escrin" (v. 110) for Bonitus to wear during the ceremony. Afterward, the "Sainte Dame" gives Bonitus the "glorius vestement" (v. 134) which, even though it was seen clearly ("nez et clers," v. 156) by all those present, was said to be "estrange" (v. 164) because it was not made by human hands ("faiture humaine," v. 166). Not only is this sacred and special garment passed as a gift ("tel dun," v. 198) from the Virgin's hand to the bishop's shoulders, it carries the added implication of having possibly been fashioned by the "Sainte Dame" herself, by her special touch. Thus does the tale resonate with another widespread narrative of the Virgin as the creator of the miraculously seamless tunic that she wove to clothe the Christ Child.[71] Interestingly, the garment bestowed by the Virgin on Saint Bonitus is not described as the kind of lavishly embroidered costly silk vestments typically worn by bishops. Rather, the onlookers in this account perceive the garment the Virgin gives to be of more humble cloth, either linen or wool ("u linge u lange," v. 163). The protection afforded by this *vestement*, like the unadorned tunic woven for Christ, resides in simplicity and direct materiality, a simple article of clothing that had been conferred if not also created by the Virgin's hand.[72] To be sure, the Virgin herself is portrayed as spinning in a number of Annunciation paintings through the thirteenth century,[73] where her symbol is the distaff.

A thirteenth-century legend featuring a penitent "fileuse" reiterates the Virgin's guiding influence in the production of woolen cloth. Having defied the proscription not to spin on Saturday, the Virgin's day, this worker suffered paralysis in her hands, body swelling, and eventual putrefaction. The only cure, we are told, is to make a pilgrimage to Chartres.[74] And what might she have found there?

We know that at Chartres piety intersected with commerce in a number of important ways. Pilgrim badges were sold at local commercial fairs organized specifically to honor the Virgin and held on her feast days.[75] On these occasions, Adolphe Lecocq explains, the cloister was studded with small boutiques and tables on which merchants could display their wares.[76] The fairs featured, among many kinds of goods, textiles manufactured in the town, which included wool (*draps de Chartres*) and, more important for our purposes, linen, which was used to make actual *chemises*. Among those selling pilgrim badges at Chartres in the thirteenth and fourteenth centuries were chandlers, tailors, curriers, casket-makers, and barbers.[77] When the market for distaffs (*quenouilles*) expanded significantly in the fifteenth century, the merchants who had been selling pilgrim badges at the fairs featuring wool and linen at Chartres took up the sale of these key implements of cloth production as well. Lecocq cites a lease from 1494, in which "Postel, a merchant and seller of distaffs" rents a stall in the cloister "as much to sell distaffs as all kinds of lead and metal objects, including tin and other metals." Only Postel, we are told, or someone authorized by him, is permitted to sell those lead items "on which the image of Notre-Dame is imprinted."[78] If the surviving badges from Chartres are any indication, these lead items would also contain an image of the *sainte chemise*. Thus, it would seem that one well-known symbol of the Virgin, her *chemise*, was displayed and sold in the market fairs alongside another: the distaff. Through both, she would have been associated visually with the production of domestic cloth.

These references to the Virgin and cloth work, along with others we have noted in Marian legends and cathedral sculpture, provide an important contrast to the robing of the Virgin figured in the apse Window of the Apostles at Chartres where the Virgin wears striped woolen cloth ostensibly made by wool merchants who donated the window.[79] In that instance, local craftsmen emphasized their skill and wares in a Pygmalion-like gesture of dressing up the Virgin in cloth produced locally, venerating her while also literally enfolding her in their commercial success. By contrast, images of the lone *chemise* on pilgrim badges feature a garment not worn by the Virgin but one that stands in for her, an iconic *chemise* that represents both the Virgin and, by extension, those women producers of cloth whose work is linked symbolically to her.

The *Denier Chartrain*

All extant versions of the *chemisettes* carry, in some form, a fictional representation of the *denier chartrain*, a feudal coin minted by the counts of Chartres and Blois (Figure 14).[80] Jane Welch Williams explains that local coins (*chartrains*) had been minted at Chartres since the ninth century. Until the four-

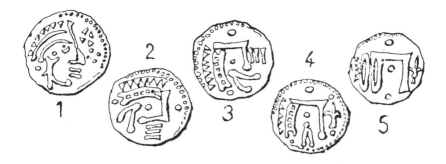

Figure 14. Development of the *denier chartrain* from René de Ponton d'Amécourt, *Monnaies au type chinonais* (Mâcon, 1895).

teenth century, the counts of Chartres and Blois minted coins and enfeoffed the right to mint to various vassals, but by the thirteenth century the bishops held some rights to mint as well. Williams suggests that the presence of the Chartrain coin on the *chemisettes* reminded pilgrims of their duty to give generously to the shrine and the church, reiterating in a sense the ideology of pious giving represented in the cathedral windows.[81] But could the *denier chartrain* also indicate participation in a larger world of commerce and trade beyond the region of Chartres where the local fairs were in fact international? Indeed, linen, from which a simple western *chemise* would have been fashioned, was both locally produced and traded on the international market as part of the second largest industry in the town of Chartres.[82]

The Virgin herself is linked perhaps most tangibly to commerce and trade at Chartres because, from the beginning of the fifteenth century at least, her image was physically stamped onto each piece of fabric produced in the town. Lengths of Chartrain cloth received both a wax stamp ("une esprainte de cire") and a lead seal ("un marc et sain publique de plom") or "plommet" that carried an image of the Virgin along with the word "Chartres" written below it, marking the textile's point of origin.[83] Commercial seals are known to have been used on textiles as early as 1361 in Rouen and 1399 in Abbeville, where ordinances record the requirement of affixing *sigilla pannorum* to cloth before it was transferred to merchants for sale.[84] Sabatier describes extant fifteenth-century lead seals from Abbeville, Amiens, Arras, Bourges, and Caen that indicate the name of the city of origin but include no visual image. However, the Chartrain seal from 1419, which he mentions, pairs the name

Chartres with an image of the Virgin. And even more important, that seal contains on the reverse, as do the Chartrain pilgrim badges, an image of the *denier chartrain*.[85]

To be sure, reading the *chemisettes* back to front, one could certainly understand them to suggest that donations of money, represented by the *denier chartrain*, to the *chemise* pictured above it would accrue to the Virgin figured on the front of the badge. Jean Le Marchant's collection of miracles includes a story that clearly describes such a process of successful fundraising. In his tale documenting how the "seinte chemise, en la chasse" (3.98) survived a devastating cathedral fire, the Virgin's garment emerges intact from the ruins and inspires onlookers, who thank "la glorïeuse dame" (3.317) for having saved their city, to pledge their generous support in money, income, and goods, each according to his means, both "clers et borjois."[86] After three years of rebuilding, when monies to pay workers wore thin, we are told, the Virgin implored God to perform additional miracles, attracting yet more pilgrims and further donations (3.469–70). The legend offers an image of local pious donation.

However, if we consider the geographic range of the *denier chartrain* and related coins—the "type Chartrain," also called "chinonais," that circulated in the mid-Loire region according to the analysis of Arthur Engel and Raymond Serrure—the spread of those coins charts movement not only toward but also away from Chartres. Engel and Serrure map in part an area that stretched initially from Chartres in the north to Châteaudun and Vendôme, then on toward Blois, and further south through Saint-Aignan and Selles to Brosse.[87] The first three cities indicated here match exactly the first three stops on the pilgrimage route to Santiago de Compostela.[88] After joining the branch that originated in Saint-Denis, the route continued across the Pyrenees and into Spain, where we know silks to have been produced and actively traded.[89]

A number of literary texts attest to the characterization, in the popular imagination, of pilgrimage sites in France and abroad as places of commercial exchange, especially regarding cloth or items of clothing. In the satirical *Fifteen Joys of Marriage* (ca. 1400) an unnamed wife is said to give her pilgrim husband a belt and beads so he can touch them to the relics and the statue of Our Lady at the Marian shrine in Le Puy. The husband, however, once arrived at the pilgrimage site, is distracted by the rich, bourgeois ladies who are caught up in buying beads of coral, jade, and amber, as well as rings and other jewels. The husband then feels his wife too should have these luxury items, despite their excessive cost.[90] Similarly, commercial exchange more than piety characterizes the pilgrimage site in a mid-eleventh-century legend concerning Sainte-Foy in the south of France. This account tells of a Gascon man who brought a piece of cloth to the shrine not, as we might expect, to touch it to the relic and derive protection or spiritual benefit, but rather, we are told, "to sell it at a profit."[91] As we saw in Chapter 5, the *Pèlerinage de Charlemagne à Jerusalem et à Constantinople* narrates Charlemagne's founding of a Church in Jerusalem dedicated to the Virgin Mary. Describing nothing more than the trade in cloth and spices that took place there, this text characterizes the holy site more in terms of merchants than pilgrims.[92] Of further significance, the *Pèlerinage* lists among a cache of relics that the Frankish king received from the patriarch in Jerusalem the "sainte chemise" that Mary wore (v. 189).[93] That same *chemise*, by a complicated twist of fate and fable, becomes the relic donated by Charles the Bald to Chartres Cathedral in Le Marchant's *Miracles de Notre Dame*.

Pilgrim Badges II

Although neither of these Old French texts details the form or fabric of the famed *chemise*, pilgrim badges from Chartres offer an imaginative possibility. We have seen how the *chemises* portrayed in one group of Chartrain badges reiterate legendary narratives of the Virgin's participation, alongside women, in local textile production. The garments in Figures 15 and 16, however, reinforce and expand the story of the Virgin's relation to international travel and trade. They bear a distinctly different cut and shape from the western, linen *chemises* depicted in Figures 8 through 10. The *chemises* in Figures 15 and 16 are flat, without gathering or pleating, seemingly cut from a single piece of cloth with dolman-like sleeves that are marked in part by a large curve along the underarm. The flatness of the garments is rendered effectively by a pattern of uninterrupted cross-hatching that contrasts significantly with the vertical lines representing the fullness and possible pleating in Figures 8 through 10.

The *chemises* in Figures 15 and 16 resemble most closely the vertically constructed shifts that Veronika Gervers attributed to Byzantine Egypt of the sixth and seventh centuries (Figure 17). Gervers observed that this style of garment, often made of silk, became increasingly common in Egypt from Islamic times on, and spread rapidly throughout North Africa and the Mediterranean world. She argued further that this originally "eastern" style of dress influenced fashion in western, northern, and Eastern Europe, serving in fact as a

Figure 15. Reproduced from Arthur Forgeais, *Collection de plombs historiés trouvés dans la Seine* (Paris: Chez Aubry, 1863), 2:33–34.

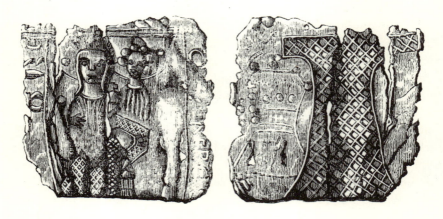

Figure 16. Reproduced from Arthur Forgeais, *Collection de plombs historiés trouvés dans la Seine* (Paris: Chez Aubry, 1865), 4:120.

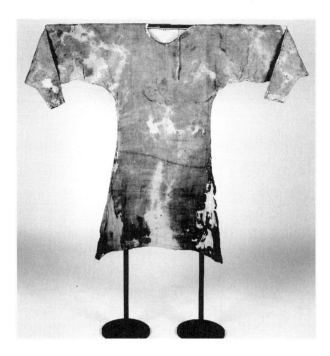

Figure 17. Shirt (linen tabby) cut in Oriental fashion. Reproduced with permission of the Royal Ontario Museum ROM.

prototype for the western European *chemise*.[94] Interestingly, the *chemise* attributed to Saint Louis and now held in the treasury of Notre-Dame Cathedral in Paris, bears this distinctive shape.[95]

The badge in Figure 18 from this group provides an interesting hybrid image. While displaying the form of garments in Figures 8 through 10—a horizontal seam at the yoke and a full lower portion composed of multiple panels (as seen in Figure 13)—the *chemise* is also rendered with the cross-hatching pattern distinctive of badges in Figures 15 and 16. However, cross-hatching is not used in this instance to indicate the flatness of a single piece of cloth (as in Figures 15 and 16). Rather, this diagonal patterning is interrupted by the multiple seams of a garment shown to be constructed of numerous pieces that would produce a fullness of folds.

The Madonnas represented on the badges in Figures 15, 16, and 18 also differ significantly from those in the first group we discussed above (Figures 8 through 10), in which the Virgin sits on a portable platform, reminiscent

Figure 18. Reproduced from A. Lecocq, "Recherches sur les enseignes de pèlerinages et les *chemisettes* de Notre-Dame-de-Chartres," *Mémoirés de la Société archéologique d'Eure et Loir* 6 (1876): 217.

perhaps of the movable Madonnas in Majesty and the crypt statue of Notre-Dame-sous-Terre. The Virgins in Figures 15, 16, and 18 appear instead to be seated on a throne. Crowned, but not haloed, they also wear a *maphorion*-like veil that would situate them in relation to similarly veiled images of the Byzantine Hodegetria.[96] And indeed, the posture of the Virgin herself in Figure 15, her head inclined toward the Christ Child held in her left hand, strikes the familiar pose of the Virgin Hodegetria.[97] The veiled heads of these Virgins further recall the enigmatic line from Jean Le Marchant's legendary account of the Virgin's *chemise* saving Chartres from invading Normans, in which he describes two textile banners, the second one not mentioned in his Latin source: a battle flag called the "voile de la Vierge":

> Avecques une autre banniere,
> Qui du voile de la Vierge yere,
> De Chartres s'en issirent tuit
> O grant effors et o grant bruit.
> En l'ost des paiens tot se mirent.
> 28.87–91

(With another banner made from the Virgin's veil, they exited Chartres with great strength and noise to engage with the pagan army.)

Tellingly, the *chemises* resembling an Egypto-Byzantine tunic in Figures 15 and 16 apparently functioned unproblematically in the medieval western Christian imagination as a viable expression of the western (French) Virgin's underclothes. Thus, while imported silk fabrics were swelling the coffers of medieval western Church treasuries, and an Islamic textile iconography was being used to decorate garments found on medieval French cathedral façades,[98] so too had Chartrain pilgrim badges absorbed and displayed eastern-style garments alongside western ones as central icons of medieval western European piety. If Chartrain legends of the Virgin's miracles had westernized to a significant degree the lavish silk garment of Gautier de Coinci's Byzantine Virgin, and if the legendary accounts had also transposed the Byzantine *maphorion* or veil, in some sense, into a *chemise*, these substantial cultural adaptations were only partial. The resulting Virgin's *chemise* at Chartres emerges as a richly hybrid garment positioned at a crossroads of both cultural and commercial exchange.

The Virgin and International Trade

Indeed, the conjunction of *chemise* and coin on the badges from Chartres, much like actual lengths of fabric stamped with the Virgin's image and that same coin in subsequent years, could mark those items not only as belonging to the Virgin or having been produced at Chartres but also more specifically as having been *sold* there. This is often the case with the naming of medieval textiles themselves, such that "toiles de Champagne" can mean either linen made in Champagne or linen sold at that site. Similarly, *panni alexandrini* can refer to silk produced or (as was more often the case) simply sold in Alexandria and thus known, as Wilhelm Heyd explains, as "d'origine sarrasine."[99] In this sense, the conjoined images of *chemise* and *denier* on pilgrim badges from Chartres would signal the importance of the Virgin in local commerce, where specific Chartrain coins were required to do business, and especially in the local cloth trade, which flourished at this site. But the paired images of cloth and coin would point as well to spheres of international trade: to the fairs in Champagne (at Lagny in particular and perhaps others as well), at Angers, Orléans and the "foires du Lendit" (between Saint-Denis and Paris) where we know that Chartrain textiles (wool and linen) were traded,[100] sometimes to Venetian, Genoese, and Spanish merchants, who delivered in exchange highly valued, imported silk.[101] Linen, in turn, was exported from Champagne to Constantinople and Famagouste in Cyprus, while Rémois linen was especially prized in Egypt.[102]

Women played at least some role in this extended commerce. The Old French *Dit des marchéans*, which depicts merchants as travelers to foreign countries and "outremer" to England, Spain and Brittany, as well as on pilgrimage to Saintiago and Saint Gilles, also describes the fairs of Champagne at "Lagnai," "Bar," and "Provins," where textiles figure among a vast array of other products. Mentioned specifically are "marcheanz de dras/ Et de toile et de chanevas" and their female counterparts. When, in closing, the narrator asks "Jesus, son of Mary" to keep all merchants safe and guide them into heaven, he requests the same protection for "les marchéandes."[103] Geneviève Aclocque further cites an ordinance of wool makers at Chartres that signals the participation of women. It prohibits "nul marcheant ne *marcheande* de hors" (italics mine) from buying lamb's wool, spun wool, long or shorter threads, except on the feast days of Our Lady.[104] The Virgin portrayed on Chartrain pilgrim badges, which feature both a garment *and* a coin, stands then at the nexus of the local clothwork in linen and wool, the work of those women featured on the Cathedral façade as pursuing the active life through clothmaking, and a larger world of trade, travel, and commerce beyond the local sphere in which they may have also participated.

Across the Sea of Silk

Within the story of the medieval Christian pilgrim's journey to venerate the Virgin's purportedly western linen *chemise* at Chartres cathedral lies a story of distant travel: a tale of trade and cross-cultural contact. In making the Virgin's *chemise* visible, the anomalous pilgrim badges, termed *chemisettes*, tell that cross-cultural story in fabric and clothing: shifting our gaze constantly back and forth between the domestic production of European linen and centers of Byzantine and Islamic manufacture of silk fabric and attire. Following the threads of the Virgin's western, linen *chemise* leads us in various geographic directions, whether across the Mediterranean to Constantinople and the Levant or across the Pyrenees to Christian and Muslim Spain, but always toward silk, which itself traveled long distances both as a fiber traded as currency and as diplomatic and ecclesiastical gifts. And yet, the *chemisettes* also return our gaze to France, to Chartres, to the Virgin seated so regally on the front of each badge, to the traditional *sedes sapientiae*, but with a significant twist. The portrait of the sedentary Virgin is now infused with the possibility of movement in a number of ways: in the active work of women represented on the cathedral's north porch or in tales of the Virgin's own spinning and sewing, in the broad gesture displayed by her silk-clad counterpart engaged in defending the city of Constantinople, in the commercial circulation of coins representing her town, and the cloth trade the coins fostered. The iconic *chemise* itself positions this Virgin at a cultural crossroads: her linen Latinate *camisia* can also take the shape of an Egypto-Byzantine *chemise* and possibly consist simultaneously of Andalusian silk. The pilgrim badges from Chartres do not reveal whether this Virgin might have been understood as black—or white or brown, as French or Moorish. The *chemisettes* do help us situate the Virgin at Chartres culturally, however, between western Christian Europe and what were often considered in the medieval French imagination to be Saracen lands. If the Virgins depicted on Chartrain pilgrim badges are not literally black, they seem nonetheless, through their long geographical reach and hybrid clothing, to be in some sense Saracen. If the eastern-style tunic featured on some pilgrim badges at Chartres Cathedral can double as the western-style *chemise* worn by the Virgin at the conception and birth of Christ, where does that place her, the Virgin of Chartres, represented as she is on the *chemisettes* both by cloth and a coin? Somewhere between France and Constantinople, Egypt and al-Andalus? Or perhaps, more accurately, right there at Chartres cathedral, a place itself made more "Saracen" by the complex resonances of the Virgin's clothes.

GLOSSARY

Based on careful study of extant silk fabrics, textile historians provide detailed technical descriptions for a number of silks that are also named in Old French literary texts. The authors of romance and epic, however, tend to use a wide range of terms for silk fabrics and silk garments, without specifying precise differences among them. The following offers a simple glossary of terms for the nonspecialist reader.

Attabi/hatebis/tabby: Silk and gold brocaded textiles.
Baudequin: From the Italian "baldichino" indicating silk named after the city of Baghdad but produced in many sites across the Mediterranean.
Camoca: Patterned silk woven in the Mongol Empire and in Italy of contrasting colors but with little or no gold thread. Can also refer to wool.
Cendal: Supple, light weight silk, sometimes called taffeta, often used for linings.
Cochinelle/cochineal: Insect used to produce carmine red dye and by analogy the red dye itself.
Dabīqī: Fine linen produced in Tinnis and Damietta, often embroidered with colored or gold thread.
Damascene: Patterned silk, originally made in Damascus.
Diapre: Patterned silk originally white or of a single color; often used to denote silk and gold brocade generally.
Dras d'areste/ dras d'ache: Silk textiles with a herringbone or chevron pattern. See above p. 94.
Dras d'or: Silk cloth interwoven with gold thread.
Ecarlate: Dark red or purple wool but also sometimes used to indicate dark red silk.
Futaine: Cotton or cotton mixed with another fiber such as linen, silk, or wool.
Grege: Raw silk, silk fiber before it is dyed or woven.
Inde/ynde: Indigo: Blue dye made from indigo plant and less commonly from one kind of Phoenician sea snail. Often associated with India, an early producer of large quantities of indigo.

Kermes: Insect, distantly related to the cochineal insect, and used to produce crimson dye which also bears the name "kermes."

Orfrois: Narrow band of silk and gold, bearing a decorative pattern that can be either woven or embroidered. Appears on secular and religious garments and often contains Arabic script. See above pp. 48–52.

Osterin: Dark colored luxury silk.

Paile: Used as a generic term for silk, often accompanied by a place of origin such as "paile alixandrine," "paile d'Aumaire." See above p. 34.

Perse: Deep blue color, often used to refer to blue-dyed wool.

Porpre: Silk cloth of a dark color.

Samit: luxurious, heavy silk cloth.

Sharb: Fine, high-grade linen.

Siglaton: Silk cloth decorated with patterned circles.

Tartaires/ panni tartarici: Cloth of silk and gold associated in particular with thirteenth-cloth production in the Mongol empire.

Toile: common linen.

Tyrian purple: purple-red dye first produced by the ancient Phoenicians in the city of Tyre, extracted from the predatory sea snail known as murex. Also known as royal purple, imperial purple, Byzantine purple.

NOTES

INTRODUCTION

1. David Jacoby, "Silk Economics and Cross-Cultural Artistic Interaction: Byzantium, the Muslim World, and the Christian West," *Dumbarton Oaks Papers* 58 (2004): 197–240.

2. S. D. Goitein, *A Mediterranean Society: The Jewish Communities of the Arab World as Portrayed in the Documents of the Cairo Geniza* (Berkeley: University of California Press, 1999), 6 vols.; Abulafia, "Mediterraneans," in *Rethinking the Mediterranean*," ed. W. V. Harris (Oxford: Oxford University Press, 2005), 63–93; *Italy, Sicily, and the Mediterranean, 1100–1400* (London: Variorum, 1987); Jacoby, "Silk Economics."

3. Exceptions include Charles Brand's discussion of "Some Byzantine Women of Thebes and Elsewhere," in *To Hellenikon: Studies in Honor of Speros Vryonis, Jr.*, vol. 1, ed. John S. Langdon et al. (New Rochelle, N.Y.: Aristide D. Carnatzas, 1993); Jacoby's description of the domestic weaving of silks and half-silks on a modest scale to produce small pieces of clothing and bedding "mainly manufactured by women" in southern Italy, Lucca, Genoa, and Venice as early as the eleventh century, "Silk Economics," 228, and "Silk Crosses the Mediterranean," in G. Airaldi, ed., *Le vie del Mediterraneo. Idee, uomini, oggetti* (Genoa: Università degli studi di Genova, 1997), 66, 71. Goitein explains that women were paid silk workers in Fustat, Alexandria, and small towns in Egypt in the eleventh and twelfth centuries, and occasionally worked as brokers who sold silk, *A Mediterranean Society*, 1: 102; 128–29; Maya Shatzmiller describes women silk workers in Islamicate silk works in the Middle East, *Labour in the Medieval Islamic World* (Leiden: Brill, 1994), 244, 249, 352; Olivia Remie Constable mentions women spinning and men weaving silk in Almería, *Trade and Traders in Muslim Spain: The Commercial Realignment of the Iberian Peninsula, 900–1500* (Cambridge: Cambridge University Press, 1994), 174. These fleeting references suggest there is much more to discover.

4. Sharon Farmer, "Biffes, Tiretaines, and *Aumonières*, The Role of Paris in the International Textile Markets of the Thirteenth and Fourteenth Centuries," *Medieval Clothing and Textiles* 2 (2006): 73–89; "Weavers and Spinners in the Wool, Linen, and Silk Industries in Thirteenth-century Paris: A Comparative Analysis," in manuscript.

5. See Chapter 6, "Saracen Silk; Dolls, Idols, and Courtly Ladies," in *Courtly Love Undressed: Reading Through Clothes in Medieval French Culture* (Philadelphia: University of Pennsylvania Press, 2002), 181–210.

6. On the Asian silk routes, see Susan Whitfield and Ursula Sims Williams, eds., *The Silk Road: Trade, Travel, War and Faith* (Chicago: Serindia Publications, 2004); Susan Whitfield, *Life Along the Silk Road* (Berkeley: University of California Press, 1999); Frances Wood, *The Silk Road: Two Thousand Years in the Heart of Asia* (Berkeley: University of California Press, 2002); Luce Boulnois, *La Route de la Soie* (Paris: Arthaud, 1963); François Bellec, ed., *A la Rencontre de Sinbad: La Route maritime de la soie* (Paris: Musée de la Marine, 1994); Kenneth Nebenzahl, *Mapping the Silk Road and Beyond: 2000 Years of Exploring the East.* (New York: Phaidon Press, 2004).

7. Goitein, *A Mediterranean Society*, vols. 1 and 4. Maurice Lombard, *Les Textiles dans le monde musulman du VIIe au XIIe siècle* (Paris: Mouton, 1978); Maya Shatzmiller, *Labour in the Medieval Islamic World*; David Jacoby, "Silk Crosses the Mediterranean"; "Silk in Western Byzantium Before the Fourth Crusade," in *Trade, Commodities, and Shipping in the Medieval Mediterranean* (Brookfield, Vt.: Variorum, 1997); Robert Lopez, "Silk Industry in the Byzantine Empire," in *Byzantium and the World Around It: Economic and Institutional Relations* (London: Variorum, 1978); Lopez, "Les Influences orientales à l'éveil économique de l'Occident," in *Byzantium and the World Around It*. See also Anna Muthesius, *Byzantine Silk Weaving: AD 400 to AD 1200* (Vienna: Verlag Fassbaender, 1997); Muthesius, "Impact of the Mediterranean Silk Trade on Western Europe Before 1200 AD," in *Textiles in Trade: Proceedings of the Second Biennial Symposium of the Textile Society of America* (Washington, D.C.: Textile Society of America, 1990), 126–35; Muthesius, "Byzantine Silk Industry: Lopez and Beyond," *Journal of Medieval History* 19 (1993): 1–67; along with Jean Ebersolt, *Constantinople Byzantine et les voyageurs du Levant* (London: Pindar Press, 1985); Janet Abu-Lughod, *Before European Hegemony: The World System A.D. 1250–1350* (Oxford: Oxford University Press, 1989); Constable, *Trade and Traders in Muslim Spain*; and Jean Favier, *De l'or et des épices: Naissance de l'homme d'affaires au Moyen Age* (Paris: Fayard, 1987).

8. The Latin term "opere saraceno" is used in 1295 to describe vestments at St. Paul's Cathedral, London, including a stole, tunic, dalmatic, and other garments with borders of *opere saraceno*. See Francisque Michel, *Recherches sur le commerce, la fabrication et l'usage des étoffes de soie, d'or et d'argent*, 1 (Paris: Imprimerie de Crapelet, 1852), 360.

9. On the gown of "porpre sarazinesche" worn by the allegorical figure Largesse in Guillaume de Lorris's *Roman de la Rose*, see vv. 1161–62 in Armand Strubel, ed. (Paris: Librairie générale française, 1992) and for an analysis of the passage, Burns, *Courtly Love Undressed*, 187–89. On "aumosnieres sarasinoises" see Farmer, "Biffes, Tiretaines, and *Aumonières*." The inventory of relics from Sens Cathedral cites, among many examples of silk fabrics and items, a "tissus sarrasinois" from the thirteenth century which "a servi d'aumônière" said to contain relics, E. Chartraire, *Inventaire du trésor de l'église primatiale et métropolitaine de Sens* (Paris: Picard, 1897), 30. Parisian guild statutes from the end of the thirteenth century cite "female makers of Saracen alms purses" (faiseuses d'aumosnieres sarrazinoises). See G. B. Depping, *Réglemens sur les arts et métiers de Paris rédigés au XIIIe*

siècle (Paris: Imprimerie de Crapelet, 1837), 382–86. On Saracen embroidery work, Francisque Michel cites the "ueuvre sarrasinoise" containing an embroidered portrait of Gauvain in one version of the Perceval story in which the knight's likeness is "brodé par une sarrasine" from Queen Guenevere's chamber. This unnamed Saracen woman is said to have embroidered the portrait on a "chier paille" with a heavily worked "Saracen" border: "a bort d'ueuvre sarrasinoise," 2:354; and the *Roman du Brut de la Montagne* similarly describes a child wrapped in "dras d'or et de soie en sarrazin ouvrés," Michel, 1:344.

10. "Des peuples païens ou mahométans," *Les Musulmans dans les chansons de geste du cycle du roi* (Aix-en-Provence: Publication de l'Université de Provence, 1982), 29. See also Jacques Le Goff, *La Civilisation de l'Occident médiéval* (Paris: Arthaud, 1967), 179–80.

11. Jean-Charles Payen, "L'Image du grec dans la chronique normande: sur un passage de *Raoul de Caen*," *Sénéfiance* 11 (1982): 269–75. See also Jeffrey Jerome Cohen, *Medieval Identity Machines* (Minneapolis: University of Minnesota Press, 2003), 208.

12. John Tolan, *Saracens: Islam in the Medieval European Imagination* (New York: Columbia University Press, 2002), 105–34. Tolan also gives examples of Saracens cast in learned texts as heretical followers of the trickster and magician Muhammad, 136–69.

13. Tolan, *Saracens*, 128. See also the thirteenth-century crusading map discussed by Alfred Hiatt that includes a rubric labeling the "Land inhabited by pagans and Saracens, ruled by the Sultan of Damascus," "Mapping the Ends of Empire," in *Postcolonial Approaches to the European Middle Ages*, ed. Ananya Jahanara Kabir and Deanne Williams (Cambridge: Cambridge University Press, 2005), 64.

14. Jeanne Wathelet-Willelm, "Les Saracens dans le 'Cycle de Vivien,'" *Sénéfiancé* 11 (1982): 364.

15. Maxime Rodinson, *La fascination de l'Islam* (Paris: Editions la Découverte, 1989), 42. In the Fourth Lateran Council, Innocent III decries Muslims and Jews together as blasphemers who parade in garish clothes while also condemning Jews, Muslims, Greeks, and Oriental Christians as heretics (Tolan, *Saracens*, 196, 198).

16. Dorothee Metlitski, *The Matter of Araby in Medieval England* (New Haven: Yale University Press, 1977), 119; Philippe Sénac, *L'Image de l'autre: l'occident médiéval face à l'Islam* (Paris: Flammarion, 1983), 22–24.

17. Norman Daniel, *The Arabs and Mediaeval Europe* (London: Longman, 1975), 53.

18. Cohen, *Medieval Identity Machines*, 190. See also Michael Uebel, "Unthinking the Monster: Twelfth-century Responses to Saracen Alterity" in Cohen, ed., *Monster Theory: Reading Culture* (Minneapolis: University of Minnesota Press, 1996), 264–91; and further Kenneth Baxter Wolf's analysis of two eighth-century Latin chronicles in which Muslims are called "arabes" and "sarraceni" and "multitudo Ishmahelitarum" but not "pagani" or "infideles" and Europeans are called "gothi" and "franci" but not "christiani, in "Christian Views of Islam in Early Medieval Spain," John Tolan, ed., *Medieval Christian Perceptions of Islam: A Book of Essays* (New York: Garland, 1996), 88. See further Denis Hüe's discussion of the Saracen as an expansive and universalizing category that encompassed Europe, Asia, and Africa in "La Chrétienté au miroir sarrasin" in *La Chrétienté au péril sarrasin*," *Sénéfiance* 40 (2000): 87. On Constantinople as a quintessentially eastern city, see Carole Bercovici-Huard, "*Partenopeus de Blois* et la couleur byzantine," *Images et signes de l'orient*

dans l'occident médiéval, Sénéfiance 11 (1982): 185–92; and Charles Diehl, *Manuel d'art byzantin,* vol. 1 (Paris: Picard, 1926), 395.

19. María Rosa Menocal, *The Arabic Role in Medieval Literary History: A Forgotten Heritage* (Philadelphia: University of Pennsylvania Press, 1987), 39–40.

20. *Medieval Identity Machines,* 190–91.

21. Rodinson, 36, 40–41. Rodinson explains further that eastern chroniclers like William of Tyre and others evince a much more nuanced understanding of political and religious complexities of the practice of Islam in the Middle East, 40.

22. Jacoby, "Silk Economics," 212.

23. Jacoby, "Silk Economics," 198.

24. "Weavers and Spinners in the Wool, Linen, and Silk Industries."

25. "Biffes, Tiretaines, and *Aumonières,*" 73–89.

26. Boulnois contends that this is the case at least from the time of the Greek writer Apollodorus of Artemita in Assyria, in the first century B.C.E. who speaks of the Seres as a distant Oriental people, without making reference to textiles, *Silk Road: Monks, Warriors, and Merchants on the Silk Road,* trans. Helen Loveday (New York: Norton, 2004), 36–37.

27. Virgil, *Bucolics, Aeneid, and Georgics of Vergil,* ed. J. B. Greenough (Boston: Ginn and Co., 1900), Book 2, vv. 125–27, "Of Aethiop forests hoar with downy wool,/ Or how the Seres comb from off the leaves/ Their silky fleece?"; and Pliny the Elder, *The Natural History,* ed. and trans. John Bostock and H. T. Riley (London: G. H. Bohn, 1855–57), Book 6, Chapter 20, pp. 2036–37; and more recently, Pliny, *Natural History,* trans. H. Rackham, 2 (Cambridge, Mass.: Harvard University Press, 1941), 377. Bostock explains that although this passage in Pliny is generally thought to refer to cloth exported by the Seres as *serica* that would correspond to our silk, Pliny refers elsewhere to silks as *bombycina,* produced by the bombyx or silkworm. See, for example, 11. 26–27, where Pliny describes silkworms as native to the isle of Cos where they don thick winter coats by "rubbing off the down that covers the leaves, by the aid of the roughness of their feet. This they compile into balls by carding it with their claws, and then draw it out and hang it between the branches of the trees, making it fine by combing it out as it were. Last of all, they take and roll it around their body, thus forming a nest in which they are enveloped" (11.27, p. 3026); and H. Rackham, trans. 3: 479. Pausanias expands the description, stating: "the threads from which the Seres make the dresses are produced from no bark, but in a different way as follows. There is in the land of the Seres, an insect which the Greeks call *ser,* though the Seres themselves give it another name. Its size is twice that of the largest beetle, but in other respects it is like the spiders that spin under trees, and furthermore it has, like the spider, eight feet. These creatures are reared by the Seres, who build them houses adapted for winter and for summer. The product of the creatures, a clue of fine thread, is found rolled around their feet," *Description of Greece,* trans. W. H. S. Jones and H. A. Ormerod (Cambridge, Mass.: Harvard University Press, 1918), 6.26. 6–7.

28. Ovid, *Amores,* Book 1, poem 14, "Vela colorati qualia Seres habent," *Amores, Epistulae, Medicamina faciei femineae, Ars amatoria, Remedia amoris,* ed. R. Ehwald (Leipzig: B. G. Teubner, 1907); Pausanias, 6.26, 8–9.

29. Boulnois, 149–55.

30. Ptolemy, *Geography: Book 6: Middle East, Central and North Asia, China*, ed. Helmut Humbach and Suzanne Ziegler (Wiesbaden: L. Reichert, 1998), 201–12. The Greek geographer Strabo uses the Seres as a point of reference to indicate the impressive reach of the Bactrians' holdings in Asia, saying they "extended their empire even as far as the Seres and Phryni," *Geography*, ed. H. C. Hamilton (London: George Bell and Sons, 1903), 11.11.1.

31. Boulnois, 197–98.

32. Seneca the Elder, *Declamations (Controversiae)*, trans. M. Winterbottom, 1 (Cambridge, Mass.: Harvard University Press, 1974), 375.

33. Rackham translates "Seres" as "the Chinese."

34. Pliny, trans. Rackham, Book 6, Chapter 20, p. 379.

35. Ibid.

36. Pliny, trans. Rackham, Book 11, Chapter 26, p. 479.

37. Pliny, trans. Rackham, Book 11, Chapter 27, p. 481.

38. See Burns, *Courtly Love Undressed*, 13–34, 38.

39. Wilhelm Heyd, *Histoire du Commerce du Levant au Moyen Age*, vol. 1 (Amsterdam: Adolf M. Hakkert, 1959), 18.

40. *Erec et Enide*, ed. Mario Roques (Paris: Champion, 1976).

41. Burns, *Courtly Love Undressed*, 187–94.

42. Félix Lecoy, ed., *Le Roman de la Rose ou de Guillaume de Dole* (Paris, Champion, 1962).

43. Translation from Jean Renart, *The Romance of the Rose or Guillaume de Dole*, trans. Patricia Terry and Nancy Vine Durling (Philadelphia: University of Pennsylvania Press, 1993), 77.

44. "Mout i ot bien ouvré Nature:/ que que li seneschaus ait dit,/ se Deu plest et Saint Esperit,/ que toz maus l'en vendra par tens" (Nature had fashioned [worked] her with great care. Whatever the seneschal might have said, God and the Holy Spirit willing, all will eventually turn against him).

45. Sharon Kinoshita has explained the phenomenon convincingly for Almeria silk, "Almería Silk and the French Feudal Imaginary," in E. Jane Burns, ed., *Medieval Fabrications: Dress, Textiles, Clothwork and Other Cultural Imaginings* (New York: Palgrave Macmillan, 2004), 165–76. Kinoshita makes a cogent argument for rethinking the geography of feudal France in a larger frame based on her readings of twelfth-century French texts in *Medieval Boundaries: Rethinking Difference in Old French Literature* (Philadelphia: University of Pennsylvania Press, 2006), esp. 1–45. For examples of how the purported opposition between pagan east and Christian west erodes in other contexts, see Michelle Warren, *History on the Edge: Excalibur and the Borders of Britain, 1100–1300* (Minneapolis: University of Minnesota Press, 2000), 183; John Ganim, "Native Studies: Orientalism and Medievalism," in *The Postcolonial Middle Ages*, Jeffrey Jerome Cohen (New York: St. Martin's, 2000), 125, 131; Glenn Burger, "Cilician Armenian Métissage and Hetoum's *La Fleur des Histoires de la Terre d'Orient*," in Cohen, ed., *The Postcolonial Middle Ages*, 79–80; Robert Bartlett, *The Making of Europe: Conquest, Colonization and Cultural Change, 950–1350* (Princeton, N.J.: Princeton University Press, 1993), 24–31. For examples of the dyadic construction of Christians against Saracens, see John Tolan, *Saracens: Islam in the*

Medieval European Imagination (New York: Columbia University Press, 2002); Jean Flori, "Mourir pour la croisade," *L'Histoire* 109 (March 1988): 13; Pierre Jonin, "Le Climat de croisade des chansons de geste," *Cahiers de civilisation médiévale* 3 (1964): 288; Paul Bancourt, *Les Musulmans dans les chansons de geste du cycle du roi*, vol. 2 (Aix-en-Provence: Université de Provence, 1982), 1005; Michelle Houdeville, "Une Arme étrange dans la *Chanson de Roland*," in *De l'Etranger à l'étrange ou la conjointure de la merveille* (Aix-en-Provence: CUERMA, 1988), 249–52. Micheline de Combarieu, "Un Personnage épique: La Jeune musulmane," *Sénéfiancé* 7 (Aix-en-Provence: CUERMA, 1979), 184.

CHAPTER 1. WOMEN AND SILK

1. The story is told by Aurel Stein in *Ancient Khotan: Detailed Report of Archaeological Explorations in Chinese Turkestan* (Oxford: Clarendon Press, 1907), 229. In his recounting and analysis of the tale, Stein refers to translations of the Chinese legend by Stanislaus Julien, *Mémoires sur les contrées occidentales traduites du Sanskrit en chinois en l'an 648 par Hiouen Thsang* (Paris: Imprimerie Impériale, 1857–58); Samuel Beal, *Si-yu-ki Buddist Records of the Western World. A Translation from the Chinese of Hiuen Tsiang (A.D. 629)* (London: Trubner and Co., 1884); and Abel Rémusat, *Histoire de la Ville de Khotan traduit du chinois* (Paris: Imprimerie Doublet, 1920). Luce Boulnois also provides a full account of the legend in *The Silk Road: Monks, Warriors and Merchants on the Silk Road*, trans. Helen Loveday (New York: W. W. Norton, 2004), 179–85.

2. Chrétien de Troyes, *Le Chevalier au Lion (Yvain)*, ed. Mario Roques (Paris: Champion, 1978), vv. 5182–5331. For a full discussion of this curious episode, see Chapter 2 below.

3. For that earlier study, see E. Jane Burns, *Courtly Love Undressed: Reading Through Clothes in Medieval French Culture* (Philadelphia: University of Pennsylvania Press, 2002), 179–210.

4. Christine Barbier-Kontler, "Les Soiries chinoises," in François Bellec, ed., *A la Rencontre de Sinbad: La Route maritime de la soie* (Paris: Musée de la Marine, 1994), 73; Susan Whitfield, *Life Along the Silk Road* (Berkeley: University of California Press, 1999), 9; Susan Whitfield and Ursula Sims-Williams, eds., *The Silk Road: Trade, Travel, War and Faith* (Chicago: Serinda Publications, 2004), 13–19, 46.

5. Frances Wood, *The Silk Road: Two Thousand Years in the Heart of Asia* (Berkeley: University of California Press, 2002), 75; Carol Michaelson, "Jade and the Silk Road: Trade and Tribute in the First Millennium," in Whitfield and Sims-Williams, eds., *The Silk Road*, 46. On nomads and silk, see Xinriu Liu, "Silk, Robes, and Relations Between Early Chinese Dynasties and Nomads Beyond the Great Wall," in Stewart Gregory, ed., *Robes and Honor: The Medieval World of Investiture* (New York: Palgrave, 2001), 23–34.

6. The network of Chinese silk routes that enabled the transport of silk fiber and fabric into the western territories and beyond also brought valuable goods into China, fostering active trading in horses, furs, gold, metal, pearls, and gems, especially jade (Boulnois, 340–52; Wood, 26). By the time of the Tang Dynasty (618–907) Chinese imports along the

silk routes included gold thread, horses, hawks, and falcons for imperial hunting; horse hides and furs; plants, including saffron from India and narcissus; foodstuffs and dyestuffs; and pistachios from Persia (Wood, 80–83). Exports of Chinese silk brought other textiles from Central Asia: felt for tents and drapes, curtains, mats, saddle covers and boots, ready-made woolen goods, linen (although China also made its own), cotton from India, and lavish silk brocades and damasks from Persia, Kaspia, and Byzantium. Also imported were noncombustible, asbestos-like fabrics, and weaponry (Boulnois, 288, 291, 295–300).

7. Barbier-Kontler, 73.

8. Wood, 12–13.

9. A number of recent studies that explain the complexity of these routes tend nonetheless to perpetuate, in their titles, the impression of a single silk road. See studies by Wood, Bellec, and Nebenzahl and edited collections by Grotenhuis and Whitfield, all reprising with variations the title of Luce Boulnois's early study: *La Route de la Soie* (Paris: Arthaud, 1963).

10. Kenneth Nebenzahl, *Mapping the Silk Road and Beyond: 2000 Years of Exploring the East* (London: Phaidon, 2004), 7–8.

11. Susan Whitfield, "Introduction," in Whitfield and Sims-Williams, eds., *The Silk Road*, 13. Whitfield explains that the silk road was composed of a series of stable regimes that fostered trade from one home market to the next and back, and emphasizes the substantial role played by the Sogdians as recognized merchants of the eastern silk road during the first one thousand years C.E. (13–14). See also Etienne de la Vaissière, "The Rise of Sogdian Merchants and the Role of the Huns," in Whitfield and Sims-Williams, eds., *The Silk Road*, 19–23.

12. The extended route was divided into three parts from west to east: Sogdiana (north of Afghanistan) from the Oxus River to the Pamir Mountains; the Tarim Basin, between the Pamir Mountains and Lop Nor; and the Gansu corridor, from Dunhuang to Chang'an (present-day Xi'an). See Whitfield, *Life Along the Silk Road*, 22–26.

13. Nebenzahl, *Mapping the Silk Road and Beyond*, 16–22; Wood, 28. Boulnois gives the example of Julius Caesar's military triumph in 43 B.C. when crowds were astounded by silk banners unfurled overhead, 44.

14. Boulnois, 186, 336–37.

15. Whitfield and Sims-Williams, eds., *The Silk Road*, 149; Boulnois, 187.

16. *Penguin Atlas of Medieval History*, ed. Colin McEvedy (Baltimore: Penguin Books, 1961), 28.

17. Maurice Lombard, *Les Textiles dans le monde musulman du VIIe au XIIe siècle* (Paris: Mouton, 1978), 85. Lombard explains further that the commercial trading of silk fiber and cloth, originally moving westward from China, eventually developed into highly complex patterns of movement that traversed the Mediterranean in both directions as some medieval silks were imported to western Europe via Italy in particular from Constantinople and the Levantine coast and other silks moved along the North African coast between Egypt and Muslim Spain.

18. S. D. Goitein, *A Mediterranean Society: The Jewish Communities of the Arab World as Portrayed in the Cairo Geniza*, vol. 1 (Berkeley: University of California Press, 1967),

222–24; and his *Letters of Medieval Jewish Traders* (Princeton, N.J.: Princeton University Press, 1974). The letters of medieval Jewish traders traveling between Egypt and the eastern Mediterranean in the eleventh and twelfth centuries indicate that silk was paid, in one instance, as a recompense for oil received and could have served, in another, as a substitute for gold (*Letters*, 156, 195).

19. Goitein, 1:104.

20. Olivia Remie Constable, *Trade and Traders in Muslim Spain: The Commercial Realignment of the Medieval Iberian Peninsula, 900–1500* (Cambridge: Cambridge University Press, 1994), 49. Earlier, in Southern Arabia, Jews and Christians contracted to send celebrated striped fabrics, possibly Yemeni silk *washi*, to the Abbasid caliph in Baghdad as partial payment of their tribute and taxes. See Patricia L. Baker, *Islamic Textiles* (London: British Museum Press, 1995), 36.

21. Philippot, "Li dit des marchéans," in Anatole de Montaiglon and Gaston Raynaud, eds., *Recueil des fabliaux des XIIIe et XIV siècles*, vol. 2 (Paris, 1877; rpt. New York: Burt Franklin, 1963), 124.

22. Lombard, 86.

23. Wood, 91–94.

24. Whitfield and Sims-Williams, eds., *The Silk Road*, 146–47, 149.

25. Boulnois, 107–8, 188.

26. Boulnois, 233; Lombard, *Les Textiles dans le monde musulman*, 80; Constable, 173. David Jacoby also describes sericulture in Gabes, Tunisia in the tenth century, "Silk Economics and Cross-Cultural Artistic Interaction: Byzantium, the Muslim World, and the Christian West," *Dumbarton Oaks Papers* 58 (2004): 200, as does Goitein, *A Mediterranean Society* 4:168.

27. Boulnois, 47–52.

28. Boulnois, 54.

29. Barbier-Kontler describes Chinese albums dedicated to agriculture and weaving that characterize this balanced distribution of labor as persisting throughout the Han dynasty, 72. See also Francesca Bray, *Technology and Gender: Fabrics of Power in Late Imperial China* (Berkeley: University of California Press, 1997).

30. Boulnois, 179–83.

31. From a collection of tales published in 1986 by Chen Yu Bian, ed. as *Dunhuang de Chuan Shuo* (Shanghai: Shanghai wen yi chu ban she), 131–34. I would like to thank my colleague Li-ling Hsiao for her help with the Chinese text. Although neither version of the story names the princess, Stein explains that local legend connects the tale with a convent founded by Lu-shê on the site where silkworms were first bred in Khotan, 229.

32. Procopius, *History of the Wars, Secret History, and Buildings*, trans. and ed. Averil Cameron (New York: Washington Square Press, 1967); Book 4:17, p. 253.

33. See note 4 above.

34. Boulnois, 184. Susan Whitfield, in *Life Along the Silk Road*, recounts a ninth-century tale of Princess Taihe, the fourth Chinese princess to be promised in marriage to an Uighur kaghan, which tells of trade negotiations between the Chinese who paid in silk for highly valuable Uighur ponies, 98–99.

35. See the account of Stein's first expedition in his two-volume report, *Ancient Khotan*, 230, 259–61, 275, 277–70, 298, Pls. LX, LXI. Mario Bussagli reproduces the image in *Central Asian Painting* (Geneva: Skira, 1979), 56. On this series of panels, currently in the British Museum in London, see Roderick Whitfield and Anne Farrer, *Caves of the Thousand Buddhas: Chinese Art from the Silk Route* (New York: George Braziller, 1990), 140–41, 160, 162–66. Whitfield and Farrer date the series of panels from Dandan-Uiliq, in the north of Khotan, to the sixth century, 158. See also Michaelson, who explains that by the fifth century, Khotan had a thriving silk-producing industry, "Jade and the Silk Road," in Whitfield and Sims-Willliams, eds., *The Silk Road*, 47.

36. This analysis of the image is provided by Whitfield and Farrer in *Caves of the Thousand Buddhas*, 160, pl. 132.

37. Whitfield and Farrer compare this figure to another image found at the same site (Dandan-Uiliq) also from the sixth century C.E. (162; pl. 134B). This votive panel of Mahésvara contains, on the reverse, an image of the God of Silk seated, as is the male figure in the image of the Silk Princess, and holding similar implements: a goblet and weaver's comb. See also Joanna Williams, "Iconography of Khotanese Painting," *East and West* 23 (1973): 109–54, who reproduces the image of the Silk Princess identified by Stein (Figure 57) and provides an additional image of the Silk Princess and her attendants smuggling silkworms in her headdress, now housed at the State Hermitage in Leningrad (Figure 64).

38. On the medieval Mediterranean trading network that included the production, exchange, and transport of silk as its most valuable commodity see S. D. Goitein, *A Mediterranean Society*, 1: 28; David Jacoby, "Silk in Western Byzantium Before the Fourth Crusade," in *Trade, Commodities, and Shipping in the Medieval Mediterranean* (Brookfield, Vt.: Variorum, 1997), 452–53; and his "Silk Economics," 197–240. See also Jean Favier, *De l'Or et des épices; Naissance de l'homme d'affaires au Moyen Age* (Paris: Fayard, 1987), 18; Maurice Lombard, *Les Textiles dans le monde musulman du VIIe au XIIe siècle* (Paris: Mouton, 1978); Anna Muthesius, *Byzantine Silk Weaving: AD 400 to AD 1200* (Vienna: Verlag Fassbaender, 1997), 145; and Muthesius, "The Impact of the Mediterranean Silk Trade on Western Europe Before 1200 AD," in *Textiles in Trade: Proceedings of the Second Biennial Symposium of the Textile Society of America* (Washington, D.C.: Textile Society of America, 1990), 126–35; Muthesius, "The Byzantine Silk Industry: Lopez and Beyond," *Journal of Medieval History* 19 (1993): 1–67; Robert Lopez, "Silk Industry in the Byzantine Empire," in *Byzantium and the World Around It: Economic and Institutional Relations* (London: Variorum, 1978); Lopez, "Les Influences orientales à l'éveil économique de l'Occident," in *Byzantium and the World Around It*; Jean Ebersolt, *Constantinople Byzantine et les voyageurs du Levant* (London: Pindar Press, 1985), 32–33.

39. The image is found in the upper right register of a Paris, BN, fr. 1433, f. 104, reproduced in *Les Manuscrits de Chrétien de Troyes*, ed. Keith Busby, Terry Nixon, Alison Stones, and Lori Walters, vol. 1 (Amsterdam: Rodopi, 1993), 477. I would like to thank Lori Walters for directing me to this image.

40. See, for one example among many, the reference in *Yvain* to Gauvain liberating damsels in distress, vv. 3682–95.

41. Silk appears on only two other occasions in this romance. When King Arthur arrives at Laudine's castle after her marriage to Yvain, the town is bedecked with silk:

Li drap de soie sont fors tret
et estandu a paremant,
et des tapiz font pavemant
que par les rues les estandent
contre le roi que il atandent.
vv. 2342–46

(Silk fabrics were brought out and hung as decorations while tapestries were spread along the streets for the king they awaited.)

Yvain himself is dressed in "cote et mantel . . . de soie en greinne" (vv. 2970–71; a tunic and cloak of scarlet silk) after being healed in the forest by the dame de Noroison (vv. 2959-69).

42. Sarah Grace Heller, "Fashion in French Crusade Literature: Desiring Infidel Textiles," in Désirée Koslin and Janet Snyder, eds., *Encountering Medieval Textiles and Dress: Objects, Texts, Images* (New York: Palgrave, 2002), 107–9.

43. *Fierabras*, ed. Marc Le Person (Paris: Champion, 2003), v. 212.

44. See, for example, Chrétien de Troyes's *Erec et Enide*: "Unes estaches de cinc aunes/ de fil de soie d'or ovrees/ a la reïne demandees" (vv. 1602–4; The queen requested some ribbons five yards long made of silk thread worked in gold); Marie de France, "Laustic," "En une piece de samit/ A or brusdé e tut escrit" (vv. 135–36; In a piece of heavy silk embroidered and written with gold); and "Yonec," "Une tumbe troverent grant/ Coverte d'un paile roé,/ D'un cier orfreis parmi bendé" (vv. 500–502; They found a large tomb covered with silk patterned with roundels and banded with a costly orphrey), both in *Les Lais de Marie de France*, ed. Jean Rychner (Paris: Champion, 1973).

45. Janet L. Abu-Lughod, *Before European Hegemony: The World System A.D. 1250–1350* (New York: Oxford University Press, 1989), 102-109. See her map of the Mediterranean routes from Genoa and Venice in the Middle Ages, 123; Goitein, *A Mediterranean Society*, 1: 212-14.

46. One obvious exception is women working in the town of Montpellier as merchants in Jean Renart's *Escoufle*. For an extended discussion, see Sahar Amer, *Border Crossings: Love Between Women in Medieval French and Arabic Literatures* (Philadelphia: University of Pennsylvania Press, 2008).

47. Wilhelm Heyd, *Histoire du commerce du Levant au Moyen Age*, vol. 1 (Amsterdam: Adolf M. Hakkert, 1959), 21.

48. Michael McCormick, *Origins of the European Economy: Communications and Commerce, A.D. 300–900* (Cambridge: Cambridge University Press, 2001), 284, 723–24, 726; Heyd, 1:18.

49. Lombard, 93; Michel Balard, *Croisades et Orient latin, XIe–XIVe siècle* (Paris: Armand Colin, 2001), 210.

50. *Le Charroi de Nîmes*, ed. J-L. Perrier (Paris: Champion, 1982). For references to wool, see "escarlates et vert et brun," (green and brown wools, v. 1065; and further, vv. 1140–43).

51. Among the list are Sicily, Lombardy, Calabria, and Apulia along with Germany and Romania, Tuscany and Hungary, Poitiers, Normandy, England, Scotland, and Wales. But he also mentions attending an ancient fair in Crac, perhaps referring to the crusader city in Acre/Antioch, having traveled there via Venice (vv. 1191–1200).

52. Some silk moved into medieval France from Muslim Spain via Genoese merchants with contacts in Provence and Languedoc. While the Venetians looked toward the eastern Mediterranean, the Aegean, and Constantinople, the Genoese controlled the western Mediterranean with ties to Muslim Spain and North Africa. Abu-Lughod, *Before European Hegemony*, 105.

53. Constable, *Trade and Traders*, 177.

54. Constable lists "Pailes d'Aumarie, soie d'Aumarie, cendals d'Aumarie, mantel d'Aumarie, siglatons d'Espagne" (179) and explains that by the early thirteenth century (1225), Montpellier was importing silk by the pound from al-Andalus and Genoa (176). Sharon Kinoshita has shown how Almerían silks featured in twelfth-century epic and romance texts play a key role in the French cultural imagination, "Almería Silk and the French Feudal Imaginary: Toward a 'Material' History of the Medieval Mediterranean," in E. Jane Burns, ed., *Medieval Fabrications: Dress, Textiles, Clothwork and Other Cultural Imaginings* (New York: Palgrave, 2004), 165–76.

55. For two recent analyses and extensive bibliography for *Floire et Blancheflor* see Kinoshita, *Medieval Boundaries*, 78–95, and Burns, *Courtly Love Undressed*, 211–29.

56. Significantly, one manuscript version offers a more complex role for the heroine, staging Blancheflor as deftly assuming a subject position after her captivity in Babiloine. I analyze the process in *Courtly Love Undressed*, 226–29.

57. *Le Conte de Floire et Blanchflor*, ed. Jean-Luc Leclanche (Paris: Champion, 1980).

58. Lombard, 94.

59. Goitein, 1:102. In fact, Jewish merchants carried brocades from Muslim Spain to other regions of the Mediterranean from the ninth century (1:214); Sicilian exports of raw silk and silk cloth ranked second in volume in the Geniza records (1:102). See also Constable, 176.

60. Lombard, 98. Yet another route carried silk from Cyprus to Egypt and the Syro-Palestinian coast, then on to sites north of Antioch in Asia Minor (Goitein, 1:214). A Maghrebi silk merchant in Alexandria writes about merchants from Constantinople, Venice, Crete, and Sicilians all trading there (Goitein 4:168), and the Cairo Geniza shows Venetians, Pisans, and Genoans in Fustat and Alexandria (Balard, 36).

61. Constable, 176–77.

62. Goitein, 1: 211–13. Constable explains that slaves were the third major commodity distributed through Andalusi markets where, as early as the ninth century, Muslim and

Jewish merchants brought slaves to al-Andalus from eastern Europe and Christian Spain. A new trade developed by the thirteenth century in Cordoba, where selling Muslim slaves to Christian buyers replaced earlier sales of northern Christian slaves. And, in fact, many slaves sold in southern France and Italian port cities are termed "Saracen" or "Moors" (207). For a history of slavery in Italy, especially in the fourteenth and fifteenth centuries, see Steven A. Epstein, *Speaking of Slavery: Color, Ethnicity, and Human Bondage in Italy* (Ithaca, N.Y.: Cornell University Press, 2001).

63. Constable, 139.

64. Lombard, 214.

65. Jacoby, "Silk Economics," 226.

66. Steven Runciman, "Byzantine Trade and Industry," in *Cambridge Economic History of Europe*, vol. 2 (Cambridge: Cambridge University Press, 1952), 105–6. Women are included among the silk workers of Constantinople described by the *Book of Eparch*, Brand, 60.

67. Lombard, 216–17. In the provinces the silk industry was carried out by magnates employing servile labor, although the later silk industry of Corinth and Thebes seems not to have used slave labor ("Byzantine Trade and Industry," 106).

68. "Silk Economics," 226.

69. Maya Shatzmiller, *Labour in the Medieval Islamic World* (Leiden: Brill, 1994), 244, 249; 352, 358–59. See Chapter 2 below for details.

70. Boulnois, 238; Lombard, 90.

71. R. B. Sergeant, *Islamic Textiles: Material for a History up to the Mongol Conquest* (Beirut: Librairie du Liban, 1972), 157.

72. Thomas T. Allsen, *Commodity and Exchange in the Mongol Empire* (Cambridge: Cambridge University Press, 1997), 38–41.

73. Jacoby, "Silk Economics," 202; 217–18.

74. Constable, 146; Lombard, 192. Imitations of Baghdad-style silks were especially popular in Almería during the most prosperous Almoravid period (1107–43), exemplified by the shroud of San Pedro de Osma. See Cristina Partearroyo, "Almoravid and Almohad Textiles," in *Al-Andalus: The Art of Islamic Spain*, ed. Jerrilynn D. Dodds (New York: Metropolitan Museum of Art, 1992), 106. On gold brocades from Almería, see also R. B. Sergeant, *Islamic Textiles*, 169; Constable, 174.

75. The Muslim expansion in the eighth through the eleventh centuries fostered the establishment of silk factories under the Umayyads in Cordoba, Almería, Seville, and Malaga and under the Alglabids and later Fatimids in Sicily (Sergeant, 165–76; Lombard, 100–101). Idrisi lists the following fabrics as being produced in Almería on 800 silk looms: "des étoffes connues sous le nom de holla, de dibâdj, de siglaton, d'ispahâni, de djordjâni; des rideaux ornés de fleurs, des étoffes ornées de clous, de petits tapis, des étoffes connues sous le nom de 'attâbî (tabis), de mi'djar . . . ," Reinhart P. A. Dozy and Michael J. De Goeje, ed. and trans., *Edrisi, Description de l'Afrique et de l'Espagne* (Amsterdam: Oriental Press, 1969), 240. See also Goitein, 4:169; Constable, 145.

76. Goitein, 4:169.

77. Lombard, 90.

78. Jacoby, "Silk Economics," 221.

79. Lombard, 100; André Guillon, "La Soie sicilienne au Xe–XIe siècle," in *Byzantino-Sicula II: Miscellanea di Scritti in Memoria Di Giuseppe Rossi Taibbi* (Palermo: Instituto Siciliano di Studi Bizantini E Neoellenici Quaderni, 1975), 286.

80. Partearroyo, 106–8. On brocades from Almería see also E. Lévi-Provençal, *Histoire de l'Espagne musulmane* (Leiden: Brill, 1953), 309–11.

81. Patricia Baker, *Islamic Textiles* (London: British Museum Press, 1995), 44, 61.

82. Anne E. Wardwell, "*Panni Tartarici*: Eastern Islamic Silks Woven with Gold and Silver," *Islamic Art* 3 (1988–89): 95. See also the museum catalogue prepared by James C. Y. Watt and Anne E. Wardwell, *When Silk Was Gold* (New York: Metropolitan Museum of Art, 1997). Not only did silk works throughout southeast Spain actively imitate textiles produced in the eastern Mediterranean, but those western "copies" of eastern silks were also subsequently admired, purchased, and used in Egypt, sometimes even traveling beyond their original destination to sites as far north as Khurasan (Lombard, 99).

83. Paula Sanders, "Robes of Honor in Fatimid Egypt," in *Robes and Honor*, 230–33; Sergeant, 158–59.

84. Lombard, 100–101.

85. On labor mobility across Christian, Jewish, and Muslim silk-working communities in the medieval Mediterranean as the result of spontaneous movement, enforced deportation, or compulsory resettlement, see Jacoby, "Silk Economics," 223–25.

86. Goitein, 1:100–102.

87. Jacoby explains that silks came to the west from crusades, pilgrimage, and commerce with the Latin states in the Levant beginning around 1100, especially from Acre but also other cities under Frankish rule such as Antioch and Tripoli, which had populations of indigenous silk workers, and from cities still under Muslim rule such as Aleppo, Damascus, and Mosul, "Silk Economics," 230–31.

88. Jacoby, "Silk Economics," 240.

89. Balard, 210.

90. André E. Sayous, "Le Commerce de Marseille avec la Syrie au milieu du XIIIe siècle," *Revue des études historiques* 95 (1929): 400–401.

91. Along with cloth, money circulated between Marseille and the east, in particular "besants sarrasins d'Acre," as well as "de l'or filé" from Genoa and Lucca and at times from Montpellier (Sayous, 400–402).

92. The fictive history of this garment records the ready transfer of silk from secular to ecclesiastical use also attested by surviving textiles. See examples in Françoise Piponnier and Perrine Mane, *Dress in the Middle Ages*, trans. Caroline Beamish (New Haven: Yale University Press, 1997), 116; Rosamund Mack, *Bazaar to Piazza: Islamic Trade and Italian Art, 1300–1600* (Berkeley: University of California Press, 2002), 27.

93. Erec's embroidered coronation robe in *Erec et Enide*, specifically "l'uevre del drap et le portret," was executed, we are told, by four fairies (vv. 6681–82). We will examine another garment attributed to the work of a fairy in the discussion of *Le Roman de la Rose ou de Guillaume de Dole* in Chapter 3 below.

94. For a fuller discussion see Sharon Kinoshita, "Almería Silk and the French Feudal Imaginary," in Burns, ed., *Medieval Fabrications*.

95. If Enide's gift charts one key silk-trading vector from Muslim Spain into medieval France, Erec's offering to the church at Carnant suggests another major medieval silk route. Erec's contribution of 60 marks of silver is accompanied by a gold cross adorned with precious gems. Described as a piece of the true cross and said to have once belonged to the emperor Constantine (v. 2323–32), Erec's offering appears to be a relic from the silk-rich city of Constantinople, a source of diplomatic silks and relics to the Frankish west from the time of Charlemagne and earlier. See McCormick, 284, 723–24, 726.

CHAPTER 2. WOMEN SILK WORKERS FROM KING ARTHUR'S FRANCE TO KING ROGER'S PALERMO

1. See especially Roberta L. Krueger, *Women Readers and the Ideology of Gender in Old French Verse Romance* (Oxford: Oxford University Press, 1993).

2. See Peter Haidu, "The Hermit's Pottage: Deconstruction and History in *Yvain*," in *The Sower and His Seed: Essays on Chrétien de Troyes*, ed. Rupert T. Pickens (Lexington, Ky.: French Forum Publishers, 1983), 127–45. Tony Hunt contends that the liberation of the silkworkers at Pesme Aventure constitutes one of the two most important adventures in this romance, revealing the extent to which the narrative subverts both courtly love and the genre of courtly romance, "Le Chevalier au Lion: *Yvain Lionheart*," in Norris J. Lacy and Joan Trasker Grimbert, eds., *A Companion to Chrétien de Troyes* (Cambridge: D. S. Brewer, 2005), 156–68.

3. *Le Chevalier au lion (Yvain)*, ed. Mario Roques (Paris: Champion, 1978).

4. Gérald Brault provides a cogent summary of scholarly work on the episode of Pesme Aventure up to 1959, aligning the social realists such as Foulon, Jonin, and Cohen against Frappier and those who argue for the predominance of mythic elements in the scene. See his "Fonction et sens de l'épisode du Château de Pesme Aventure dans l'*Yvain* de Chrétien de Troyes," in *Mélanges de langue et de littérature françaises du Moyen Age et de la Renaissance offerts à Charles Foulon*, vol. 1 (Rennes: Institut de français, Université de Haute Bretagne, 1980), 59–64. Most recently, Monica Wright has analyzed the episode in relation to contrasting gift and merchantile economies. See her "De Fil d'Or et de Soie: Making Textiles in Twelfth-Century French Romance," *Medieval Clothing and Textiles* 2 (2006): 61–72. A pathbreaking essay by Danielle Régnier-Bohler discussed the function of domestic space among aristocratic heroines, some of whom do cloth work but in settings very different from the silkworks in *Yvain*. See her "Geste, parole, et clôture: Les représentations du gynécée dans la littérature médiévale du XIIIe au XVe siècle," in *Mélanges de langue et de littérature médiévales offerts à Alice Planche* (Paris: Les Belles Lettres, 1984), 393–404.

5. The lord later remarks, "En cest chastel a establie/ une molt fiere deablie/ qu'il me convient a maintenir" (vv. 5461–63; In this castle a powerful devilry was established that I am forced to observe). The custom was established through the weakness of a young king

visiting this realm from the Isle of Maidens: "Et li rois qui grant peor ot/ s'an delivra si com il pot: si jura qu'il anvoieroit/ chascun an, tant con vis seroit,/ ceanz, de ses puceles, trante;/ si fust quites par ceste rante;/ et devisié fu a jurer/ et cist treüz devoit durer/ tant con li dui maufé durroient" (vv. 5273–81; And the king, terrified, survived as best he could: he swore to send thirty maidens from his kingdom every year for as long as he lived. This payment secured his release. It was settled by oath that the tribute would last as long as the two demons were alive).

6. For a description of the more standard plot see Jean Frappier, *Etude sur* Yvain ou le Chevalier au lion *de Chrétien de Troyes* (Paris: SEDES, 1969), 125–28.

7. As *Yvain* looks these maidens over from head to toe, the standard catalogue of female attributes is replaced by details of the women's famished bodies and ragged clothing. One telling detail remains from the usual line-up: their eyes are downcast, not in blushing modesty, as is the case with many other romance heroines, but because they are so abused and beleaguered (*acorees*), "ne lor ialz n'en pueent retreire/ de terre, tant sont acorees"(vv. 5204–5; They cannot raise their eyes because they are so abused/beleaguered).

8. To be sure, the model of aristocratic marriage advanced in many courtly narratives does not convey the complexity or nuance of historical conjugal households and the significant rights often exercised by women within them as recorded in abundant documentation recently analyzed by Theodore Evergates. See his *The Aristocracy in the County of Champagne, 1100–1300* (Philadelphia: University of Pennsylvania Press, 2007), esp. 82–100.

9. Krueger, *Women Readers*, 71, 74.

10. Perhaps the closest literary parallel is found in a medieval Spanish ballad. One of the "romances juglarescos" features a curious scene of "Dona Alda" in Paris accompanied by three hundred ladies who are said to perform a number of tasks, among them "Las ciento hilaban oro,—las ciento tejen cendal (One hundred of them spin gold, one hundred weave silk cloth), XXXIX, v. 6, *Spanish Ballads*, ed. S. Griswold Morley (New York: Henry Holt, 1912), 55. The ballad likely postdates the French text, however.

11. David Herlihy, *Opera Muliebria: Women and Work in Medieval Europe* (Philadelphia: Temple University Press, 1990), 81–83.

12. Ibid.

13. A similar lapse occurs in Peter Haidu's article on *Yvain*, where allusion to the small scale production of wool and linen are invoked to explain silk making, "The Hermit's Pottage," 140.

14. This despite David Jacoby's curious assertion that Chrétien's *Yvain* does not mention silk weaving, "Silk Crosses the Mediterranean," in G. Airaldi, ed., *Le vie del Mediterraneo. Idee, uomini, oggetti* (Genoa: Università degli studi di Genova, 1997), 67, n. 83.

15. Krijnie Ciggaar, "Chrétien de Troyes et la matière byzantine: Les demoiselles du château de Pesme Aventure," *Cahiers de civilisation médiévale* 32 (1989): 328. Ciggaar suggests further that the story of women working in Palermo might have been carried to France by Eleanor of Aquitaine, who transited the island en route to France on her return from the Second Crusade or by Henry the Liberal, who could have learned of the Palermitan silk works while in Constantinople, 329. To be sure, Roger II's lavish palace in

202 NOTES TO PAGES 43–44

Palermo with its enclosed silk workshop and many enclosed courtyards provides a striking corollary for the configuration of buildings represented in the silk workers scene in *Yvain*. See Hubert Houben, *Roger II of Sicily: A Ruler Between East and West*, trans. Graham A. Loud and Diane Milburn (Cambridge: Cambridge University Press, 2002), 129. Following Roger II, his son William I ruled from 1154 to 66 and subsequently his grandson, William II or "William the Good" from 1166 to 89, the latter during the time that Chrétien's *Yvain* was composed (1178–82). See Karla Mallette, *The Kingdom of Sicily, 1100–1250: A Literary History* (Philadelphia: University of Pennsylvania Press, 2005), 5.

16. Philippe Sénac, *Le Monde musulman: Des origines au XIe siècle* (Paris: SEDES, 1999), 185; Jacoby, "Silk in Western Byzantium," in *Trade, Commodities and Shipping in the Medieval Mediterranean* (Brookfield, Vt.: Variorum, 1997), 467–68; Wilhelm Heyd, *Histoire du Commerce du Levant au Moyen Age*, vol. 2 (Amsterdam: Adolf M. Hakkert, 1959), 695; Maurice Lombard, *Les Textiles dans le monde musulman du VIIe au XIIe siècle* (Paris: Mouton, 1978), 100; Jacoby, "Silk Economics and Cross-cultural Artistic Interaction: Byzantium, the Muslim World, and the Christian West," *Dumbarton Oaks Papers* 58 (2004): 227. Robert A. Hall, Jr., suggested in 1941, in fact, that the maidens might represent Christian slaves employed in Muslim silk works, "The Silk Factory in Chrestien de Troyes' Yvain," *Modern Language Notes* 56 (1941): 418–22.

17. S. D. Goitein, "Sicily and Southern Italy in the Cairo Geniza Documents," *Archivio storico per la Sicilia orientale* 67 (1971): 9–33; David Abulafia, "The Italian Other: Greeks, Muslims, and Jews," in *Italy in the Central Middle Ages*, ed. David Abulafia (Oxford: Oxford University Press, 2004), 223.

18. S. D. Goitein, *A Mediterranean Society: The Jewish Communities of the Arab World as Portrayed in the Documents of the Cairo Geniza*, vol. 1 (Berkeley: University of California Press, 1967), 102.

19. Jacoby, "Silk Economics," 227; Michael Angold, *The Byzantine Empire 1025–1204* (London: Longman, 1985), 250. The Arab geographer records the presence of Muslim embroiderers in the artisan's quarter of Palermo as early as the tenth century. See Sénac, *Le Monde musulman*, 152.

20. Jacoby, "Silk Economics," 226–27.

21. David Abulafia, "The Crown and the Economy Under Roger II and His Successors," in *Italy, Sicily, and the Mediterranean, 1100–1400* (London: Variorum Reprints, 1987), 7. Records from the Cairo Geniza document Palermo as the hub of Mediterranean trade in the eleventh century with silk as its main export (Goitein, *A Mediterranean Society*, 1:102; and his "Sicily and Southern Italy.") The city was known as a center of Mediterranean trade where merchants from Muslim North Africa and Spain interacted with Italian Christians and developed strong mercantile ties with Cairo, Alexandria, and Egypt generally (Houben, 12; Goitein, ed. and trans., *Letters of Medieval Jewish Traders* [Princeton, N.J.: Princeton University Press, 1974], 23). Jeremy Johns has documented in detail the close relation between the Norman court in Palermo and court culture in Cairo, "The Norman Kings of Sicily and the Fatimid Caliphate," *Anglo-Norman Studies* 15 (1993): 145–47.

22. "She opens up a silk cloth on her knees and sews with one gold thread and an-

other of silk," Michel Zink, ed., *Les Chansons de toile* (Paris: Champion, 1977), vv. 2–3, p. 96.

23. *Guillaume de Palerne, roman du XIIIe siècle*, ed. Alexandre Micha (Geneva: Droz, 1990), vv. 8635–42.

24. "in auro pannisque sericis imperator Bizancius et rex Siculus gloriantur," *De Nugis curialium: The Courtier's Trifles*, ed. M. R. Jones, revised C. N. L. Brooke and R. A. B. Mynors (Oxford: Oxford University Press, 1983), translated as "The emperor of Constantinople and the King of Sicily boast themselves in gold and silken webs," 45. The account of textiles actually produced at the Norman silk works in Palermo included in *The History of the Tyrants of Sicily*, ascribed to Hugo Falcandus (ca. 1190), gives few specifics, but also mentions ornamentation of "gold threaded into silk": "multa ornamenta in quibus et sericis aurem intexitur," *La Historia o liber de regno sicilie* (Rome: Gia Corsini, 1897), 180; and *The History of the Tyrants of Sicily by "Hugo Falcandus" 1154–69*, trans. Graham A. Loud and Thomas Wiedemann (Manchester: Manchester University Press, 1998), 259.

25. Desrosiers, *Soieries et autres textiles de l'Antiquité au XVIe siècle* (Paris: Réunion des musées nationaux, 2004), 152–54; Cat. 70, Cl. 3054.

26. Félix Bourquelot, *Etudes sur les foires de Champagne, sur la nature, l'étendue et les règles du commerce qui s'y faisait au XIIe, XIIIe et XIVe siècles* (Brionne, France: Le Portulan, 1865), 268.

27. *Le Quotidien au temps des fabliaux*, ed. Danielle Alexandre-Bidon and Marie-Thérèse Lorcin (Paris: Picard, 2003), 211 cites "tissu d'or" in the fabliau "Pleine bourse de sens," v. 63. For "draz dorez" see the "Dit des Marchéans," in *Recueil des fabliaux des XIIIe et XIVe siècles*, ed. Anatole de Montaiglon and Gaston Raynaud, (Paris, 1877; rpt. New York: Burt Franklin, 1963), 126.

28. Francisque Michel, *Recherches sur le commerce, la fabrication et l'usage des étoffes de soie, d'or et d'argent et autres tissus précieux en Occident, principalement en France pendant le Moyen Age*, vol. 2 (Paris: Imprimerie de Crapelet, 1852), 112–13, 118, 122, 140–44.

29. Lombard, 234.

30. Bourquelot, 269–70. He also cites tax records indicating that "fil d'or" was sold at the fairs of Champagne, possibly even alongside "draps d'or," 270.

31. Goitein, 1:102, 212.

32. See, for example, Marco Polo, *Le Devisement du monde*, ed. Philippe Ménard, vol. 1 (Geneva: Droz, 2001), 139, 141–42 and note p. 198. For an English translation see *The Description of the World*, ed. A. C. Maile and Paul Pelliot (London: George Routledge and Sons, 1938; rpt. New York: AMS Press, 1976), 98, 100–101.

33. Thomas T. Allsen, *Commodity and Exchange in the Mongol Empire* (Cambridge: Cambridge University Press, 1997), 44, quoting Maile and Pelliot, 183. Anne Wardwell explains that although Marco Polo refers repeatedly to these two kinds of brocade (*nasich* and *nac*), he does not indicate what they look like, "*Panni Tartarici*: Eastern Islamic Silks Woven with Gold and Silver (Thirteenth and Fourteenth Centuries)," *Islamic Art* 3 (1988–89): 95. Allsen explains that in the case of *nasij*, ornamental gold threads were added to silk cloth to produce a form of silk brocade that was literally cloth of silk and gold, "Robing in the Mongolian Empire," in Stewart Gregory, ed., *Robes and Honor*, 305. For a

detailed categorization of Central Asian and Middle Eastern cloths of silk and gold silks see Wardwell's appendix I, 133.

34. Allsen, "Robing," 2–4; Wardwell, 115–17.

35. Allsen, *Commodity and Exchange*, 1–25.

36. Frédéric Godefroy, *Dictionnaire de l'ancienne langue française* (Paris, 1888; rpt. Vaduz: Liechtenstein: Scientific Periodicals Establishment, 1961), 632.

37. Godefroy cites examples from *Raoul de Cambrai*, "La damoisele a fait mander li rois/ Et ele vint vestue d'un orfrois" and from *Floire et Blanchflor*, "Lors vesti un bliaut d'orfroiz," 631.

38. For examples of extant "banded" Spanish silks from the thirteenth century in which the bands are woven into the fabric itself, see Rosamond Mack, *Bazaar to Piazza: Islamic Trade and Italian Art 1300–1600* (Berkeley: University of California Press, 2002), 33, Figure 21.

39. A more expansive use of the term is found in the description of Richesse's gown in the thirteenth-century *Roman de la Rose* where "orfrois" refers to designs woven in golden thread on silk cloth: "La porpre fu toute orfroisie/ Si ot portraites a orfrois/ Estoires de dus et de rois" (vv. 1055–57; the silk was completely covered with gold thread; stories of dukes and kings were portrayed on it in gold thread).

40. R. Glazier offers this definition in his *Historic Textile Fabrics* (New York: Scribner's, 1923), 112.

41. "Un galon tissé ou brodé d'or," Desrosiers, *Soieries*, 483.

42. Françoise Piponnier, "Usages et diffusion de la soie en France à la fin du Moyen Age," in *La Seta in Europa Sec. XIII-XX*, ed. Simonetta Cavaciocchi (Florence: Instituto internazionale di storia economica, 1993), 788. Piponnier defines "orfrois" as "des bandes brodéees en application." Victor Gay defines "orfrois" simply as "parement, galon brodé, frangéé d'or" and gives examples from the fourteenth and fifteenth centuries that specify "orfrois" in terms of place such as "orfrois de Rome . . . de Paris . . . de Florence . . . de Venise," *Glossaire archéologique du Moyen Age et de la Renaissance*, vol. 2 (Paris: Librairie de la société bibliographique, 1887), 181–82.

43. Desrosiers, *Soieries*, 381–91.

44. Sophie Desrosiers catalogues an embroidered "fragment de galon de Palerme," of "soie et fil d'or" from the second half of the twelfth century, used for the king of Sicily's clothing (*Soieries*, number 68, p. 150) and a "fragment de galon" in "soie et fil d'or" made in Palermo in the eleventh or twelfth century (number 67, p. 148). By contrast, she provides documentation of a "fragment de tapisserie de soie sur fond d'or" from Palermo, dated to the second or third quarter of the 12th century (number 69, p. 151), along with the well-known Palermitan silk at the Cluny Museum described here as a "fragment d'une bande en tapisserie" (number 70, p. 153 and Figure 4 above). The latter three fabrics (numbers 68, 69, 70) are thought to be related to the lining fabrics of Roger II's famous mantle, discussed below. On William's hose see Ruth Grönwoldt, "Sicilian Textiles Employed in the Imperial Coronation in Vienna," in *La Seta in Europa*,

45. Sophie Desrosiers, "Les Soieries comme source historique (Europe, XIII–XXe siècle)" in *La Seta in Europa*, 498–502.

46. Florence Lewis May, *Silk Textiles of Spain: Eighth to Fifteenth Century* (New York: Hispanic Society of America, 1957), 11–13, 66.

47. May, *Silk Textiles*, 17. Shared textile construction continues between Spain and Sicily into the thirteenth century, when Muslim weavers at the Aragonese court produce fabrics related to those manufactured in Sicily. See Dominique Cardon, "De L'Espagne à l'Italie: Hypothèses concernant un groupe de soieries médiévales à fond de losanges lisérés et bandes de samit façonné," *Techniques et culture* 34 (1999): 139–57.

48. Desrosiers, *Soieries*, catalogue number 64.

49. May, 51. The Spanish cope of St. Valerio dated to the thirteenth century bears an orphrey of white silk with blue borders and a woven pattern of confronted birds in gold thread amid images of the tree of life (p. 72, figure 45 and detail p. 56, figure 38). On this textile see also Rosa María Martín i Ros, "Les vêtements liturgiques dits de Saint Valère: Leur place parmi les tissus hispano-mauresques du XIIIe siècle," *Techniques et culture* 34 (1999): 49–66, and Gabriel Vial, "Les Vêtements liturgiques dits de Saint Valère: Etude technique de pseudo-lampas à fond (ou effet) double-étoffe," *Techniques et culture* 34 (1999): 67–81.

50. "Usages et diffusion," 788–89.

51. Mack, 29, #14; Jacoby, "Silk Economics," 204; See Anabelle Simon-Cahn, "The Fermo Chasuble of St. Thomas Becket and Hispano-Mauresque Cosmological Silks: Some Speculations on the Adaptive Reuse of Textiles," *Murquanas* 10 (1993): 1–5.

52. Mack, 27. Mack here defines "orphrey" as an ornamental band, usually embroidered.

53. Sharon Kinoshita has shown how Almerían silks featured in twelfth-century epic and romance texts play a key role in the French feudal imaginary, "Almería Silk and the French Feudal Imaginary: Toward a 'Material' History of the Medieval Mediterranean," in E. Jane Burns, ed., *Medieval Fabrications*, 165–76.

54. Jean Rychner, ed., *Les Lais de Marie de France* (Paris: Champion, 1973).

55. Cristina Partearroyo, "Almoravid and Almohad Textiles," in *Al-Andalus: The Art of Islamic Spain*, ed. Jerrilynn D. Dodds (New York: Metropolitan Museum of Art, 1992), 112.

56. E. Chartraire, *Inventaire du trésor de l'église primatiale et métropolitaine de Sens* (Paris: A. Picard, 1897), 20, 29–32.

57. "Un vaisselet ad fet forgier;/ Unques n'i ot fer ne acier,/ Tuz fu d'or fin od bones pieres,/ Mut precïuses e mut chieres;/ Covercle i ot tres bien asis./ Le laüstic ad dedenz mis,/ Puis fist la chasse enseeler./ Tuz jurs l'ad fete od lui porter," vv. 149–56. (He had a vessel made, not from iron or steel, but entirely of gold and costly precious gems with a nicely fitted cover. He put the nightingale inside, had the reliquary sealed, and carried it with him forever.)

58. Grönwoldt postulates several additional pieces of tablet weaving that might have been made in the royal workshop in Palermo: a sword-belt of the twelfth and thirteenth century with stylized tree and animal motifs on a golden ground, and the small gold braids in tablet-weave that decorate the Utrecht alb; "Sicilian Textiles," 899.

59. "By order of the magnificent Holy King Guljälm who is highly honoured

through God, supported by his Majesty and victorious by His vigour," translated by Grönwoldt, 896.

60. See accounts given by Grönwoldt, "Sicilian Textiles," and Rotraud Bauer, "The Mantle of King Roger II and Related Textiles in the Schatzkammer of Vienna: The Royal Workshop at the Court of Palermo," in *Interdisciplinary Approach to the Study and Conservation of Medieval Textiles*, ed. Rosalia Varoli-Piazza (Palermo: International Council of Museums, 1998).

61. Grönwoldt, 896.

62. Grönwoldt, 898.

63. *Encyclopedia of Islam*, ed. P. J. Bearman et al. (Leiden: Brill, 2000), 534–37.

64. See Yedida Stillman, *Arab Dress from the Dawn of Islam to Modern Times: A Short History* (Leiden: Brill, 2000), 120–37. For examples of *tiraz* fabrics see Desrosiers, *Soieries*, catalogue numbers 14–22, pp. 75–88; and Florence Day, "Dated Tiraz in the Collection of the University of Michigan," *Ars Islamica* 4 (1937).

65. Patricia L. Baker, *Islamic Textiles* (London: British Museum Press, 1995), 53.

66. R. B. Serjeant, *Islamic Textiles: Material for a History up to the Mongol Conquest* (Beruit: Librairie du Liban, 1972), 147.

67. Baker, 57; Lombard, 220.

68. Baker, 57.

69. H. A. Elsberg and R. Guest, "The Veil of Saint Anne," *The Burlington Magazine for Connoisseurs* 68, No. 396 (1936): 140–47. Byzantine textiles also survive that bear the names, either woven or embroidered, of what seem to be the owner or maker of the workshop in which they were manufactured (Jacoby, "Silk Economics," 202). Indeed, Byzantine rulers had their own *gynaecea* in Egypt as elsewhere where they developed a distinctive Coptic style marked by embroidered decorative patches: squares or roundels and banded shoulder seams. By the tenth century, the Byzantines were well aware of Islamic tiraz bands and fascinated by Kufic calligraphy (Jacoby, "Silk Economics," 220; Georgette Cornu and Marielle Martiniani-Reber, "Etoffes et Vêtements dans le Ménologe de Basile II: Reflets des courants d'échange entre Byzance et le monde Islamique," *Quaderni di Studi Arabi* 15 [1997]: 51–52). In iconography from the Middle Byzantine period, the square and circular attachments on Early Byzantine tunics begin to be replaced by armbands often bearing pseudo-Kufic inscriptions, probably inspired, according to Maria Parani, by *tiraz* worn by Muslim nobles in early Islamic times (Maria G. Parani, *Reconstructing the Reality of Images; Byzantine Material Culture and Religious Iconography, Eleventh– Fifteenth Centuries* [Leiden: Brill, 2003], 54).

70. Janet Snyder, "Cloth from the Promised Land: Appropriated Islamic Tiraz in Twelfth-century French Sculpture," in E. Jane Burns, ed., *Medieval Fabrications*, 147–64; and Snyder's "Clothing as Communication: A Study of Clothing and Textiles in Northern French Early Gothic Sculpture," Ph.D. diss., Columbia University, 1996.

71. Lombard, 219.

72. Stillman, 120–37. The tiraz system of Muslim silk factories flourished in Spain under the Umayyads (780–1013) and in Egypt under the Fatimids (910–1171) and had been equally highly valued by the Abassids in Iraq (750–1258). See Lombard, 220.

73. Baker, 53.

74. *Encyclopedia of Islam*, 537.

75. Lombard, 234.

76. The earliest known Islamic *tiraz* workshop was set up by the Umayyad caliph Hisham in the eighth century, but soon all major Muslim textile centers included them. See Baker, 53; Lombard, 220.

77. Lombard, 220; Serjeant, 117; Bourquelot, 1, 269.

78. See Haidu, "The Hermit's Pottage," 127–45.

79. See also the earlier reference to "Moorish" or dark-skinned enemies such as the guardian of the wild bulls, "Un vileins qui resanbloit Mor,/ leiz et hideus a desmesure" (vv. 286–87; A peasant who resembled a Moor, extremely ugly and hideous), dressed in skins (vv. 307–10); and to a "vilain lez," "hideus," and "noirs" (vv. 711–13).

80. This possibility was suggested by R. A. Hall, in *Modern Language Notes*, 1941.

81. For the substantial bibliography of rape in medieval French literature see Kathryn Gravdal, *Ravishing Maidens: Writing Rape in Medieval French Literature* (Philadelphia: University of Pennsylvania Press, 1991), and more generally, Elizabeth Robertson and Christine M. Rose, eds., *Representing Rape in Medieval and Early Modern Literature* (New York: Palgrave, 2001). Stephen Steele's article "Rape in the Eye of the Reader: Sexual Violence in Chrétien's *Yvain*" curiously does not mention this key passage. *Dalhousie French Studies* 30 (1995): 11–16.

82. Maya Shatzmiller, *Labour in the Medieval Islamic World* (Leiden: Brill, 1994), 244, 249; 352, 358–59.

83. Mallette, 2–3.

84. Serjeant, 192.

85. Translation is from Jeremy Johns, *Arabic Administration in Norman Sicily: The Royal Diwan* (Oxford: Oxford University Press, 2002), 213.

86. Mallette, 150; translation from Johns, *Arabic Administration*, 213.

87. "puellisque et eunuchis qui regi regineque serviunt deputate," *Historia*, 178. For further discussion of both Ibn Jubayr and Hugo Falcandus's accounts of slaves in Palermo, see Johns, *Arabic Administration*, 247–56.

88. Falcandus, 259–60.

89. Falcandus, 259; my emphasis.

90. Herlihy, 85. Speaking of female slaves in the west more generally, Wilhelm Heyd contends that they were preferred to males because they could be used as domestic servants and to please their masters sexually in contrast to the paradigm in force in Egypt, where male slaves were considered most desirable as recruits for the army. *Histoire du Commerce du Levant au Moyen Age*, vol. 1 (Amsterdam: Adolf M. Hakkert, 1959), 561–63.

91. See David Abulafia, *Italy, Sicily, and the Mediterranean*, 8; and Anna Muthesius, "Sicily," in *Cambridge History of Western Textiles*, ed. David Jenkins (Cambridge: Cambridge University Press, 2003), 331.

92. Jacoby shows that in both Greece and Palermo men were employed alongside women, "Silk in Western Byzantium Before the Fourth Crusade," 467–68, 485–88; "Silk Crosses the Mediterranean," 67.

93. Angold, 249, citing J. L. Van Dieten, ed., *Nicetae Choniate Historia* (Berlin, 1975), 74; Charles Brand "Some Byzantine Women of Thebes and Elsewhere," in *To Hellenikon: Studies in Honor of Speros Vryonis, Jr.*, ed. John S. Langdon et al., vol. 1 (New Rochelle, N.Y.: Aristide D. Carnatzas, 1993), 59–60; Ciggaar, 328. Jacoby disagrees, claiming that although Niketas Chionates suggests that Greek women of high social status and skilled in weaving were among the artisans abducted from Corinth, "such women may have occasionally engaged in domestic silk weaving [but] it is inconceivable that they should have worked full-time in market-oriented industrial enterprises," 467–68. He does not explain why such female participation might be "inconceivable," suggesting only that the Greek chronicler's reference to women's fine weaving of luxury textiles might be a literary topos, "Silk in Western Byzantium," 468. In another context, see Ruth Mazo Karras's explanation of weaving as an index of feminine virtue in medieval England in her "'This Skill in a Woman Is by No Means to Be Despised': Weaving and the Gender Division of Labor in the Middle Ages," in Burns, ed., *Medieval Fabrications*, 89–104.

94. Jacoby, "Silk in Western Byzantium," 458–59.

95. See E. Jane Burns, *Courtly Love Undressed: Reading Through Clothes in Medieval French Culture* (Philadelphia: University of Pennsylvania Press, 2002), 88–118.

96. And later, "La cortine qu'ele ot tissue" (v. 1185), Chrétien de Troyes, *Philomena*, ed. C. de Boer (Paris: Editions Paul Geuthner, 1909). See also "Avuec c'iert si bone ovriere/ D'ovrer une porpre vermoille/ Qu'an tot le mont n'ot sa paroille" (In addition she was such an accomplished weaver/embroiderer that no one in the world could equal her at weaving/embroidering red silk), vv. 188–90.

97. With the help of an old woman who "knows how to spin and weave" ("vilaine filer et tistre savoit," v. 871), Philomena communicates her plight to her sister Progne, enabling the latter to secure the mutilated innocent *pucele*'s release. For an extended discussion see E. Jane Burns, *Bodytalk: When Women Speak in Old French Literature* (Philadelphia: University of Pennsylvania Press, 1993), 111–18.

98. Chrétien de Troyes, *Cligès*, ed. Alexandre Micha (Paris: Champion, 1957).

99. "li deus d'Amors, s'il la veïst,/ ne ja amer ne la feïst/ autrui se lui meïsmes non./ Por li server devenist hon" (vv. 5370–74; If the God of love had seen her, he would have made her fall in love with no one but himself. He would have served her as a liegeman).

100. I find no evidence in these statements to support Yvan G. Lepage's contention that the freed workers have no interest in earning money but want simply to return to the Isle of Maidens and pursue their "oisiveté"! "Encore les Trois Cents Pucelles," *Cahiers de civilisation médiévale* 34 (1991): 159–66.

101. Jean Renart, *Galeran de Bretagne: Roman du XIIIe siècle*, ed. Lucien Foulet (Paris: Champion, 1925). For a discussion of a similar reference to silk making in Jean Renart's *Escoufle*, see Sahar Amer, *Border Crossings: Love Between Women in Medieval French and Arabic Literatures* (Philadephia: University of Pennsylvania Press, 2008).

102. This failed knight, who leaves his homeland to seek "news" (noveles, v. 5252) from courts in neighboring regions, falls victim to "mal ëur" (v. 5256) endemic at the Chastel de Pesme Aventure, and succumbs as would a vulnerable "lamb" (aignelet, v. 5272), we are told. It seems his sinister bargain to send an annual tribute of thirty maidens results

not from previously exploitive practices or some character flaw, but from the terror he experiences when confronted with the violent practices in these foreign lands (v. 5273).

CHAPTER 3. WOMEN WORKING SILK FROM CONSTANTINOPLE TO LOTHARINGIA

1. Eva Rodhe Lundquist, *La Mode et son vocabulaire* (Goteborg, Sweden: Wettergren and Kerber, 1950), 75–77. For the reference to sewing supplies see Jean Renart, *Le Roman de la Rose ou de Guillaume de Dole*, ed. Félix Lecoy (Paris: Champion, 1962), vv. 275–76, where "fil de filieres" rimes with "*aumosnieres*," and for an important example of the *aumosniere* as a love token containing the heroine's brooch, vv. 1228, 4412, 4432. See below pp. 86–87.

2. Guillaume de Lorris et Jean de Meun, *Le Roman de la Rose*, ed. Armand Strubel (Paris: Librairie générale française, 1992).

3. E. Chartraire, *Inventaire du trésor de l'église primatiale et métropolitaine de Sens* (Paris: A. Picard, 1897), 29–32, 41.

4. G. B. Depping, *Régelemens sur les arts et métiers de Paris rédigés au XIIIe siècle* (Paris: Imprimerie de Crapelet, 1837), 382–86. See Sharon Farmer, "Biffes, Tiretaines, and Aumônières: The Role of Paris in the International Textile Markets of the Thirteenth and Fourteenth Centuries," in *Medieval Clothing and Textiles*, ed. Robin Netherton and Gale R. Owen-Crocker, 2 (2006): 87.

5. "Silk Economics and Cross-Cultural Artistic Interaction: Byzantium, the Muslim World, and the Christian West," *Dumbarton Oaks Papers* 58 (2004): 208.

6. Farmer, "Weavers and Spinners in the Wool, Silk, and Linen Industries in Thirteenth-Century Paris: A Comparative Analysis," in manuscript; Boileau, *Le livre des métiers et corporations de la ville de Paris, XIIIe siècle*, ed. René de Lespinasse and François Bonnardot (Paris: Imprimerie Nationale, 1879).

7. *La légende de l'Empereur Constant*, ed. James Coveney (Paris: Société d'Edition les Belles Lettres, 1955).

8. "Car tout cil de Griesse a cel jour/ Paiien et masicreant estoient" (vv. 192–93; at that time all Greeks were pagans and unbelievers).

9. Chrétien de Troyes, *Le Chevalier au Lion*, ed. Mario Roques (Paris: Champion, 1964).

10. To be sure, some references to *aumosnieres* indicate no special decoration, as is the case with repeated allusions to the *aumosniere* filled with "besans" in Chrétien de Troyes, *Guillaume d'Angleterre*, ed. A. J. Holden (Geneva: Droz, 1988), vv. 739, 743, 2793, 2799, 2802.

11. *L'Escoufle: roman d'aventure*, ed. H. Michelant and P. Meyer (Geneva: Droz, 1894). For an extended discussion of the function of this *aumosniere* as an indication of female same-sex attachments in *Escoufle*, see Sahar Amer, *Border Crossings: Love Between Women in Medieval French and Arabic Literatures* (Philadelphia: University of Pennsylvania Press, 2008).

12. The term "opere saraceno" is used in the thirteenth century to describe the bor-

ders of vestments at St. Paul's Cathedral, London. See Francisque Michel, *Recherches sur le commerce, la fabrication et l'usage des étoffes de soie, d'or et d'argent, et autres tissus précieux en Occident, principalement en France pendant le Moyen Age*, vol. 1 (Paris: Imprimerie de Crapelet, 1852), 360.

13. The text of the *Empereur Constant* survives in two versions, a 630-line *dit* in octosyllabic rimed couplets and a 408-line *conte* in prose, both in the Picard dialect and published together as *La Légende de l'Empereur Constant*, ed. James Coveney. The *dit*, which is the subject of this chapter, exists in a single manuscript that also contains *Le Roman de la Rose*, an untitled love poem, and *Le Plait de droit et de l'evesque* (Coveney, 7–8).

14. See Jean Rychner, "Fresne," in *Les Lais de Marie de France* (Paris: Champion, 1973), vv. 123–15; and on the significance of the silk coverlet in *Le Fresne*, E. Jane Burns, *Courtly Love Undressed: Reading Through Clothes in Medieval French Literature* (Philadelphia: University of Pennsylvania Press, 2002), 191–92. The silk coverlet in *Le Dit de l'Empereur Constant* underwrites Constant's father's earlier prediction that his newly born son will eventually become emperor, "De Griesse(s) sera cournonnés,/ Empereres de ceste ville,/ Rois del roiaume de Sesille,/ De Romme emper[er]es sera" (vv. 148–51; He will be crowned emperor of Greece, King of Sicily, and he will be emperor of Rome).

15. The text explains that the boy is called "Coustant" because the medical treatments necessary to heal the substantial wounds he suffered from Florien were very "costly" (vv. 235–36). But of course another resonance accompanies this one since Constantinople, in the medieval western European imagination, stood as one of the most extravagantly wealthy and opulent cities.

16. Sebelinne states, "A il ichi rice tresor? Ciertes, veés chi la plus bielle piersonne d'onme ke jou onkes mes veïse a nul jour mais de ma vie. Et il aporte laitres . . . Les deux pucielles s'aprocierent dou varlet et li enblerent ses laitres, et les lut la fille l'enpereur " (vv. 243–48; Isn't this a rich treasure? To be sure, this is the handsomest man I have even seen in my life and he's carrying a letter. . . . The two young women approach the young man, take the letter, and the emperor's daughter reads it).

17. See for example, Guillaume de Lorris, *Le Roman de la Rose*, ed. Armand Strubel, vv. 2153–54: "aumoniere de soie" (a small silk purse); Jean Renart, *L'Escoufle*, ed. H. and P. Meyer, vv. 3828–32: "L'anel mist en une aumosniere/ D'un samit vermeil, fin et frois/ Ki pent a son tissu d'orfrois/ K'ele ot le jor au primes chaint" (She put the ring in a small purse made of heavy red silk, refined and enhanced with gold, that she had put on at daybreak); and *Le Roman du Castelain de Couci et de la Dame de Fayel*, ed. Maurice Delbouille (Paris: SATF, 1936), vv. 5338–41, where we are told that the lady "Est a son coffre alee prendre/ Deniers, s'emplit une aumoniere/ Qui de soie estoit boinne et ciere" (went to her coffer to get coins, which she put in a small purse made of high quality costly silk).

18. Judith Herrin, *Women in Purple: Rulers of Medieval Byzantium* (Princeton, N.J.: Princeton University Press, 2001), 100. In the thirteenth century, the Egyptian Shajarat-al-Durr forges the Sultan's signature before literally becoming Sultan herself in 1249. See Sahar Amer, "Traveling Sexualities," in manuscript.

19. *La Légende de l'Empereur Constant*, ed. James Coveney, 94.

20. *Macaire*, ed. F. Guessard (Paris: A. Frank, 1866), ii.

21. See lines 403–6 of the prose version included in Coveney's edition.

22. See also the exordium to Spring that opens the tale and the allusion to Fortune, vv. 1–45. The character Florien in the *Dit de l'Empereur Constant* may bear some textual reference to the protagonist Florien, son of Flore, in *Le Roi Flore et la Belle Jeanne*, identified as a future king of Constantinople, Coveney, 93–94.

23. Coveney, 100.

24. See E. Jane Burns, "Love's Stitches Undone: Women's Work in the *chansons de toile*," in *Courtly Love Undressed*, 88–118.

25. Danièle Alexandre-Bidon and Marie Thérèse Lorcin, *Le Quotidien au temps des fabliaux* (Paris: Picard, 2003), cite the following: "Boivin" vv. 6–19, which describes a young man disguised as a peasant with "douze deniers" in his "bourse" (vv. 17–18; p. 173); "Du pretre et des deux ribauds" details even poorer individuals who, without the benefit of a leather bourse, would simply tie their coins in a knot in their chemise (vv. 68–77, p. 267); and "Des braies au cordelier" (vv. 275–82) tells of a man reaching into his "bourse" to pay his "ecot" (v. 277; p. 267).

26. Alexandre Bidon, 279, figs. 180–81.

27. Alexandre-Bidon, 274, fig. 174; 278, fig. 179.

28. Alexandre-Bidon, fig. 181.

29. Alexandre-Bidon, 278. See the inventory provided in E. Chartraire, 29–32, 41.

30. Brian Spencer, *Pilgrim Souvenirs and Secular Badges: Medieval Finds from Excavations in London*: vol. 7 (London: Stationery Office, 1998), 314–15.

31. Cited in Francisque Michel, *Recherches sur le commerce*, vol. 2, 353.

32. Alexandre-Bidon, 278, figure 179, derived from British Library MS Egerton 1894, fol. 17.

33. Alexandre-Bidon, 279, figure 182; Oxford, Bodleian Library, ms Bodley 264, fol. 59.

34. The scene's key commentators are summarized by David Hult, who further reveals androgynous overtones in an expanded linguistic nexus of *coilles, coillir, cueillir, Bel Acueil*, "Language and Dismemberment: Abelard, Origen and the *Romance of the Rose*," in *Rethinking the Romance of the Rose: Text, Image, Reception*, ed. Kevin Brownlee and Sylvia Huot (Philadelphia: University of Pennsylvania Press, 1992), 101–30.

35. See examples in Marcel and Pierre-Gilles Girault, *Visages de pèlerins au moyen âge: Les Pèlerinages européens dans l'art et l'épopée* (Paris: Zodiaque, 2001), figures 1, 20, 24, 39, 77, 147 among others. Medieval pilgrims are most often depicted as carrying a larger, more practical *escharpe* or *sacoche* worn typically "en bandolière" across the chest, leaving the hands free and providing more ample room to carry provisions while traveling.

36. I do not mean to argue here for influence or direct borrowing. Whereas the first part of the *Rose* is typically dated ca. 1230, the *Empereur Constant* has been ascribed more broadly to the thirteenth century (Coveney, 6).

37. Coveney, 100.

38. See also ll. 9–12 in contrast to the *Dit*'s characterization of Florien simply as "poissans et redoutés,/ Rices e tres larges donneres, vv. 48–49.

39. The union had been sanctioned by the "haus homes" of the realm at Sebelinne's request but in Florien's absence, vv. 512, 518–19.

40. "Ge, rois Muselins, enperes de Grese et de Bisanche la chité," vv. 285–86.

41. Jean Renart, *Le Roman de la Rose ou de Guillaume de Dole*, ed. Félix Lecoy (Paris: Champion, 1962).

42. Sarah Kay explains how the romance plays these traditional topoi off against one another, *Subjectivity in Troubadour Poetry* (Cambridge: Cambridge University Press, 1990), 189–91.

43. Roger Dragonetti, *Le Mirage des sources: l'art du faux dans le roman médiéval* (Paris: Editions du Seuil, 1987), 183, 187–89. Roberta L. Krueger has shown in detail how Lienor is ultimately reduced to a potent sign of femininity manipulated by the narrator to shore up aristocratic marriage while displacing the subjectivity of historical women, an argument forged in response to a spate of readings that had emphasized the heroine as a rhetorical ploy in the narrative. See Krueger's response to Michel Zink, Jean-Charles Huchet, and Henri Rey-Flaud in particular, *Women Readers and the Ideology of Gender in Old French Verse Romance* (Cambridge: Cambridge University Press, 1993), 143–55. Regina Psaki extends the analysis in this vein, seeing Lienor as the image of a "fragmented woman" used by Jean Renart to explore the possibilities and limitations of literary language, generating at her trial an illusory reality born of multiple perspectives that is also favored by the author of this romance, "Jean Renart's Expanded Text: Lïenor and the Lyrics of *Guillaume de Dole*," in Nancy Vine Durling, ed., *Jean Renart and the Art of Romance* (Gainesville: University Press of Florida, 1977), 122–41. By contrast, Sarah Kay emphasizes Lienor's contribution itself as forcefully rhetorical: *Subjectivity*, 194.

44. Kay, *Subjectivity*, 192; Burns, *Courtly Love Undressed*, 198.

45. John W. Baldwin, "Once there was an emperor . . . A Political Reading of the Romances of Jean Renart," in Durling, ed., *Jean Renart and the Art of Romance*, 54.

46. Baldwin, 51, 54–55.

47. Baldwin, 53.

48. "Et ses contesses en samiz/ et en draz d'or emperials/ em pur lor biax cors sans mantiaus,/ et ces puceles en cendez" (vv. 200–203; And countesses in heavy silk and imperial cloth of gold, their bodies visible without cloaks, and maidens in light weight silks).

49. Françoise Piponnier explains that decorative *ceintures* were especially widespread by the fifteenth century, most made of "tissue de soie," sometimes embroidered or embellished with gold, and often termed simply "tissus," as is the case is this thirteenth-century example. "Ceintures de soie," she explains, were often accompanied by "bourses" of satin, samite, velvet or cloth of gold. They were embroidered, embellished with gold, decorated with buttons or small silver bells, "Usages et diffusions de la soie en France à la fin du Moyen Age," in Simonetta Cavaciocchi, ed., *La Seta in Europa Sec. XIII-XX* (Florence: Instituto internazionale di storia economica, 1993), 793–94.

50. Kay, *Subjectivity*, 194.

51. Helen Solterer was one of the first to emphasize the significance of Lienor using textiles to stage her mock defloration of the seneschal, arguing that through Lienor's embroidery, the text comments symbolically on the force of women's representation, "At the Bottom of a Mirage, a Woman's Body: *Le Roman de la rose* of Jean Renart," in *Feminist Approaches to the Body in Medieval Literature*, ed. Sarah Stanbury and Linda Lomperis (Philadelphia: University of Pennsylvania Press, 1993), 225–27. Nancy A. Jones's pathbreaking essay "The Uses of Embroidery in the Romances of Jean Renart: Gender, History, Textuality," in Durling, ed., *Jean Renart and the Art of Romance*, analyzed the author's works as examples of what Jones termed femino-centric romances with an embroidery subplot, narratives in which the pivotal figures are resourceful heroines who rely on clothworking skills, 13–43.

52. See also vv. 4964–65.

53. The ring and brooch, which figure among the love tokens, stand apart from the cloth items that could be "worked" by women's hands. And yet, even these material objects fall within the "feture" of the *aumosniere* in a sense since Lienor stipulates from the outset that the *aumosniere* contains a ring that should never be removed from it, "Cest teissu et cest aumosniere./ Tot est brodé d'une maniere,/ et si a dedenz un anel/ a une esmeraude, mout bel,/ et gardez bien que nuls nel voie" (vv. 4292–96; This belt and almspurse are embroidered in the same way and there is a beautiful emerald ring inside. Be careful that no one sees it); and when the seneschal wants to wear the brooch, the messenger makes clear that Lienor orders that it too remain enclosed in the *aumosniere*, "Fet il: 'Ele me rouva dire/ qu'il remainsist en l'aumosniere'" (vv. 4431–32; [The messenger] said 'She asked me to tell you to keep it in the purse'").

54. For a fuller discussion of this topic and accompanying bibliography see E. Jane Burns, *Bodytalk: When Women Speak in Old French Literature* (Philadelphia: University of Pennsylvania Press, 1993), 115–50.

55. Piponnier catalogues silk fabrics used for liturgical purposes inventoried in fourteenth-century registers as including many of the silks mentioned here: *samit, baudequin, disapre, damas, cendal,* explaining that some contain symbolic images of peacocks, stags, or lambs while others are marked by secular motifs of dogs, lions, or birds. Many have geometric forms and most are purely decorative rather than figurative, "Usages et diffusion," 788.

56. Ed. Suzanne Duparc-Quioc (Paris: Librairie Orientaliste Paul Guethner, 1977).

57. Jacoby, "Silk Economics and Cross-cultural Artistic Interaction: Byzantium, the Muslim World, and the Christian West," *Dumbarton Oaks Papers* 58 (2004): 218, 229.

58. Corbaran's trans-Mediterranean reach emerges further when he is said to load fifteen pack mules from Syria with gold coins and gold from Palestine, while also charging twenty pack horses with Almerían silks, "pailes d'Aumarie" (vv. 397–99).

59. Patricia Baker, *Islamic Textiles* (London: British Museum Press, 1995), 43, 45, 55.

60. Sophie Desrosiers, *Soieries et autres textiles de l'Antiquité au XVIe siècle* (Paris: Editions de la Réunion des musées nationaux, 2004), catalogue numbers 47, 53, 64, 67a.

61. Desrosiers, "Draps d'Areste (II): Extension de la classification, comparaisons et lieux de fabrication," 89–117; Donald King, "Two Medieval Textile Terms: "Draps d'ache"

and "draps de l'arest," 83–88; and Dominique Cardon, "De l'Espagne à l'Italie," 139–57, all in "Soieries médiévales," *Techniques et Culture* 34 (1999).

62. Wardwell, "Panni Tartarici," 140.

63. Interestingly, the heroine Philomena is credited with just such powers, that is, the ability to portray in silk cloth even the noise made by Hellequin's followers, that is, to make cloth tell a story. See Burns, *Bodytalk*, 122.

64. In Krueger's reading, Lienor's marriage to Conrad reinscribes her within the "Helen of Troy narrative": as the embroidered marriage cloak enfolds this heroine, she is marked visibly as being reabsorbed into the system of exchange in which men have traded women from the outset of this text, *Women Readers*, 152. That is true. But Lienor's manipulation of other textiles tells a different story.

65. Patricia Terry and Nancy Vine Durling, trans. and eds., *The Romance of the Rose or Guillaume de Dole* (Philadelphia: University of Pennsylvania Press, 1993), 15 n. 11.

CHAPTER 4. FOLLOWING TWO "LADIES OF CARTHAGE" FROM TYRE TO NORTH AFRICA AND SPAIN TO FRANCE

1. Alternate spellings in the *Roman d'Enéas* include "Cartaige," "Cartauge," "Cartaje," "Cartauje": *Le Roman d'Enéas*, ed. Aimé Petit (Paris: Livre de Poche, 1997).

2. Rebuilt after its destruction by the Romans in the Punic Wars, Carthage flourished as a center of Roman Africa from the first century, passing to the Byzantines in the sixth century, and to Muslim control in the eighth, Bernard Reilly, *The Medieval Spains* (Cambridge: Cambridge University Press, 1993), 2, 14–16, 26. Not until the end of the thirteenth century was Cartagena (in modern-day Spain) under Christian control, Reilly, 1; Olivia Remie Constable, *Trade and Traders in Muslim Spain: The Commercial Realignment of the Medieval Iberian Peninsula, 900–1500* (Cambridge: Cambridge University Press, 1994), 188.

3. David Jacoby "Silk Crosses the Mediterranean," in G. Airaldi, ed., *Le vie del Mediterraneo. Idee, uomini, oggetti* (Genoa: Università degli studi di Genova, 1997), 56, n. 5, who explains further that by the eighth century *tyria* had become a generic term for a type of purple cloth.

4. "The Medieval Scarlet," in *Cloth and Clothing in Medieval Europe*, ed. N. B. Harte and K. G. Ponting (London: Heinemann Educational Books, 1983), 14–18. *The Book of the Eparch*, which regulated silk production in Constantinople under Leo VI (886–912), stipulated that red and purple silks could not be transported outside the capitol, citing Gratian's edict from 383, which names two purples for the emperor's use only: Tyrian purple (silk) and dark red silk. See *The Book of the Eparch; Le Livre du Préfet, Edit de l'empereur Léon le Sage sur les corporations et métiers de Constantinople* (London: Variorum, 1970), 150. On kermes (cochineal) see also Maurice Lombard, *Les Textiles dans le monde musulman du VIIe au XIIe siècle* (Paris: Mouton, 1978), 119–22.

5. Commenting on the *Roman d'Enéas*, among other *romans d'antiquité*, Jean Frappier argued a number of years ago that the characters were often "modernized" to conform to

twelfth-century western tastes in décor, architecture, and costume. In fact, however, the lavish attire of twelfth-century courtly heroines in particular, the dress that gives them what Frappier believed to be a recognizably "French" character, owe that putatively western "identity" to the features of imported eastern luxury goods including silk, gold, and precious gems. See E. Jane Burns, *Courtly Love Undressed: Reading Through Clothes in Medieval French Culture* (Philadelphia: University of Pennsylvania Press, 2002), 185.

6. Desmond, *Reading Dido: Gender, Textuality, and the Medieval* Aeneid (Minneapolis: University of Minnesota Press, 1994), 108.

7. Desmond, 101–3. Sarah Spence argues similarly that Virgil portrays Dido in Carthage as a figure at once removed and chaste, since she rules her city like a female king, who later becomes tragically vulnerable through her passion for Aeneas, *Rhetorics of Reason and Desire* (Ithaca, N.Y.: Cornell University Press, 1988), 30–31.

8. *Historia Regum Britanniae of Geoffrey of Monmouth*, ed. and trans. Neil Wright (Cambridge: D. S. Brewer, 1991), 131.

9. Linguistic evidence shows how systematically the *Enéas* poet equates Dido with land, repeating the rime "feme/regne" and its non-riming lexical couplet "terre/femme," building to the more overt equation of Dido with her city in the lexical couplet "Carthage/Didon." See Christiane Marchello-Nizia, "De l'Enéide à l'Enéas: Les Attributs du fondateur," in *Lectures médiévales de Virgile*, ed. Jean Yves Tilliette (Paris: CID, 1985), 251–66.

10. Marie-Luce Chênerie, "Le Motif des présents dans le *Roman d'Enéas*," in *Relire le "Roman d'Enéas,"* ed. Jean Dufournet (Paris: Champion, 1985), 56–57.

11. Eunice Rathbone Goddard, *Women's Costume in French Texts of the Eleventh and Twelfth Centuries* (Baltimore: Johns Hopkins Press, 1927), 130–31.

12. Ed. Alexandre Micha (Paris: Champion, 1957), vv. 1607–14, 1618. For an analysis see Burns, *Courtly Love Undressed*, 63–64.

13. For a fuller discussion, see Burns, *Courtly Love Undressed*, 19–56.

14. *Tertullian: Disciplinary, Moral, and Ascetical Works*, trans. Rudolph Arbesmann et al. (New York: Fathers of the Church, 1959), 125.

15. See also vv. 9533–37.

16. Lombard, 93.

17. Lombard, 93.

18. Michel Balard, *Croisades et Orient Latin XIe-XIVe siècle* (Paris: Armand Colin, 2001), 110; Steven Runciman, *A History of the Crusades: The Kingdom of Jerusalem and the Frankish State, 1100–1187*, vol. 2 (Cambridge: Cambridge University Press, 1951), 317.

19. *A History of the Crusades*, 2: 316.

20. Fulcher of Chartres, *A History of the Expedition to Jerusalem 1095–1127*, trans. Frances Rita Ryan, ed. Harold S. Fink (Knoxville: University of Tennessee Press, 1969), 271. On this passage, see the analysis of Jaroslav Folda, *The Art of the Crusaders in the Holy Land, 1099–1187* (Cambridge: Cambridge University Press, 1995), 86–87.

21. Fulcher, 271.

22. On Reims as producing the highest quality linen see Sharon Farmer, "Biffes, Tiretaines, and Aumonières: The Role of Paris in the International Textile Markets of the

Thirteenth and Fourteenth Centuries," in *Medieval Clothing and Textiles*, ed. Robin Netherton and Gale R. Owen-Crocker, 2 (2006), 80. On linen production at Chartres see André Chédeville, *Chartres et ses campagnes, XIe–XIIIe siècles* (Paris: Klincksieck, 1973), 448, 451.

23. Lombard, 93.

24. *Le Conte de Floire et Blancheflor*, ed. Jean-Luc Leclanche (Paris: Champion, 1980).

25. *Aucsasin et Nicolette: chantefable du XIIIe siècle*, ed. Mario Roques (Paris: Champion, 1977). See also: "Nicolete est cointe et gaie;/ jetee fu de Cartage,/ acatee fu d'un Saisne" (p. 3).

26. Along with possessing courtly speech, "Nicolete est cointe et gaie" (III, 8); "ses gens cors et son viaire,/ sa biautés . . ." (III, 15–16); "ele avoit blonde la cringe/ et bien faite la sorcille,/ la face clere et traitice;/ ainc plus bele ne veïstes" (V, 7–10); "de s'amie o le vis cler" (VII, 3); "douce amie" (VII, 20); "flor de lis" (XII, 12); "tant par estoit blance la mescinete (XII, 28).

27. Jacqueline de Weever, *Sheba's Daughters: Whitening and Demonizing the Saracen Woman in Medieval French Epic* (New York: Garland, 1998), 3–52.

28. Maria Rosa Menocal, "Signs of the Times: Self, Other, and History in *Aucassin et Nicolette*," *Romanic Review* 53, 4 (1989): 506.

29. See Sarah Kay, *The* Chansons de geste *in the Age of Romance: Political Fictions* (Oxford: Oxford University Press, 1995), 25–48; Lynn Tarte Ramey, *Christian, Saracen, and Genre in Medieval French Literature* (New York: Routledge, 2001), 43–50; Sharon Kinoshita, *Medieval Boundaries: Rethinking Difference in Medieval French Literature* (Philadelphia: University of Pennsylvania Press, 2006), 46–73, 176–99.

30. Menocal, "Signs," 497–511. The bulk of scholarship on this brief narrative has focused on the question of parody and on the analysis of competing literary and social discourses, including the discourse of money stimulated by the rising bourgeois class. Studies of parody beginning with Urban Tigner Holmes in 1947 and continuing with Alexandre Micha in 1959 persist through the 1980s. See, for select examples, Micha, "En relisant *Aucassin et Nicolette*," *Le Moyen Age* 65 (1959): 282–83; Omer Jodogne, "La parodie et le pastiche dans *Aucassin et Nicolette*," *Cahiers de l'Association Internationale des études françaises* 12 (1960): 53–65; Barbara Nelson Sargent, "Parody in *Aucassin et Nicolette*: Some Further Considerations," *French Review* 43, 4 (1970): 597–605; June Hall Martin, *Love's Fools: Aucassin, Troilus, Calisto, and the Parody of the Courtly Lover* (London: Tamesis, 1972); Nathaniel B. Smith, "The Uncourtliness of Nicolette," in *Voices of Conscience*, ed. Raymond Cormier (Philadelphia: Temple University Press, 1977), 169–82; Norris J. Lacy, "Courtliness and Comedy in *Aucassin et Nicolette*," in *Essays in Early French Literature Presented to Barbara M. Craig* (York, S.C.: French Literature Publishing Company, 1982). Arguing against parody: Tony Hunt, "La Parodie médiévale: Le cas d'*Aucassin et Nicolette*," *Romania* 100 (1979): 341–81. On discourse analysis see Eugene Vance, "A Word at Heart: *Aucassin et Nicolette* as a Medieval Comedy of Language," *Yale French Studies* 45 (1970): 33–51 and Kevin Brownlee, "Discourse and *Prouece* in *Aucassin et Nicolette*," *Yale French Studies* 70 (1986): 167–82; and for studies raising the issue of economics in *Aucassin et Nicolette*, Eugene Vance, "*Aucassin et Nicolette* as a Medieval Comedy of Significance and

Exchange," in *The Nature of Medieval Narrative*, ed. Minnette Grunmann-Gaudet and Robin F. Jones (Lexington, Ky.: French Forum Publishers, 1980): 58–73; and R. Howard Bloch, "Money, Metaphor, and the Mediation of Social Difference in the Old French Romance," *Symposium* 35 (1981): 18–33.

31. Nicolete, disguised as a *jongleur*, later answers the question, explaining to Aucassin that "si est fille au roi de Cartage, qui le prist la u Aucassins fu pris, si le mens en le cite de Cartage tant qu'il seut bien que c'estoit se fille, si en fist molt grant feste; si li veut on doner cascun jor baron un des plus haus rois de tote Espaigne" (XL, 6–10; She is the daughter of the king of Carthage, who took her at the same time Aucassin was taken, and transported her to the city of Carthage, until he realized that she was his daughter, and then rejoiced and laid plans to give her one day one of the most highly placed kings in Spain as her lord).

32. "Je l'avoie acatee de mes deniers" (IV, 11; I bought her with my own money) and "Si l'acatai de mon avoir a Sarasins" (VI, 15–16; I bought her from Saracens with my own means).

33. Even during the verbal contest between the lovers over who experiences love more intensely, men or women, Aucassin contrasts the metaphorical seat of love in the male heart ("cué") with the love that exists only in a woman's anatomical extremities, citing, in addition to her eyes, the tip of her nipple and the toe at the end of her foot (XIV, 20–21).

34. See also XIV, 1–2, "Qant Aucassins oï dire Nicolete qu'ele s'en voloit aler en autre païs" (When Aucassin heard Nicolette say she wanted to flee to another country).

35. Chrétien de Troyes, *Le chevalier de la charette*, ed. Mario Roques (Paris: Champion, 1970), vv. 1294–1321, esp. "sa volenté en poïst faire," v. 1315.

36. Wilhelm Heyd, *Histoire du Commerce du Levant au Moyen Age*, 1 (Amsterdam: Adolf M. Hakkert, 1959), 561–63.

37. A. J. Greimas, *Dictionnaire de l'ancien français* (Paris: Larousse, 1969), 601.

38. See glossary to *The Crowning of Louis*, ed. and trans. Nirmal Dass (Jefferson, N.C.: McFarland and Co., 2003), 104.

39. John Tolan, *Saracens: Islam in the Medieval European Imagination* (New York: Columbia University Press, 2002), 187.

40. Tolan, 187–88.

41. Philip K. Hitti, *The Arabs: A Short History* (Washington D.C.: Regnery Publications, 1996), 198. Carthage in North Africa was the point where the Muslim western expansion began. After taking Syria, Iraq, Persia, and Egypt in the first stage of expansion, Muslims made their most spectacular advance westward from the city of Carthage, which they already held (Hitti, 80–81). By the thirteenth century, when the Old French *Aucassin et Nicolette* is thought to have been composed, the original Phoenician colony established at Cartagena in southern Spain had been governed by Muslims since the eighth century.

42. Constable, 205–7.

43. Constable, 234.

44. Constable, 234. Constable provides the example of the conquest of Valencia by James I of Aragon in 1238, which is followed by many sales of Valencian Muslim slaves in 1239 (235).

45. Constable, 223.

46. And later the same formulation: "Vos n'en donriiés mie un des menbres por cinc cens mars d'argent ne por nul avoir" (XXII, 34–36).

47. See especially Vance, "*Aucassin et Nicolette* as a Medieval Comedy of Significance and Exchange," 65–67; and Brownlee, 171–72.

48. McCormick, *Origins of the European Economy: Communications and Commerce, A.D 300–900* (Cambridge: Cambridge University Press, 2001), 319.

49. McCormick, 776; S. D. Goitein, *A Mediterranean Society*, vol. 1 (Berkeley: University of California Press, 1967), 101.

50. McCormick, 351.

51. Goitein, 1: 222–24.

52. Constable, 202, 204.

53. *Le Couronnement de Louis*, ed. Ernest Langlois (Paris; Champion, 1966), vv. 594–98.

54. The transformation offers a potent antidote to misogynous texts such as the early thirteenth-century "Dit de la Femme," in which comparison of the woman to a strange "beste" allows the author to elaborate an antifeminist portrait of women as fickle, prideful, deceitful, and vainglorious. See Monique Léonard, "Le Dit de la femme," in *Ecrire pour dire: Etudes sur le dit médiéval*, ed. Bernard Ribémont (Paris: Klincksieck, 1990), 29–45.

55. The portrait of Nicolette as a curative relic also contrasts starkly with the pat description of her as an immobilized lovely lady rendered, interestingly, just after her daring and wholly unladylike escape from the tower prison using "dras de lit et touailes" (XII, 13). Even this relatively predictable catalogue of the courtly heroine's static body parts: her blonde curls, her smiling light eyes, her oval face with a well-formed nose, lips redder than a cherry or rose in summer, small white teeth . . . is accompanied in the case of this heroine by a description of her feet swinging through the daisies that she breaks off with her toes (XII, 19–26).

56. *The Songs of Jaufré Rudel*, ed. Rupert T. Pickens (Toronto: Pontifical Institute of Mediaeval Studies, 1978), 166.

57. *The Songs of Bernart de Ventadorn*, ed. Stephen G. Nichols, Jr. (Chapel Hill: University of North Carolina Press, 1962), 110–11.

58. Alexandre Micha, ed. (Paris: Champion, 1957).

59. Pickens, ed., 102.

60. In fact, the medieval traffic in relics was highly developed and lucrative in its own right, in stark contrast to the ideal of religious veneration of relics as being beyond earthly pursuits.

CHAPTER 5. WOMEN MAPPING A SILK ROUTE FROM SAINT-DENIS TO JERUSALEM AND CONSTANTINOPLE

1. *Le Voyage de Charlemagne à Jerusalem et à Constantinople*, ed. Paul Aebischer (Geneva: Droz, 1965). Aebischer and M. G. Favati prefer the title "Voyage" while Jules

Horrent and Gaston Paris use the more traditional French title of "Pèlerinage," as Aebischer explains in his introduction, pp. 11–12. A thorough accounting of studies of the *Pèlerinage* to 1995 is provided by Anne Elizabeth Cobby in *Ambivalent Conventions: Formula and Parody in Old French* (Amsterdam: Rodopi, 1995), 82–86. Subsequent studies that bear on the arguments advanced here include: Margaret Burrell, "The Specular Heroine: Self-Creation Versus Silence in *Le Pèlerinage de Charlemagne* and *Erec et Enide*," *Parergon: Bulletin of the Australian and New Zealand Association for Medieval and Early Modern Studies* 15, 1 (1997): 83–99; Joel Thompson Argote, "Charlemagne's Women," *RLA: Romance Languages Annual* 9 (1997): 1–5; François Suard, "Constantinople dans la littérature épique française jusqu'au XIV siècle," in *Sauver Byzance de la barbarie du monde*, ed. Liana Nissim and Silvia Riva (Milan: Cisalpino, 2004), 91–112; Annalee Rejhon, "L'Itinéraire de Saint-Denis à la Terre Sainte dans *Le Pèlerinage de Charlemagne à Jerusalem et à Constantinople* (British Library MS Royal 16.E.VIII)," *Revue belge de philologie et d'histoire* 83, 3 (2005): 829–39.

2. Jonathan Riley-Smith explains that at the time of the First Crusade Pope Urban II considered women unsuitable for the crusading mission. They could only participate when given special permission from Church authorities to accompany their brothers or husbands, *The Crusades: A Short History* (New Haven: Yale University Press, 1987), 8.

3. Odo of Deuil, *De profectione Ludovici VII in orientem*, ed. and trans. Virginia Gingerick Berry (New York: Columbia University Press, 1948), 87. See also Jacques Le Goff, *La Civilisation de l'Occident médiéval* (Paris: Arthaud, 1967), 179–80, 190.

4. See Alexandre Leupin, "La Compromission: Sur le *Voyage de Charlemagne à Jerusalem et à Constantinople*," *Romance Notes* 25, 3 (1985): 222–38.

5. Sharon Kinoshita has discussed Charlemagne's wife and Hugh's daughter as the "text's two women," showing how they function in the narrative to reinstate a reassuring binary opposition between the rival rulers while also "redeeming western masculinity." *Medieval Boundaries*, 68. There is yet another woman, however, and she is the Byzantine empress. For two other studies that address female protagonists in the *Pèlerinage* see Burrell, "The Specular Heroine," and Argote, "Charlemagne's Women."

6. Eugene Vance, "Semiotics and Power: Relics, Icons, and the *Voyage de Charlemagne à Jerusalem et à Constantinople*," *Romanic Review* 79, 1 (1988): 174–75; Michael Angold, *The Byzantine Empire, 1025–1204* (New York: Longman, 1985), 164.

7. She has specified earlier that her assessment refers to King Hugh's wealth: "Plus est riche d'aver e d'or e de deners" (v. 27; He is richer in goods, gold and coins).

8. "Cele ne fud pas sage, folement respondeit" (v. 12; She was not wise; she answered foolishly); "Ma dame la reïne folie dist e tord" (v. 813; My lady the queen spoke foolishly and wrongly).

9. For an analysis of the importance of the itinerary into "foreign lands" mapped by this text, see Rejhon, "L'Itinéraire de Saint-Denis à la Terre Sainte."

10. One brief reference to "seie blanc" describes tents carried by Charlemagne's men as they depart, heavily laden with gold and silver accoutrements, "Faudestoulz d'or i portent e treis de seie blanc" (v. 85; They carried golden thrones and tents of white silk).

11. "Un bon paile grizain" (v. 294; a fine piece of grey silk); "Le paleis e la sale, de

pailes purtendues" (v. 332; The palace and the hall hung with silk); "Li reis fait en sa cambre acunduire sa fille:/ Purtendue est trestute de pailles e de curtines" (vv. 705–6; The king
has his daughter taken to her chamber. Its walls are completely covered with silks and
curtains).

12. Le Goff, *La Civilisation de l'Occident médiéval*, 179–80; The *Couronnement de
Louis* repeatedly figures Saracen wealth in terms of gold alone, as the denier becomes a
metaphor for evil, the currency of pagan devils, *Le Couronnement de Louis*, ed. Ernest
Langlois (Paris: Champion, 1966), vv. 84, 179, 226.

13. *La Prise d'Orange*, ed. Claude Régnier (Paris: Klincksieck, 1983).

14. Ronald Walpole, ed., *An Anonymous Old French Translation of the Pseudo-Turpin
Chronicle* (Cambridge, Mass.: Medieval Academy of America, 1979), 86.

15. Notker, "De Carolo Magno" in *Two Lives of Charlemagne: Einhard and Notker the
Stammerer*, trans. Lewis Thorpe (Harmondsworth: Penguin, 1967), 167; and Einhard, *Vita
Karolini*, describes Charlemagne as wearing the relatively modest national dress of the
Franks: a linen shirt and linen drawers, a tunic edged in silk, long hose, shoes, a jerkin of
otter or ermine, a blue cloak (Thorpe, 77). Notker characterizes Charlemagne similarly as
wearing the dress of Franks in wartime: a long cloak, gilded boots with leather laces, scarlet wrappings on his legs, linen undergarments with elaborate embroidery, and a white
linen shirt (Thorpe, 132).

16. Thorpe, 165–66.

17. See Burns, *Courtly Love Undressed*, Chapters 6 and 7 on "Saracen Silk " and
"Golden Spurs," respectively, 179–229.

18. *The* Chansons de geste *in the Age of Romance: Political Fictions* (Oxford: Oxford
University Press, 1995), 178–82.

19. For an extended discussion of the implications of the relic of the Virgin's *chemise*,
see Chapter 6.

20. With the exception of Olivier who colludes with Hugh's daughter to lie, vv.
714–33.

21. We have already seen proof that these abundant and powerful relics can perform
miracles in Jerusalem when they cure a severely ill paralytic (vv. 191–95).

22. Tertullian, *Disciplinary, Moral, and Ascetical Works*, trans. Rudolph Arbesmann
(New York: Fathers of the Church, 1959), 124.

23. Tertullian, 123.

24. "Faites .c. mulz receivre d'or e d'argent trusset"/ E dist li patriarches : "Ja mar en
parlerez!" (vv. 220–21; "Have one hundred mules packed with gold and silver," but the patriarch says, "Don't even mention it!").

25. See also vv. 224–25.

26. This is the only time the *Pèlerinage* makes specific reference to "Saracens."

27. Riley-Smith, *The Crusades*, 6–7.

28. The translation of "coste" as "alecost" is from Glynn S. Burgess and Anne
Elizabeth Cobby, trans., *The Pilgrimage of Charlemagne and Aucassin and Nicolette* (New
York: Garland, 1988), 79, notes to ll. 210–12. Drawing on the *Assizes de Jerusalem*, Jean

Richard notes further that "li language" refers to diverse national communities that inhabited Jerusalem in the early twelfth century, each governed by specific laws and regulations, "Sur un passage du *Pèlerinage de Charlemagne*: Le marché de Jerusalem," *Revue Belge de Philologie et d'Histoire* 43, 2 (1965): 554.

29. Richard, 252–55.

30. Burgess, 79 (notes to lines 210–12); Tobler-Lommatsch, *Altfranzösisches Wörterbuch* (Wiesbaden: Franz Steiner Verlag, 1973), vol. S-SY, 678 gives the example from Fergus, 124: "sa kote deskire, ki faite fu d'un drap de syre" and his notation: "(l. Syre, Syria)." He also cites Jean Renart's *Escoufle*, v. 4728, "dras de Sire."

31. Lombard, *Les Textiles dans le monde musulman du VIIe au XIIe siècle* (Paris: Mouton, 1978), 93; Michel Balard, *Croisades et Orient Latin XIe–XIVe siècle* (Paris: Armand Colin, 2001), 210.

32. Balard, 211.

33. Lombard, 93.

34. Steven Runciman, *A History of the Crusades*, vol. 3 (Cambridge: Cambridge University Press, 1987), 353.

35. Balard, 210.

36. This considerable transfer of eastern silks westward from Latin crusader states, whether the fabrics are of Islamic or Christian manufacture, simply extends a process already well established during the Carolingian era when France imported large numbers of silks from Constantinople. See Michael McCormick, *Origins of the European Economy: Communications and Commerce, A.D 300–900* (Cambridge: Cambridge University Press, 2001), 284, 723–24, 726.

37. Once again, then, we find that the anomalous *Pèlerinage* adds an odd twist to the more familiar scenario featured in many Old French epic poems that reflect a distinct resistance to and critique of a rising economy, as Sarah Kay has suggested (*Chansons de geste*, 183–84). Whereas the eastern King Hugh is clearly criticized in the *Pèlerinage* for his lavish display of wealth in gold and silk, the Christian site of Jerusalem emerges simultaneously as an active hub of unfettered trading in the most costly of medieval commodities, silk.

38. Joseph Bédier, *Les Légendes épiques: Recherches sur la formation des* chansons de geste, vol. 4 (Paris: Champion, 1926–66), 125–27, 137.

39. Bédier, 473–76, 122–37, 155. Bédier explains that in 1108 the cathedral of Notre Dame in Paris received from Jerusalem a valued relic: a piece of the holy cross (137), and that the following year a procession in the direction of St. Denis was established to venerate this relic in the "champ du Lendit," a fief of the bishop of Paris (138).

40. Indeed, the Old French epic *Fierabras* critiques the royal tax levied on sales at the Lendit fair as a form of greed (vv. 15–21), suggesting that mercantile interests have taken over the initial religious impetus for the fair, all profits of which went to the monks of St. Denis, *Fierabras*, ed. Marc Le Person (Paris: Champion, 2003), 35.

41. *Dit du Lendit rimé*, in Gustave Fagniez, ed., *Documents relatifs à l'histoire de l'industrie et du commerce en France*, vol. 2 (Paris: Jacques Picard, 1974), 176, v. 81ff.

42. Félix Bourquelot, *Etudes sur les foires de Champagne, sur la nature, l'étendue et les*

règles du commerce qui s'y faisait au XIIe, XIIIe et XIVe siècles. Brionne, France: Le Portulan, 1865; 269–70; Janet Abu-Lughod, *Before European Hegemony: The World System A.D. 1250–1350* (New York: Oxford University Press, 1989), 56.

43. Vance, "Semiotics and Power," 171, following Angold, 206. Of further interest for the current argument, Angold explains that Manuel I Comnenus and Conrad III had discussed a joint invasion and partition of Italy and Sicily, the Byzantine share of which was to count as the dowry due to Manuel from his marriage to Berthe-Eirene. The plan faltered when Conrad joined ranks instead with Louis VII on the Second Crusade, 619.

44. Angold, 163. On Manuel Comnenus's first two foreign brides, Bertha Sulzbach, sister-in-law of the German Emperor Conrad III, and Maria of Antioch, daughter of Raymond of Poitiers and Constance of Antioch, see also Carolyn Connor, *Women of Byzantium* (New Haven: Yale University Press, 2004), 211; and Barbara Hill, *Imperial Women and Byzantine Power, Patronage, and Ideology: 1025–1204* (London: Longman, 1999), 171.

45. Angold, 249.

46. J. L. Van Dieten, ed., *Nicetae Choniate Historia* (Berlin: de Gruyter, 1975), 74. Cited in Angold.

47. Charles Brand, "Some Byzantine Women of Thebes and Elsewhere" in John S. Langdon et al., eds., *To Hellenikon: Studies in Honor of Speros Vryonis, Jr.*, vol. 1 (New Rochelle, N.Y.: Aristide de Carnatzas, 1993), 60.

48. Connor, 160–61; Marie-France Auzépy, "La Destruction de l'icône du Christ de la Chalcé par Léon III: Propagande ou réalité?" *Byzantion* 60 (1990): 445–92, esp. 449.

49. Judith Herrin, *Women in Purple: Rulers of Medieval Byzantium* (Princeton, N.J.: Princeton University Press, 2001), 78–79, 91. Connor, 209.

50. Herrin, 102–3.

51. Herrin, 105–7.

52. Herrin, 102–3.

53. Herrin, 49, 103 fn. 93.

54. Herrin, 103.

55. Herrin, 164.

56. Herrin, 51.

57. Herrin, 71–72.

58. Herrin, 91, 99–100,

59. Herrin, 75.

60. See Bédier, 130 ff. Charlemagne did fund the building of a church in Jerusalem, as well as Rome, and was tagged by a number of Latin chroniclers as the new Constantine, emperor crowned by God. See Bédier, 439. For Charles as an ideal crusader, see the windows at Chartres Cathedral, based on the *Descriptio* and *Pseudo-Turpin Chronicle*.

61. See *Visages de pèlerins au Moyen âge*, ed. Marcel et Pierre-Gilles Girault (Paris: Zodiaque, 2001), 76.

62. The historical Charlemagne had three wives, according to his biographer Einhard, all of them foreign women: the daughter of Desiderius, King of the Longobards, Hildigard from Swabia, and Fastrada, who came from the region of eastern Franks (Thorpe, 73).

63. Theodor Heinermann, "Zeit und Sinn der Karlsreise," *Zeitschrift für romanische*

Philologie 61 (1936), 550. Notker's biography of Charlemagne provides fictive support for this effort with a curiously reversed version of the voyage recounted in the *Pèlerinage*. In Notker's account, envoys of the Persian king, named Harun-al-Raschid (who was the actual caliph of Baghdad from 786 to 809), explain that Charlemagne, unfortunately disrespected by his own men in the west, wields significant influence in the east among Persians, Medes, Armenians, Indians, Parthians, Elamites, and others who stand in greater awe of Charlemagne than of their own ruler, Harun. Harun himself recognizes the superior might of Charlemagne as a leader capable of conquering anything under heaven and agrees, as does King Hugh of the Greeks, Persians, and Cappadocians at the end of the *Pèlerinage*, to become Charles's vassal: "I will give the land to him-he may hold it. I will rule over it as his representative. I will be a most faithful steward," Thorpe, 146–48.

64. Régine Pernoud, *La Femme au temps des croisades* (Paris: Stock, 1990), 107–8. Elizabeth A. R. Brown, "Eleanor of Aquitaine: Parent, Queen, and Duchess," in *Eleanor of Aquitaine: Patron and Politician*, ed. William W. Kibler (Austin: University of Texas Press, 1976), 9–34.

65. Peter Edbury, "Looking Back on the Second Crusade: Some Late Twelfth-Century English Perspectives," in *The Second Crusade and the Cistercians*, ed. Michael Gervers (New York: St. Martin's Press, 1992), 163–69. On adulterous queens in Old French literature, see Peggy McCracken, *The Romance of Adultery: Queenship and Sexual Transgression in Old French Literature* (Philadelphia: University of Pennsylvania Press, 1998).

66. Edbury, 167.

67. Pernoud, 97. Aebischer notes that Koschwitz's diplomatic edition reproduces the title of the manuscript as follows: "Ci commence le liuere cumment charels de fraunce voiet in ierhusalem Et pur parolz sa feme a constantinople pur vere roy hugon" (15), thus reinforcing Aebischer's view that the text's primary subject is a comical and secular journey to Constantinople rather than a religious pilgrimage. But the title also conveys pointedly that it is "because of his wife's words" that Charles's proposed journey to Jerusalem is rerouted toward Constantinople.

68. Pernoud, 109.

69. Matthew Bennett, "Virile Latins, Effeminate Greeks, and Strong Women: Gender Definitions on Crusade?" in *Gendering the Crusades*, ed. Susan B. Edgington and Sarah Lambert (New York: Columbia University Press, 2002), 23. On later medieval representations of Eleanor's infidelity see McCracken, 132–33. Of course, in traveling with Louis to the Latin Kingdom of Antioch ruled by Raymond, Eleanor also journeyed toward the site of her grandfather William IX's own colonizing forays into the Holy Land during the First Crusade. Those efforts were said to have failed in part because of the excessive debauchery and bawdiness that Guillaume IX, like his granddaughter after him, embraced. See Edbury, 167; Riley-Smith, 38; Pernoud, 107.

70. Michael R. Evans, "Unfit to Bear Arms: The Gendering of Arms and Armour in Accounts of Women on Crusade," in *Gendering the Crusades*, ed. Susan B. Edgington, 51–52; David Townsend, "Sex and the Single Amazon in Twelfth-Century Latin Epic," in *The Tongue of the Father: Gender and Ideology in Twelfth-century Latin*, ed. Townsend and Andrew Taylor (Philadelphia: University of Pennsylvania Press, 1998), 136.

71. "Trop de coffres a ferrures contenants les manteaux, robes, voiles de ces dames, oignieres, basins, vaisselle et grandes quantities de linge et d'accessoires de toilette; cuvettes, savons, miroirs, peignes, brosses, pots a fards et crèmes," as well as "bijoux, bracelets, colliers, fibulas, diadems," quoted in Pernoud, 95–96.

72. Ronald Walpole made this case convincingly in 1954, demonstrating the impossibility of accurately dating the city of Constantinople as it is depicted in the *Pèlerinage*, or of aligning Charlemagne's pilgrimage/crusade with a single, specific, historical crusade. Rather, Walpole asserted that the *Pèlerinage* narrates a legend about Charlemagne and his voyage east that remained as fictive as it was factual, "The *Pèlerinage de Charlemagne*: Poem, Legend, and Problem," *Romance Philology* 8 (1954–55): 173–86, esp. 180. In 1988, Eugene Vance made the case in terms of discourse analysis and offered a compellingly detailed reading of the poem that moves productively between its historical and fictive registers, "Semiotics and Power."

73. The relics held in St. Denis under the abbot Suger, a nail from the cross and the crown of thorns, were reputed to have been deposited at the abbey church by Charlemagne, Girault, ed., *Visages*, 184.

CHAPTER 6. SILK BETWEEN VIRGINS

1. Jean Le Marchant, *Miracles de Notre-Dame de Chartres*, ed. Pierre Kuntsmann, *Mémoires de la Société Archéologique d'Eure-et-Loir* 26 (Ottawa: Publications de l'Université d'Ottawa, 1973), 3.98 and his Latin source, *Les miracles de Notre-Dame de Chartres*, ed. Antoine Thomas, Bibliothèque de l'Ecole des Chartes 42 (1881), 505–50. Chartres's *Vieille Chronique* of 1389 similarly describes the relic as a "sancta camisia" (Fernand de Mély, *Les Chemises de la Vierge* [Chartres, 1885]), 3, n. 1, as do most Latin sources from William of Malmesbury's twelfth-century *De gestis regum Anglorum* to John of Garland's thirteenth-century mention of the "camisia virginis." See Yves Delaporte, *Le Voile de Notre Dame* (Chartres, 1927), 8; and Evelyn Faye Wilson, ed., *The "Stella maris" of John of Garland*, Mediaeval Academy of America Publications (Cambridge, Mass., Harvard University Press, 1946), 123-24. Most Old French versions of the miracles at Chartres describe a "chemise": Wace's *Roman de Rou*, ed. A. J. Holden, vol. 1 (Paris: Picard, 1970), 68–71; and William Adgar's *Marien Legenden nach der Londoner Handschrift Egerton 612*, ed. Carl Neuhaus (Wiesbaden, 1968), as well as Jean Le Marchant's account. Other variations exist in accounts by Dudo of Saint-Quentin, who calls the Virgin's garment the *tunicam sacrosanctae Mariae virginis* (*De gestis Normannorum*, cited in E. Cartier, "Recherches sur l'origine des types des monnaies chartraines," in *Suite au Mélanges d'archéologie*, eds. Charles Cahier and Arthur Martin [Paris, 1844], 51–73 at 57, n. 1) and Etienne de Bourbon, who speaks of the Virgin's "tunicam" (*Anecdotes historiques, légendes et apologues*, ed. A. Lecoy de La Marche [Paris: Librairie Renouard, 1877], 112). Some eleventh- and twelfth-century documents refer to the same garment as a *supparum* (shawl) and "interiorem tunicam" (undertunic), see Delaporte, 6–8; Cartier, "Recherches sur l'origine," 56, nn. 1 and 2. Hilding Kjellman prints two versions, one referring to a "cote," the other to a "gonele," both tunic-

like outer garments, the "gonele" generally shorter and of coarser fabric, *Les miracles de la Sainte Vierge* (Paris: Champion, 1922).

2. "a char nue," Jean Le Marchant, *Miracles*, 21.36.

3. See E. Jane Burns, "Ladies Don't Wear *Braies*: Underwear and Outerwear in the French *Prose Lancelot*," in *The Lancelot-Grail Cycle: Text and Transformations*, ed. William W. Kibler (Austin: University of Texas Press, 1994), 154–58.

4. Jannic Durand, *Le trésor de la Sainte-Chapelle* (Paris: Réunion des musées nationaux, 2001), 231.

5. The most complete account of the relic's history is provided by Delaporte, who explains that sometime between 968 and 1003 the "Sainte Chemise" was enclosed in a wooden "châsse," covered in gold, and decorated with jewels (*Le voile*, 8).

6. A thorough study of French pilgrim badges is provided by Denis Bruna, *Les enseignes de pèlerinage et les enseignes profanes au moyen âge* (doctoral thesis Paris, 1995); and his catalogue for the Cluny Museum, *Enseignes de pèlerinage et enseignes profanes: Musée national du moyen âge* (Paris: Réunion des musées nationaux, 1996). According to Bruna, badges were worn on hats from the fourteenth to sixteenth centuries and on *surcots* from the seventeenth to eighteenth centuries (*Enseignes*, thesis, 167–68). See also his *Enseignes de plomb et autres menus chosettes du Moyen Age* (Paris: Editions du Léopard d'or), 2006.

7. Arthur Forgeais, *Collection de plombs historiés trouvés dans la Seine*, 5 vols. (Paris: Chez Aubry, 1862–66), 2:28–34 provides engravings of two badges from Chartres and at 4:115–21 shows two others. A fifth Chartrain badge is pictured in Brian Spencer, *Pilgrim Souvenirs and Secular Badges: Medieval Finds from Excavations in London*, 7 (London: Stationary Office, 1998), 224, pl. 239b. A sixth badge, along with the four printed by Forgeais, is reproduced by A. Lecocq, "Recherches sur les enseignes de pèlerinages et les chemisettes de Notre-Dame-de-Chartres," *Mémoires de la Société archéologique d'Eure et Loir* 6 (1876): 194–242. The precise dates assigned to individual badges by Forgeais and Lecocq need to be reassessed.

8. Bruna explains how badges sometimes became "secondary relics" (*Enseignes*, thesis, 204). See also Esther Cohen, "*In haec signa*: Pilgrim Badge Trade in Southern France," *Journal of Medieval History* 2 (1976): 193–214, at 194–95. Michael McCormick describes the phenomenon more generally by which textiles and other objects that came into contact with saints' tombs could take on characteristics of secondary relics, *Origins of the European Economy: Communications and Commerce, A.D. 300–900* (Cambridge: Cambridge University Press, 2001), 284. An example pertinent to Chartres is found in an account from the *Liber miraculorum* at Rocamadour (ca. 1172), which describes a priest from Chartres near death who is miraculously revived by a pilgrimage badge procured at Rocamadour by the priest's mother, who pins it to his clothing and beseeches the Virgin to save him (Bruna, *Enseignes*, thesis, 92; Robert Worth Frank, Jr., "Pilgrimage and Sacral Power," in *Journeys toward God: Pilgrimage and Crusade*, ed. Barbara Nelson Sargent-Bauer [Kalamazoo, Mich.: Medieval Institute Publications, 1992], 31–43, at 38). On pilgrims and pilgrimage more generally see Edmond René Labande, "Recherches sur les pèlerins dans l'Europe des XIe et XIIe siècles," *Cahiers de civilisation médiévale* 1 (1958): 159–69.

9. Mély, *Les chemises*, 3.

10. A. Chédeville, *Chartres et ses campagnes: XIIe-XIIIe siècles* (Paris: Klincksieck, 1973), 451, n. 134. Félix Bourquelot cites the *Compte de la chevalerie d'Alphonse, compte de Poitiers, 1241* from the *Bibliothèque de l'Ecole des chartes*, 14 (1853), 35 in his *Etudes sur les foires de Champagne, sur la nature, l'étendue et les règles du commerce qui s'y faisait au XIIe, XIIIe et XIVe siècles* (Brionne, France: Le Portulan, 1865), 280.

11. R. Vaultier, "Les Enseignes de pèlerinage de Notre-Dame de Chartres," *Sanctuaires et pèlerinages* 12 (1958): 40. Vaultier cites the custom in Chartres of producing "petites chemises" of linen, satin, and damask that had been touched to the "sainte châsse" and then worn for protection.

12. Vaultier, *Enseignes*, 43. Vaultier also notes J. Lesaige, who describes in his *Voyage en Terre Sainte* of 1518 having been saved from drowning by a *chemise de Chartres* that he wore next to his skin (43–44).

13. Mély, *Les chemises*, 3.

14. Mély, *Les chemises*, 4–16.

15. The *Cartulaire de Notre-Dame de Chartres*, ed. E. de Lépinois and Lucien Merlet, 1 (Chartres, 1862), cxlvi–cxlvii, lists donations from the eleventh through thirteenth centuries of jewels and gemstones for the reliquary. By the fourteenth century, decorations included many precious stones, among them the famous cameo given by Charles V (Delaporte, *Le voile*, 8). Fernand de Mély provides an engraving of this elaborately decorated reliquary he contends was made before the Revolution, *Le trésor de Chartres: 1310–1793* (Paris, 1886), pl. VIII.

16. Delaporte, *Le voile*, 13. Fernand de Mély gives the description of the relic from the *procès verbal* from 1712 as follows: "In ea (la Ste Châsse) invenimus sindonem seu linteum, lineis distinctum, in quo animalium, florumque figurae filis intertextis depictae sunt; cujus extremitates segmentis multicoloribus variogatae terminantur limbo imaginibus animalium ex filis aureis decoro cum fimbria serica rubra; quae quidem sindon obducebat aliud linteum tenuissimum et per antiquum ex tela partier serica, vetustate et humore detritum et aliquibus in locis concisum, longum circiter quatuor ulnis cum dimidia, cujus duae extremitates filatim dissolutae," *Le trésor de Chartres*, 118. Delaporte also describes other items that were removed from the "châsse": a leather belt with an ivory buckle, a small manuscript containing the text of the fourth evangelist, shreds of fabric, some bones and pieces of hair, some in small boxes with canonical lids, others inside gloves, some inscriptions on parchment, one stating that the belt and book were from St. Lubin, bishop of Chartres who died in the sixth century. All of these were put back into the "Sainte Châsse" when the two bands of fabric, the principal relics, as he calls them, were transferred to a new gold reliquary to protect them from worms (13–14).

17. Delaporte, *Le voile*, 28.

18. Delaporte details the process of reconstituting the "Sainte Chemise," which had been cut into pieces in 1793, as follows. In 1806 a former bishop of Chartres discovered several fragments of the "étoffe orientale," which was the covering for the *chemise*, and put them in a new reliquary of silver in the form of a monstrance. In 1809, more fragments were collected along with documentation from the *abbé* Barthélemy describing the holy

chemise as "étoffe de soye" more than a thousand years old, resembling the veils of Oriental women. These fragments were placed in a sack of yellow silk and put in a "reliquaire de vermeil" in the form of a "coffret" and sent to Chartres, where they were later enclosed in a "châsse de bronze doré" in the form of a Gothic building. In 1820 the new bishop of Chartres recognized the authenticity of the relics as part of the act of reestablishing the episcopal see (*Le voile*, 16–18).

19. Delaporte, *Le voile*, 31.

20. At this point, according to Delaporte, the veils are removed from the "coffret" of 1820 and placed in another that still exists: a cedar box enclosed in a copper "châsse," decorated in enamel and goldwork (22). Marcel Bulteau quotes the *procès verbal* of 1849, which refers to the holy garment as both a "tunique" and a "chemise," saying "elle se compose de deux morceaux de la même étoffe de soie blanche ecrue" (*Description de la Cathédrale de Chartres* [Chartres, 1850], 163). In 1855, the church receives a final fragment of approximately 130 by 140 centimeters and a fragment of the patterned covering, which were put in a new reliquary, placed in the crypt in 1857, and still venerated today (Delaporte, *Le voile*, 23). J.-B. Souchet's *Histoire du diocèse de la ville de Chartres* 2 (Chartres: Garnier, 1868) seeks to prove the authenticity of the Virgin's *chemise* at Chartres using church chronicles and miracle stories. Although this author had never seen the contents of the reliquary, he describes having touched them with a special golden rod and having determined them to be some kind of folded *linge* (101). When the reliquary was opened for the last time in 1927, its contents included two pieces of white silk, 2 meters by 12 centimeters by 46 centimeters, and 26 centimeters by 18 centimeters, and fragments of the "étoffe orientale" along with the *procès verbaux* from 1712, 1820, 1822, 1849, and 1876 (this last date being when the veil, then called the "Carnutum Tutela," was paraded through the streets of Chartres in celebration of the original donation in 876, Delaporte, *Le voile*, 23–24).

21. Bulteau, *Description*, 163.

22. Mély cites an undated *vieil cartulaire* that described two textiles constituting the famed relic, "a white fabric such as linen or rough silk" (une étoffe blanche comme linge ou soie salye) and another fabric "like a striped, whitish, Egyptian-like cloth" (comme un droguet rayé, blanchastre à peu près comme celui des Egyptiens), *Le trésor*, 49, n. 2.

23. André Chédeville, ed., *Histoire de Chartres et du pays chartrain* (Toulouse: Privat, 1983), 61. Roger Joly calls it "Muslim work," *Histoire de Chartres* (Le Coteau: Editions Horvath, 1982), 2.

24. "Threads of Authority: The Virgin Mary's Veil in the Middle Ages," in *Robes and Honor: The Medieval World of Investiture*, ed. Stewart Gregory (New York: Palgrave, 2001), 73.

25. William of Malmesbury describes a "camisiam quoque ejusdem Virginis quam Carolus Calvus cum aliis reliquiis a Constantinopoli advexerat"; the *Chronique de Saint-Martin de Tours* portrays a "camisia Beatae Mariae, quam Carolus Calvus detulit a Bizantio"; and the *Miracles de Notre-Dame de Chartres* reports that "cives attoniti . . . Beate Marie auxilium implorant camisiamque gloriosissime Virginis quam a Constantinopoli ibi allatam unus ex Karolis, qui Calvus dictus est, ibi posuerat, super propugnacula in modum

vexilli ventis imponunt" (Delaporte, *Le voile*, 8). In his thirteenth-century Old French account (ca. 1262), Jean Le Marchant describes the "seinte chemise" as originating from "Constentinoble" (28.49–51), and Adgar similarly portrays Mary's "chemise" as having come from "Costentinoble la bele" (vv. 33–37). Jean Le Marchant's account mentions two garments, as noted above: a *chemise* and *voile* (27.151–52), although only one garment (*camisia*) is recorded in the Latin text he translates and adapts (Delaporte, *Le Voile*, 12; Joly, *Histoire*, 2).

26. Marcel Bulteau, *Monographie de la cathédrale de Chartres*, 1 (Chartres, 1887), 106.

27. Ilene H. Forsyth, *The Throne of Wisdom: Wood Sculptures of the Madonna in Romanesque France* (Princeton, N.J.: Princeton University Press, 1972), 1–2.

28. Adolf Katzenellenbogen, *The Sculptural Programs of Chartres: Christ, Mary, Ecclesia* (Baltimore: Johns Hopkins University Press, 1959), 9–11 and pl. 9; Jane Welch Williams, *Bread, Wine, and Money: The Windows of the Trades at Chartres Cathedral* (Chicago: University of Chicago Press, 1993), 56–57. The pose is also found on Palestinian *ampullae* of the sixth century and on sixth-century ivories, Katzenellenbogen pl. 17 and 18.

29. See Willliams, color pl. 4 and pl. 54 along with the Cult of the Carts in the Miracle of the Virgin window, pl. 64. For high-quality recent photographs see Colette and Jean-Paul Deremble, *Vitraux de Chartres* (Paris: Zodiaque, 2003): the Life of Christ window, 24–28; the Belle Verrière, 50–53; and two quatrefoils in the Miracles of the Virgin Window, 62–64. For corresponding images in Colette Mahnes-Deremble, *Les Vitraux narratifs de la Cathédral de Chartres: Etude iconographique* (Paris: Léopard d'or, 1993), see pls. 50, 30a, and 38. For a listing of the many and varied depictions of the Virgin in stained glass at Chartres, see Colette Mahnes-Deremble, *Les Vitraux narratifs*, 169–70.

30. The statue seen at Chartres today is a replica made in 1857 according to Forsyth, *The Throne of Wisdom*, 109, note 67. Laura Spitzer in "The Cult of the Virgin and Gothic Sculpture: Evaluating Opposition in the Chartres West Façade Capital Frieze," GESTA 33.2 (1994): 132–50 discusses the relation between folkloric aspects of the cult of the Virgin and the narrative of her life depicted on the capital frieze of the west façade, which emphasizes family, fertility, and local worship by women in particular, in contrast to what Spitzer views as the more canonical imagery of the *sedes sapientiae*, in which Mary is subservient iconographically to the Christ Child seated on her lap, as on a throne. My analysis will show another aspect of the *sedes sapientiae* that relates it directly to popular piety and cultic practice, a dimension born of pilgrimage, cloth production, and trade.

31. Forsyth, *Throne of Wisdom*, 109. On the cult statue in the crypt see Forsyth, 105–11; and Yves Delaporte, *Les trois Notre-Dames de la Cathédrale de Chartres* (Chartres, 1955), 6–32.

32. "La vierge est dans une chaise, tenant son fils assis sur ses genoux . . . La vierge est revestue, par dessus sa robe, d'un manteau à l'antique, en forme de dalmatique, qui, se retroussant sur le bras, semble arrondie par le devant sur les genoux jusqu'où elle descend; le voile qui lui couvre la teste porte sur ses deux épaules," cited in Forsyth, *Throne of Wisdom*, 108.

33. See Sophie Cassagnes-Brouquet, *Vierges noires* (Parc Saint-Joseph: Editions de Rouergue, 2000), 74, 79, 81, 151–53, and 166–70. Williams, *Bread, Wine and Money*, pls.

62–63, provides images of Nostre-Dame-sous Terre along with the sculpted "Virgin enthroned" on the west façade.

34. Forsyth, *Throne of Wisdom*, 8 and 23. Katzenellenbogen, *Sculptural Programs*, 60. Forsyth, however, understands the Madonnas in Majesty in the main as part of a tradition of Northern French sculpture (20–22).

35. The most famous medieval statues of black Virgins (now both destroyed) were located at Chartres and Le Puy (Cassagnes-Brouquet, *Vierges noires*, 135). Legendary accounts of the statue at Le Puy trace its provenance from Egypt to Babylon and Jerusalem before being brought to France by a French king, thought perhaps to be Louis IX (Forsyth, *Throne of Wisdom*, 103).

36. Forsyth, *Throne of Wisdom*, 16.

37. Delaporte, *Les trois Notre-Dames*, 35–40; Williams, *Bread, Wine, and Money*, 57. See the Gothic ambulatory window shown in Williams, pl. 65; and the Miracle of the Virgin window in the south aisle, pl. 64. In addition, the window dedicated to the Miracles of Notre Dame includes, in the second quatrefoil, a modern reconstruction of an intriguing scene of men carrying what appears to be a reliquary honored by pilgrims, Deremble, *Vitraux*, 62; and Mahnes-Deremble, pl. 38.

38. Bruna, *Enseignes*, thesis, 7–9, 84, and 94; *Enseignes*, catalogue, 82, 95, and 96–98. Bruna cites production of badges at Le Puy from 1182 (*Enseignes*, catalogue, 95) and possible production in Paris from 1260, noting Etienne Boileau's *Livre des métiers*, which describes lead and tin workers making "autres menus choseites apartenans a plon et a estain" (Bruna, *Enseignes*, thesis, 34). Secular badges, some with highly profane images, were sold to pilgrims alongside religious badges beginning in the fourteenth century (Bruna, *Enseignes*, thesis, 7 and 35). See also Brian Spencer, "Medieval Pilgrim Badges: Some General Observations Illustrated Mainly from English Sources," in *The Rotterdam Papers: A Contribution to Medieval Archaeology*, ed. J. G. N. Renaud (Rotterdam, 1968), 139; and his *Pilgrim Souvenirs, and Secular Badges*; Cohen, "*In haec signa*," 195; Colette Lamy-Lassalle, "Recherches sur un ensemble de plombs trouvés dans la Seine: Musée des antiquités de Rouen et Collection Bossard de Lucerne," *Revue de la Société des savants de Haute Normandie, Lettres et Sciences Humaines* 49 (1968): 10; and Vaultier, "Enseignes," 40.

39. In another context, a letter of Innocent III in 1199 speaks of "the emblems of lead or tin . . . bearing the image of the apostles Peter and Paul, with which those who visit their shrines distinguish themselves, as evidence of their devotion and proof of their completed journey," cited in Diana Webb, *Pilgrims and Pilgrimage in Medieval Europe* (London: I. B. Tauris, 1999), 129. Bruna notes, however, that by the thirteenth century in France, pilgrim badges, while distinguishing pilgrims from other travelers, no longer indicated penitence (*Enseignes*, thesis, 172).

40. Bruna, *Enseignes*, catalogue, 24–25, reports that Forgeais sold some 3,300 lead objects to the Cluny Museum in 1861, with others arriving in 1863–64, that he sold still others to the Musée Carnavalet in Paris and the Musée des beaux arts in Chartres, and donated others to the Musée des beaux arts in Rouen.

41. Badges from Boulogne-sur-Mer are equally unusual in depicting a miracle performed by the Virgin. See Forgeais, 2:7–18.

42. Weyl Carr, "Threads of Authority," 64–66. Weyl Carr explains (72) that the image is recorded in Anna Komnene's description of Alexios I carrying a *maphorion* and in a translation of a hymn by a Venetian bishop who was in France from 807 to 815; the image then made its way into the Chartrain legends as seen, for example, in William of Malmesbury's text, in which the *chemise* is displayed on the ramparts like a banner.

43. *Les miracles de Nostre Dame par Gautier de Coinci*, ed. V. Frederic Koenig, (Geneva: Droz, 1970), 31–41. Sirarpie Der Nercessian, "Two Miracles of the Virgin in the Poems of Gautier de Coincy," *Dumbarton Oaks Papers* 41 (1987): 157–63, provides an image of the siege from an Old French manuscript, explaining that it is the oldest preserved example depicting the victory of the Byzantines over their enemies during the siege of 717–18.

44. Kjellman, *Miracles*, 234–36, prints a version of another legend that tells how the Virgin's image, rather than her silk cloak, protects a city thought to be Constantinople from Saracen attack, "Comment une image de la Sainte Vierge protégea les chrétiens contre les sarrasins." The text describes "une cite de la terre seinte" initially protected by a painted image of "la gloriouse Marie" (vv. 1–22), and a later incident in the time of emperor "Leoine," when "Sarazins" besiege the city for three years and again the painted image of the "seinte figure" saves the city (vv. 23–50). Previously, this same image, carried into battle by the emperor Aracle against a "gent perverse au royaume de Perse," had also ensured victory (vv. 55–66).

45. Ed. Lucien Merlet (Chartres, 1885), 192–94.

46. Although Félix Bourquelot contends that the majority of fabrics used in Christian churches in the west came from the Christian Orient (*Etudes sur les foires*, 694), Olivia Remie Constable explains that before the thirteenth century, al-Andalus exported Muslim silk to Europe and that by the end of the eleventh century northern Spain enjoyed Muslim textiles of both Andalusian and eastern manufacture, *Trade and Traders in Muslim Spain: The Commercial Realignment of the Iberian Peninsula, 900–1500* (Cambridge: Cambridge University Press, 1994), 178. For silk production in Paris in the thirteenth century, see Sharon Farmer, "Biffes, Tiretaines, and *Aumonières*: The Role of Paris in the International Textile Markets of the Thirteenth and Fourteenth Centuries," *Medieval Clothing and Textiles* 2 (2006): 73–89; and her "Weavers and Spinners in the Wool, Linen, and Silk Industries in Thirteenth-Century Paris: A Comparative Analysis." In manuscript.

47. Mély, *Le trésor*, i., pl. XI (my Figure 11).

48. Delaporte, *Le voile*, plate VI.

49. Dominique Cardon, "De l'Espagne à l'Italie: Hypothèses concernant un groupe de soieries médiévales à fond de losanges lisérés et bandes de samit façonnée," in *Techniques et culture* 34 (1999): 139–57.

50. Constable, *Trade and Traders*, 178. On Cordoban textiles see R. B. Serjeant, *Islamic Textiles: A History up to the Mongol Conquest* (Beirut: Librairie du Liban, 1972), 165 and 169–77.

51. Bourquelot, *Etudes sur les foires*, 68–69.

52. Kuntsmann has published the most comprehensive set of legends involving the Virgin's *chemise* at Chartres: three Old French accounts by Jean Le Marchant, "De l'arsure de l'iglise de Chartres et comment li legas sarmona aus gens de la ville" (66–78), "Coment

la cité de Chartres fut delivree de ses anemis par la seinte chemise de Chartres" (217–21), and "Dou Chevalier qui fu sauvé de mort a vie por ce qu'il avoit vestue des chemises de Chartres" (162–66); as well as two related tales concerning the Virgin at Chartres and clothwork: "D'une fame a cui il mesavint por ce qu'el filla au semadi au seir" (190–205), and "D'une fame qui ofri une töaille a l'autel Nostre Dame de Chartres" (213–16). Collections of legends dedicated to the Virgin in France were compiled beginning in the early twelfth century at Marian shrines such as Coutances, Nogent, Laon, Soissons, Rocamadour, Fécamp, and Chartres. See Wilson, ed. *Stella maris*, p. 4; and *Vierge et merveille: Les miracles de Norte-Dame narratifs au moyen âge*, ed. Pierre Kuntsmann (Paris, 1981). 17. Kunstmann notes the existence of two thousand medieval miracle stories in Latin, 490 in Old French verse and six hundred in prose (20).

53. On Dudo of Saint-Quentin, Etienne de Bourbon, John of Garland, Wace, Jean le Marchant, William Adgar, and the texts published in Kjellman, *Miracles*, see note 1 above. See also William of Jumièges, *Gesta Normannorum ducum*, ed. Jean Marx (Rouen, 1914), 26–27; William of Malmesbury, *De gestis regum Anglorum*, 1 (Oxford, 1998); and Vincent of Beauvais's *Speculum historiale*, ed. Michel Tarayre (Paris, 1999).

54. Although the soldiers are said to witness a miracle "Que leur fist la dame charteine," 28.79, she works entirely through the *chemise*.

55. Jean Le Marchant, *Miracles*, 162–66, "Dou Chevalier qui fu sauvé de mort a vie por ce qu'il avoit vestue des chemises de Chartres."

56. And earlier, 21.59–64.

57. See, for example, the badges Forgeais (vol. 2) gives from Vauvert (4), Liesse (35, 39, 40, 41, 42, 44, and 45), Tombelaine (48, 50, 51), Roc-Amadour (52 and 57–60), and others (63 and 64). On pilgrim badges from Boulogne-sur-Mer, the Virgin also holds the Child in a similar pose but she is most often standing (14, 15, 17, 18, 19, 21, 25, and 26).

58. Bruna gives five examples of the tunic at Argenteuil (*Enseignes*, thesis, 58–60); Forgeais provides four images of Christ's holy tunic on pilgrim badges (4:99, 101, 102, and 104). Spencer provides images from Aachen (*Pilgrim Souvenirs*, 256–60). Badges featuring the veronica also depict cloth or drapery (Forgeais, 4:87, 89, 91, and 93). Among the secular badges, there is at least one example of a pair of shoes, another of a hat, and ten of alms purses, ranging from the fourteenth to the sixteenth centuries (Bruna, *Enseignes*, thesis, 246, 349, and 313–16, respectively). In England, St. Thomas of Canterbury's gloves are featured on a number of surviving badges (Spencer, "Medieval Pilgrim Badges," 141), and there are isolated stunning examples of detailed clothing worn by individual figures portrayed on badges in Spencer, *Pilgrim Souvenirs*, such as 263d, 263e, 246c, 211a, and 211. The badges of "métiers" published by Forgeais in volume 1 feature a purse for the "boursiers" (37), a belt for the "ceinturonniers" (42–44), a hat for the "chapeliers" (49–52), and a stocking for the "chaussetiers" (56). As for other textile relics, Forsyth lists various tunics, robes, and *chemises* of the Virgin, sometimes in fragmentary form, venerated at Clermont-Ferrand, Cologne, Schaffhausen, Senlis, Stavelot, Trier, and Vézelay, explaining further that Cluny had a sleeve and Le Puy a slipper (*Throne of Wisdom*, 32).

59. Cohen, "*In haec signa*," 196. Bruna cites the few rare exceptions of pilgrimage badges, including those from Chartres, that carry an image on the reverse (*Enseignes*,

thesis, 147). Badges from Boulogne-sur-Mer are unusual in depicting a miracle performed by the Virgin (Forgeais, 2:7–18); by contrast, the "méreaux" reproduced by Forgeais typically have images on both front and back (Forgeais, vol. 1). So too pewter *ampoules*, or portable reliquaries brought west from Palestine by medieval pilgrims returning from the Holy Land, which were adapted in the west in the seventh century and persisted, especially at sites with water, until the sixteenth century in France, often had images on two sides. See Bruna, *Enseignes*, thesis, 77–94.

60. Lamy-Lassalle, "Recherches," 9; Spencer, "Medieval Pilgrim Badges," 141; Bruna, *Enseignes*, thesis, 98. Brigitte Bedos-Rezak explains that the Virgin appears on ecclesiastical seals, crowned and enthroned, as early as 1150, "Women, Seals, and Power in Medieval France, 1150–1350," in Mary Erler and Maryanne Kowaleski, eds. *Women and Power in the Middle Ages* (Athens: University of Georgia Press, 1988), 75.

61. Forsyth cites this pose as a variation found among the sculpted Madonnas in Majesty (*Throne of Wisdom*, 23). Actually, the Virgin figured on these first three Chartrain badges resembles most closely images of the Virgin on certain medieval seals, both Byzantine and French, a seal of Nicephor I from the ninth century and seals from the abbey of Breteuil in 1183 and the city of Narbonne in 1218. The Byzantine seal differs most dramatically from the Chartrain badge in that the Virgin is standing; see *Byzantine Women and Their World*, ed. Ioli Kalavrezou (New Haven: Yale University Press, 2003), fig. 3, 201. In the French examples, as on Chartrain pilgrim badges, the Virgin is seated; see Germain Demay, *Le costume au moyen âge d'après les sceaux* (Paris: Librairie de D. Dumoulin, 1880), 390 and 392. The Virgin appears on Byzantine seals beginning in the sixth century, with imperial seals tending to favor over time the image of the Virgin Hodegetria, the icon of Blachernai reputed to have protected the capital in 626 (*Byzantine Women*, 200).

62. Deremble, *Vitraux*, 236.

63. Forsyth, *Throne of Wisdom*, 114 and 135–36.

64. Forgeais, 4:103, provides this image as a point of reference for the *sainte tunique* at Argenteuil.

65. Jean Le Marchant, Miracles, 213–16, "D'une Fame qui ofri une töaille a l'autel Nostre Dame de Chartres."

66. Although the "toaille" does not bear the cut and shape of a medieval chemise, nor does it hold the privileged ancestry of having been worn by the Virgin herself, it does function in other Marian legends as an extension of the Virgin's body, as when she is shown to use a "touaille blance" to wipe the "neck, body, and face" of a deserving follower in need of comfort (Adgar, *Marien Legenden*, 84). Among the "eastern" Marian miracles recounted by Gregory of Tours in his *Libri miraculorum*, "De leproso mundato in loco ubi Dominus est baptizatus, et reliquiis B. Mariae" tells of another piece of linen cloth that miraculously survives a fire, this time set by thieves. A leper from Gaul who traveled to Jerusalem to be cured then takes to Rome some unspecified "relics of the Virgin" enclosed in a chest. When attackers, who break open the chest hoping to find gold, see only the relics, they set a fire that reduces the chest to ashes. Not only do the relics survive, but more specifically the linen in which they were wrapped, "linteum quo involutae," *Les livres des miracles et autres*

opuscules de Georges Florent Grégoire, évêque de Tours, ed. and trans. H. L. Bordier, vol. 1 (Paris, 1857), 55.

67. Chédeville, *Chartres et ses campagnes*, 448 and 451. Geneviève Aclocque claims that linen weavers at Chartres had formed their own guild by the fifteenth century: *Les corporations, l'industrie et le commerce à Chartres du XIe siècle à la révolution* (Paris, 1917; rpt. New York, 1967), 303. See also George Henderson, *Chartres* (Harmondsworth: Penguin, 1968), 72. Aclocque attributes the early stages of wool production to male workers, while asserting that the spinning was done by women using distaffs (108). She explains further that master weavers of wool at Chartres could teach their heirs, male or female, to replace them as masters of the trade (332).

68. Katzenellenbogen, *Sculptural Programs*, 74. Margaret and Ernest Marriage, *The Sculptures of Chartres Cathedral* (Cambridge: Cambridge University Press, 1909), pls. 47–48, describe the first two figures as washing and carding wool (102). Aclocque follows their reading (*Les corporations*, 318), as does Chédeville (*Chartres et ses campagnes*, 448); Dominique Cardon, *La Draperie au Moyen Age: Essor d'une grande industrie européene* (Paris: CNRS, 1999), 146, 180. For images of female figures working cloth at Chartres see 187, 285.

69. Marriage, *The Sculptures*, 102.

70. Adgar, *Marien Legenden*, 116–21.

71. The garment, which expanded as Christ grew, became the object of Roman soldiers' gambling at his death. Gregory of Tours refers to the garment only generically as a "vestimentum." See *Les livres des miracles*, 25–27.

72. A more metaphorical version of the story is provided by the thirteenth-century poet and playwright Adam de la Halle, who stages a repentant narrator asking the "Glorïeuse Virge Marie" to be his "cover and cloak" ("couvreture et mantiaus," P. J. M. Ashmann, ed., *Le Culte de la Vierge et la littérature profane du moyen âge* [Utrecht, 1930], 105). In this instance, rather than making or conferring a holy garment, the Virgin has actually become, metaphorically, the garment itself: she is the mantle that wraps her devoted followers in safety and reassurance. Although the fabric of the Virgin's metaphorical cloak in this poem is not specified, the sentiment expressed here resonates with other contemporary calls to abandon the luxurious garments and goods of this world (often made of silk) and embrace an alternative kind of luxury in the celestial realm (See Burns, *Courtly Love Undressed*, 37–41). Here, the faithful do not physically touch a garment previously touched by the Virgin but are instead enfolded metaphorically by her luxurious, garment-like body. A similar legend is told of St. Dominic who, having arrived in heaven felt sad and lonely until the Virgin opened her mantle to reveal numerous other Dominicans who had been accepted into heaven because of their Marian devotion (Ashmann, *Culte*, 34).

73. See, for example, Gail McMurray Gibson, *Theater of Devotion: East Anglian Drama and Society in the Late Middle Ages* (Chicago: University of Chicago Press, 1989), 161; Nancy A. Jones, "The Uses of Embroidery in the Romances of Jean Renart: Gender, History, Textuality," in *Jean Renart and the Art of Romance*, ed. Nancy Vine Durling (Gainesville: University Press of Florida, 1997), 13–44.

74. Jean Le Marchant, *Miracles*, 190–205, "D'Une Fame a cui il mesavint por ce qu'el filla au semadi au seir."

75. Aclocque, *Les corporations*, 171 and 174–75.

76. Lecocq, "Recherches," 208.

77. Cohen, "*In haec signa*," 206. Vaultier cites evidence from 1390 of a "vendeur d'image de plomb" at Chartres ("Enseignes," 40). For the conflicting views held by the medieval church on merchants, see Jacques Le Goff, *Marchands et banquiers du moyen âge* (Paris: Presses Universitaires de France, 1956). Lester Little notes further that Franciscans and Dominicans, the very orders that furthered Marian legends, also often appealed to urban audiences using metaphors of the marketplace and were denounced for their avarice, wealth, and merchandising, in brief, for their similarity to merchants, *Religious Poverty and the Profit Economy in Medieval Europe* (Ithaca, N.Y.: Cornell University Press, 1978), 201–2.

78. "Postel, quenoiller et marchant," rents a stall in the cloister "tant à vendre quenoilles que toute espèce de plomb et metal, estain ou autre espèce que ce puist estre, et sans ce que autre que ledit Postel, ou de par luy, dedans ledict Cloistre y en puisse vendre, où soit imprimé l'ymage Nostre-Dame, sans le congié et licence dudit Postel" ("Recherches," 207). At Chartres, by the late Middle Ages, *quenouilles* were sold exclusively in the cloister of Notre-Dame: Claudine Billot, *Chartres à la fin du Moyen Age* (Paris: Edition de l'Ecole des hautes études en sciences sociales, 1987), 226.

79. Williams, *Bread, Wine, and Money*, pl. 4 and her compelling discussion of the wool as an offering by local merchants, 60–62.

80. Vaultier, "Enseignes," 41. In one instance (Figure 16), the image of the Virgin's *chemise* is accompanied on the left by a shield-like form that retains only some of the patterned details of the *denier chartrain* represented on other badges. For details of local coinage at Chartres, see Chédeville, *Chartres et ses campagnes*, 431–39; and René de Ponton d'Amécourt, *Monnaies au type chinonais* (Mâcon, 1895).

81. Williams, *Bread, Wine, and Money*, 119 and 137–42.

82. Chédeville contends that in terms of revenue, the sale of food was the major contributor to profit making at Chartrain fairs, with the sale of textiles and furs second in volume, and small objects (including pilgrim badges) third (*Chartres et ses campagnes*, 446–47 and 456).

83. Aclocque, *Les corporations*, 116.

84. Antoine Sabatier, *Sigillographie historique des administrations fiscales, communautés ouvrières et institutions diverses ayant employé des sceaux en plomb: XIVe-XVIIIe siècles* (Paris, 1912), 196–97, and 247.

85. Sabatier, *Sigillographie*, 235–37, 240, and 512. Interestingly, Forgeais (5:898) describes Byzantine coins from the eleventh and twelfth centuries as typically bearing the emperor's image on the front and the Virgin on the reverse. Forgeais also reproduces tokens (*méreaux*) accorded to merchants, he surmises, as an indication of taxes and tolls paid (5:128–34). Chédeville claims that all cloth sold at Chartres, in the fairs and markets alike, was taxed in the amount of an *obole, Chartres et ses campagnes*, 449.

86. Jean Le Marchant, *Miracles* 3.325–34, "De l'arsure de l'iglise de Chartres et comment li legas sarmona aus gens de la ville": "Et loërent, o vois joieuse,/ Dieu et sa mere glo-

rïeuse/ Qui la seinte chasse ennoree/ Avoient dou feu delivree./ Lors pristrent trestuit a promestre/ Dou leur agent donner et mestre/ En feire riche iglise et noble;/ Clers et borjois et rente et mueble/ Abandonerent en aïe,/ Chascun selonc sa menantie." Historically, the relics were circulated in public to raise money (Chédeville, *Chartres et ses campagnes*, 515–16); Williams, *Bread, Wine, and Money*, 31 and 168 n. 94.

87. Williams provides a map, *Bread, Wine, and Money*, 136. Arthur Engel and Raymond Serrure reproduce a range of coins of the "type chartrain" also called "chinonais" because they circulated in the mid-Loire region in their *Traité numismatique du Moyen Age*, vol. 2 (Bologna: Arnaldo Forni, 1964), 394–410. See also Chédeville, *Chartres et ses campagnes*, 431–39; and C. Cartier, *Essai sur les monnaies chartraines frappées par les comptes de Chartres et de Blois jusqu'au 14e siècle* (Tours, 1883). Chartrain coins generally have been dated between 1256 and 1319 based on different configurations of the *fleur de lys* that they display. Cartier's argument in "Recherches sur l'origine," 51–73, that the image of the denier found on the pilgrim badges from Chartres represents the actual bands of cloth housed in the reliquary, has not been substantiated by later scholars.

88. Alison Stones and Jeanne Krochalis, *The Pilgrim's Guide: A Critical Edition*, vol. 1 (London: Harvey Miller, 1998), inside back cover, not paginated.

89. Constable, *Trade and Traders*, 4–45. In addition, Chartres was also a rallying point for crusaders departing for the Holy Land in 1106, after attending the wedding of Bohémond of Tarent, prince of Antioch, to Constance, sister of Louis VI (Chédeville, *Histoire de Chartres*, 73).

90. *Les Quinze joies de marriage*, ed. Jean Rychner (Paris: Champion, 1963), 69–70.

91. Pamela Sheingorn, *The Book of Sainte Foy* (Philadelphia: University of Pennsylvania Press, 1995), 182–83.

92. The confusion of merchants and pilgrims was commonplace. McCormick has documented the fluid boundaries that existed between ambassadors, pilgrims, and merchants as early as the Carolingian era (*Origins*, 242). Webb adds further that in the Holy Land, pilgrims generated business for both Christian and Muslim merchants (*Pilgrims*, 24 and 27). Pilgrims were often confused with merchants because the two shared certain special legal rights regarding wills, contracts, and safe conduct accorded only to travelers (*Pilgrims*, 84–105). Innocent IV appeals to the queen of France in 1251 not to levy taxes or tolls on the horses and goods carried by Danish pilgrims passing through "as if they were merchants" because, as he explains "they are not merchants at all" (*Pilgrims*, 101). And yet the confusion arises because both merchants and pilgrims held the distinction of traveling and circulating geographically and because they both transported goods. Indeed, many pilgrims were in fact merchants.

93. Abeischer, *Le Voyage*, 41 and 85.

94. Veronika Gervers, "Medieval Garments in the Mediterranean World," in *Cloth and Clothing in Medieval Europe*, ed. N. B. Harte and K. G. Ponting (London: Heinemann Educational Books, 1983), 279–315.

95. See *Le trésor de la Sainte-Chapelle*, 231.

96. The most widely copied of all types of the Virgin in Byzantium, the Hodegetria, derived from an icon originally in the Hodegon monastery in Constantinople, generally

refers to a Virgin holding the Child in her left arm and gesturing toward him with her right hand while gazing at the viewer or off in the distance. The Christ Child typically holds a scroll in his lap and makes the gesture of blessing: see Alexander P. Kazhdan, ed., *Oxford Dictionary of Byzantium* (Oxford: Oxford University Press, 1991), 2172–73.

97. See, for example, the Virgin Hodegetria on the twelfth-century cameo seal from Constantinople, *Byzantine Women*, figure 199, p. 286. The badge in Figure 18 bears a distinctively different architectural shape from the others, but Figures 15 and 18 are further related in the repetition of the brooch on the Virgin's mantle.

98. Janet Snyder, "Cloth from the Promised Land," in E. Jane Burns, ed. *Medieval Fabrications*, 147–64; and her "The Regal Significance of the Dalmatic: The Robes of *le sacre* as Represented in Sculpture of Northern Mid-Twelfth Century France," in Stewart Gregory, ed., *Robes and Honor*, 291-304.

99. Bourquelot, *Etude sur les foires*, 281, Wilhelm Heyd, *Histoire du commerce du Levant*, vol. 2 (Amsterdam: Adolph Hakkert, 1959), 694.

100. Chédeville, *Chartres et ses campagnes*, 446–47 and 454; Billot, *Chartres*, 226 and 228. Bourquelot, *Etudes sur les foires*, 144. The *Dit du Lendit rimé* lists both wool and linen merchants among the many vendors at the Foire du Lendit (vv. 64, 73–74, and 85), and it lists Chartres as one of the seventeen cities that participated in the fair (v. 102), Gustave Fagniez, *Documents relatifs à l'histoire de l'industrie et du commerce en France*, vol. 2 (Paris: Picard, 1974), 173–76.

101. Janet Abu-Lughod in *Before European Hegemony: The World System A.D. 1250–1350* (Oxford: Oxford University Press, 1989) explains that Champagne had early and prolonged contact with the Middle East, 56-57, 62, 65, 186, and 189. See also Bourquelot, *Etudes sur les foires*, 260–63.

102. Heyd, *Histoire du commerce*, 707; Abu-Lughod, *Before European Hegemony*, 65; Bourquelot, *Etude sur les foires*, 280.

103. "Le dit des marchéans," *Recueil général et complet des fabliaux des XIIIe et XIVe siècles*, ed. Anatole de Montaiglon and Gaston Raynaud, 2 (Paris, 1872–90; rpt. New York, Burt Franklin, 1963), 124–128.

104. *Les corporations*, 332.

WORKS CITED

PRIMARY SOURCES

Adgar, William. *Marien Legenden Nach der Londoner Handschrift Egerton* 612. Ed. Carl Neuhaus. Wiesbaden, 1968.

Aucassin et Nicolette: Chantefable du XIIIe siècle. Ed. Mario Roques. Paris: Champion, 1977.

Beal, Samuel. *Si-yu-ki Buddist Records of the Western World. A Translation from the Chinese of Hiuen Tsiang* (A.D. 629). London: Trubner and Co., 1884.

Boileau, Etienne. *Le livre des métiers et corporations de la ville de Paris. XIIIe siècle*. Ed. René de Lespinasse and François Bonnardot. Paris: Imprimerie nationale, 1879.

The Book of the Eparch; Le Livre du Préfet, Edit de l'empereur Léon le Sage sur les corporations et métiers de Constantinople. London: Variorum, 1970.

La Chanson d'Antioche. Ed. Suzanne Duparc-Quioc. Paris: Librairie Orientaliste Paul Guethner, 1977.

Le Charroi de Nimes. Ed. J.-L. Perrier. Paris: Champion, 1982.

Chartraire, E. *Inventaire du trésor de l'Eglise primatiale et métropolitaine de Sens*. Paris: A. Picard, 1897.

Chrétien de Troyes. *Le chevalier au lion (Yvain)*. Ed. Mario Roques. Paris: Champion, 1978.

———. *Le chevalier de la charette*. Ed. Mario Roques. Paris: Champion, 1970.

———. *Cligès*. Ed. Alexandre Micha. Paris: Champion, 1957.

———. *Erec et Enide*. Ed. Mario Roques. Paris: Champion, 1976.

———. *Guillaume d'Angleterre*. Ed. A. J. Holden. Geneva: Droz, 1988.

———. *Philomena*. Ed. C. de Boer. Paris: Editions Paul Geuthner, 1909.

Le Conte de Floire et Blancheflor. Ed. Jean-Luc Leclanche. Paris: Champion, 1980.

Le Couronnement de Louis. Ed. Ernest Langlois. Paris: Champion, 1966.

The Crowning of Louis. Ed. and trans. Nirmal Dass. Jefferson, N.C.: McFarland, 2003.

Depping, G. B., ed. *Régelemens sur les arts et métiers de Paris rédigés au XIIIe siècle*. Paris: Imprimerie de Crapelet, 1837.

Dit du Mercier. In Philippe Menard, ed. *Mélanges offerts à Jean Frappier*, vol. 2. Geneva: Droz, 1970. 797–810.

Dit du Lendit. In Gustave Fagniez, ed. *Documents relatifs à l'histoire de l'industrie et du commerce en France*, vol. 2. Paris: Picard, 1974.

Dit des Marchéans. In Anatole de Montaiglon and Gaston Raynaud, eds. *Recueil des fabliaux des XIIIe et XIVe siècles*, vol. 2. Paris, 1877; rpt. New York: Burt Franklin, 1963.

Dunhuang de Chuan Shuo. Ed. Chen Yu Bian. Shanghai: Shanghai wen yi chu ban she, 1986.

Edrisi. *Description de l'Afrique et de l'Espagne*. Ed. and trans. Reinhart P. A. Dozy and Michael J. De Goeje. Amsterdam: Oriental Press, 1969.

Encyclopedia of Islam. Ed. P. J. Bearman et al. Leiden: Brill, 2000.

Fagniez, Gustave, ed. *Documents relatifs à l'histoire de l'industrie et du commerce en France*, vol. 2. Paris: Picard, 1974.

Falcandus, Hugo. *"The History of the Tyrants of Sicily" by "Hugo Falcandus" 1154–69*. Trans. Graham A. Loud and Thomas Wiedemann. Manchester: Manchester University Press, 1998.

———. *La Historia o liber de regno sicilie*. Rome: Gia Corsini, 1897.

Fierabras. Ed. Marc Le Person. Paris: Champion, 2003.

Forgeais, Arthur. *Collection de plombs historiés trouvés dans la Seine*. 5 vols. Paris: Chez Aubry, 1862–66.

Fulcher of Chartres. *A History of the Expedition to Jerusalem 1095–1127*. Trans. Frances Rita Ryan. Ed. Harold S. Fink. Knoxville: University of Tennessee Press, 1969.

Gautier de Coinci. *Les miracles de Nostre Dame par Gautier de Coinci*. Ed. V. Frederic Koenig. Geneva: Droz, 1970.

Godefroy, Frédéric. *Dictionnaire de l'ancienne langue française*. Paris, 1888; rpt. Vaduz, Liechtenstein: Scientific Periodicals Establishment, 1961.

Goitein, S. D., ed. and trans. *Letters of Medieval Jewish Traders*. Princeton, N.J.: Princeton University Press, 1974.

Greimas, A. J. *Dictionnaire de l'ancien français*. Paris: Larousse, 1969.

Gregory of Tours. *Les livres des miracles et autres opuscules de Georges Florent Grégoire, évêque de Tours*. Ed. and trans. H. L. Bordier, vol. 1. Paris: J. Renouard, 1857.

Guillaume de Lorris and Jean de Meun. *Le Roman de la Rose*. Ed. Felix Lecoy. 3 vols. Paris: Champion, 1965–66, 1970.

———. *Le Roman de la Rose*. Ed. and trans. Armand Strubel. Paris: Librairie générale française, 1992.

Guillaume de Palerne, roman du XIIIe siècle. Ed. Alexandre Micha. Geneva: Droz, 1990.

Historia Regum Britanniae of Geoffrey of Monmouth. Ed. and trans. Neil Wright. Cambridge: D. S. Brewer, 1991.

Jean le Marchant, *Miracles de Notre-Dame de Chartres*. Ed. Pierre Kuntsmann. Mémoires de la Société Archéologique *d'Eure-et-Loir* 26, Ottawa: Publications de l'Université d'Ottawa, 1973.

Jean Renart. *L'Escoufle: Roman d'aventure*. Ed. H. Michelant and P. Meyer. Paris: Firmin Didot, 1894.

———. *Galeran de Bretagne: Roman du XIIIe siècle*. Ed. Lucien Foulet. Paris: Champion, 1925.

———. *Le Roman de la Rose ou de Guillaume de Dole*. Ed. Félix Lecoy. Paris: Champion, 1962.

Julien, Stanislaus. *Mémoires sur les contrées occidentales traduites du Sanskrit en chinois en l'an 648 par Hiouen Thsang*. Paris: Imprimerie Impériale, 1857–58.

Kazhdan, Alexander P., ed. *Oxford Dictionary of Byzantium*. Oxford: Oxford University Press, 1991.

Kjellman, Hilding, ed. *Les Miracles de la Sainte Vierge*. Paris: Champion, 1922.

Les Lais de Marie de France. Ed. Jean Rychner. Paris: Champion, 1973.

Lecoy de la Marche, A., ed. *Anecdotes historiques, légendes et apologues*. Paris: Librairie Renouard, 1877.

La Légende de l'Empereur Constant. Ed. James Coveney. Paris: Société d'Edition les Belles Lettres, 1955.

Lépinois, E. de, and Lucien Merlet, eds. *Cartulaire de Notre-Dame de Chartres*, vol. 1. Chartres, 1862.

Macaire. Ed. F. Guessard. Paris: A. Frank, 1966.

Les Manuscrits de Chrétien de Troyes. Ed. Keith Busby, Terry Nixon, Alison Stones, and Lori Walters. Amsterdam: Rodopi, 1993.

Map, Walter. *De Nugis curialium: The Courtier's Trifles*. Ed. M. R. Jones. Revised C. N. L. Brooke and R. A. B. Mynors. Oxford: Oxford University Press, 1983.

Michel, Francisque. *Recherches sur le commerce, la fabrication et l'usage des étoffes de soie, d'or et d'argent et autres tissus précieux en Occident, principalement en France pendant le Moyen Age*. Paris: Imprimerie de Crapelet, 1852.

Les miracles de Notre-Dame de Chartres. Ed. Antoine Thomas. Bibliothèque de l'Ecole des Chartes 42 (1881): 505–50.

Odo of Deuil, *De profectione Ludovici VII in orientem*. Ed. and trans. Virginia Gingerick Berry. New York: Columbia University Press, 1948.

Ovid, *Amores, Epistulae, Medicamina faciei femineae, Ars amatoria, Remedia amoris*. Ed. R. Ehwald. Leipzig: B. G. Teubner, 1907.

Pausanius. *Description of Greece*. Trans. W. H. S. Jones and H. A. Ormerod. Cambridge, Mass.: Harvard University Press, 1918.

Penguin Atlas of Medieval History. Ed. Colin McEvedy. Baltimore: Penguin, 1961.

Pliny the Elder, *The Natural History*. Ed. and trans. John Bostock and H. T. Riley. London: G. H. Bohn, 1855–57.

Pliny, *Natural History*, vol. 2. Trans. H. Rackham. Cambridge, Mass.: Harvard University Press, 1941.

Polo, Marco. *The Description of the World*. Ed. A.C. Maile and Paul Pelliot. London: George Routledge and Sons, Ltd., 1938. rpt. New York: AMS Press, 1976.

———. *Le Devisement du monde*. Ed. Philippe Ménard. 3 vols. Geneva: Droz, 2001.

La Prise d'Orange. Ed. Claude Régnier. Paris: Kliencksiek, 1983.

Procopius. *History of the Wars, Secret History, and Buildings*. Ed. and trans. Averil Cameron. New York: Washington Square Press, 1967.

Ptolemy. *Geography: Book 6: Middle East, Central and North Asia, China*. Ed. Helmut Humbach and Suzanne Ziegler. Wiesbaden: L. Reichert, 1998.

Les Quinze joies de marriage. Ed. Jean Rychner. Paris: Champion, 1963.

Recueil général et complet des fabliaux des XIIIe et XIVe siècles. Ed. Anatole de Montaiglon and Gaston Raynaud, vol. 2. Paris, 1872–90; rpt. New York, 1963.

Rémusat, Abel. *Histoire de la ville de Khotan traduit du chinois.* Paris: Imprimerie Doublet, 1920.

Le Roman d'Enéas. Ed. Aimé Petit. Paris: Livre de Poche, 1997.

Le Roman du Castelain de Couci et de la Dame de Fayel. Ed. Maurice Delbouille. Paris: SATF, 1936.

Seneca the Elder. *Declamations (Controversiae).* Trans. M. Winterbottom. Cambridge, Mass.: Harvard University Press, 1974.

The Songs of Bernart de Ventadorn. Ed. Stephen G. Nichols, Jr. Chapel Hill: University of North Carolina Press, 1962.

The Songs of Jaufré Rudel. Ed. Rupert T. Pickens. Toronto: Pontifical Institute of Mediaeval Studies, 1978.

Spanish Ballads. Ed. S. Griswold Morley. New York: Henry Holt, 1912.

Strabo. *Geography.* Ed. H. C. Hamilton. London: George Bell and Sons, 1903.

Stones, Alison, and Jeanne Krochalis. *The Pilgrim's Guide: A Critical Edition*, vol. 1. London: Harvey Miller, 1998.

Terry, Patricia, and Nancy Vine Durling, trans. and eds. *The Romance of the Rose or Guillaume de Dole.* Philadelphia: University of Pennsylvania Press, 1993.

Tertullian. *Disciplinary, Moral, and Ascetical Works.* Trans. Rudolph Arbesmann. New York: Fathers of the Church, 1959.

Tobler-Lommatzsch, Adolph. *Altfranzösisches Wörterbuch.* Wiesbaden: Franz Steiner Verlag, 1973.

Two Lives of Charlemagne: Einhard and Notker the Stammerer. Trans. Lewis Thorpe. Harmondsworth: Penguin, 1967.

Van Dieten, J. L., ed. *Nicetae Choniate Historia.* Berlin, 1975.

Vierge et merveille: Les miracles de Norte-Dame narratifs au moyen âge. Ed. Pierre Kuntsmann. Paris, 1981.

Vincent of Beauvais. *Speculum historiale.* Ed. Michel Tarayre. Paris, 1999.

Virgil. *Bucolics, Aeneid, and Georgics of Vergil.* Ed. J. B. Greenough. Boston: Ginn and Co., 1900.

Le Voyage de Charlemagne à Jerusalem et à Constantinople. Ed. Paul Aebischer. Geneva: Droz, 1965.

Wace. *Roman de Rou.* Ed. A. J. Holden. Paris: Picard, 1970.

Walpole, Ronald, ed. *An Anonymous Old French Translation of the Pseudo-Turpin Chronicle.* Cambridge, Mass.: Medieval Academy of America, 1979.

William of Jumieges. *Gesta Normannorum ducum.* Ed. Jean Marx. Rouen: A. Lestringant, 1914.

William of Malmesbury. *De gestis regum Anglorum*, vol. 1. Oxford, 1998.

Zink, Michel, ed. *Les Chansons de toile.* Paris: Champion, 1977.

SECONDARY SOURCES

Abulafia, David. *Italy, Sicily, and the Mediterranean, 1100–1400*. London: Variorum, 1987.
———. "The Crown and the Economy Under Roger II and His Successors." In *Italy, Sicily, and the Mediterranean 1100–1400*.
———. "The Italian Other: Greeks, Muslims, and Jews." In *Italy in the Central Middle Ages*. Ed. David Abulafia. Oxford: Oxford University Press, 2004,
———. "Mediterraneans." In *Rethinking the Mediterranean*. Ed. W. V. Harris. Oxford: Oxford University Press, 2005. 63–93.
Abu-Lughod, Janet. *Before European Hegemony: The World System A.D. 1250–1350*. Oxford: Oxford University Press, 1989.
Aclocque, Geneviève. *Les corporations, l'industrie et le commerce à Chartres du XIe siècle à la révolution*. Paris, 1917; rpt. New York, 1967.
Alexandre-Bidon, Danielle, and Marie-Thérèse Lorcin. *Le Quotidien au temps des fabliaux*. Paris: Picard, 2003.
Allsen, Thomas T. *Commodity and Exchange in the Mongol Empire*. Cambridge: Cambridge University Press, 1997.
———. "Robing in the Mongolian Empire." In Stewart Gregory, ed., *Robes and Honor*.
Amer, Sahar. *Border Crossings: Love Between Women in Medieval French and Arabic Literatures*. Philadelphia: University of Pennsylvania Press, 2008.
———. "Traveling Sexualities," in manuscript.
Anderson, Glaire. "Byzantine Islamic Diplomacy and Islamic Buildings in Constantinople (10th–13th c)." In manuscript.
Angold, Michael. *The Byzantine Empire 1025–1204*. London: Longman, 1985.
Argote, Joel Thompson. "Charlemagne's Women." *RLA: Romance Languages Annual* 9 (1997): 1–5.
Ashmann, P. J. M., ed. *Le Culte de la Vierge et la littérature profane du moyen âge*. Utrecht, 1930.
Auzépy, Marie-France. "La Destruction de l'icône du Christ de la Chalcé par Léon III: Propagande ou réalité?" *Byzantion* 60 (1990): 445–92.
Baker, Patricia L. *Islamic Textiles*. London: British Museum Press, 1995.
Balard, Michel. *Croisades et Orient Latin XIe–XIVe siècle*. Paris: Armand Colin, 2001.
Baldwin, John W. "Once there was an emperor . . . A Political Reading of the Romances of Jean Renart." In Nancy Vine Durling, ed., *Jean Renart and the Art of Romance*. Gainesville: University Press of Florida, 1977.
Bancourt, Paul. *Les Musulmans dans les chansons de geste du cycle du roi*, vol. 2. Aix-en-Provence: Université de Provence, 1982.
Barbier-Kontler, Christine. "Les Soiries chinoises." In François Bellec, ed., *A la Rencontre de Sinbad: La Route maritime de la soie*. Paris: Musée de la Marine, 1994.
Bartlett, Robert. *The Making of Europe: Conquest, Colonization, and Cultural Change, 950–1350*. Princeton, N.J.: Princeton University Press, 1993.

Bautier, Robert-Henri. *Sur l'histoire économique de la France médiévale.* Brookfield, Vt.: Variorum, 1991.

Bauer, Rotraud. "The Mantle of King Roger II and Related Textiles in the Schatzkammer of Vienna: The Royal Workshop at the Court of Palermo." In Rosalia Varoli-Piazza, ed., *Interdisciplinary Approach to the Study and Conservation of Medieval Textiles.* Palermo: International Council of Museums, 1998.

Bédier, Joseph. *Les Légendes épiques: Recherches sur la formation des chansons de geste.* Paris: Champion, 1926–66.

Bedos-Rezak, Brigitte. "Women, Seals, and Power in Medieval France, 1150–1350." In Mary Erler and Maryanne Kowaleski, eds., *Women and Power in the Middle Ages.* Athens: University of Georgia Press, 1988.

Bennett, Matthew, "Virile Latins, Effeminate Greeks, and Strong Women: Gender Definitions on Crusade?" In Susan B. Edgington and Sarah Lambert, eds., *Gendering the Crusades.* New York: Columbia University Press, 2002.

Bercovici-Huard, Carole. "*Partenopeus de Blois* et la couleur Byzantine." *Images et signes de l'orient dans l'occident médiéval, Sénéfiance* 11 (1982): 185–92.

Billot, Claudine. *Chartres à la fin du Moyen Age.* Paris: Edition de l'Ecole des hautes études en sciences sociales, 1987.

Bloch, R. Howard. "Money, Metaphor, and the Mediation of Social Difference in the Old French Romance." *Symposium* 35 (1981): 18–33.

Boulnois, Luce. *La Route de la Soie.* Paris: Arthaud, 1963.

———. *La Route de la Soie: Dieux, Guerriers et Marchands.* Geneva: Olizane, 2001, 2003.

———. *Silk Road: Monks, Warriors, and Merchants on the Silk Road.* Trans. Helen Loveday. New York: Norton, 2004.

Bourbon, Etienne. *Anecdotes historiques, légendes et apologues.* Ed. A. Lecoy de la Marche. Paris: Librairie Renouard, 1877.

Bourquelot, Félix. *Etudes sur les foires de Champagne, sur la nature, l'étendue et les règles du commerce qui s'y faisait au XIIe, XIIIe et XIVe siècles.* Brionne, France: Le Portulan, 1865.

Brand, Charles. "Some Byzantine Women of Thebes and Elsewhere." In John S. Langdon et al., eds., *To Hellenikon: Studies in Honor of Speros Vyronis, Jr.,* 1. New Rochelle, N.Y.: Aristide D. Carnatzas, 1993.

Brault, Gérald. "Fonction et sens de l'épisode du Château de Pesme Aventure dans l'*Yvain* de Chrétien de Troyes." In *Mélanges de langue et de littérature du Moyen Age et de la Renaissance offerts à Charles Foulon,* vol. 1. Rennes: Institut de français, Université de Haute Bretagne, 1980, 59–64.

Bray, Francesca. *Technology and Gender: Fabrics of Power in Late Imperial China.* Berkeley: University of California Press, 1997.

Brown, Elizabeth A. R. "Eleanor of Aquitaine: Parent, Queen, and Duchess." In William W. Kibler. ed., *Eleanor of Aquitaine: Patron and Politician.* Austin: University of Texas Press, 1976, 9–34.

Brownlee, Kevin. "Discourse and *Proueces* in *Aucassin et Nicolette.*" *Yale French Studies* 70 (1986): 167–82.

Bruna, Denis. *Enseignes de pèlerinage et enseignes profanes: Musée national du moyen âge.* Catalogue. Paris: Réunion des musées nationaux, 1996.

———. *Les enseignes de pèlerinage et les enseignes profanes au moyen âge.* Doctoral thesis. Paris, 1995.

———. *Enseignes de plomb et autres menus chosettes du Moyen Age.* Paris: Editions du Léopard d'or, 2006.

Bulteau, Marcel. *Description de la Cathédrale de Chartres.* Chartres, 1850.

———. *Monographie de la cathédrale de Chartres*, vol. 1. Chartres: R. Selleret, 1887.

Burger, Glenn. "Cilician Armenian Métissage and Hetoum's *La Fleur des Histoires de la Terre d'Orient.*" In Jeffrey Jerome Cohen, ed., *The Postcolonial Middle Ages.*

Burgess, Glynn S. and Anne Elizabeth Cobby, trans. *The Pilgrimage of Charlemagne and Aucassin and Nicolette.* New York: Garland, 1988.

Burns, E. Jane. *Bodytalk: When Women Speak in Old French Literature.* Philadelphia: University of Pennsylvania Press, 1993.

———. *Courtly Love Undressed: Reading Through Clothes in Medieval French Culture.* Philadelphia: University of Pennsylvania Press, 2002.

———. "Ladies Don't Wear *Braies*: Underwear and Outerwear in the French *Prose Lancelot.*" In William W. Kibler, ed., *The Lancelot-Grail Cycle: Text and Transformations.* Austin: University of Texas Press, 1994.

———. "Saracen Silk and the Virgin's *Chemise*: Cultural Crossings in Cloth." *Speculum* 81 (2006): 365–97.

Burns, E. Jane, ed. *Medieval Fabrications: Dress, Textiles, Cloth Work and Other Cultural Imaginings.* New York: Palgrave Macmillan, 2004.

Burrell, Margaret. "The Specular Heroine: Self-Creation Versus Silence in *Le Pèlerinage de Charlemagne* and *Erec et Enide.*" *Parergon: Bulletin of the Australian and New Zealand Association for Medieval and Early Modern Studies* 15:1 (1997): 83–99.

Bussagli, Mario. *Central Asian Painting.* Geneva: Skira, 1979.

Byzantine Women and Their World. Ed. Ioli Kalavrezou. New Haven: Yale University Press, 2003.

Cardon, Dominique. "De l'Espagne à l'Italie: Hypothèses concernant un groupe de soieries médiévales à fond de losanges lisérés et bandes de samit façonné." *Techniques et culture* 34 (1999): 139–57.

———. *La Draperie au Moyen Age: Essor d'une grande industrie européene.* Paris: CNRS, 1999.

Cartier, C. *Essai sur les monnaies chartraines frappées par les comptes de Chartres et de Blois jusqu'au 14e siècle.* Tours, 1883.

Cartier, E. "Recherches sur l'origine du type des monnaies chartraines." In Charles Cahier and Arthur Martin, eds., *Suite au Mélanges d'archéologie.* Paris, 1844.

Cassagnes-Brouquet, Sophie. *Vierges noires.* Parc Saint-Joseph: Editions de Rouergue, 2000.

Cavaciocchi, Simonetta, ed. *La Seta in Europa Sec. XIII-XX.* Florence: Instituto internazionale di storia economica, 1993.

Chapin, Elizabeth. *Les Villes des foires de Champagne: Des origines au début du XIVe siècle.* Paris: Champion, 1937.

Chédeville, André. *Chartres et ses campagnes. XIIe-XIIIe siècles.* Paris: Klincksieck, 1973.

Chédeville, André, ed. *Histoire de Chartres et du pays chartrain.* Toulouse: Privat, 1983.

Chênerie, Marie-Luce. "Le Motif des présents dans le *Roman d'Enéas.*" In Jean Dufournet, ed., *Relire le* Roman d'Enéas." Paris: Champion, 1985.

Ciggaar, Krijnie. "Chrétien de Troyes et la matière byzantine: Les demoiselles du château de Pesme Aventure." *Cahiers de civilisation médiévale* 32 (1989).

Cobby, Anne Elizabeth. *Ambivalent Conventions: Formula and Parody in Old French.* Amsterdam: Rodopi, 1995.

Cohen, Esther. "*In haec signa*: Pilgrim Badge Trade in Southern France." *Journal of Medieval History* 2 (1976): 193–214.

Cohen, Jeffrey Jerome. *Medieval Identity Machines.* Minneapolis: University of Minnesota Press, 2003.

Cohen, Jeffrey Jerome, ed. *Monster Theory: Reading Culture.* Minneapolis: University of Minnesota Press, 1996.

———. *The Postcolonial Middle Ages.* New York: St. Martin's, 2000.

Combarieu, Micheline. "Un Personnage épique: la jeune musulmane." *Sénéfiance* 7 (Aix-en-Provence: CUERMA, 1979).

Connor, Carolyn. *Women of Byzantium.* New Haven: Yale University Press, 2004.

Constable, Olivia Remie. *Trade and Traders in Muslim Spain: The Commercial Realignment of the Medieval Iberian Peninsula, 900–1500.* Cambridge: Cambridge University Press, 1994.

Cornu, Georgette, and Marielle Martiniani-Reber. "Etoffes et Vêtements dans le Ménologe de Basile II: Reflets des courants d'échange entre Byzance et le monde Islamique." *Quaderni di Studi Arabi* 15 (1997).

Daniel, Norman. *The Arabs and Mediaeval Europe.* London: Longman, 1975.

Day, Florence. "Dated Tiraz in the Collection of the University of Michigan." *Ars Islamica* 4 (1937).

Delaporte, Yves. *Les Trois Notre-Dames de la Cathédrale de Chartres.* Chartres, 1955.

———. *Le Voile de Notre Dame.* Chartres, 1927.

Demay, Germain. *Le costume au moyen âge d'après les sceaux.* Paris: Librairie de D. Dumoulin, 1880.

Deremble, Colette, and Jean-Paul Deremble. *Vitraux de Chartres.* Paris: Zodiaque, 2003.

Der Nercessian, Sirarpie. "Two Miracles of the Virgin in the Poems of Gautier de Coincy." *Dumbarton Oaks Papers* 41 (1987): 157–63.

Desmond, Marilynn. *Reading Dido: Gender, Textuality, and the Medieval Aeneid.* Minneapolis: University of Minnesota Press, 1994.

Desrosiers, Sophie. "Draps d'Areste (II): Extension de la classification, comparaisons et lieux de fabrication." In "Soieries médiévales," *Techniques et culture* 34 (1999): 89–117.

———."Les Soieries comme source historique (Europe, XIII–XXe siècle)." In Simonetta Cavaciocchi, ed., *La Seta in Europa.*

———. *Soieries et autres textiles de l'Antiquité au XVIe siècle.* Paris: Editions de la Réunion des musées nationaux, 2004.

De Weever, Jacqueline. *Sheba's Daughters: Whitening and Demonizing the Saracen Woman in Medieval French Epic*. New York: Garland, 1998.

Diehl, Charles. *Manuel d'art byzantin*, 1. Paris: Picard, 1926.

Dodds, Jerrilynn D., ed. *Al-Andalus: The Art of Islamic Spain*. New York: Metropolitan Museum of Art, 1992.

Dragonetti, Roger. *Le Mirage des sources: l'art du faux dans le roman médiéval*. Paris: Editions du Seuil, 1987.

Dubois, Henri. "Le Commerce et les foires au temps de Philippe Auguste." In Robert-Henri Bautier. ed. *La France de Philippe Auguste: Le Temps des mutations*. Paris: CNRS, 1982.

Durand, Jannic. *Le trésor de la Saint Chapelle*. Paris: Réunion des musées nationaux, 2001.

Ebersolt, Jean. *Constantinople Byzantine et les voyageurs du Levant*. London: Pindar Press, 1985.

Edbury, Peter. "Looking Back on the Second Crusade: Some Late Twelfth-century English Perspectives." In Michael Gervers, ed., *The Second Crusade and the Cistercians*. New York: St. Martin's Press, 1992.

Edgington, Susan B., and Sarah Lambert. *Gendering the Crusades*. New York: Columbia University Press, 2002.

Elsberg, H. A., and R. Guest. "The Veil of Saint Anne." *The Burlington Magazine for Connoisseurs* 68, no. 396 (1936): 140–47.

Engel, Arthur, and Raymond Serrure. *Traité numismatique du Moyen Age*, 2. Bologna. Arnaldo Forni, 1964.

Epstein, Steven A. *Speaking of Slavery: Color, Ethnicity, and Human Bondage in Italy*. Ithaca, N.Y.: Cornell University Press, 2001.

Evans, Michael. "Unfit to Bear Arms: The Gendering of Arms and Armor in Accounts of Women on Crusade." In Susan Edgington and Sarah Lambert, eds., *Gendering the Crusades*.

Evergates, Theodore. *The Aristocracy in the County of Champagne, 1100–1300*. Philadelphia: University of Pennsylvania Press, 2007.

Farmer, Sharon. "Biffes, Tiretaines, and *Aumonières*: The Role of Paris in the International Textile Markets of the Thirteenth and Fourteenth Centuries." *Medieval Clothing and Textiles* 2 (2006): 73–89.

———. "Weavers and Spinners in the Wool, Linen, and Silk Industries in Thirteenth-Century Paris: A Comparative Analysis." In manuscript.

Favier, Jean. *De l'Or et des épices; Naissance de l'homme d'affaires au Moyen Age*. Paris: Fayard, 1987.

Flori, Jean. "Mourir pour la croisade." *L'Histoire* 109 (March 1988).

Folda, Jaroslav. *The Art of the Crusaders in the Holy Land (1099–1187)*. Cambridge: Cambridge University Press, 1995.

Forsyth, Ilene. *The Throne of Wisdom: Wood Sculptures of the Madonna in Romanesque France*. Princeton, N.J.: Princeton University Press, 1972.

Frank, Robert Worth, Jr. "Pilgrimage and Sacral Power." In Barbara Nelson Sargent-Bauer, ed., *Journeys Toward God: Pilgrimage and Crusade*. Kalamazoo, Mich.: Medieval Institute Publications, 1992, 31–43.

Frappier, Jean. *Etude sur* Yvain ou le Chevalier au lion *de Chrétien de Troyes*. Paris: SEDES, 1969.

Ganim, John. "Native Studies: Orientalism and Medievalism." In Jeffrey Jerome Cohen, ed., *The Postcolonial Middle Ages*.

Gay, Victor. *Glossaire archéologique du Moyen Age et de la Renaissance*. Paris: Librairie de la société bibliographique, 1887.

Gervers, Veronika. "Medieval Garments in the Mediterranean World." In N. B. Harte and K. G. Ponting, eds., *Cloth and Clothing in Medieval Europe*. London: Heinemann Educational Books, 1983. 279–315.

Gibson, Gail McMurray. *Theater of Devotion: East Anglian Drama and Society in the Late Middle Ages*. Chicago: University of Chicago Press, 1989.

Girault, Marcel, and Pierre-Gilles Girault. *Visages de pèlerins au moyen âge: Les Pèlerinages européens dans l'art et l'épopée*. Paris: Zodiaque, 2001.

Glazier, R. *Historic Textile Fabrics*. New York: Scribner's, 1923.

Goddard, Eunice Rathbone. *Women's Costume in French Texts of the Eleventh and Twelfth Centuries*. Baltimore: Johns Hopkins Press, 1927.

Goitein, S. D., trans. *Letters of Medieval Jewish Traders*. Princeton, N.J.: Princeton University Press, 1974.

———. *A Mediterranean Society: The Jewish Communities of the Arab World as Portrayed in the Documents of the Cairo Geniza*. Berkeley: University of California Press, 1967–93.

———. "Sicily and Southern Italy in the Cairo Geniza Documents." *Archivio storico per la Sicilia orientale* 67 (1971).

Gravdal, Kathryn. *Ravishing Maidens: Writing Rape in Medieval French Literature*. Philadelphia: University of Pennsylvania Press, 1991.

Gregory, Stewart, ed. *Robes and Honor: The Medieval World of Investiture*. New York: Palgrave, 2001.

Grönwoldt, Ruth. "Sicilian Textiles Employed in the Imperial Coronation in Vienna." In Simonetta Cavaciocchi, ed., *La Seta in Europa*.

Grotenhuis, Elizabeth Ten, ed. *Along the Silk Road*. Seattle: University of Washington Press, 2002.

Guillon, André. "La Soie sicilienne au Xe-XIe siècle." In *Byzantino-Sicula II: Miscellanea di Scritti in Memoria Di Giuseppe Rossi Taibbi*. Palermo: Instituto Siciliano di Studi Bizantini E Neoellenici Quaderni, 1975.

Haidu, Peter. "The Hermit's Pottage: Deconstruction and History in *Yvain*." In Rupert T. Pickens, ed., *The Sower and His Seed: Essays on Chrétien de Troyes*. Lexington, Ky.: French Forum Publishers, 1983.

Hall, Robert A. Jr. "The Silk Factory in Chrestien de Troyes' *Yvain*." *Modern Language Notes* 56 (1941): 418–22.

Heinermann, Theodor. "Zeit und Sinn der Karlsreise." *Zeitschrift für romanische Philologie* 61 (1936).

Heller, Sarah Grace. "Fashion in French Crusade Literature: Desiring Infidel Textiles." In

Désirée Koslin and Janet Snyder, eds., *Encountering Medieval Textiles and Dress: Objects, Texts, Images*. New York: Palgrave, 2002.

Henderson, George. *Chartres*. Harmondsworth: Penguin, 1968.

Herlihy, David. *Opera Muliebria: Women and Work in Medieval Europe*. Philadelphia: Temple University Press, 1990.

Herrin, Judith. *Women in Purple: Rulers of Medieval Byzantium*. Princeton, N.J.: Princeton University Press, 2001.

Heyd, Wilhelm, *Histoire du Commerce du Levant au Moyen Age*. Amsterdam: Adolf M. Hakkert, 1959.

Hiatt, Alfred. "Mapping the Ends of Empire." In Ananya Jahanara Kabir and Deanne Williams, eds., *Postcolonial Approaches to the European Middle Ages*. Cambridge: Cambridge University Press, 2005.

Hill, Barbara. *Imperial Women and Byzantine Power, Patronage, and Ideology: 1025–1204*. London: Longman, 1999.

Hitti, Phillip K. *The Arabs: A Short History*. Washington D.C.: Regnery Publications, 1996.

Houben, Hubert. *Roger II of Sicily: A Ruler Between East and West*. Trans. Graham A. Loud and Diane Milburn. Cambridge: Cambridge University Press, 2002.

Houdeville, Michelle. "Une Arme étrange dans la *Chanson de Roland*." In *De l'Etranger à l'étrange ou la conjointure de la merveille*. Aix-en-Provence: CUERMA, 1988. 249–52.

Hüe, Denis. "La Chrétienté au miroir sarrasin." *Sénéfiance* 40 (2000).

Hult, David. "Language and Dismemberment: Abelard, Origen, and the *Romance of the Rose*." In Kevin Brownlee and Sylvia Huot, eds., *Rethinking the Romance of the Rose: Text, Image, Reception*. Philadelphia: University of Pennsylvania Press, 1992.

Hunt, Tony. "La Parodie médiévale: Le cas *d'Aucassin et Nicolette*." *Romania* 100 (1979): 341–81.

———. "Le Chevalier au Lion: *Yvain Lionheart*." In Norris J. Lacy and Joan Trasker Grimbert, eds., *A Companion to Chrétien de Troyes*. Cambridge: D.S. Brewer, 2005. 156–68.

Jacoby, David. "Silk Crosses the Mediterranean." In G. Airaldi, ed., *Le vie del Mediterraneo. Idee, uomini, oggetti*. Genoa: Università degli studi di Genova, 1997.

———. "Silk Economics and Cross-cultural Artistic Interaction: Byzantium, the Muslim World, and the Christian West." *Dumbarton Oaks Papers* 58 (2004).

———. "Silk in Western Byzantium Before the Fourth Crusade." In *Trade, Commodities, and Shipping in the Medieval Mediterranean*. Brookfield, Vt.: Variorum, 1997.

Jodogne, Omer. "La parodie et le pastiche dans *Aucassin et Nicolette*." *Cahiers de l'Association Internationale des études françaises* 12 (1960): 53–65.

Johns, Jeremy. *Arabic Administration in Norman Sicily: The Royal Diwan*. Oxford: Oxford University Press, 2002.

———. "The Norman Kings of Sicily and the Fatimid Caliphate." *Anglo-Norman Studies* 15 (1993).

Joly, Roger. *Histoire de Chartres*. Le Coteau, Roanne: Editions Horvath, 1982.

Jones, Nancy A. "The Uses of Embroidery in the Romances of Jean Renart: Gender, History, Textuality." In Nancy Vine Durling, ed., *Jean Renart and the Art of Romance*.

Jonin, Pierre. "Le Climat de croisade des chansons de geste." *Cahiers de civilisation médiévale* 3 (1964).

Karras, Ruth Mazo. "'This Skill in a Woman Is By No Means to Be Despised': Weaving and the Gender Division of Labor in the Middle Ages." In E. Jane Burns, ed., *Medieval Fabrications*, 89–104.

Katzenellenbogen, Adolf. *The Sculptural Programs of Chartres: Christ, Mary, Ecclesia.* Baltimore: Johns Hopkins University Press, 1959.

Kay, Sarah. *The* Chansons de geste *in the Age of Romance: Political Fictions.* Oxford: Oxford University Press, 1995.

———. *Subjectivity and Troubadour Poetry.* Cambridge: Cambridge University Press, 1990.

King, Donald. "Two Medieval Textile Terms: 'Draps d'ache' and 'draps de l'arest.'" In "Soieries médiévales." *Techniques et Culture* 34 (1999): 83–88.

Kinoshita, Sharon. "Almería Silk and the French Feudal Imaginary: Toward a 'Material' History of the Medieval Mediterranean." In E. Jane Burns, ed., *Medieval Fabrications*, 165–76.

———. *Medieval Boundaries: Rethinking Difference in Medieval French Literature.* Philadelphia: University of Pennsylvania Press, 2006.

Krueger, Roberta L. *Women Readers and the Ideology of Gender in Old French Verse Romance.* Oxford: Oxford University Press, 1993.

Labande, Edmond René. "Recherches sur les pèlerins dans l'Europe des XIe et XIIe siècles." *Cahiers de civilisation médiévale* 1 (1958): 159–69.

Lacy, Norris J. "Courtliness and Comedy in *Aucassin et Nicolette.*" In *Essays in Early French Literature Presented to Barbara M. Craig.* York, S.C.: French Literature Publishing Company, 1982.

Lamy-Lassalle, Colette. "Recherches sur un ensemble de plombs trouvés dans la Seine: Musée des antiquités de Rouen et Collection Bossard de Lucerne." *Revue de la Société des savants de Haute Normandie, Lettres et Sciences Humaines* 49 (1968).

Lepage, Yvan G. "Encore les Trois Cents Pucelles." *Cahiers de civilisation médiévale* 34 (1991): 159–66.

Lecocq, A. "Recherches sur les enseignes de pèlerinages et les chemisettes de Notre-Dame-de-Chartres." *Mémoires de la Société archéologique d'Eure et Loir* 6 (1876): 194–242.

Le Goff, Jacques. *La Civilisation de l'Occident médiéval.* Paris: Arthaud, 1967.

———. *Marchands et banquiers du moyen âge.* Paris: Presses Universitaires de France, 1956.

Léonard, Monique. "Le Dit de la femme." In Bernard Ribémont, ed., *Ecrire pour Dire: Etudes sur le dit médiéval.* Paris: Klincksieck, 1990. 29–45.

Little, Lester. *Religious Poverty and the Profit Economy in Medieval Europe.* Ithaca, N.Y.: Cornell University Press, 1978.

Leupin, Alexandre. "La Compromission: Sur le *Voyage de Charlemagne à Jerusalem et à Constantinople.*" *Romance Notes* 25, 3 (1985): 222–38.

Lévi-Provençal, E. *Histoire de l'Espagne musulmane.* Leiden: Brill, 1953.

Lombard, Maurice. *Les Textiles dans le monde musulman du VIIe au XIIe siècle.* Paris: Mouton, 1978.

Lopez, Robert. "Les Influences orientales à l'éveil économique de l'Occident." In *Byzantium and the World Around It: Economic and Institutional Relations*. London: Variorum, 1978.

———. "Silk Industry in the Byzantine Empire." In *Byzantium and the World Around It: Economic and Institutional Relations*.

Lundquist, Eva Rhode. *La Mode et son vocabulaire*. Goteborg; Sweden: Wettergren and Kerber, 1950.

Mack, Rosamond E. *Bazaar to Piazza: Islamic Trade and Italian Art 1300–1600*. Berkeley: University of California Press, 2002.

McCormick, Michael. *Origins of the European Economy: Communications and Commerce, A.D. 300–900*. Cambridge: Cambridge University Press, 2001.

McCracken, Peggy. *The Romance of Adultery: Queenship and Sexual Transgression in Old French Literature*. Philadelphia: University of Pennsylvania Press, 1998.

Mahnes-Deremble, Colette. *Les Vitraux narratifs de la Cathédrale de Chartres: Etude iconographique*. Paris: Léopard d'or, 1993.

Mallette, Karla. *The Kingdom of Sicily, 1100–1250: A Literary History*. Philadelphia: University of Pennsylvania Press, 2005.

Marchello-Nizia, Christiane. "De l'Enéide à l'Enéas: Les Attributs du fondateur." In Jean Yves Tilliette, ed., *Lectures médiévales de Virgile*. Paris: CID, 1985.

Marriage, Margaret, and Ernest Marriage. *The Sculptures of Chartres Cathedral*. Cambridge: Cambridge University Press, 1909.

Martín i Ros, Rosa María. "Les vêtements liturgiques dits de Saint Valère: Leur place parmi les tissus hispano-mauresques du XIIIe siècle." *Techniques et culture* 34 (1999): 49–66.

Martin, June Hall. *Love's Fools: Aucassin, Troilus, Calisto, and the Parody of the Courtly Lover*. London: Tamesis, 1972.

May, Florence Lewis. *Silk Textiles of Spain: Eighth to Fifteenth Century*. New York: Hispanic Society of America, 1957.

Mazzaoui, Maureen Fennell. *The Italian Cloth Industry in the Later Middle Ages, 1100–1600*. Cambridge: Cambridge University Press, 1981.

Mély, Fernand de. *Le trésor de Chartres: 1310–1793*. Paris, 1886.

———. *Les Chemises de la Vierge*. Chartres, 1885.

Menocal, Maria Rosa. "Signs of the Times: Self, Other, and History in *Aucassin et Nicolette*." *Romanic Review* 53, 4 (1989): 497–511.

Metlitski, Dorothee. *The Matter of Araby in Medieval England*. New Haven: Yale University Press, 1977.

Micha, Alexandre. "En relisant *Aucassin et Nicolette*." *Le Moyen Age* 65 (1959): 282–83.

Michaelson, Carol. "Jade and the Silk Road: Trade and Tribute in the First Milllenium." In Whitfield and Sims-Williams, eds., *The Silk Road*.

Michel, Francisque. *Recherches sur le commerce, la fabrication et l'usage des étoffes de soie*. Paris, Imprimerie de Crapelet, 1852; rpt. Amsterdam: International General, 2001.

Mola, Luca. *The Silk Industry of Renaissance Venice*. Baltimore: Johns Hopkins University Press, 2000.

Morize, J. "Aigues Mortes au 13e siècle." *Annales du Midi* 26 (1914).

Munro, John H. "The Medieval Scarlet." In N. B. Harte and K. G. Ponting, eds., *Cloth and Clothing in Medieval Europe*. London: Heinemann Educational Books, 1983.

Muthesius, Anna. "The Byzantine Silk Industry: Lopez and Beyond." *Journal of Medieval History* 19 (1993): 1–67.

———. *Byzantine Silk Weaving: A.D. 400 to A.D. 1200*. Vienna: Verlag Fassbaender, 1997.

———. "The Impact of the Mediterranean Silk Trade on Western Europe Before 1200 A.D." In *Textiles in Trade: Proceedings of the Second Biennial Symposium of the Textile Society of America*. Washington, D.C.: Textile Society of America, 1990.

———. "Sicily." In David Jenkins, ed., *Cambridge History of Western Textiles*. Cambridge: Cambridge University Press, 2003.

Nebenzahl, Kenneth. *Mapping the Silk Road and Beyond: 2000 Years of Exploring the East*. London: Phaidon, 2004.

Parani, Maria G. *Reconstructing the Reality of Images; Byzantine Material Culture and Religious Iconography (Eleventh–Fifteenth Centuries)*. Leiden: Brill, 2003.

Partearroyo, Cristina. "Almoravid and Almohad Textiles." In Jerrilynn D. Dodds, ed., *Al-Andalus: The Art of Islamic Spain*. New York: Metropolitan Museum of Art, 1992.

Payen, Jean-Charles. "L'Image du grec dans la chronique normande: sur un passage de *Raoul de Caen*." *Sénéfiance* 11 (1982).

Pernoud, Régine. *La Femme au temps des croisades*. Paris: Stock, 1990.

Piponnier, Françoise. "Usages et diffusion de la soie en France à la fin du Moyen Age." In Simonetta Cavaciocchi, ed., *La Seta in Europa*.

Piponnier, Françoise, and Perrine Mane. *Dress in the Middle Ages*. Trans. Caroline Beamish. New Haven: Yale University Press, 1997.

Ponton d'Amécourt, René de. *Monnaies au type chinonais*. Mâcon, 1895.

Psaki, F. Regina. "Jean Renart's Expanded Text: Lïenor and the Lyrics of *Guillaume de Dole*." In Nancy Vine Durling, ed., *Jean Renart and the Art of Romance*, 122–41.

Ramey, Lynn Tarte. *Christian, Saracen, and Genre in Medieval French Literature*. New York: Routledge, 2001.

Régnier-Bohler, Danielle. "Geste, parole, et clôture: Les représentations du gynécée dans la littérature médiévale du XIIIe au XVe siècle." In *Mélanges de langue et de littérature médiévales offerts à Alice Planche*. Paris: Les Belles Lettres, 1984, 393–404.

Reilly, Bernard. *The Medieval Spains*. Cambridge: Cambridge University Press, 1993.

Rejhon, Annalee. "L'Itinéraire de Saint-Denis à la Terre Sainte dans *Le Pèlerinage de Charlemagne à Jérusalem et à Constantinople* (British Library MS Royal 16.E.VIII)." *Revue belge de philologie et d'histoire* 83.3 (2005): 829–39.

Richard, Jean. "Sur un passage du *Pèlerinage de Charlemagne*: Le marché de Jérusalem." *Revue belge de philologie et d'histoire* 43, 2 (1965).

Riley-Smith, Jonathan. *The Crusades: A Short History*. New Haven: Yale University Press, 1987.

Robertson, Elizabeth, and Christine M. Rose, eds. *Representing Rape in Medieval and Early Modern Literature*. New York: Palgrave, 2001.

Rodinson, Maxime. *La fascination de l'Islam*. Paris: Editions la Découverte, 1989.

Runciman, Steven. "Byzantine Trade and Industry." *Cambridge Economic History of Europe*, vol. 2. Cambridge: Cambridge University Press, 1952.

————. *A History of the Crusades: The Kingdom of Jerusalem and the Frankish State, 1100–1187*, vol. 2. Cambridge: Cambridge University Press, 1951.

Sabatier, Antoine. *Sigillographie historique des administrations fiscales, communautés ouvrières et institutions diverses ayant employé des sceaux en plomb: XIVe–XVIIIe siècles*. Paris, 1912.

Sanders, Paula. "Robes of Honor in Fatimid Egypt." In Stewart Gregory, ed., *Robes and Honor*.

Sargent, Barbara Nelson. "Parody in *Aucassin et Nicolette*: Some Further Considerations." *French Review* 43, 4 (1970): 597–605.

Sayous, André E. "Le Commerce de Marseille avec la Syrie au milieu du XIIIe siècle." *Revue des études historiques* 95 (1929): 391–408.

Sénac, Philippe. *L'Image de l'autre: L'occident médiéval face à l'Islam*. Paris: Flammarion, 1983.

————. *Le Monde musulman: des origines au XIe siècle*. Paris; SEDES, 1999.

Serjeant, R. B. *Islamic Textiles: Material for a History up to the Mongol Conquest*. Beirut: Librairie du Liban, 1972.

Shatzmiller, Maya. *Labour in the Medieval Islamic World*. Leiden: Brill, 1994.

Sheingorn, Pamela. *The Book of Sainte Foy*. Philadelphia: University of Pennsylvania Press, 1995.

Simon-Cahn, Anabelle. "The Fermo Chasuble of St. Thomas Becket and Hispano-Mauresque Cosmological Silks: Some Speculations on the Adaptive Reuse of Textiles." *Murquanas* 10 (1993): 1–5.

Smith, Nathaniel B. "The Uncourtliness of Nicolette." In Raymond Cormier, ed., *Voices of Conscience*. Philadelphia: Temple University Press, 1977, 169–82.

Snyder, Janet. "Cloth from the Promised Land: Appropriated Islamic *Tiraz* in Twelfth-century French Sculpture." In E. Jane Burns, ed., *Medieval Fabrications*, 147–64.

————. "Clothing as Communication: A Study of Clothing and Textiles in Northern French Early Gothic Sculpture." Ph.D. diss., Columbia University, 1996.

————. "The Regal Significance of the Dalmatic: The Robes of *le sacre* as Represented in Sculpture of Northern Mid-Twelfth Century France." In Stewart Gregory, ed., *Robes and Honor*, 291–304.

Solterer, Helen. "At the Bottom of a Mirage, a Woman's Body: *Le Roman de la rose* of Jean Renart." In Sarah Stanbury and Linda Lomperis, eds., *Feminist Approaches to the Body in Medieval Literature*. Philadelphia: University of Pennsylvania Press, 1993.

Souchet, J.-B. *Histoire du diocèse de la ville de Chartres*, vol. 2. Chartres: Garnier, 1868.

Spence, Sarah. *Rhetorics of Reason and Desire*. Ithaca, N.Y.: Cornell University Press, 1988.

Spencer, Brian. *Pilgrim Souvenirs and Secular Badges: Medieval Finds from Excavations in London*: 7. London: Stationery Office, 1998.

————. "Medieval Pilgrim Badges: Some General Observations Illustrated Mainly from English Sources." In J. G. N. Renaud, ed., *The Rotterdam Papers: A Contribution to Medieval Archaeology*. Rotterdam, 1968.

Spitzer, Laura. "The Cult of the Virgin and Gothic Sculpture: Evaluating Opposition in the Chartres West Façade Capital Frieze." *GESTA* 33, no. 2 (1994): 132–50.

Steele, Stephen. "Rape in the Eye of the Reader: Sexual Violence in Chrétien's *Yvain.*" *Dalhousie French Studies* 30 (1995): 11–16.

Stein, Aurel. *Ancient Khotan: Detailed Report of Archaeological Explorations in Chinese Turkestan.* Oxford: Clarendon Press, 1907.

Stillman, Yedida. *Arab Dress from the Dawn of Islam to Modern Times: A Short History.* Leiden: Brill, 2000.

Stuard, Susan Mosher. *Gilding the Market: Luxury and Fashion in Fourteenth-century Italy.* Philadelphia: University of Pennsylvania Press, 2006.

Suard, François. "Constantinople dans la littérature épique française jusqu'au XIV siècle." In Liana Nissim and Silvia Riva, eds., *Sauver Byzance de la barbarie du monde.* Milan: Cisalpino, 2004. 91–112.

Tolan, John. *Saracens: Islam in the Medieval European Imagination.* New York: Columbia University Press, 2002.

Townsend, David. "Sex and the Single Amazon in Twelfth-century Latin Epic." In David Townsend and Andrew Taylor, eds., *Tongues of the Fathers: Gender and Ideology in Twelfth-Century Latin.* Philadelphia: University of Pennsylvania Press, 1998.

Uebel, Michael. "Unthinking the Monster: Twelfth-century Responses to Saracen Alterity." In Jeffrey Jerome Cohen, ed., *Monster Theory.*

Vaissière, Etienne de la. "The Rise of Sogdian Merchants and the Role of the Huns." In Whitfield and Sims-Williams, eds., *The Silk Road.*

Vance, Eugene. "A Word at Heart: *Aucassin et Nicolette* as a Medieval Comedy of Language." *Yale French Studies* 45 (1970): 33–51.

———. "*Aucassin et Nicolette* as a Medieval Comedy of Significance and Exchange." In Minnette Grunmann-Gaudet and Robin F. Jones, eds., *The Nature of Medieval Narrative.* Lexington, Ky.: French Forum Publishers, 1980, 58–73.

———. "Semiotics and Power: Relics, Icons, and the *Voyage de Charlemagne à Jerusalem et à Constantinople.*" *Romanic Review* 79, no. 1 (1988): 174–75.

Vaultier, R. "Les Enseignes de pèlerinage de Notre-Dame de Chartres." *Sanctuaires et pèlerinages* 12 (1958): 40–44.

Vial, Gabriel. "Les Vêtements liturgiques dits de Saint Valère: Etude technique de pseudo-lampas à fond (ou effet) double-étoffe." *Techniques et culture* 34 (1999): 67–81.

Walpole, Ronald. The *Pèlerinage de Charlemagne*: Poem, Legend, and Problem." *Romance Philology* 8 (1954–55): 173–86.

Wardwell, Anne E. "*Panni Tartarici*: Eastern Islamic Silks Woven with Gold and Silver." *Islamic Art* 3 (1988–89).

Warren, Michelle R. *History on the Edge: Excalibur and the Borders of Britain, 1100–1300.* Minneapolis: University of Minnesota Press, 2000.

Watt, James C. Y., and Anne E. Wardwell. *When Silk Was Gold.* New York: Metropolitan Museum of Art, 1997.

Webb, Diana. *Pilgrims and Pilgrimage in Medieval Europe.* London: I. B. Tauris, 1999.

Welch Williams, Jane. *Bread, Wine, and Money: The Windows of the Trades at Chartres Cathedral.* Chicago: University of Chicago Press, 1993.

Weyl Carr, Anne Marie. "Threads of Authority: The Virgin Mary's Veil in the Middle Ages." In Stewart Gregory, ed., *Robes and Honor.*

Whitfield, Roderick, and Anne Farrer. *Caves of the Thousand Buddhas: Chinese Art from the Silk Route.* New York: George Braziller, 1990.

Whitfield, Susan. *Life Along the Silk Road.* Berkeley: University of California Press, 1999.

Whitfield, Susan, and Ursula Sims-Williams, eds. *The Silk Road: Trade, Travel, War, and Faith.* Chicago: Serindia Publications, 2004.

Williams, Joanna. "Iconography of Khotanese Painting." *East and West* 23 (1973): 109–54.

Wilson, Evelyn Faye, ed. *The "Stella Maris" of John of Garland.* Mediaeval Academy of America Publications. Cambridge, Mass.: Harvard University Press, 1946.

Wolf, Kenneth Baxter. "Christian Views of Islam in Early Medieval Spain." In John Tolan, ed. *Medieval Christian Perceptions of Islam: A Book of Essays.* New York: Garland, 1996.

Wood, Frances. *The Silk Road: Two Thousand Years in the Heart of Asia.* Berkeley: University of California Press, 2002.

Wright, Monica. "De Fil d'Or et de Soie: Making Textiles in Twelfth-Century French Romance." *Medieval Clothing and Textiles* 2 (2006): 61–72.

Xinriu Liu. "Silk, Robes, and Relations Between Early Chinese Dynasties and Nomads Beyond the Great Wall." In Stewart Gregory, ed., *Robes and Honor.*

INDEX

Desmond, Marilynn, 105–6

Desrosiers, Sophie, 94, 204n44

diapre, 49, 185

Dido: of Carthage, 101–3, 215n9; corrupt silk and gold, and courtly love of, 13, 101, 108–14, 117; depiction of, 106; gender assumptions about, 105–6, 214–15n5; lavish garments of, 104–6, 114, 214–15n5; maps of cloth and, 113–14; ox hide, and manipulation by, 106–8; pyre of, 114–15, 117; of Tyre, 101–2, 117

Le Dit de l'Empereur Constant: aumosnieres in, 73, 78, 82; Constant in, 74–77, 82, 210nn14–15; Florien in, 74–75, 77, 78, 82, 210n15, 211n22; narrative of, 70–78, 210n12, 210nn13–16. *See also* Sebelinne

Le Dit des marchéans, 19, 182

Le Dit du Lendit rimé, 149

dras d'ache, 94, 185

dras d'areste: defined, 185

dras d'or, 45, 141, 185, 188–89n9

dyers, 3, 30

ecarlate: defined, 185

economics, of silk work, 1–4, 19, 26–29, 73, 130, 196n46, 197nn51–52, 59–60

Egypt: Cairo Geniza records in, 29, 41, 130, 197nn59–60, 202n21; gynaecea in, 54, 206n69; linen in, 182; men as slaves in, 207n90; Palermo, and trade with, 202n21; silk payments in, 193–94n18; silk production in Fatimid, 19, 30, 32, 52–54, 94, 106–7n72, 115–16, 206–7n72; silk trade with, 193n17, 197n60, 199n82; *tiraz* production in, 52–54, 206–7n72; Virgin's *chemise* and, 160, 177, 181–83; women silk workers in, 187n3

Eleanor of Aquitaine, 138, 152–54, 201–2n15, 223n69

embroiderers, 3, 11, 43, 52

embroidering, 36, 52, 53, 57, 78, 90; in *chanson de toile*, 78, 90

embroidery: Charlemagne's garments with, 220n15; femino-centric romances with subplot of, 213n51; gold, 44, 50, 52, 54, 57; Lienor's identity in, 89, 90, 97, 98; Muslim/Islamic, 5, 52, 53, 54, 57; *ouvré*, use of term, 5, 26, 44; Saracen, 50, 188–89n9; silk, 44, 49, 50; of Soredamor, 63, 67, 70, 72, 113; *tiraz* production, 53, 54, 57; Virgin's *chemise* with, 159

enseignes, 164, 229n39

epic texts, 4, 5, 10, 25–26, 36

Erec et Enide (Chrétien): courtly silk in, 10, 40, 61; Dido depiction in, 106; displaced woman in, 40, 61; fairy silk worker in, 199–200n93; gendered silk work in, 34–36, 199nn92–93, 200n95; marriage in, 60–61; *orfrois* production in, 48–49

L'Escoufle (Jean Renart), 73, 196n46

Estoria de España, 125

Evergates, Theodore, 201n8

fairs, Champagne, 149, 182, 221n40

Falcandus, Hugo, 57, 203n24

Farmer, Sharon, 3, 7, 72

Farrer, Anne, 195nn35–37

Fatimid Egypt, 19, 30, 32, 52–54, 94, 106–7n72, 115–16

Fatimid Sicily, 32, 52, 198n75

feture, and identity of Lienor, 89–90, 94–96, 213n53, 213nn53, 55, 58

Fierabras, 221n40

Fifteen Joys of Marriage, 176

Floire et Blancheflor, 29, 31, 118, 130, 197n56

Florien, 74–75, 77, 78, 82, 210n15, 211n22

floss silk, 19

foreign: Jews, as, 189n51; Muslims as, 5, 189–90nn15, 18, 21; Saracen/Saracens as, 2, 4–6, 189–90nn12, 15, 18, 21; women as, 42–43, 63–65. *See also outremer* sites; Saracen/Saracens

Forgeais, Arthur, 164, 171, 225n7, 229n40, 231n58, 232n64, 234n85

Forsyth, Ilene, 161, 163, 171, 228n30, 229n34, 232n61

France: linen produced in, 33; relics in, 221n39, 224n73; silk production in, 3, 6–7, 33, 72, 199nn91; slave trade in, 29, 197–98n62; wool produced in, 33

Franks, 5, 93, 116–17, 138, 145, 151, 220n15

Frappier, Jean, 214–15n5

Fulcher of Chartres, 116–17

futaine: defined, 185

Galeran de Bretagne (Renart), 67

Gautier de Coinci, 168

gender: assumptions about, 105–6, 214–15n5; of participants in silk geography, 3, 11, 16, 187n3; of silk workers, 34–36, 187n3, 199nn92–93, 200n95, 208nn92–93; ungendered participants in silk geography and, 3, 26, 33. *See also* men

gendered subjectivities, in literature, 78, 97–99

ACKNOWLEDGMENTS

I WOULD LIKE to thank the many people whose thoughtful suggestions over the years have improved the quality of these pages. I have benefited from the intellectual generosity of Sahar Amer, Glaire Anderson, Judith Bennett, Matilda Bruckner, Eglal Doss-Quinby, Theodore Evergates, Sharon Farmer, Jaroslav Folda, Roberta Krueger, Ann Marie Rasmussen, Elizabeth Robertson, Helen Solterer, and Kathryn Starkey. Sharon Kinoshita's careful reading of the entire manuscript proved invaluable.

I received further help and encouragement from members of the North Carolina Research Group on Medieval and Early Modern Women and from participants at the Institute for the Arts and Humanities at the University of North Carolina, Chapel Hill.

Generous research support from the Druscilla French Distinguished Professorship, the American Council of Learned Societies, the Institute for the Arts and Humanities, and the College of Arts and Sciences at UNC made this book possible.

Thanks, yet again, to Jerry Singerman, this time for his interest in silk.

Special thanks are due, as always, to Fred Burns (who thought of the title) and to Ned.

I would also like to thank my mother, Elizabeth Marootian Dilworth, who taught me how to sew, embroider, knit, and crochet.

Part of Chapter 3 appeared previously as "A Cultural Performance in Silk: Sebelinne's *aumousniere* in the *Dit de l'Empereur Constant*" in *Cultural Performances in Medieval France: Essays in Honor of Nancy Freeman Regalado*, ed. Eglal Doss-Quinby, Roberta L. Krueger, and E. Jane Burns (Cambridge, England: D. S. Brewer, 2007): 71–78, and is reprinted here with permission of Boydell and Brewer.

A slightly altered version of Chapter 6 was published as "Saracen Silk and the Virgin's *Chemise*: Cultural Crossings in Cloth," *Speculum* 81 (2006), and is reprinted here with permission of *Speculum: A Journal of Medieval Studies*.